Modelling Learning in Economics

To Sabine

Modelling Learning in Economics

Thomas Brenner
Research Associate
Evolutionary Economics Unit
Max-Planck-Institute for Research into Economic Systems
Jena, Germany

Edward Elgar
Cheltenham, UK · Northampton, MA, USA

Published by
Edward Elgar Publishing Limited
Glensanda House
Montpellier Parade
Cheltenham
Glos GL50 1UA
UK

Edward Elgar Publishing, Inc.
136 West Street
Suite 202
Northampton
Massachusetts 01060
USA

20262957

A catalogue record for this book
is available from the British Library

Library of Congress Cataloguing in Publication Data

Brenner, Thomas, 1968–
    Modelling learning in economics / Thomas Brenner.
    Includes bibliographical references and index.
    1. Economics—Study and teaching. 2. Economics—Research.
  I. Title.
  HB74.5.B74 1999
  330—dc21   99–14860
                                                                              CIP

ISBN 1 84064 134 7

Printed and bound in Great Britain by MPG Books Ltd, Bodmin, Cornwall

Contents

CONTENTS

List of Figures

List of Tables

List of Symbols

$a, \tilde{a}$ index of possible actions (also capital assets and procedures)

$a_i(t)$ action of individual i at time t

$\bar{a}(t)$ average behaviour on the population level at time t

$a_i^{(j)}(t)$ action committed by individual j of type i at time t

$\mathbf{a}(t)$ $= (a_i(t))_{i \in \mathcal{I}}$: action of all individuals at time t

$\mathbf{a}_{i_-}$ index of possible actions of all individuals except individual i

$\mathbf{a}_{i_-}(t)$ action of all individuals at time t except individual i

A number of possible actions

A_i number of possible actions for individuals of type i

$\mathcal{A}$ set of possible actions

$\mathcal{A}_i$ set of possible actions for individuals of type i

$\mathbf{A}$ set of possible action profiles $\mathbf{a}$

$B_i(t)$ budget of individual i at time t

$b_{i,c}(g)$ extent to which good g has the characteristic c according to the subjective believe of individual i

$\mathbf{b}(g)$ attributes of good g

c index of characteristics of goods or events

$\mathcal{C}, \mathcal{C}_i$ set of characteristics of goods or events

C constant of normation

$C(.,.)$ correlation function of two variables

$d(a, \tilde{a})$ distance between alternative a and $\tilde{a}$

$e(t)$ event or outcome at time t

$\mathcal{E}$ set of events or outcomes

$E(.)$ expected value

$f(.,t)$	probability density of a variable at time t
$f_i(a,t)$	probability that individual i commits action a at time t
$f_i(\mathbf{p},t)$	probability that $\mathbf{p}$ describes the distribution of action of individual i or an individual of type i at time t
$f_a(p,t)$	probability that the behaviour a is realised with probability p at time t
$f(\mathbf{x},t)$	probability of a system to be in state $\mathbf{x}$ at time t
$f_{st}(\mathbf{x})$	stable probability density
$F(.)$	function in different applications
g	index of goods
$g_i(t)$	good consumed by individual i at time t
$g(t)$	function in least squares learning
$\mathcal{G}$	set of goods
$h, \tilde{h}$	index of hypotheses in Bayesian learning
$\mathcal{H}$	set of hypotheses in Bayesian learning
$\mathbf{H}(\mathbf{a})$	matrix in the context of reinforcement learning
$h_i(.)$	function without economic meaning (only for mathematical convenience)
$H_i(t)$	mathematical abbreviation similar to the average reinforcement obtained by individual i
I	social impact
i, j	index of the individuals, players, or types of individuals
$\mathcal{I}$	set of individuals or players
k	number of previous plays that are remembered
$k_{i,a}(t)$	number of occasions in which individual i committed action a and which are remembered by this individual at time t
$k_{i,a}(\tilde{a},t)$	number of occasions in which individual i realised action a while the opponent realised action $\tilde{a}$ and which are remembered by individual i at time t
L, L_a, L_i	general operator describing the dynamics of learning
L_e	learning operator used in the original Bush-Mosteller model
$\mathbf{L}_e$	learning matrix operator in the original Bush-Mosteller model
l_a	parameter in the original Bush-Mosteller model
l_i	parameter in utility function of individual i
$M(t)$	function without economic meaning in the Robbins-Monro model

$m_i(t)$	motivation of individual i at time t
$m_{i,0}$	basis motivation of individual i
N	number of individuals or players
N_i	number of individuals of type i
n	number of interacting individuals
$p(a,t)$	probability of an individual to commit action a at time t
$p_i(a,t)$	probability of individual i to commit action a at time t
$\mathbf{p}(t)$	probability distribution of actions at time t
$\mathbf{p}_i(t)$	probability distribution of actions of individual i at time t
$p(\mathbf{a}_{-i},t)$	probability of all individuals except individual i to commit the actions given by $\mathbf{a}_{-i}$ at time t
$p_i^{(j)}(a,t)$	probability of individual j of type i to realise action a at time t
$\mathbf{p}_i^{(j)}(t)$	probability distribution of actions for individual j of type i at time t
$p_i(g,t)$	probability that individual i consumes good g at time t
$p(h,t)$	probability assigned with hypothesis h at time t
$P_g(t)$	price of good g at time t
$P(.\vert.)$	conditional probability
$P(e(t)\vert h)$	probability that event $e(t)$ occurs according to hypothesis h
$\mathbf{q}_i(t)$	satiety of individual i at time t
$q_i(g,t)$	satiety of individual i with respect to good g at time t
$Q(g,t)$	consumption of good g by the whole population
$Q_i(g,t)$	consumption of good g by the other consumers $j \neq i$
$r(\mathbf{x} \to \tilde{\mathbf{x}},t)$	transition rate from state $\mathbf{x}$ to state $\tilde{\mathbf{x}}$ at time t
$r_i(a \to \tilde{a},t)$	transition rate for individual i to change from action a to action $\tilde{a}$ at time t
$r_{i,I}(j,t)$	probability of individual i to imitate individual j at time t
$r_{i,v}(a,t)$	probability of individual i to vary action at time t and realise action a next
$r_i(a,t)$	probability of individual i to start investing in asset a at time t
$s_i(t)$	satisfaction of individual i at time t
$s_{i,0}$	indulgence towards new choices
$S_i(t)$	satiety from money of individual i at time t

$t, \tilde{t}$	time (if time is discrete, the unit of time is one)
$\mathcal{T}_{i,a}(t)$	set of particular points in time in which individual i realised action a and which are remembered by this individual at time t
$T_i(a)$	average period of time that individual i invests in asset a
$u(a, t)$	utility that action a gives rise to at time t
$u_i(a, t)$	subjective utility that individual i derives by choosing action a at time t
$u(a, \theta(t))$	utility that action a gives rise to given the circumstance $\theta(t)$
$\bar{u}(a)$	average utility that action a gives rise to
$u_p(a)$	risk preference function
$u_{i,c}(b, t)$	utility function assigned by individual i to characteristic c at time t
$u_{i,r}(t)$	average utility observed by individual i at time t
$u_{\rightarrow}(a)$	pull factor of procedure a
$V(t)$	strength of classical conditioning in the Rescorla-Wagner theory
$x(a, t)$	probability to meet an individual who realises action a at time t in a population
$x_i(a, t)$	share of individuals of type i who commit action a at time t
$x(i, t)$	frequency of the type or behaviour i in a population at time t
$\mathbf{x}(t)$	state of a system at time t
$\check{\mathbf{x}}$	stable value of $\mathbf{x}$
$\mathcal{X}$	set of possible states of a system
$y(t), \tilde{y}(t)$	variables in least squares learning
$z_i(t)$	aspiration level of individual i at time t
Γ	stochastic disturbance
Δ	change in the net returns of all assets
Δs_i	change in satisfaction of individual i after the change in net returns
Δt	small period of time
$\Delta \Pi_i$	tolerance of individual i to a decrease in net returns
$\Pi(t)$	payoff obtained at time t
$\Pi_i(\mathbf{a})$	payoff for individual i if the interacting individuals realise action profile $\mathbf{a}$

$\Pi(a_i, \mathbf{a}_{i_-})$	payoff for an individual that realises action a_i if the behaviour of the other individuals is given by $\mathbf{a}_{i_-}$
$\Pi(a, t)$	payoff for action a at time t
$\Pi_i(a, t)$	payoff for an individual of type i for action a at time t
$\hat{\Pi}_i(a, t)$	average payoff remembered by individual i or an individual of type i with respect to action a at time t
$\bar{\Pi}_i(a, t)$	average payoff obtained by the individuals of type i committing action a at time t
$\langle \Pi(t) \rangle$	average payoff of a population at time t
$\Pi_i(g)$	reinforcing strength of good g with respect to individual i
$\Phi_i(j, t)$	function for the effect of individual j's performance on the imitation of individual j by individual i
Φ_0	preparedness to change investment behaviour
$\Psi(\eta)$	function for the effect of experience on variation and imitation
α_e	reinforcing strength in the original Bush-Mosteller model
$\alpha, \alpha(\Pi)$	speed of learning in Cross's version and the generalised version of the Bush-Mosteller model and in melioration learning
β, γ	parameters and functions used in different occasions
$\delta(a = a(t))$	conditional function that is 1 if the condition is fulfilled and 0 otherwise
$\epsilon, \epsilon_i, \epsilon_j$	infinitesimally small positive values
$\eta_i(a, t)$	experience of individual i regarding action a at time t
$\eta_{i,0}$	neutral value of experience of individual i
$\hat{\eta}_i$	least value of experience so that an asset may still be chosen by individual i
θ	variable that represents all influences which are not explicitly considered (used in different circumstances)
κ_{ij}, κ	influence of communicated outcomes on experience
λ	parameter in the Rescorla-Wagner theory
ν_m	speed of learning in melioration learning
$\nu(t)$	selection pressure
$\nu_{i,I}$	imitation factor
$\nu_{i,V}$	variation factor
ρ	parameter in the context of social pressure
$\sigma(.)$	variance of the variable defined by the argument

ς_s	speed of the deminishing of satiety from goods
ς_m	speed of the deminishing of satiety from spare money
$\varsigma_{i,e}$	influence of neutral experience on experience
$\varsigma_{i,m}$	influence of satisfaction on motivation
$\varsigma_{i,o}$	influence of own outcome on the aspiration level
$\varsigma_{i,r}$	influence of other's outcomes on the aspiration level
$\varsigma_{i,s}$	influence of new outcomes on satisfaction
τ	denoting time in sums and integrals
$\phi(x)$	potential function
φ_{ij}	likelihood that individual i imitates individual j
$\omega(i\|j,t)$	mutation rate from type j to type i in the mutation-selection-equation
ω_{ij}	influence of observed outcomes on experience
ω_i	influence of the personal outcome on experience

Acknowledgements

I started to study learning processes in 1993 when I was at the University of Stuttgart. Since then I have changed my location several times, had many different colleges and attended many conferences. All these provided me with numerous opportunities to discuss my ideas and to gather a lot of helpful comments. The final result is the present book and there are many people I would like to thank.

The main work on this book was done at the Max-Planck-Institute for Research into Economic Systems in Jena which offered me great opportunities for research. During this time I profited much from the huge knowledge and experience of Ulrich Witt, who supervised me, and from his critical comments. It always felt comfortable and I think it was very helpful to be supervised by someone who shares many basic notions so that there is a good basis for discussion but has much more experience so that he is a good point for orientation.

Furthermore, I wish to thank my colleges at the Max-Planck-Institute for the good atmosphere within the unit which was helpful as much for my personal well-being as for the productivity in my research. I received many good comments during my presentations at the institute and from the colleges who read the first manuscript and helped me to improve the book, especially Armin Haas, Guido Bünstorf, Silke Stahl, Norbert Koch and Marcie Matthews. I also thankfully remember the sometimes vehement discussions with Burkhard Flieth, which often caused my thoughts to become clearer and more structured. The book also profited from the comments on its first version by Hans-Walter Lorenz and Marco Lehmann-Waffenschmidt.

Finally, I wish to thank my family, my friends and especially Sabine. In my opinion, recreation is an important factor for scientific work. However the people around me, especially Sabine, have not only provided me with the opportunity for recreation, they have also supported me with a lot of understanding, they have offered me the chance to discuss my ideas with people outside science, and they have prevented me from getting lost in science and divorced from reality.

Chapter 1

Introduction

In recent years the basic assumptions concerning economic actions have been discussed controversially. It was assumed for a long time that economic agents behave rationally, that is to say optimally with respect to their preferences. Today many economists claim that learning is the basis of behaviour. Subsequently they have shown that learning leads to rational behaviour in the long run so that rational behaviour can be explained as the result of learning. Few economists claim that learning does not converge to rational behaviour in general, that is, that the rational concept fails in many cases. An important aspect is often overlooked, however: people differ and so do situations, and, as a result, there exists a multitude of different behaviours which cannot be confined to only one explanation. Individuals may decide to learn on the basis of comprehensive calculations, on the basis of rules, on the basis of imitation, or on the basis of non-cognitive processes.

The present book presents a categorisation of different learning processes and gives some clues about the types of situations in which they occur. Furthermore it presents a number of applications of these different learning processes to various economic research topics.

What is learning?

Since this book is devoted to learning, I should first of all define what has to be understood by *learning*. In the economic literature it is rarely defined. In psychology the notion of learning is more elaborated but remains controversial. Learning is usually defined "as a relatively permanent change in behavioral potentiality that occurs as a result of reinforced practice" (Kimble 1961, p. 6). Furthermore most psychologists agree that learning cannot be observed directly. Learning processes have to be inferred from a change in behaviour. As a consequence learning theories themselves can not be directly tested. Different theories can only be evaluated based on their implications for behaviour.

In economics the focus is slightly different. Economists are mainly interested in describing economic behaviour and psychological aspects are important only in so far as they help to understand or predict economic behaviour. Learning belongs to the group of psychological aspects which is helpful in an economic context.

Definitions are always made within a certain context. The definition of learning given above was made in a psychological context. Thus it is necessary to reflect on this definition with respect to economics. I shall do so by considering each aspect of the above definition separately.

The definition of learning given by Kimble is based on the understanding of psychology as a behavioural science. Therefore learning is defined by its consequences, altered behaviour, although this change is not necessarily immediately observable. In economics a similar view is adequate for a different reason. While most psychologists believe that learning processes cannot be studied by themselves, economists are simply not interested in the study of learning processes. In the context of economics, only the implications for economic behaviour are relevant. Thus a definition of learning by its consequences seems to be adequate.

The basic statement of the above definition of learning is that learning is a "relatively permanent change in behavioral potentiality". This means that, first of all, learning is defined by its implication. Learning is understood as the process that changes behaviour or at least behavioural potentiality. In other words, learning changes something within the individual that alters behaviour in certain situations. Behavioural potentiality in this context means that the result of learning can only be observed if these situations occur.

Furthermore by virtue of the fact that Kimble's definition restricts learning processes to those processes that change the behaviour in a "relatively permanent" manner, all short-lived changes of behaviour, caused for example by fatigue or illness, are excluded. Changes of behaviour that are caused by learning remain until they are replaced by subsequent learning processes, or vanish due to the process of forgetting. Changes in behaviour provoked by changes of the circumstances do not indicate learning processes either.

The definition given by Kimble also contains a statement about the causes of learning. Learning is defined as the "result of reinforced practice". This implies that learning is a result of practice in an environment which provides reinforcement.

The first part of this implication does not place much restriction on the definition of learning. It just states that learning results from practice. By this, Kimble excludes behavioural changes that result from reflexes or instinct. Learning focuses on behaviours that evolve during life. Thus learning is a response to reinforced experience gathered in the past.

The second part of the above implication restricts learning to reinforcement learning. This is used very often in the psychological literature, although not all learning theorists agree on it. In the context of economics I feel it is too restrictive to define learning as a result of reinforcement processes only. I deviate from Kimble's definition on this point. The definition of learning to be used in the present book should only require that, due to past experience, a behavioural change may result. Experience may also include cognitive processing. Of course cognitive processing follows rules that have been learnt themselves. Consequently the definition of learning processes is expanded to include processes that do not change behaviour directly but change the rules of learning and therefore future changes of behaviour.

To sum up, by *learning* I understand any cognitive or non-cognitive processing of experience that leads to a direct or latent change in economic behaviour, or to a change of cognitive pattern that influences future learning processes.

Why do we need to consider learning processes in economics?
Learning has played a minor role in economic theory. It is the concept of rationality that has dominated economics for many decades. Following the assumption that economic agents behave rationally, there is neither a place nor a need for an understanding of learning processes within the agenda of economics. A rational individual, according to the neoclassical definition, always considers all information that is available and realises the optimal action. Neoclassical individuals only change their behaviour if there is some new information about the situation that they face. By this, learning is reduced to a process of information gathering. A psychological explanation of what is involved in learning is completely irrelevant in this context and the process of information gathering can be described in a normative manner as is done, for example, in the concept of Bayesian learning: It is claimed that individuals collect and process information in a way that serves their goals best.

From the assumption that individuals behave optimally, provided the information they have gathered is understood and the adequate interpretation of it is used, we are able to deduce their behaviour directly. The complex mechanisms of learning need not be understood. When applying rationality in a static approach, we only have to analyse the information available to an individual in a specific situation and calculate the adequate action. In a dynamic approach we have, in addition, to analyse the sources of new information. The static approach to economic action is simpler to handle and quite convincing. Therefore it is no surprise that this view has dominated economics for decades.

We may wonder instead why there have been economists all through the history of economics who have claimed that learning has to be taken more seriously. Many of these economists focus on the dynamic aspect of learning. However the dynamics of economic processes in general have rarely been analysed in the economic literature. This neglect of dynamics, especially on the micro level, has provoked a more detailed consideration of learning processes from time to time. Another group of economists concerned with the role of learning in economic behaviour, instead, challenge the notion of learning as a process of information gathering. Although some of them are inspired by the more complex notion of learning in psychology, most of them simply realise that a theory based on the rational processing of information fails to correspond with reality.

Moreover in recent years, the discrepancy between theory and reality has become more apparent due to the increase in data available from experimental research. Especially where the intensified study of decision making is concerned, the concept of the maximisation of the expected utility has been proven to be refutable (cf. e. g. Hey 1991 or Camerer 1995). Furthermore some experiments directly suggest that the dynamics of learning processes should be included in models of economic behaviour (cf. e. g. Roth & Erév 1995 or El-Gamal & Palfrey 1995 for the proposal of dynamic models in the context of games and the experimental evidence that confirms such dynamic models). Despite much evidence to the contrary, the idea of rational behaviour is still convincing enough for most economists.

In recent years the rational concept claiming that individuals behave optimally, at least in the long run, gained support by economists who turned their attention to biological evolution. They claim that human behaviour has to be rational in the sense of optimality because it would otherwise have been eliminated by the *biological selection* process. C. B. Harley (1981) formalised this claim. He proved that if a learning rule exists that enables an individual to learn the optimal behaviour in every situation, this learning rule will supersede all the others. However he also stated that such a learning rule would be too complicated to be realistic. Nevertheless the argument that human behaviour is determined by biological selection, and therefore is optimal, is frequently used in the context of economics.

Let me follow this biological selection argument for a moment, to show what it implies for economic behaviour. *Biological evolution* supports behavioural traits that increase the average ability to reproduce. Behaviours that hamper reproduction, instead, are eliminated by biological evolution. Affected by this selection process are all behavioural traits determined by genes. Geneticists are, however, not able to identify for sure which behaviours are determined genetically and which behaviours have to be learnt during life. Consequently there is a controversy about whether human behaviour is genetically determined at all (see e. g. Wuketits 1990, Symons 1992, and Tooby & Cosmides 1992). In this debate it is known that the number of behavioural traits that can be determined genetically is restricted by the number of genes. Hence it is unrealistic to assume that the adequate behavioural outcome for each specific situation a person encounters is inscribed in the genes. However from psychological studies dealing with twins raised separately, it seems somewhat plausible that the general way a person deals with decision-making situations is influenced genetically. This means that behaviour only has to be adequate with respect to the principles of biological selection, not that each behaviour in a specific situation needs to be the optimal one. This aspect generally supports the assumption of "rationality" as a basic principle of behaviour with regard to fundamental characteristics of behaviour, in other words behavioural tendencies, but not on the level of single actions in specific situations. The result of biological evolution should be a set of rules that determine behaviour and learning generally. Classical rationality in economics, by contrast, assumes that individuals behave in each isolated situation optimally with respect to their aims and capabilities.

The above considerations indicate that, although the *normative* argumentation about the rationality of human behaviour may well have descriptive power, rationality cannot be expected in a simple situation-based manner, as has often been described in the literature. If, instead, rationality is defined in the context of behavioural principles that hold for a variety of situations, it will be less helpful in deducing predictions and explanations for specific situations or for specific periods of time. Some approaches have been put forward to attempt to analyse and compare rules of behaviour, learning rules or decision rules, in the light of their success in different situations (cf. e. g. Heiner 1988, Kirchkamp 1995, and Pasche 1997). Such approaches, however, face two crucial problems.

Firstly they have to define the set of general behavioural rules that they allow and secondly, they have to categorise the possible situations and determine which situations are tackled with the same behavioural rule. Both problems are far from being solved.

An alternative approach to economic action is the *phenomenological* analysis of empirical and experimental data. Such an approach neglects any biological or normative considerations. Instead it tries to condense the empirical and experimental findings to theories or models, or to confirm and falsify theories and models by empirical and experimental studies. Subsequently the theories and models enable the scientists to explain and predict economic behaviour in comparable situations.

A phenomenological approach can be conducted in a static or a dynamic manner. A static approach analyses the relations between the characteristics of situations and economic behaviour without predicting reasons for behavioural changes. A dynamic approach, instead, analyses the reasons for behavioural changes. In recent years it has been frequently shown that *path dependence* plays an important role in economic dynamics (e. g. David 1985 and Arthur 1992). Path dependence implies that the behaviour in a situation depends on the individual's history, the events previous to the situation at hand. With modelling dynamic processes it is necessary to understand path dependencies and to make predictions of the resulting features. On the macro level the relevant changes are institutional, social, or political changes. On the micro level it is necessary to analyse behavioural changes. Consequently a dynamic phenomenological approach to economic behaviour has to be based on an understanding of the learning processes which affect behaviour.

To sum up, two alternative ways to study economic behaviour, and thus economic processes, can be distinguished. One is based on the concept of rationality and derives predictions in a deductive manner from the specific assumptions of rational behaviour. The other is based on a phenomenological approach to economic behaviour and its dynamics. Both ways can be justified. Moreover from a scientific point of view both ways should be used, as long as they prove helpful to understanding economic processes. However if one decides to follow the phenomenological approach and intends to study economic processes, learning will be a central aspect of the study.

How should we model learning in economics?

The understanding and modelling of learning processes should not be seen as an independent field of research of preferences in the context of learning in economics, it is only a tool necessary for a phenomenological theory on the micro level. The question remains open of how we should handle learning processes. There is a need for a theoretical learning concept to arise applicable to economic topics. Such a concept can be developed within economics itself or be adopted from other sciences.

In the history of economic thought, five different strategies have been used to obtain theoretical concepts about learning: (1) Repeatedly, economists have tried to deduce a model of learning from their own view about human behaviour. They have assumed that learning has to converge to optimal behaviour through individuals collecting information about specific situations. Bayesian learning, as well as many other learning models, resulted from such considerations. (2) From time to time, psychological learning theories have been applied to economic topics (cf. e.g. the Bush-Mosteller model and its applications in Cross 1983). In this context nobody has ever systematised the various learning theories used. They have rather been fitted in whenever they seemed to explain observed behaviour. (3) Some economists have tried to establish a general notion of learning. They developed models describing learning as changes in behaviour, either in a general sense (cf. Cross 1983) or as improvements with respect to individual performance (cf. e.g. Marimon 1993). (4) In the last decade economists have started to conduct their own experiments in the context of learning. With the intention of finding a learning model inductively with the help of these experiments. The prime example is R. Selten who developed the *learning direction theory* (cf. Selten & Stoecker 1986). (5) In recent years more and more economists are adopting algorithms from biology, mathematics, and technical optimisation to describe learning processes. While the use of biological algorithms is usually justified by the analogy between social and biological evolution, the use of algorithms from mathematics and physics is usually left unjustified.

This heterogeneity in the modelling of learning is necessary due to a lack of a generally accepted concept.

Bayesian learning, although it is most frequently used, is a theoretical construct that lacks any thorough empirical or experimental justification. It is a normative statement about how people ideally should learn rather than a realistic description of learning processes. The same holds for all other learning models based on the assumption that individuals collect information and behave optimally in accordance with their incomplete knowledge about the situation.

The second approach, utilising a psychological understanding of learning, seems to be a more promising one. However, psychologists have a different intention when they study learning processes, so that it is not simple to transfer their findings to an economic context. I shall discuss this problem in more detail in the next chapter.

So far, general mathematical formulations of learning processes allow for almost any dynamics, since only minor assumptions are made (cf. e. g. Cross 1983). Cross himself specified his learning model for each of his applications. Formulations of learning based on the assumption that learning always improves the performance of individuals are misleading for two reasons. First, they converge to a locally optimal behaviour by definition. Therefore they do not consider whether and when individuals behave optimally. Second, learning processes may lead to a deterioration of performance in some situations. For example, both unreflected imitation of other individuals (known as *social learning*) and *trial and error* behaviour, which leads to more information about the situation, can have a negative impact on the performance of the individual.

The fourth approach, conducting *experiments* wherein learning can be studied in an economic context, seems promising. Experiments have improved the understanding of learning processes. However, economists have not yet developed a substantive theoretical concept from this understanding.

The fifth approach to developing an economic model of learning has found a lot of acceptance in recent years. It is claimed that there are sufficient similarities between learning and *biological evolution* so that *evolutionary algorithms* can be used to describe learning processes. However, the utilisation of analogies to transfer mathematical models without testing their validity, contains the danger of engaging misleading models. In recent years some economists have analysed the analogy between learning and biological evolution in more detail (cf. Börgers & Sarin 1997, Brenner & Witt 1997 and Brenner 1997). The results have been manifold. In some cases, however, the use of evolutionary algorithms has been justified by these studies.

The above discussion of various approaches to model learning presents a set of tools for building models of economic behaviour. Some of these tools are reasonably well justified and others rather questionable. Also, there is neither a categorisation of the various approaches nor a comparison of their results. Each author uses the model that seems to be the most adequate or personally preferable. Often, learning models are chosen after the fact in such a way as to fit the results. By doing so, the understanding of learning and its influence on economic action has not been increased significantly.

To tackle this problem it is first of all necessary to clarify what learning is and what it is not. Two notions of learning should be avoided.

First, learning is sometimes interpreted as the attempt of boundedly rational individuals to reach optimal behaviour. As a consequence, every algorithm that optimises successively is seen by many economists as an adequate tool to describe learning. Such a view is misleading because it neglects the dynamics of learning and focuses only on the result of learning, which it defines right at the beginning. By this it does not increase the understanding of economic action, and it excludes the fact that individuals have motives and cognition; these may influence the learning process and prevent convergence to optimal behaviour. Second, learning in all situations cannot be described by one model. The research into learning processes has shown that learning may take various routes. It is impossible, at least at the moment, to establish one unifying theory describing learning in general. Instead, a better understanding of the prerequisites for the occurrence of certain learning processes is needed.

Because the type of learning employed depends upon the situation, if we want to apply concepts of learning in economics it seems helpful to develop a classification of learning processes according to the situations in which they occur. To this end, first the different kinds of processes have to be identified. In a second step, these different kinds of learning have to be related to the characteristics of the situations in which they occur. Finally, adequate learning algorithms have to be found for each kind of learning. The result is a taxonomy of situations, related learning processes, and appropriate learning models. This will be dealt with in the first part of this book.

Where does a consideration of learning lead?
With the help of a taxonomy of situation characteristics and related learning processes, we will be able to distinguish relevant economic situations. Of course the assignment of economic situations to learning processes is not always unequivocal. It often depends on the individuals and their experiences. Nevertheless, the taxonomy enables us to develop models of learning processes active in many economic situations, and give some suggestions as to which processes may be occurring.

We can then apply the knowledge about learning adequately to the different topics in economics as is done in the second part of the book. By this some new insights into economic behaviour can be gained.

However a consideration of learning does not imply the abandonment of all the theories that have been used before. Two processes have to be distinguished. Learning is the basic way to deal with situations in a world that is changing. As will be described later, psychological experiments have revealed a type of learning process that occurs in animals and humans alike, called *reinforcement learning*. Besides this learning process other types can be observed requiring, for example, cognition. Individuals develop ideas and theories about their surroundings. Subsequently they process information on the basis of their ideas and cognitive theories. As a result they learn in a way that is in keeping with their own ideas.

Let me discuss an example to clarify this point. Assume that economists have found that the best way to invest money, under the assumption that people are risk averse, is to distribute it between many uncorrelated assets. If, then, people are instructed to understand or believe in this advice, they will act accordingly. In other words, they will not apply their innate learning rules, but, will sit down and make the calculations they have learnt to do. They are behaving rationally in the way defined by the economists who have established this common notion of how to invest money. If people believe in the advantage of the advice of the economists, the normative theory about appropriate behaviours in specific situations becomes a positive theory, in this case. However, this works only in situations when people believe in the normative theory and have the time and the cognitive ability to adopt it.

From this we learn that there are two opposite ways to make decisions. One is innate, according to reinforcement learning, the other one is trained, according to the advice of professionals, or may be developed for other reasons. Neither of these assumes optimal rational behaviour but, in the latter case, individuals may behave rationally if they have already learnt the optimal way to deal with a situation. Therefore the assumption of rational behaviour is often not a bad approximation of real behaviour. This book seeks to describe other kinds of behaviour and therefore concentrates on learning processes. However, it is not intended to claim that rational behaviour is not important. Yet, alone, it does not provide a complete picture of economic behaviour and so there is a need to examine other behaviours and the learning processes underlying them.

How this book deals with learning

This book is divided into two parts. In the first part the theoretical knowledge about learning is presented. The second part gives some examples for the application of learning models to economic topics, and the implications of these applications.

The first part comprises Chapters 2, 3 and 4. In Chapter 2, learning processes are categorised according to the conditions under which they occur   and   the   resulting   categorisation   is   compared   with   the existing learning theory in psychology. Chapter 3 discusses possible ways to model the different kinds of learning found in Chapter 2. In Chapter 4, some general mathematical characteristics of learning processes are examined. The second part is divided into six chapters. In the fifth chapter the evolution of preferences and the relevance of preferences for learning processes is discussed. The last five chapters are devoted to the three different learning processes identified in Chapter 3. The sixth chapter is devoted to the application of *reinforcement learning* in a game theoretic context, while in the seventh chapter reinforcement learning is applied in the context of consumer behaviour. In Chapter 8, *routine-based learning* is studied in the context of capital investment. Chapter 9 comprises an analysis of routine-based learning in the context of the diffusion of products or ideas, and in Chapter 10, *associative learning* processes are modelled in the context of dilemma situations.

Part I

Theoretical Aspects of Learning

Chapter 2

Categorisation of Learning

In the literature, economic as well as psychological, many different models and theories of learning exist. If these models and theories are to be used in economic studies, a categorisation of learning processes, according to the conditions of their occurrence, has to be established. This categorisation should answer the question of what kind of learning occurs in which situations, and what the implications are for each kind of learning process. To this end, the important characteristics of a situation are first analysed from the point of view of the individuals involved. With the help of the results of this analysis a categorisation of learning processes is proposed with respect to the individual subjective awareness. Then a review of the psychological theories of learning is given. Finally, I relate this categorisation to the distinction made in the psychological literature.

2.1 LEARNING AND THE SITUATION

An adequate categorisation of learning should distinguish learning processes according to their features and the circumstances necessary for their occurrence. If we intend to understand economic processes as influenced by learning, first of all we have to know which kind of learning takes place, or if the individuals are learning at all. T. Börgers stated that a "fruitful approach for theoreticians is to identify different categories of learning rules, and to try to find properties which learning rules in the same category share" (1996, p. 1381).

The classification of learning processes is determined by two aspects; the characteristics of the situation and the individual perception of the situation. The latter means that the individuals' cognitive awareness, that is, the amount of cognitive capacity spent on the situation, and the comprehension of the situation, that is, the individuals' understanding of the situation, are aspects that should be considered while classifying learning processes. They are discussed below.

2.1.1 Cognitive Awareness

Cognitive awareness means that agents are aware of the situation they face and actively try to make the best out of it. This assumption is far from being a natural one. During any normal day we face an enormous number of decision-making tasks of varying degrees of importance and difficulty. Most decisions are made automatically, without spending a single thought on them. An obvious example is driving a car on the left- or right-hand side of the street. In a familiar locality this is luckily an unconscious decision, however, many people have experienced this non-cognitive behaviour in a foreign country, where people drive on the other side of the street. When turning a corner onto an empty street, they have sometimes automatically chosen the side of the road that they are used to. Some stimulation, such as another car driving in the opposite direction on the same side of the road, is needed to direct *cognitive attention* to the decision whether to drive on the right- or left-hand side of the street.

The same holds for many other decisions, for example in consumption behaviour. Some economists claim that the reluctance to try new alternatives is a question of *decision costs*. The underlying idea is that it takes time and effort to gain information about alternatives. Consequently, the search for different behaviours or decisions that might be better or even optimal is costly. Thus, before individuals search for behavioural alternatives, they estimate whether the expected improvement of their performance is greater than the decision costs of the search. It may be claimed that the consideration of decision costs leads to an infinite regress, because the estimation of the expected improvement itself is costly, so that this estimation has to be questioned in the same way (a similar argument is made by Simon 1987). Moreover, it is often claimed that individuals behave as if they calculated decision costs. An approach based on decision costs is believed to be a good approximation to describing the reluctance of people towards change. Such a claim can only be

evaluated either by empirical evidence or by a comparison of the results
with the results of a model based on more realistic assumptions about
individual behaviour. Experimentally this topic has been rarely studied
(see Brown 1995, for a study that claims decision costs to be irrelevant
for decision making).

For a positive theorist the question remains: why are individuals
reluctant to change their behaviour? Put somewhat differently: when
do individuals change their behaviour? A straightforward answer would
be: whenever they can improve their outcome by changing. Generally,
individuals do not know whether they can improve their performance by
changing their behaviour.

Consequently, to understand and describe economic action we have to
know in which situations individuals reflect their action cognitively and
in which situations they do not. To this end, it has first to be understood
why individuals do not reflect every action cognitively. The answer to
this question is quite obvious but helpful: cognitive considerations take
time and require *cognitive capacity*. Both these resources are scarce (cf.
similar arguments in Simon 1978). In other words, individuals are simply
not able to think about all decisions they have to make; the cognitive
capacity has to be distributed between many different tasks. As a consequence only some decisions are made cognitively while others are made
non-cognitively.

However, the question remains of how to identify situations in which
individuals decide cognitively. Generally it can be claimed that individuals pay cognitive attention to a situation only if they have an incentive
to do so. Various situations provide obvious motives provoking cognitive
attention:

- In a new situation in which individuals have no established rules
  to rely on, a cognitive effort is likely to pay because an arbitrary
  choice may cause a poor performance. Nevertheless, in many new
  situations individuals utilise rules transferred from similar ones.
  Thus the expression "new" has to be handled carefully. Individuals are not usually able to classify situations according to the
  situations' objective logical or theoretical structure, but must classify according to their own cognitive understanding. A situation is
  subjectively new if it is not related to any other situation according to this cognitive understanding. In a subjectively new situation
  individuals are likely to pay cognitive attention.

- Dissatisfaction is strong motivation for dealing with a situation cognitively. When a repeatedly faced situation leads to unsatisfactory

outcomes, individuals are motivated to change their behaviour. To this end, they pay attention to the situation and reflect upon it cognitively, in an attempt to improve their performance. In this context the aspiration level plays an important role.

- Certain situations and decisions are regarded as important to the individual for personal reasons, such as personal pride or aesthetic aspirations or sympathy concerning the outcome. Such a desire to direct cognitive attention may be explained by the large variance of outcomes in these situations, from quite positive to possibly negative. However if outcomes vary significantly, there is a great potential to improve one's performance, so that the cognitive attention paid to these situations may be interpreted as a recognised opportunity to increase well-being.

These three situations provoking cognitive attention share one aspect, which indicates one general rule for predicting cognitive learning. Each of them states that attention is directed towards situations in which the outcome is either unsatisfactory or can be anticipated to be unsatisfactory with a high probability.

Thus, I claim the following; *non-cognitive learning* is the normal route to behavioural changes. Individuals generally do not pay cognitive attention to the repeated situations they face. Paying *cognitive attention* is inspired by unsatisfactory results or their anticipation. Although this assumption is a theoretical abstraction of the aspects analysed above, it offers a sound basis for the categorisation of learning processes.

In reference to the above simplification, however, it must be noted that in the course of a repeated situation faced by an individual, two non-cognitive processes should be distinguished. A behaviour may originate and be guided further non-cognitively until a problem develops, or may originate cognitively and then be guided further non-cognitively. In the case of a non-cognitively learnt behaviour, when asked for the reasons for it, individuals can only answer "Oh, I have never really thought about this". Such a response signals that these behaviours have been learnt by non-cognitive processes. In the case of a cognitively learnt behaviour, individuals may, as soon as they have found a satisfying behaviour, direct their cognitive attention to other situations. Subsequently the behaviour becomes subject to non-cognitive learning and, since it is repeatedly chosen, this behaviour is confirmed as long as it is reinforcing, that is, satisfying. Individuals act habitually, again and again, without reflecting on their behaviour. If, however, the outcomes prove dissatisfying, individuals usually switch to learning cognitively.

2.1.2 Comprehension of Situations

In the following, learning will be discussed for situations in which individuals are motivated strongly enough to pay cognitive attention. They are assumed to reflect on their situation and try to behave in a way that suits them, however, they do not necessarily succeed in reaching their aims. They may fail to use all available information, there may not be enough information available, or they may misunderstand the situation entirely. Consequently, different degrees of comprehension of the situation occur depending on the characteristics of the situation as well as those of the individuals. Comprehension of a situation has a crucial impact on the way individuals behave and learn, if they are cognitively aware of the situation.

Individuals feeling competent

Individuals who feel *competent* behave according to their own considerations because these considerations are assumed to be the best advice. These individuals maximise their *expected utility*, that is, they *optimise* their behaviour preferably according to their own understanding of the situation. Whether their expectations about the outcomes are realistic or not has no influence on their decision to optimise.

I agree with T. Börgers when he claims that economists have lately directed their research too much towards learning as an explanation of optimising behaviour (cf. Börgers 1996). If individuals are to *optimise* their expected utility, they have to be both cognitively aware of the situation and to have a feeling of competence within it. Furthermore, their expectations have to be correct. When information and a feeling of competence are present, individuals do not, in general, actively search for clues about appropriate behaviour so that they may rely on wrong expectations. However, their feeling of competence or their expectations may change due to certain events. Thus individuals may switch between different kinds of learning behaviours.

Individuals lacking competence

According to the usual economic point of view, if individuals do not have complete information about the situation they are facing and if they are aware of this, they collect and process this information until they finally realise optimal behaviour. In this case, economists talk of adaptive expectations that converge to rational expectations (cf. e.g. Canning 1995). In other words, individuals are assumed to possess learning rules which help them to reach optimal behaviour. In the literature the expression "adaptive learning" is often used in this context. Sometimes *adaptive learning* is even defined as a process that changes behaviour in such a way that less successful behaviours disappear (cf. e. g. Milgrom & Roberts 1991). However it is difficult to develop a learning rule that secures convergence to optimal behaviour in real situations (e. g. Bullard and Duffy (1994a) have shown that least squares learning does not always converge to optimal behaviour, even though least squares learning is based on a procedure that processes stochastic information about the situation optimally).

Thus, cognitively learning individuals face a difficult task. They are cognitively aware of the situation, but they are also aware of the fact that they have insufficient knowledge of that situation (otherwise they do not cognitively attempt to learn). Nevertheless individuals aim to behave at least adequately (that means in a way that satisfies their goals) if not optimally. How should they deal with this predicament?

One may suggest that people should learn in a way that converges to optimal behaviour, as many economists believe individuals to behave anyway. However, the question remains what such an optimising learning process looks like. Many algorithms have been proposed, *Bayesian learning, least squares learning* or *Robbins-Monro algorithm*, just to name a few. In the economic literature, however, none of them has proven to describe the behaviour of individuals adequately. Experiments suggest that individuals apply behaviour according to relatively simple learning rules dependent on the situation, their attitudes, and their past experiences. If this is so, it implies that individuals need some insight into the logic of the situation to know which rule to apply. If they lack understanding of the logic of the situation they need at least a *cognitive model* about the learning behaviour that roughly suits the situation they are failing to understand.

Whenever individuals repeatedly face a situation, and they are cognitively aware of it and motivated to make the best out of it, they choose some dynamic rule of how to behave and how to react to the resulting experience. This rule may be called a learning rule. This rule determines how the collection and processing of information proceeds. It directs behaviour as long as the cognitive model about the situation stays the same. However the cognitive model, and therefore the learning rule, may be changed by the individuals if its performance is too inadequate.

The learning rule applied by an individual depends on the individual's cognitive understanding of the situation, that is, the individual's cognitive model of the situation. Cognitive learning without the existence of cognitive models is not possible. Cognitive models are necessary to recognise the need for learning and they interact automatically with every cognitive behaviour. Absence of the use of cognitive models implies that individuals are not consciously aware of the situation and are therefore learning only non-cognitively. If cognitive models are being used, the following three cases can be distinguished, depending upon how individuals evaluate their cognitive models.

- First, individuals may be prepared to modify their cognitive models because the models are believed by them to be inadequate. Nevertheless they must show some behaviour. In this case, two processes interact: a change of behaviour according to the current cognitive model and the simultaneous change of the cognitive model itself.

- Second, individuals may assume their cognitive models to be adequate or correct. Nevertheless the cognitive model may imply that they must gather information before they are able to make the optimal choice. Consequently, they are not prepared to change their cognitive models, but they deduce an appropriate adaptive learning rule from their cognitive model. In this case, individuals only utilise learning rules.

- Third, individuals may believe they already have the right information to know the optimal way to act. This means that they have a "fixed" cognitive model of the situation, and have what they consider to be all the information necessary to identify the adequate behaviour. In this case, the individuals' behaviour is stationary and can be described by the maximisation of expected utility.

To sum up, a theoretical approach to an individual's learning behaviour, in repeatedly-occurring situations in which there is cognitive awareness, can be categorised into three cases, according to the feeling of competence in the situation faced. First, situations in which no behavioural changes, that is, no learning processes take place because individuals believe their behaviour to be adequate; behaviour in such cases is described by the behaviour that learning converges to, which can be interpreted as the behaviour maximising expected utility. Second, situations in which individuals learn according to a learning rule. The learning rule is determined by their cognitive model of the situation. Third, situations in which individuals change their cognitive models because they feel incompetent in the situation.

2.2   CATEGORISATION OF LEARNING PROCESSES

In the section above we have seen that learning processes can be distinguished according to the cognitive awareness of individuals and their feeling of competence, that is, their preparedness to follow and change learning rules. The first aspect suggests a distinction of non-cognitive and cognitive learning processes. Only for the latter kind is the feeling of personal competence relevant. It leads to a further distinction between cognitive learning processes that follow a learning rule which I call *routine-based learning* processes, and cognitive learning processes that establish or change cognitive models of the situation, and therefore the routines which I call *associative learning* processes.

2.2.1   Non-cognitive Learning

Non-cognitive learning is not accompanied by any cognitive reflection of the situation (cf. e. g. Biel & Dahlstrand 1997, who also argue that reinforcement learning takes place whenever individuals do not reflect on their behaviour). Individuals are not aware of a learning process in progress and thus are not able to direct it; the learning process occurs automatically. Two "non-directed" learning processes have been found by psychological studies, *classical* and *operant conditioning*, which are described in the next section. They are generally assumed to be innate in humans and animals. These learning processes have in common that they are not intentionally brought about. Therefore non-cognitive learning occurs in every situation. However, they can be consciously overridden by cognitive learning.

The implications of non-cognitive learning are double-edged. On the one hand, conditioning leads to a more frequent use of behaviours that were helpful in the past, while inappropriate behaviours slowly diminish. On the other hand, non-cognitive learning is a short-sighted learning process. Actions are only repeated after they have led to reinforcing outcomes within a very short period of time. Later-occurring consequences of actions do not cause non-cognitive learning. This short-sightedness may lead to the "least preferred state of affairs" in the long run (for example, Brenner and Witt (1997) show that reinforcement learning leads to defection in a temporal dilemma situation).

Moreover, non-cognitive learning processes are always accompanied by stochastic fluctuations. Two reasons exist for these fluctuations. First, according to the observations about conditioning, individuals never eliminate a behaviour totally from their set of behaviours, although this behaviour may occur with only an infinitesimal small probability. Second, according to Scitovsky (1992), individuals are attracted to something new. Novelty is a reinforcer itself and therefore reinforces behaviours that lead to something new from time to time.

To sum up, non-cognitive learning is a process that takes place automatically and cannot be influenced by the individuals. Two non-cognitive processes have to be distinguished: classical and operant conditioning. They both are short-sighted and independent of consequences appearing later on.

2.2.2 Routine-based Learning

Routine-based learning is a cognitive way of learning requiring that individuals are aware of the situation, of possible alternative behaviours, and of the freedom to choose between two or more of these behaviours. This cognitive learning process, of course, consumes time and cognitive capacity. Since time and cognitive capacity are scarce resources, the question arises why individuals engage in this and other forms of cognitive learning. Here motivation to learn and improve one's own performance play, obviously, a crucial role for the occurrence of cognitive learning processes. The different reasons for this motivation are discussed in the section 2.1.

Routine-based learning is a process where reactions to an experience follow a certain rule which I call a learning rule. Learning rules are developed by individuals according to their cognitive understanding of the situation faced. A learning rule may be, for example, the rule to imitate any individual who is observed to perform better. Some learning rules are applied in very different situations, while in some situations, specific learning rules are applied. Whenever a fixed learning rule is applied, that is when the behaviour of individuals follows learning rules mechanically, I call the resulting process a routine-based learning process.

In any situation, the learning rule may have various features. The following are examples describing routine-based learning. *Observational imitation* is one example of a routine in routine-based learning also considered in psychology. In this case, individuals watch others and their performance and imitate the most successful and/or most frequently committed actions. Another routine is the collection of knowledge about the situation, for example *trial-and-error learning*. In this case, individuals try different actions and memorise the outcomes. This way they learn about the appropriateness of actions and are able to choose the one that will lead to the most comfortable results. Routines may also be defined in a more specific way. If possible, actions in a certain situation can be ordered in a meaningful way, individuals may learn according to the *learning direction theory*. This means that the individuals change their behaviour towards the direction where, according to the most recent outcomes, performance improves (cf. Selten and Stoecker 1986). In the literature many other rules have been proposed to describe routine-based learning, and they all have in common that individuals try to improve performance using their experience and understanding of the situation, i. e., their cognitive models.

These cognitive models may change as well, which is discussed in the next paragraph as associative learning. Both processes, routine-based and associative learning, together describe the cognitive learning process, i. e. the process in which the individuals are aware of the situation and try actively to improve their performance. However, cognition is far from being completely understood. The distinction between routine-based and associative learning is somewhat artificial and arbitrary because there is no clear evidence that cognitive learning can be divided into two separate processes. This distinction is made for modelling reasons to separate well understood processes, here called routine-based learning, from less well understood processes, here described as associative learning. By separating these situations and learning processes from the more complicated processes, it is possible to model cognitive learning at least approximately in some situations. However, it should not be forgotten that this is only a technical distinction and that each routine-based learning event is supported by cognitive models. Routine-based learning is an abstraction, based on empirical observations of some reoccurring structures of learning, and supported by the search for a possibility to model cognitive learning mathematically.

In economics, it is usually assumed that routine-based learning results in optimal behaviour. However, all that can be stated for sure is that individuals who engage in routine-based learning try to improve their performance. Whether they succeed in doing so depends on several circumstances. Not every rule applied is equally successful. Different situations may require different learning rules. Thus, the understanding of the situation is crucial for performance. It is unrealistic to assume that individuals comprehensively understand all situations they face, life is too complicated. Furthermore, situations often change while individuals are trying to adapt their behaviour. Often they do not realise the change of the situation immediately, if at all, and continue to follow their learning routine despite its ineffectiveness. Finally, individuals may stop adapting actively before they reach optimal behaviour. Since routine-based learning is an active process, individuals have to be motivated to engage in this kind of learning. If motivation fades, this learning process subsides and will be replaced by a non-cognitive learning process.

To sum up, routine-based learning has to be motivated. It is time-consuming and requires cognitive capacity. Many different learning routines exist. Some of them can be applied to nearly every situation, e. g. imitation or trial-and-error learning, while others are very specific and are useful only in specific contexts. Although routine-based learning is always intended to result in optimal behaviour, it does not always attain this goal because, for example, the particular cognitive models of the situation may be incorrect.

2.2.3   Associative Learning

Associative learning is the learning process least comprehensively understood. Nevertheless it is important to many economic processes. Similar to routine-based learning, it occurs only if individuals are motivated to engage in cognitive reflection. Again the motivation may result from dissatisfaction or from the importance of the outcome.

However, the two learning processes take place on different levels. As stated above, routine-based learning changes behaviour itself according to experience, knowledge of events, while associative learning changes learning rules according to uncovered mistakes in the cognitive models. Associative learning enables individuals to build or change associations and understand relations, causes, and interdependencies. The models established by associative learning are called *cognitive models*.

Cognitive models represents a picture of the world. This picture is in general neither correct nor complete, yet this is the information that individuals utilise whenever they make decisions cognitively.

Associative learning is the process that changes a person's picture of the world. These changes can be an enrichment of the picture by addition of new cognitive models, a falsification and therefore the abandonment of existing structures, or the restructuring of elements. Whether cognitive models are ordered in fixed structures in the brain or are combined with each other in a loose way is not known yet. However, experimental results imply cognitive models are connected together in a larger structure or framework. This interconnectedness is important for the cognitive learning process; it implies that cognitive models cannot be changed individually. They belong to a "big picture" and each change has an impact on the rest of the picture. Consequently, a learning process is rarely a pure addition of a new cognitive model to fit to the already existing knowledge. Changes always have to fit roughly into the big picture of

the world. This may cause discontinuities in the learning process as well
as resistance towards new information.

Since the process of integrating new information into the existing cognitive structure is time consuming, not every new piece of information
can be considered. Therefore, individuals have to decide which pieces of
information to process and which ones to neglect (this decision may be
made non-cognitively). The processing of new information is influenced
by two aspects: the interest of the individual and the concordance with
the existing picture. Individuals process information, they fit it into a
part of their world picture only if it attracts their attention (cf. Witt
1996). Information may attract attention because it is interesting or
helps to achieve a goal or because it is related to other facts of interest.
Attention is a scarce resource that is directed to various tasks according to current desires and present topics. However, not every piece of
information that attracts attention fits into the cognitive picture easily.
Individuals are able to suppress information if it contradicts their picture of the world. A simple example is brand loyalty. Once a person is
convinced that one brand is better than the others, it takes a great deal
of evidence against it before the person revises her/his opinion. Small
indications that the product of this brand may not be worth its price are
simply ignored, that is, not processed cognitively.

Associative learning is important for individuals because it enables
them to think in causal lines, identify relations, and think strategically.
In associative learning processes individuals explore reasons and influences. In this way associative learning shapes learning routines.

To sum up, associative learning is a complex process that is sketchily
understood so far. We know only some features: for example, that individuals combine pieces of information into a cognitive structure; that
new information is inserted into this structure; that the processing of
new information is selective; and that the resulting picture of the world
is subjective and neither complete nor necessarily correct. The fact that
our knowledge of associative learning is still partial may also be a reason
for the neglect of the subject in economics, although some single aspects
have found their way into the analysis of specific issues (cf. e. g. Denzau
& North 1994, Gößling 1996, or Kubon-Gilke 1997).

2.3 PSYCHOLOGICAL KNOWLEDGE ABOUT LEARNING

The above categorisation of learning processes was made with respect to economic interests, mainly the necessity to model learning in different situations, well aware of the fact that learning processes have different features dependent on the situation. However, learning is an essential human occupation and is therefore of central interest in psychology. If learning processes are being studied, although from an economic perspective, the psychological knowledge about learning should not be neglected. Therefore the psychological theories on learning are reviewed below.

Psychological research into learning processes can be classified into different schools. Four main kinds of learning theories exist, each focusing on a different aspect of learning: classical conditioning, operant conditioning, imitative learning, and cognitive theories. These theories have been proposed at different points in the history of psychology. Classical and operant conditioning date from the beginning of the 20th century, while imitative learning was intensively studied in the middle of the 20th century. The theories of cognitive learning are the most recent and the only ones that are still frequently reconsidered. Nevertheless, most psychologists consider all four theories to be valuable.

2.3.1 Classical Conditioning

This school of learning theory developed out of the famous experiments by I. P. Pavlov at the beginning of the 20th century. It is based on the findings that individuals react to certain external sensations, called *stimuli*, always with the same action, called *response*. A pair consisting of a stimulus and the corresponding response is usually called a *stimulus-response association*. In a series of experiments with animals, he was able to establish new stimulus-response associations (these works can be found in Pavlov 1953). Today this mechanism is known as *classical conditioning*. Classical conditioning makes use of an already existing stimulus-response association, i. e., a response elicited automatically by a stimulus such as an innate or instinctive response. If this association is innate we talk of an *unconditioned stimulus* and an *unconditioned response*. In the most famous study by Pavlov, a dog was served with some food (stimulus) that caused its saliva to flow (response). This stimulus-response association was utilised to create a new stimulus. When the dog was presented with food a bell was rung. After a short time the ringing of the bell itself caused the same salivating response in the dog as the presentation of food had done.

In order for classical conditioning to work, a neutral stimulus, that is a stimulus that causes no response, is presented to the subject together with the unconditioned stimulus. The timing of presentation of the two stimuli, the unconditioned and the neutral, is important for the process of classical conditioning (cf. Pavlov 1953). If the neutral stimulus is presented to the subject in a certain period of time before and during the presentation of the unconditioned stimulus, it becomes a stimulus on its own. It is then called a *conditioned stimulus*. After a number of simultaneous presentations of both stimuli, the conditioned stimulus causes a response without the presence of the unconditioned stimulus. The response caused by the conditioned stimulus is called *conditioned response*. It is similar to the unconditioned response although it may deviate from it with respect to its magnitude.

The pre-existence of an unconditioned stimulus-response reaction is crucial for classical conditioning. The stimulus of such a stimulus-response reaction is called a *reinforcer*. As long as it is a natural, i.e. an innate, stimulus, it is called a *primary reinforcer*. The conditioned stimulus can be utilised to condition further stimuli. This is called second-order conditioning. Due to this capability of a conditioned stimulus it is called a *secondary reinforcer*. Nevertheless not every stimulus can be conditioned by any primary or secondary reinforcer. Classical conditioning is subject to some restrictions and the reasons for these restrictions are still being examined.

Once a stimulus-response association is established, it persists on its own for some time. However if the conditioned stimulus does not occur coincidentally with the unconditioned stimulus for some time, the conditioned stimulus-response association slowly disappears. This is called *extinction*. After a rest without the presentation of the conditioned stimulus, the conditioned stimulus-response association is re-established spontaneously, at least partly. This is called *spontaneous recovery*.

A mathematical formulation of classical conditioning is proposed by R. A. Rescorla and A. R. Wagner (cf. Rescorla & Wagner 1972). They define the strength of a conditioned stimulus at time t by $V(t)$ and the change of this strength by $\Delta V(t)$. Furthermore, a coefficient γ refers to the "conditionability" of the conditioned stimulus, while a coefficient β represents the ability of the unconditioned stimulus to condition the neutral stimulus. Finally, maximal strength of conditioning is denoted by λ. Rescorla and Wagner suppose that the change in strength of the conditioned stimulus is given by

$$\Delta V(t) = \gamma \cdot \beta \cdot \left(\lambda - V(t) \right).$$ (2.1)

This formulation is known as the *Rescorla-Wagner theory*.

Classical conditioning was controversially discussed within psychology with regard to many aspects (cf. e.g. Hergenhahn & Olson 1997). However, the crucial findings have repeatedly been confirmed. Nevertheless, one dissenting view may be worth mentioning here. R. C. Bolles (1972) suggests that what we call classical conditioning is not the establishment of new stimulus-response associations but rather the learning of *expectancies*. In other words, R. Bolles claims that the conditioned stimulus becomes a signal for the immediate occurrence of a relevant stimulus. Subsequently the individual is guided by such stimulus expectancies. By this, Bolles claims that the findings in the context of classical conditioning are a result of cognitive processes. In his argumentation he borrows some elements from *gestalt theory*. I will describe gestalt theory in more detail below.

However it is interesting to know that in many experiments related to classical conditioning, people were not able to control their learning response intentionally (for example, the subject in the experiment of R. I. Watson and R. Rayner (1920) who developed a fear of rats). Similar processes of classical conditioning that cannot be intentionally influenced by the individual are also utilised in behaviour therapy.

2.3.2 Operant Conditioning / Reinforcement Learning

The theory of *operant conditioning* or *reinforcement learning* originates from E. L. Thorndike, J. B. Watson, and B. F. Skinner. Thorndike was the first to study *stimulus-response association* in the context of learning. He believed that the most basic form of learning is *trial-and-error learning*. Already, before the turn of the century, Thorndike had made some important statements about the kind of learning which is today known as reinforcement learning. He claimed that this kind of learning is incremental and not mediated by thinking or reasoning (cf. Thorndike 1932). The central aspect of Thorndike's notion of learning, however, is the *law of effect*. It states that the strengthening of stimulus-response associations depends on the consequences of the response. He claims that a response followed by a satisfying state of affairs strengthens the corresponding stimulus-response association. Such a consequence is called *reinforcing*. The opposite is a punishing consequence. Although Thorndike first believed that such a consequence weakens the stimulus-response association, later he claimed that punishment has no impact on stimulus-response associations.

The second important person to be mentioned in the context of *operant conditioning* is B. F. Skinner (see Skinner 1938). He became famous for his experiments (where he used the Skinner-box) that aided much in the understanding of operant conditioning. Between his notion of operant conditioning and Thorndike's, there are only minor differences concerning the features of operant conditioning. For example, Skinner primarily analysed the rate of response while Thorndike focused on the time needed by his subjects to find a solution to the given problem. Today, the notion of Thorndike is known as *instrumental conditioning*, while Skinner's theory is termed *operant conditioning*. However, the differences between both concepts are rarely important so that the expression *reinforcement learning* is often used for both types (sometimes this expression is also used for classical conditioning but in the present work it will be only used for operant and instrumental conditioning).

Another important contribution of Skinner to the understanding of learning processes was that he clarified some of the notions and expressions used at that time. In his book (1953) he describes the differences between classical conditioning and operant conditioning very eloquently. While classical conditioning connects existing responses to new stimuli, operant conditioning establishes new behaviours. These behaviours are not caused by a stimulus but are established because they lead to appreciated consequences. Therefore Skinner proposed calling these behaviours "operants" instead of "responses".

Furthermore, Skinner refused to call operant conditioning "trial-and-error learning". For him, behaviour is naturally stochastic so that there is nothing which could be described as "trial" or "error". Behaviour establishes itself by the reinforcement through its consequences, which means that reinforcing consequences increase the probability that individuals repeat the corresponding action. Skinner defines all consequences that are able to reinforce action as *reinforcers*. Two kinds of reinforcers are distinguished: the primary reinforcers which are innate and the secondary reinforcers which are created by classical conditioning. Skinner distinguishes *positive* and *negative reinforcers*. Positive reinforcers are consequences that add something desirable to the state of affairs for the individual, such as food or social contact; they lead to positive reactions. Negative reinforcers are consequences that remove something from the state of affairs unpleasant for the individual, like noise or fear; they also lead to positive reactions.

The opposite of reinforcement is *punishment*.   A punishing consequence is one that either removes a positive reinforcer or adds a negative one. According to Skinner and Thorndike, punishment has no influence on the probability of a response. They hold that punishment does not destroy the habit of carrying out a certain action, although it suppresses this action as long as the punishment is present. Thus punishment has only a temporary influence on behaviour. Reinforcement, instead, changes behaviour permanently. Only the process of reinforcement is considered when psychologists talk about *reinforcement learning*.

A quantification of reinforcement learning was given by R. J. Herrnstein (1961). He studied the behaviour of pigeons that had been offered two operant keys to peck. With these the pigeons had two alternative, possible actions. If the reinforcement associated with each key is given by a reinforcement schedule (a certain rule that determines at which time the pigeons were reinforced, dependent on the key they have pressed last), he found, the frequency B_1 (B_2) of pecking key 1 (2) and the frequency of reinforcement R_1 and R_2 for each behaviour follow the condition

$$\frac{B_1}{B_1 + B_2} = \frac{R_1}{R_1 + R_2} \tag{2.2}$$

or

$$\frac{R_1}{B_1} = \frac{R_2}{B_2} . \tag{2.3}$$

This condition is called the *matching law*. It states that subjects change their behaviour until each possible action leads either to the same number of reinforcements per action or vanishes if it leads to a smaller average number of reinforcements.

2.3.3   Observational Learning

Observational learning is strongly associated with the name of A. Bandura. He wrote the most comprehensive and most often cited book on observational learning (Bandura 1977). However the first systematic study of *imitation* was conducted by N. E. Miller and J. Dollard (1941). They could show that imitation is a crucial aspect of learning and that a number of abilities are learnt by imitation.

Miller and Dollard distinguished three kinds of imitative behaviour.

1) People may carry out the same behaviour committed by others just because they have learnt the same behaviour before and now face the same stimulus. For example, people applaud at the end of a concert. According to the definition of learning given at the beginning of this

book, where learning is defined as a permanent change in behaviour, the realisation of the same behaviour in this sense is no process of learning.

2) Miller and Dollard talk about *copying behaviour* if the imitation is guided by the person that is to be imitated. Such a process of learning occurs whenever an expert trains a novice in any kind of activity. During this process the expert demonstrates actions that are to be imitated and gives a corrective feedback to the novice's attempts.

3) In the case of *matched-dependent behaviour*, imitation is provoked by the reward another individual gets for a certain behaviour. Individuals who observes this behaviour and the resulting reward, hope to get the same reward. To this end, they realise the same action. If their action is rewarded as well, it is reinforced and stabilises.

This classification of different kinds of imitative behaviours does not include the possibility that individuals reflect on the behaviour observed and its consequences. Bandura, however, took such cognitive processes into account. He distinguished between *imitation* and *observational learning*. According to Bandura, imitation is a process by which individuals carry out the action that they observe while watching others. Observational learning, however, is more than that. Observational learning also includes the aspect that people may learn from the mistakes made by others. Thus, observational learning is the process of gathering information about consequences of behaviour by observing other individuals. By this, Bandura takes into consideration the cognitive processing that accompanies the observation of other individuals' actions and the related results.

Nevertheless, the process of observational learning is seen by Bandura as a process directed by reinforcement where reinforcement is understood in a broader context. This becomes obvious in the categorisation of observational learning proposed by Bandura (1965). He distinguished three kinds of observational learning.

1) The first kind of observational learning is similar to the matched-dependent behaviour of Miller and Dollard. In this case, observers imitate the behaviour of a model who is rewarded for this very behaviour. If the observers are rewarded themselves the behaviour is reinforced and thus learnt.

2) The second kind of observational learning can be identified as the process Miller and Dollard called "copying behaviour". In this case, the model rewards the observer for the imitation of the model's behaviour, and so imitation is reinforced by the person who wants to be imitated. This kind of observational learning primarily occurs in the context of training.

3) The central contribution of Bandura to the understanding of observational learning was the introduction of the third kind of learning; this does not require reinforcement of the observer's behaviour. Bandura claims that individuals adopt the behaviour of others if they observe positive consequences for the model. A positive consequence for themselves is not necessary at the beginning. Furthermore, individuals avoid behaviours that they observed giving negative consequences to others. Bandura talks about *social-cognitive learning.*

Individuals, however, do not imitate all behaviours they observe giving positive consequences. It is therefore important to have some hints about what and when individuals may imitate. To this end, Bandura discusses four different aspects of imitative learning.

Before individuals can imitate a behavioural pattern, they have to become aware of this pattern in another individual. Attention is necessary for imitative learning. In everyday life there are so many sense stimuli that perception is necessarily selective. Consequently, the behaviour to be imitated has to attract our attention in one way or another.

In addition, the motivation to imitate the behaviour observed also plays an important role. First of all, imitation only occurs if the observer perceives a positive outcome. Whether this outcome is objectively positive, or only in the opinion of the observer, does not make any difference. It is only necessary that the observer, the one who imitates, regards the behaviour of the model as rewarding. Furthermore, imitation is more likely if the observed person has high status or is a respected character, if similarities between model and observer exist, and if behaviour and consequences are not ambiguous. Freedom of choice of the observers also plays an interesting role. If observers are free to decide whether to imitate the observed behaviour or not, imitative learning is more likely to occur.

Analogously, individuals have to be motivated to show the learnt behaviour. Motivation depends on the individuals' expectations. If they regard the learnt behaviour to be helpful for their own aims or if they see strong similarities between their situation and the situation observed, they are motivated to behave as the model did.

In addition to these influences, the individuals have to be able to conduct the same behavioural pattern as the model and they have to be able to remember the observed pattern. The first condition may or may not be fulfilled in a specific context; there is not much to theorise about. The second condition points out the importance of memory for the learning process. I will discuss this aspect later in this section.

In addition to observational learning the theory of *social impact* should

be mentioned in the context of imitative learning. It was proposed by
B. Latané (1981). Latané found through experiments that the impact of
the behaviour of a group of people on the behaviour of an observer depends on three aspects: (1) the strength of people in the observed group,
i. e. the strength of character, the status, and the relationship to the observer, (2) the immediacy of the situation, and (3) the number of people
in the observed group. The first and the second aspect are included in
the Bandura's considerations. The third aspect was intensively studied
by Latané. He found that a dependency of the form

$$I = \beta \cdot N^\gamma \qquad (2.4)$$

exists in many different situations where I is the impact on the observer,
N the number of people in the observed group, and β and γ $(0 < \gamma < 1)$
are problem-specific parameters. The impacts of the strength of the
observed people or the immediacy of the situation are multiplicative.

2.3.4   Further Cognitive Learning Models

Apart from the three well elaborated learning theories described above,
some other learning models exist in psychology. These are often subsumed under the label of cognitive learning theories. I will present some
of them below.

Insightful learning (gestalt theory)

Gestalt theory builds on the notion that it is not possible to subdivide the
organisation of life into small units that can be studied independently.
Therefore it is not possible to break down psychological phenomena into
primitive perceptual elements. Gestalt psychologists always consider the
whole environment. This is defined as a dynamic interrelated system
of many parts that influence each other. Such an environment is called
a *field* (cf. Lewin 1963). Gestalt theory is a holistic, subjective, and
cognitive theory. In contrast to the theories of conditioning, gestalt theorists assume that behaviour is not determined by the physical world.
Instead, they claim that the observed reality is transformed in the brain
into a subjective reality which, in turn, determines the behaviour of the
individuals.

   From this perspective, learning means subjective perception of the
whole situation and establishment of relations between its elements. W.
Köhler (1925) conducted many experiments with apes. In these experiments he confronted the apes with difficult tasks. The apes tried different
strategies until they found the right one by chance. After this, they had

developed an understanding of the situation and the instrumental value of different tools so that they were able to solve the same problem immediately afterwards. In other words, learning in the sense of gestalt psychology means to recognise some interactive relations and to understand their meaning in a life context.

Furthermore, gestalt theorists suggest that learning proceeds as follows. An individual faces a problem that has to be solved. The problem provides a stimulus that remains present until the problem is solved. This stimulus motivates the individual to recombine the elements of the situation in various ways. The combination is changed until the solution of the problem suddenly appears. Through this an insight into the situation is obtained. Therefore gestalt theorists call this process *insightful learning*.

Insightful learning has three crucial characteristics that should be mentioned. First, learning occurs suddenly. The elements of the situation are mentally rearranged until they fit reality and the solution is found. Therefore, only two states can be reached with respect to each specific problem: it is either solved or not solved. Second, insightful learning leads to an understanding of the situation that makes possible an error-free and constant behaviour. Furthermore, the obtained insights can be transferred to similar situations. Third, it is claimed that knowledge obtained by insightful learning remains available for some considerable time. During this period it can be applied.

The notion of insightful learning was further developed by the consideration of *memory traces* (cf. Koffka 1963). According to Koffka, each learning process results in a memory trace in the brain, which contains the experience made by solving the problem. This memory trace will, in the future, direct the behaviour in similar situations. It will also interact with experience gained in other learning processes, and so a trace system is developed. The memory, which consists of this trace system, becomes complete and meaningful. Again the whole system is assumed to be more than a simple collection of memory traces. Only the trace system as a whole represents the individual's subjective knowledge about the world.

Neo-behaviourism

Neo-behaviourism, in contrast to the learning models of behaviourism (the classical and operant conditioning), also considers cognitive processes. E. C. Tolman (1949) showed, in experiments, that animals learn even if they have no incentive to do so, that is, even if they are not rewarded for their learning. In Tolman's experiments rats were put into a maze with no incentive to do anything. After some time he rewarded them for one action (for example, for visiting a certain place in the maze where he had put some food). The rats performed as well as a control group of rats that was rewarded for this very action right from the beginning. This means individuals learn even if they are not immediately rewarded for learning.

According to Tolman, they do so because they expect the knowledge to be helpful later on. In this sense, learning is motivated by expectations while the corresponding action is motivated by ends. The drives and desires of individuals are regarded as the motivating elements of learning. Tolman assumes that individuals learn permanently and not only if they are reinforced or if they have to solve problems. In other words, individuals continually explore the world around them. While doing so they direct their attention to those aspects which they assume to be most relevant with respect to their current aims. The exploration of the world leads to a picture of the world called a *cognitive map*. The cognitive map shapes the actions taken to reach personal goals.

The cognitive map consists of a set of expectations, also called *hypotheses*, about the world. These hypotheses are confirmed or refuted with respect to personal experience. This process is similar to the one of reinforcement learning, in the sense that hypotheses are negatively or positively reinforced depending on the outcomes. However it is important to state that it applies to the cognitive map with its hypotheses, and not to the behaviour itself.

Neural patterns and learning

The better understanding of *neurons* and their interaction resulted in some new theories about learning. D. O. Hebb (1949) was the first who used neuro-psychological knowledge to construct hypotheses about learning. In his theory, neurons or groups of neurons in the brain represent specific elements of meaning or acting. Hebb assumed that infants are born with a *neural network* of random interconnections. During life, especially the first years, the neural network is structured according to individual experience. In other words, learning reconstructs inter-neural connections.

According to Hebb, neurons stimulated simultaneously persistently become related. He called a system of related neurons a *cell assembly*. Single neurons join or leave such assemblies depending on the individual's experiences. Hebb assigned cell assemblies to specific real-world objects. The different parts of the cell assemblies represent different aspects of the objects. For example if a child learns that fire is hot the visual element "fire" and the sensual element "hot" will become connected, that is, they will join the same cell assembly. Subsequently, if one of them is stimulated the other becomes stimulated as well.

While cell assemblies are pools of neurons representing different aspects of an object, thoughts are represented by *phase sequences*. A phase sequence is a collection of interrelated cell assemblies. The mechanisms in a phase sequence are the same as in a cell assembly. If one of the elements is stimulated, for example, if the neurons of one cell assembly sense, the other elements are stimulated as well. Furthermore, phase sequences are also established by experience and change according to it.

The development of cell assemblies, according to Hebb, takes place in an early phase of life. Interrelations between neurons are learnt by reinforcement. Cell assemblies are simple associative features relating aspects of objects to each other. They contain no logical structure. Cell assemblies are the basic framework for logical insights into processes. These insights are represented by phase sequences. Hebb claims that the learning of phase sequences differs from the one for learning cell assemblies, although he does not characterise this learning process in more detail. Furthermore, the learning of phase sequences which becomes possible after a certain point in early childhood lasts throughout life.

More recent experimental studies with animals showed that interrelations between neurons, similar to cell assemblies, do indeed build up according to individual experience. The development of the interrelations follows principles that are similar to reinforcement learning (cf. Kandel & Schwartz 1982).

Theory of mental models

The theory of *mental models* is mainly propagated by P. N. Johnson-Laird (1983). The basic idea is that individuals develop mental models about their surroundings. These models influence their own behaviour. In this context, learning can be seen as the development or change of these mental models. However the processes of such development and change are difficult to study. Therefore most of the literature on mental models analyses their characteristics and their impact on decision making.

With respect to learning, the theory of mental models has many similarities to other cognitive learning theories described above. It is somehow a synthesis of several cognitive learning models and can be seen as the state of the art of understanding cognitive learning processes. Nevertheless, it is built on the subjective understanding of Johnson-Laird.

Other cognitive theories

In addition to the theories described above, many others exist about cognitive learning (e. g. the theories of J. S. Bruner (1973) or J. Piaget (1976)). These theories have one thing in common: they consider *cognitive structures* (the notion of cognitive structures originates from Piaget) as the central element of learning. In this view, individuals learn by developing cognitive structures. These structures contain categories, elements of meaning, plots or thought patterns. Connecting existing elements and including new ones are regarded as the crucial processes within these theories.

Decisions are made on the basis of cognitive structures. All cognitive learning theories presented in this section agree on this. They differ in the perspective they take with respect to cognition. However, they all have in common the idea that certain kinds of cognitive beliefs or understandings are developed as a consequence of experience.

In the context of economics, it is difficult to find helpful implications that can be quantitatively exploited on the basis of these theories. It may be claimed that it is impossible to come up with precise predictions in the context of cognitive learning or that research into cognitive learning is still at its beginning. Whichever is the case, one implication may be worth mentioning: the development of cognitive structures causes learning processes to be very complex. If we only consider some elements of this structure, as is usually done in economic learning models, we can only obtain an approximation of the real processes. We should keep this in mind because for mathematical reasons we are forced to neglect the cognitive structure most of the time.

2.3.5   Further Psychological Knowledge in the Context of Learning

Memory and learning

An important aspect in the context of learning is the ability to recall facts and procedures that have been learnt before. The study of *memory* is a large field in psychology. It is also a field in which a number of new ideas and theories have been put forward in recent years. Not all of this knowledge of memory is important for the study of learning processes. In economics we are mainly interested in the ability to recall in the future what was learnt in the past. Therefore I focus on the long-term memory in the following.

The long-term memory is usually subdivided into two kinds of memory: the *procedural memory* and the *declarative memory*. The procedural memory contains all skills that an individual has learnt during life. In this context a skill is the ability to do something. It is not necessarily connected with the ability to explain the sequence of actions. Skills are hard to learn and hard to forget. Thus the procedural memory does not decay significantly through time.

The declarative memory contains the memory of facts and events (*episodic memory*) as well as the memory of associations that have been built during a lifetime (*semantic memory*). The episodic memory is often claimed to contain every event that has occurred during the life of an individual. Be that as it may, the episodic memory only contains sensual perceptions. Their interpretation or association is not part of the episodic memory. Associations of sensual perceptions are stored in the semantic memory. For example, the connection between the visual picture of water and the tactile sensation of water belongs to the semantic memory according to this definition. The episodic and semantic memory are not claimed to exist separately in the brain. It is rather a construct that explains the different experimental results concerning the ability of individuals to memorise facts, events and associations.

In contrast to the procedural memory, the declarative memory is subject to changes and decay. Four principal theories exist concerning the decay of memory traces:

1) The memory of facts (declarative memory, especially the episodic memory) vanishes with time. This theory originates from H. Ebbinghaus (1913) who found that the memory of senseless syllables vanishes with time. Especially during the first five days, the subjects forgot most of the syllables they had learnt. Later on the memory stabilised and some of the syllables were stored permanently. Nowadays this theory is seen in a much more elaborated way. Individuals certainly forget some of the facts they learn in the course of a day (for example, what we ate last day, last week, last month or last year). At the same time, there are events or facts we never forget. Therefore a theory that states that all memory fades over time cannot be sustained, although it is true for many facts and events. Ebbinghaus neglected the aspect that facts are seen in the context of other facts and evaluated according to their subjective importance. Nevertheless he was right to claim that, in general, recall of facts becomes more and more difficult over time.

2) The memory of facts and associations fades due to other facts and associations that interfere with them. If we learn some foreign vocabulary and afterwards some mathematical formulas, it will be harder to remember the foreign vocabulary than if we had taken a break in between. It would be even harder if we had learnt some vocabulary of

another foreign language in the meantime. Results like this were obtained in many experiments (cf. e. g. Underwood 1948). The memory of facts and associations is disturbed by the storage of new facts and associations. In particular if the pieces of information are related, one piece of information is able to supplant the other or at least to reduce its availability. In this sense, memory traces compete for availability in the memory.

3) People are sometimes unable to recall memory traces because they do not find the right link; this is named error of recall. Memory traces are linked with each other in the memory. To recall them we have to activate the right links. So although we do not find the answer to a question, we may find it if the question is reformulated.

4) People are able to exclude parts of the memory from consciousness. This motivated forgetting occurs, for example, in connection with events that hurt the individual's psyche too much. In the context of learning this process is of no interest.

Since I want to study learning in economics, I have to keep in mind the first two theories of the loss of memory. This means, (1) most memory traces decay with time and (2) memory traces interfere in such a way that one may reduce the availability of another. The third theory of loss of memory may be interesting in connection with the identification of situations. Learning takes place if a situation recurs. In most cases the situation does not recur in exactly the same form. However, as long as the changes are small it is identified as the same situation. By this, recall of the right link is crucial for the learning process. If a situation is presented differently, it might be perceived as a new situation although it is exactly the same as the one before. In other words, individuals relate different situations to each other and regard them as similar. This connection is a subjective act and is not necessarily identical to the objective similarity of the situations. Learning takes place within the set of situations that are connected with each other through the subjective experience of the person her/himself.

Motivation and learning

Motivation is one more psychological aspect that is important in the context of learning. The learning theories described above can be classified into active and passive learning models. The theories of conditioning are more passive, where the individual is the object of the learning process and is not able to initiate or avoid it. In other theories, for example, observational learning, the individual is quite active. During learning, they are deciding whether they want to learn and what they want to learn (although this decision may be made unconsciously). Learning processes of the latter type involve motivation. Other cognitive learning theories draw a mixed picture of when and how learning becomes active. On the one hand, in cognitive learning, the cognitive structure is assumed to be shaped by reinforcement, that is, passively. On the other hand, utilisation of cognitive models or maps is an active process where individuals consciously apply and reconsider their cognitive knowledge.

When psychologists speak about *motivation*, they also discuss *drives* and *needs*. These are the basic reasons for action and therefore the basic motivations. Many models exist that attempt to list, order and categorise human desires (most famous is that of A. H. Maslow (1970)). In the context of learning, such models are not very helpful. What we need is a theory that explains the motivation to learn, that is, to change behaviour, as a result of former experience. Three well-known theories are often stated in this context: *field theory* (Lewin 1963), *dissonance theory* (Festinger 1957) and the theory of *optimal arousal* (Hebb 1955). I will give a short description of these theories below.

Lewin models the individual as situated in a field made up by a number of objects. Each object is either attractive or repellent. Individuals try to reach the attractive objects while avoiding the repellent ones. In doing so, they are hindered by barriers or restrictions. In addition, Lewin presents many ideas about the way individuals arrange themselves within such a field. Nevertheless his theory is quite abstract and has not much to offer in the context of learning in economics.

The dissonance theory is based on field theory. It also assumes that individuals have a subjective perception of the elements in their surroundings. These perceptions are called *cognitions*. Cognitive dissonance occurs if one cognition is in contradiction with another cognition, for example, if someone is a friend of mine (cognition 1) and yet behaves in a way I cannot accept (cognition 2). In such a case, dissonance theory states that the individual tries to counterbalance the dissonance. The individual is motivated to change one of the two cognitions (I either change my opinion about the observed behaviour or abandon my friend) or to find a new cognition that explains the dissonance (I may find an explanation why my friend behaves like this). According to dissonance theory, a cognitive dissonance always leads to a change in behaviour or opinion. In the context of learning this means that the motivation to learn may be a result of cognitive dissonance, for example, the dissonance between an aim, in this case to honour a friendship, and the present outcome of one's action, the unfortunate result of the friend's behaviour.

The theory of optimal arousal differs very much from the former two.

The theory itself originates from D. O. Hebb, but it is based on the experimental findings of D. B. Lindsley (1951) and many others. The theory is based on a physiological phenomenon, namely that sensual stimuli increase the activity of the reticular activating system, an area located in the brain. This stimulation is called the arousal function of a sensual stimulus. The amount of activity of the reticular activating system is called the level of arousal. The sum of the stimuli that an individual faces determines the actual level of arousal. Hebb (1955) analysed the dependence of the performance of an individual on the arousal level. He found that both a high level of arousal and a low level of arousal have a negative impact on performance. Consequently he claimed that there is an optimal level of arousal which may vary for different tasks. Deviations from this optimal level of arousal decrease performance.

Moreover, Hebb stated that deviations from the optimal level of arousal motivate individuals to act in a way to retain optimal circumstances, circumstances that offer the right amount of stimulation so that the level of arousal is optimal. Thus the wish to reduce stimulation, when too much, as well as the wish to increase it, in the case of boredom, are basic motivations. T. Scitovsky (1992) has convincingly translated the theory of optimal arousal into the context of economics. He utilised the statement that high as well as low arousal levels are uncomfortable and that the individual tries to maintain an intermediate arousal level. Furthermore, he claimed that the effect of stimuli diminish if they are faced very often. Something which may be exciting initially becomes boring if it occurs too often. This way Scitovsky is able to explain the search for *novelty* as well as the desire for alternation.

In addition to these three theories of motivation, there are two other psychological aspects that are often linked to *motivation*. One is the *aspiration level*, the other the *level of comparison*. The aspiration level was first studied extensively by L. Festinger (1942) and by K. Lewin, T. Dembo, L. Festinger, and P. S. Sears (1944). They investigated changes of the aspiration level due to the performance of the individual or due to information about the performance of other individuals. By doing this they enriched the model of Escalona (1939) by a social aspect. Escalona proposed that the aspiration level is caused by two motives: the desire to be successful, expressed by the valence of success; and the fact that it is disagreeable to fail, expressed by the potency of success. The aspiration level of individuals, according to Escalona, lies where a certain mixture of these values is maximal. Festinger and others found that, in addition to the theory of Escalona, the performance of others plays an important role in the determination of aspiration level. Thus the aspiration level is determined by pleasures, expectations, and comparison with others.

A different but fairly related approach was taken by J. W. Thibaut and H. H. Kelley (1959). They assumed the existence of a *level of comparison*. According to them, the level of comparison is determined by the outcomes of all similar situations in the past, with the most recent outcomes considered more intensively. Thus the level of comparison is the weighted average of former experiences. It determines whether new results are judged to be negative, positive, or neutral. Each outcome above the level of comparison is evaluated as positive, while outcomes below the level of comparison are seen as negative. In contrast to the aspiration level, as defined above, the level of comparison is not influenced by any expectations or likes; it only depends on observations in the past.

In experiments it has been shown that experiences below the level of comparison motivate individuals for activities (like learning, interacting with other people, or working harder) that enable them to compensate for the dissatisfaction. Similarly, it has been found that people show a more variable behaviour and are more likely to change their situation if the performance has been below the aspiration level (cf. e. g. Sears 1942 or Hoppe 1975). In other words, they are motivated for one reason or another to perform to their aspiration level or level of comparison.

To sum up, motivational aspects play a role in all active learning processes. Three aspects are important in this context; (1) cognitive dissonance motivates individuals to change their behaviour or beliefs, (2) boredom motivates individuals to search for new impressions and activities, and (3) if individuals are dissatisfied by the present outcomes, which are below their aspiration level or level of comparison, they are motivated to change their behaviour.

2.4 SUMMARY

In this chapter a categorisation of learning processes has been proposed and the psychological literature on learning has been reviewed. The categorisation was motivated by the intention to model learning in an economic context. The different learning theories that are found in the psychological literature are based on the attempt to understand learning and different views on learning processes. For the following analysis, especially the search for a mathematical model in the next chapter, it is helpful to relate the system of categorisation proposed here to the various ideas about learning.

In the categorisation, three kinds of learning processes have been distinguished according to two characteristics: whether they are cognitive or non-cognitive, and whether they influence the behaviour itself or the cognitive models of the situation. The first distinction is made between non-cognitive and cognitive models can be found in a similar form in the psychological literature. There a distinction between the theories of behaviourism, classical conditioning and reinforcement learning, and the cognitive theories, including observational learning and all the different cognitive learning models. Classical conditioning and reinforcement learning are assumed to take place unconsciously. Thus they correspond to what has been called above *non-cognitive learning*. The cognitive learning theories in psychology correspond to the category of associative learning processes because, for both, the creation and change of cognitive models is a crucial aspect. The category of routine-based learning processes, instead, is difficult to relate to the psychological literature. This category contains all learning processes that proceed according to specific rules, due to individuals cognitively believing in these rules. They are a consequence of the cognitive belief of individuals about their surroundings and are therefore not of central interest in psychology. However, they allow modelling of cognitive learning in some situations quite convincingly, and are therefore important in an economic context. Imitation is one kind of routine-based learning; nevertheless the psychological notion of imitation, or observational learning, has nothing to do with a routine. Dependent on the form of the observational learning employed, it is either based on a non-cognitive reinforcement process or on a change of cognitive models due to observed facts. Thus observational learning, as defined in psychology, belongs either to the category of non-cognitive learning or to the category of associative learning, but not to the category of routine-based learning.

The categorisation, which will be used throughout this book, can be summarised as follows: The most important distinction concerning learning situations relates to the presence or absence of cognitive awareness by the individuals. Individuals do not have enough cognitive capacity to reason out every decision-making situation they face. Consequently, cognitive capacity is divided between several situations that seem to be important enough for the individual to pay attention. Other situations are neglected. In the neglected situations the individuals learn non-cognitively (see Figure 2.1). If individuals reflect cognitively about a situation, they form a cognitive model of the situation. If it is new, they have in general no understanding of the situation. Consequently, with the gathering of knowledge of the situation, they also learn about causes, relations and interdependencies. They adapt their cognitive model to this knowledge, that is, they learn associatively (see Figure 2.1). Each state of associative learning is characterised by the corresponding cognitive model. This model causes the individuals to apply a certain course of behaviour, known as a learning rule. If the associative learning has been settled upon, the learning rule is fixed. From this point on, individuals engage in routine-based learning, with some degree of non-cognitive learning always present (see Figure 2.1). The distinction between associative learning and routine-based learning is somewhat artificial but helpful in the context of modelling. Whether routine-based learning or associative learning occurs depends on the degree to which the individuals are used to the situation. New information or a slightly changed situation may reactivate the associative learning process at any time. If the routine-based learning process has been settled upon as well, the behaviour becomes static (see Figure 2.1). This static behaviour may be optimal if the individual has a realistic cognitive model and sufficient information.

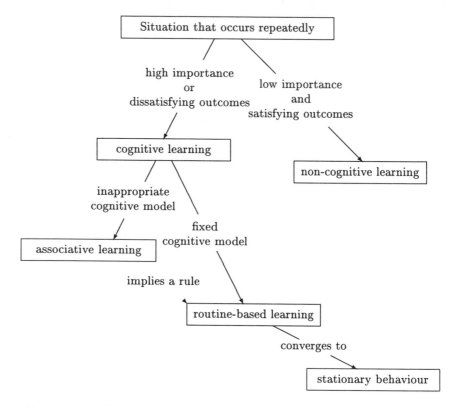

Figure 2.1: *Categorisation of learning processes according to the characteristics of the repeated situation*

Chapter 3

Modelling Learning Processes

The previous categorisation of learning processes provides a tool for deducing the main features of behaviour expected, depending on the characteristics of the corresponding situation. In the context of economic research these behavioural features determine the dynamics of economic processes. Therefore, for an economic application of these learning processes a precise formulation of the three different kinds of processes appears to be necessary.

In this chapter, each of the three kinds of learning processes will be considered separately. For each of them the possible ways of modelling are discussed on the basis of their features. To this end, the literature on learning models is summarised. Section 1 starts with the description of the processes of non-cognitive learning. In the case of routine-based learning, a huge number of learning models can be found in the literature. Therefore, the discussion of routine-based learning is divided into three parts; Section 2 describes how individuals should learn from a normative perspective, Section 3 describes specific features of routine-based learning observable in various situations and often modelled in economic contexts, and Section 4 describes a general model of routine-based learning. Finally, Section 5 discusses the different possibilities for modelling associative learning.

3.1   NON-COGNITIVE LEARNING

Non-cognitive learning contains two different kinds of learning: *classical conditioning* and *reinforcement learning*. Both are quite different with respect to their features.

In the literature, only one model can be found describing classical conditioning: the *Rescorla-Wagner theory* (cf. Chapter 2). This model represents quite well the speed of learning and the interaction of different stimuli that are conditioned at the same time. It is, however, not able to capture the process of spontaneous recovery or to explain why conditioning does not work with every pair of a neutral stimulus and a reinforcer. In the economic literature, no models of classical conditioning can be found because this kind of learning is generally not thought to be important in economic processes. An exception is the change of preferences (cf. Witt 1987b) which is discussed in more detail in Chapter 5.

In the case of reinforcement learning, two models are frequently used to describe the dynamics: the *Bush-Mosteller model* and the principle of *melioration*. Both models capture quite well two major dynamic aspects of reinforcement learning: the asymptotic increase of the frequency of behaviours that lead to better results than their alternatives, and the slow disappearance of behaviours if the reinforcement is removed. However they are not able to describe the aspect of spontaneous recovery.

3.1.1   Bush-Mosteller Model

At the beginning of this century *reinforcement learning* became a central topic in psychology (cf. the previous chapter). This finally led to the development of a mathematical learning model by R. R. Bush and F. Mosteller (1955) on the basis of the psychological knowledge about learning. Their model, called the *Bush-Mosteller model*, is based on the considerations of W. K. Estes (1950) who took the first steps towards a mathematical formulation of reinforcement learning. It is based on the idea of representing behaviour by a *frequency distribution* of behaviour patterns given by a probability vector $\mathbf{p}(t)$ $(= (p(a,t))_{a \in \mathcal{A}})$. This vector assigns a probability $p(a,t)$ $(0 \leq p(a,t) \leq 1, \sum_{a \in \mathcal{A}} p(a,t) = 1)$ to each behavioural alternative a $(a \in \mathcal{A})$ at each time t. $p(a,t)$ is sometimes called *habit strength*. The Bush-Mosteller model is a stochastic model that predicts probabilities for the occurrence of behaviour patterns rather than the behaviour pattern itself.

The probability vector $\mathbf{p}(t)$ changes during the learning process according to the theory of reinforcement. Dependent on the event e ($e \in \mathcal{E}$ where $\mathcal{E}$ is the set of all possible events) some actions are rewarded while others are punished (events that are neither rewarding nor punishing are neglected in their formulation of reinforcement learning). The resulting modification of probabilities $p(a, t)$ is assumed to be linear. This linearity is the most important restriction that Bush and Mosteller impose on their model. It allows them to model the change of the probability vector by a matrix operation $\mathbf{p}(t + 1) = \mathbf{L}_e \mathbf{p}(t)$. Consequently for each event e they only have to define a matrix $\mathbf{L}_e$ that represents the change of behaviour mathematically in that case.

The matrix operation can be explained most easily if we consider only two behavioural alternatives. In this case, the probability $p(t) = p(a, t)$ of one behavioural alternative a is sufficient to describe the situation because the probability of choosing the other behavioural alternative is given by $(1 - p(t))$. In this case, the operation $\mathbf{L}_e$ can be written as

$$\mathbf{L}_e p(t) = p(t) + \gamma_e (1 - p(t)) - \beta_e p(t) \qquad (3.1)$$

where γ_e is the reinforcing character of event e and β_e is its punishing character ($\beta_e, \gamma_e \in [0, 1]$ where for every event one of the two is zero). Thus if an event is reinforcing with respect to the behaviour, $p(t)$ increases by a proportion γ_e of the largest possible increase $(1 - p(t))$ (an increase larger than $(1 - p(t))$ would violate the condition $p(t) \leq 1$). The same holds for a punishing event. Equation (3.1) can be transformed to

$$\mathbf{L}_e p(t) = \alpha_e p(t) + (1 - \alpha_e) l_e \qquad (3.2)$$

where α_a determines the speed of the learning process. The smaller α_a, the faster the individuals learn. l_e determines the final state to which the learning process converges if only event e occurs repeatedly. Equation (3.2) can be generalised for every finite number of behavioural alternatives. In this case operation $\mathbf{L}$ reads

$$\mathbf{L}_e \mathbf{p}(t) = \alpha_e \mathbf{p}(t) + (1 - \alpha_e) \mathbf{l}_e \ . \qquad (3.3)$$

The characteristics and results of such a learning algorithm are discussed comprehensively by Bush and Mosteller (cf. Bush & Mosteller 1955). However although equation (3.3) is mathematically convenient, the question of how the parameters α_e and $\mathbf{l}_e$ are to be determined in an application is not discussed by Bush and Mosteller.

J. G. Cross (1973) further developed the Bush-Mosteller model by answering the question of how to define the parameters. He argued in

an economical context and defined the reinforcing character of an event
by the utility to which it gives rise. In future I will call this utility in the
context of reinforcement learning *reinforcement strength*. It is denoted by
$\Pi(a, t)$ for realisation of action a at time t. Cross defined reinforcement
learning by

$$p(a, t+1) = p(a, t) + \begin{cases} \alpha(\Pi(t)) \cdot (1 - p(a, t)) & \text{if } a = a(t) \\ -\alpha(\Pi(t)) \cdot p(a, t) & \text{if } a \neq a(t) \end{cases} \quad (3.4)$$

where $\Pi(t) = \Pi(a(t), t)$ is the reinforcement strength that the individual obtains at time t. $\alpha(\Pi(t))$ is a monotonously increasing function
in the reinforcement strength $\Pi(t)$. Since the probabilities $p(a, t)$ are
bounded by $0 \leq p(a, t) \leq 1$, the function $\alpha(\Pi(t))$ also has to be bounded
by $0 \leq \alpha(\Pi(t)) \leq 1$. In most applications (cf. e.g. Cross 1983 and
Börgers & Sarin 1997) $\alpha(\Pi(t))$ is defined as a linear function in $\Pi(t)$, i.e.
$\alpha(\Pi(t)) = \alpha \cdot \Pi(t)$. If we compare Cross's version with the original Bush-
Mosteller model, that is, equation (3.4) with equation (3.1), we notice
two differences. First, Cross defines the formerly undefined reinforcement
character α_e as a function of Π. Second, Cross eliminates the punishing character of events. In other words, in Cross's model every possible
outcome of a behaviour is assumed to be reinforcing. An outcome that
leads to a decrease of the frequency of the respective behaviour cannot
be modelled using Cross's model. Thus, although Cross enriched the
Bush-Mosteller model by the introduction of a reinforcement strength,
he lost generality because of the neglect of negative reinforcement.

This shortcoming of Cross's version of the Bush-Mosteller model has
been overcome by the *modified Bush-Mosteller model* proposed by T.
Brenner (cf. Brenner 1997) and by the work of Börgers and Sarin
(1996). In the model of Brenner, reinforcement strengths are defined
such that all rewarding outcomes are reflected by positive reinforcement
strengths, while all punishing outcomes are reflected by negative reinforcement strengths. Apart from this, the generalised Bush-Mosteller
model is identical to the version proposed by J. G. Cross. The change of
the probability $p(a, t)$ of the individual to realise action a is given by

$$p(a, t+1) = p(a, t) + \begin{cases} \alpha(\Pi(t)) \cdot (1 - p(a, t)) & \text{if } a = a(t) \\ -\alpha(\Pi(t)) \cdot p(a, t) & \text{if } a \neq a(t) \end{cases} \quad (3.5)$$

if action $a(t)$ is realised and the resulting reinforcement strength $\Pi(t)$ is positive, and by

$$p(a, t+1) = p(a, t) + \begin{cases} -\alpha(-\Pi(t)) \cdot p(a, t) & \text{if} \quad a = a(t) \\ \alpha(-\Pi(t)) \cdot \frac{p(a,t)\,p(a(t),t)}{1-p(a(t),t)} & \text{if} \quad a \neq a(t) \end{cases} \tag{3.6}$$

if action $a(t)$ is realised and the resulting reinforcement strength $\Pi(t)$ is negative. $\alpha(\Pi)$ is a monotonously increasing function in Π ($\Pi > 0$) with $\alpha(0) = 0$ and $0 \leq \alpha(\Pi) \leq 1$. A reinforcement strength of $\Pi = 0$ can be interpreted as *aspiration level* (as it is done in Börgers & Sarin 1996).

In this book the modified Bush-Mosteller model (Brenner 1997) is used in the simplified version with $\alpha(\Pi) = \alpha \cdot \Pi$. Using this formulation, the learning process is described by

$$p(a, t+1) = p(a, t) + \begin{cases} \alpha \cdot \Pi(t) \cdot (1 - p(a, t)) & \text{if} \quad a = a(t) \wedge \Pi(t) \geq 0 \\ \alpha \cdot \Pi(t) \cdot p(a, t) & \text{if} \quad a = a(t) \wedge \Pi(t) < 0 \\ -\alpha \cdot \Pi(t) \cdot p(a, t) & \text{if} \quad a \neq a(t) \wedge \Pi(t) \geq 0 \\ -\alpha \cdot \Pi(t) \cdot \frac{p(a,t) \cdot p(a(t),t)}{1-p(a(t),t)} & \text{if} \quad a \neq a(t) \wedge \Pi(t) < 0 \end{cases}$$

$$\tag{3.7}$$

The generalised Bush-Mosteller model comprises Cross's formulation as well as the original Bush-Mosteller model. Nevertheless, it modifies these models by the consideration of rewarding and punishing outcomes of different strength. A further version of the Bush-Mosteller model was proposed by Roth and Erév (1995). They assumed the speed of learning decreases with time and tested this version of reinforcement learning successfully in experiments (for details see Roth & Erév 1995).

All versions of the Bush-Mosteller model assume that an outcome has an impact on the frequency distribution $\mathbf{p}(t)$ in the moment of its occurrence only. This means that individuals do not remember previous actions and outcomes. The past is implicitly contained in the value of frequency distribution $\mathbf{p}(t)$. Learning is assumed to be a *Markov process*.

3.1.2 Melioration Learning

The concept of melioration learning is based on experimental findings about *reinforcement learning*. R. J. Herrnstein found that reinforcement learning under concurrent schedules leads to behaviour that can be described by the *matching law* (cf. Herrnstein 1970 and Chapter 2). Under concurrent schedules individuals have to distribute their time between different activities. For each of the activities the subjects obtain a reinforcer from time to time, according to a rule unknown by the subjects.

Herrnstein found that the percentage of time spent with each of the activities equals the percentage of the total number of reinforcers that have been obtained while performing this activity (cf. Herrnstein 1970). Later Herrnstein transferred the matching law to an economic context to describe consumer behaviour (cf. Herrnstein & Prelec 1991). To this end, he adopted the concept of a cardinal utility function. He claimed that, in the realm of consumer behaviour for example, the matching law describes economic behaviour adequately as well. This leads to the statement that the frequency of each action a is such that the average utility each action gives rise to is the same for all actions that are realised (cf. Vaughan & Herrnstein 1987):

$$\bar{u}(a) = \bar{u}(\tilde{a}) \qquad \forall\, a, \tilde{a} \in \mathcal{A} \text{ with } p(a,t), p(\tilde{a},t) \neq 0 . \qquad (3.8)$$

Actions that give rise to a smaller average utility disappear, i. e.,

$$p(a,t) \to 0 \qquad \forall\, a, \tilde{a} \in \mathcal{A} \text{ with } p(\tilde{a},t) \neq 0 \wedge \bar{u}(a) < \bar{u}(\tilde{a}) . \qquad (3.9)$$

The average utility $\bar{u}(a,t)$ was assumed by Herrnstein to reflect the average utility remembered from past experiences. According to this assumption, individuals have an imperfect memory and remember only part of their actions and outcomes from the recent past. Subsequently, they evaluate each action by the average utility it has given rise to on the occasions remembered.

The works of Herrnstein and others mainly focused on the implications of the matching law in the context of consumer behaviour (cf. Vaughan & Herrnstein 1987 and Herrnstein & Prelec 1991). They were less interested in the learning process itself. However, a formulation of the dynamics of learning which they assumed can be found in Vaughan & Herrnstein 1987. There they describe a time continuous adjustment formulation for a case with two possible actions a and $\tilde{a}$ by

$$\frac{dp(a,t)}{dt} = \alpha\Big(\bar{u}(a,t) - \bar{u}(\tilde{a},t)\Big) \qquad (3.10)$$

where $p(a,t)$ denotes the proportion of income spent on activity a and $\alpha(..)$ is a monotonously increasing function with $\alpha(0) = 0$.

In contrast to the general application of the matching law (distribution of time between various activities) Vaughan and Herrnstein (1987) assumed that the matching law also holds for budgeting of money. Hence they deal with proportions of income spent on several activities. In most of the experiments, the subjects had to distribute time between several

actions or had to decide how to act at several moments in time. Consequently, their behaviour is better described by the frequency of the occurrence of each choice, that is, the probability $p(a, t)$ that they choose
an action a at time t. In the following equation (3.10) is interpreted
according to the distribution of time.

Vaughan and Herrnstein (1987) neglect cases in which the individuals
can choose between more than two alternative actions. Nor do they
define the average utilities $\bar{u}(a, t)$ in detail. They simply state that $\bar{u}(a, t)$
denotes the average utility obtained by individuals from action a in the
past. A discussion of the average utility or payoff can be found in Brenner
& Witt 1997. I follow their proposal and define $\mathcal{T}_{i,a}(t)$ as the set of
moments of time in which an individual i has realised action a and which
individual i has memory of at time t. $k_{i,a}(t)$ denotes the number of these
occasions. Consequently the average utility $\bar{u}_i(a, t)$ is given by

$$\bar{u}_i(a, t) = \frac{1}{k_{i,a}(t)} \cdot \sum_{\tau \in \mathcal{T}_{i,a}(t)} u_i(a, \tau) \,. \tag{3.11}$$

Brenner and Witt (1997) also claim that it is more adequate to multiply
equation (3.10) by $p(a, t) \cdot (1 - p(a, t))$ instead of the artificial additional
condition that the dynamics stop if $p(a, t)$ becomes smaller than zero for
at least one action a. Consequently equation (3.10) can be written for
individual i as

$$\frac{dp_i(a, t)}{dt} = p_i(a, t) \cdot \left(1 - p_i(a, t)\right) \cdot \alpha\left(\bar{u}_i(a, t) - \bar{u}_i(\tilde{a}, t)\right) \,. \tag{3.12}$$

We may further simplify the dynamics and assume that $\alpha(..)$ is a linear
function. As before, equation (3.12) only holds for cases in which the individuals have to choose between two alternative actions, which I denote
by a and $\tilde{a}$. Therefore if $\alpha(..)$ is a linear function, equation (3.12) can be
written as

$$\frac{dp_i(a, t)}{dt} = p_i(a, t) \cdot \alpha \cdot \left(\bar{u}_i(a, t) - p_i(a, t) \cdot \bar{u}_i(a, t) - p_i(\tilde{a}, t) \cdot \bar{u}_i(\tilde{a}, t)\right) \,. \tag{3.13}$$

This formulation can be generalised to cases in which the individual can
choose from a set $\mathcal{A}$ of alternative actions. The dynamics are then given
by

$$\frac{dp_i(a, t)}{dt} = p_i(a, t) \cdot \alpha \cdot \left(\bar{u}_i(a, t) - \sum_{\tilde{a} \in \mathcal{A}} p_i(\tilde{a}, t) \cdot \bar{u}_i(\tilde{a}, t)\right) \,. \tag{3.14}$$

Equation (3.14) still converges to the *matching law* and seems to be an adequate description of the dynamics of *melioration learning.*

Since both melioration learning and the *Bush-Mosteller model* claim to describe *reinforcement learning*, the differences between the two models will be pointed out below.

When people meliorate they are assumed to utilise only the information gathered from the last several experiences. This means they remember the average utility that the most recent $k_{i,a}(t)$ realisations of action a have given rise to. Consequently, the updating of the probability distribution not only depends on current distribution and present outcome but also on a given number of previous outcomes. Melioration learning is not a Markov process; in contrast to the Bush-Mosteller model, information from past experience is not held. Of course melioration learning can be transformed into a Markov process, by constructing additional variables that carry the information about the experience in the past that influences future behaviour.

Furthermore in the Bush-Mosteller model, each action is evaluated separately. The outcome of an action first of all is assumed to change the probability of realising this very action. Other probabilities are only affected because the sum of the probabilities has to remain one. In melioration learning, it is assumed that individuals compare the outcomes of different actions and change the probability distribution $\mathbf{p}_i(t)$ accordingly.

However, as long as payoffs or utilities are positive and the remembered time period of melioration learning is sufficiently long, both models converge to the same behaviour in the long run. This behaviour is given by the *matching law*, which has been confirmed in many studies.

3.2   NORMATIVE ROUTINE-BASED LEARNING

In the economic literature, many learning models have been proposed on the basis of rational considerations. These models are constructed to describe an optimal learning process that leads to utility maximising behaviour. No attempt was made in the literature to verify the correspondence with reality of these models. Instead it has been claimed that these learning models should be chosen by every rational individual. These models are based on normative considerations rather than on psychological knowledge.

In recent years it has been proved that some of these learning processes do not converge to the utility maximising behaviour in all situations (cf. Bullard & Duffy 1994a). As a consequence the study of convergence characteristics of different learning processes has become a major subject of the investigation of learning (cf. Brenner 1997 and the references therein).

In the following three examples of normative learning processes will be described, however this is not to be considered a complete list. These are Bayesian learning, the Robbins-Monro algorithm, and least squares learning.

3.2.1 Bayesian Learning

Bayesian learning is the most well known of these normative concepts. The individuals are assumed to act rationally with respect to considering all available information and maximising their own profit on the basis of this information.

If we accept the rationality assumption that individuals take the best action according to the information available, the concept of Bayesian learning is a natural approach, but only if the individuals have sufficient knowledge about the situation to build up an adequate set of hypotheses. Bayesian learning assumes individuals establish a set of *hypotheses* about the situation they face. Each hypothesis h makes a probabilistic statement $P(e|h)$ about the occurrence of each event e of a set of events $\mathcal{E}$. This means that hypothesis h implies that event e occurs with probability $P(e|h)$. The set of hypotheses has to be complete and complementary, meaning that every possible state of reality has to be represented by one, and only one, hypothesis. The set of hypotheses is denoted by $\mathcal{H}$ in the following equations. At the beginning of the learning process the individuals generally assign the same probability $p(h, 0)$ to each hypothesis $h \in \mathcal{H}$. If the individuals have initial information about the situation they face, the initial probabilities $p(h, 0)$ are different from each other according to this information. $p(h, t)$ denotes the individual estimation of the probability that hypothesis h is correct. In other words, $p(h, t)$ is the belief of the individuals in hypothesis h at time t. The sum $\sum_{h \in \mathcal{H}} p(h, t)$ has to equal one.

After each event $e(t)$ the individuals update their presumed probabilities. The updating proceeds as follows (cf. e.g. Easley & Kiefer 1988 or Jordan 1991). The individuals calculate the probability $P(e(t)|h)$ for each hypothesis h. Subsequently they update their beliefs according to the following equation (I neglect the index for the individuals because the learning process is the same for all of them although they may obtain different information).

$$p(h, t+1) = \frac{P(e(t)|h) \cdot p(h,t)}{\sum_{\tilde{h}\in\mathcal{H}} P(e(t)|\tilde{h})\, p(\tilde{h},t)} \ . \tag{3.15}$$

By this, the presumed probabilities of hypotheses predicting the occurrence of the observed event with a high probability increase, while the presumed probabilities of the other hypotheses decrease. The condition $\sum_{h\in\mathcal{H}} p(h,t) = 1$ is maintained while updating the probabilities according to equation (3.15). After many observed events, the probability $p(h,t)$ should converge to $p(h,t) \approx 1$ for the correct hypothesis about reality, and to $p(h,t) \approx 0$ for all other hypotheses.

Decisions are made according to the following consideration. For each hypothesis h the individuals calculate the average utility $\bar{u}(a,t)$ that the action a gives rise to. To this end, they have to assign a utility $u(e)$ to each event e. $\bar{u}(a)$ is given by

$$\bar{u}(a,t) = \sum_{h\in\mathcal{H}} \sum_{e\in\mathcal{E}} p(h,t) \cdot P(e|h) \ . \tag{3.16}$$

The average utility is that which they expect to result from action a. In economics it is called *expected utility*. Since it is learnt adaptively it is also called *adaptive expected utility*. Subsequently, the individuals decide in such a way that they maximise their expected utility $\bar{u}(a,t)$.

There are two objections that can be advanced against Bayesian learning. First, Bayesian learning is a very complicated procedure. It has to be doubted whether people are really capable of such a complicated calculation for all their decisions and behaviours. Restrictions of time, capability, and cognitive capacity make Bayesian learning look rather unrealistic. Second, the set of hypotheses is not unequivocally determined. Different sets can be claimed to be adequate. The learning process, in turn, may depend crucially on the choice of hypotheses.

Nevertheless Bayesian learning has an advantage that is overlooked in the literature. Since it is based on a set of hypotheses, it offers a simple method of considering the *cognitive perception* of situations by individuals. Individuals perceive their environment in the framework of their cognitive picture of the world. Consequently, individual hypotheses about the world are never complete or consistent (although it is generally assumed that the hypotheses are consistent in the context of Bayesian learning, the concept is, in principle, able to capture inconsistent sets of hypotheses). They are rather influenced by the *cognitive models* that individuals have developed about the world. If we are able to make more precise statements about these cognitive models and the hypotheses of individuals, Bayesian learning may become a helpful tool for the description of associative learning. This aspect of Bayesian learning, however, has still to be developed.

3.2.2 Robbins-Monro Algorithm

Another specific model of adaptation is the Robbins-Monro algorithm (cf. Révész 1973 and Sargent 1993). It is defined for a continuous decision variable a (e.g. $a \in [0, \infty)$) and a discrete time t. The decision at time t is denoted by $a(t)$. Furthermore, the individuals are assumed to be well aware of their utility functions $u(a, \theta(t))$ which depend on the decision variable a and an ex ante unknown value $\theta(t)$. $\theta(t)$ represents the realisation of the relevant circumstances. Ex post the individuals are able to calculate $u(a, \theta(t))$ as well as $du(a, \theta(t))/da$ and $d^2u(a, \theta(t))/da^2$. In addition to their decision variable $a(t)$ at each time step, the individuals also update a second variable $M(t)$ that is defined recursively by

$$M(t+1) = M(t) + \frac{1}{t}\left(\frac{d^2u(a, \theta(t))}{da^2} - M(t)\right). \qquad (3.17)$$

This variable represents the average value of all former realisations of $d^2u(a, \theta(t))/da^2$. The dynamics of the decision variable $a(t)$ are given by

$$a(t+1) = a(t) - \frac{1}{t} \cdot \frac{\frac{d^2u(a, \theta(t))}{da^2}}{M(t)}. \qquad (3.18)$$

The concept for such a complex algorithm is taken from the Newton algorithm used to find the zero elements of a function $du(a, \theta(t))/da$ in numerical mathematics. Not surprisingly, the Robbins-Monro algorithm converges to a value $a(t)$ that causes $du(a, \theta(t))/da$ to be zero, i.e. $u(a, \theta(t))$ to be maximal (cf. e.g. Yin & Zhu 1990) in the case of a constant concave utility function. The Robbins-Monro algorithm represents an algorithm that enables the individuals to find optimal behaviour without full information about the situation. Information about the utility $u(a, \theta(t))$ is local. This means that the individuals only know the utility and its derivatives for the action a that was taken. The complete utility function $u(a, \theta(t))$ is not necessarily known by the individuals.

Nevertheless, the assumption that individuals learn according to the Robbins-Monro algorithm is unrealistic, because it requires that the individuals are able to recognise the two first derivatives of the utility function, and to do the calculations given by the equations (3.17) and

(3.18). It is not obvious why the individuals should be able to calcu-
late $u(a, \theta(t))$ and its derivatives $du(a, \theta(t))/da$ and $d^2u(a, \theta(t))/da^2$ for
$a = a(t)$ but not for any other value of a in general. Furthermore, most
people neither understand the algorithm above nor are they able to apply
it without technical tools and some training.

3.2.3   Least Squares Learning

Another well-known normative learning model is least squares learning
(cf. Bray 1982, Marcet & Sargent 1989, and Bullard & Duffy 1994a).
Similar to the Robbins-Monro algorithm the idea of this algorithm is
taken from mathematics, in this case from regressions of statistical data.
In the context of regression, the relation between an independent and
a dependent variable is often approximated by a linear function. The
linear function is chosen in such a way that the sum of the squares of
the differences, between the values predicted by the linear function and
the empirical values of the dependent variable, becomes minimal. Such
a procedure is named *linear regression*.

In the least squares learning model, it is assumed that two variables
$y(t)$ and $\tilde{y}(t)$ exist that depend linearly on each other with $\tilde{y}(t) = \beta \cdot$
$y(t)$ (the additive constant is neglected in the context of least squares
learning). The individuals, it is assumed, intend to learn about the
value of β. In order to predict the value of β, it is expected that they
approximate the relationship of $y(t)$ and $\tilde{y}(t)$ by linear regression, i.e.,
by

$$\hat{\beta}(t + 1) = \frac{\sum_{t'=1}^{t} y(t') \, \tilde{y}(t')}{\sum_{t'=1}^{t-1} y^2(t')} . \tag{3.19}$$

$\hat{\beta}(t)$ is the prediction of β at time $(t+1)$. The formula for linear regression
can also be written recursively by (the respective proof can be found in
Ljung & Söderström 1983)

$$\hat{\beta}(t + 1) = \hat{\beta}(t) + g(t) \left(\frac{\tilde{y}(t)}{y(t)} - \hat{\beta}(t) \right) \tag{3.20}$$

and

$$g(t) = \left(\frac{y^2(t)}{y^2(t - 1) \, g(t - 1)} + 1 \right)^{-1} . \tag{3.21}$$

where $\hat{\beta}(t)$ is the prediction of β and $g(t)$ exists only for mathematical
reasons and has no economic meaning.

Least squares learning is defined by equations (3.20) and (3.21). This way of modelling assumes that these equations describe the learning process of an unknown relation between $y(t)$ and $\tilde{y}(t)$ adequately. Besides the general hesitation to agree with this assumption, such an algorithm can be used only if individuals face a situation in which they have to estimate a linear relation between two observable variables. The decision is then made on the basis of the estimated value. In the long run, the algorithm converges to the real value of β if this value is constant (cf. Marcet & Sargent 1989).

Similar to the Robbins-Monro algorithm there is neither a psychological nor an empirical reason for the assumption that individuals behave according to least square learning. Least square learning was propagated because it seemed to be the analogue to Bayesian learning in the case of the estimation of parameters (see the respective considerations in Bray 1982).

The three models, *Bayesian learning*, the *Robbins-Monro algorithm* and *least square learning*, can only be justified by the normative argument that they converge under certain circumstances to optimal behaviour or correct prediction, respectively. In general, if we model learning by an algorithm designed to converge to optimal behaviour, in the long run we obtain exactly the optimal behaviour that has indirectly been assumed. This was proven for all three learning algorithms by various authors (cf. e. g. Jordan 1991, Yin & Zhu 1990 and Bray 1982).

However least squares learning does not always converge to the behaviour that maximises the expected utility (cf. Bullard & Duffy 1994a). In the study of Bullard and Duffy, the linear relation that is to be estimated by the individuals, changes according to their previous actions. The result is a dynamic interaction between the real value and the estimated value that may not come to a rest and converges to a limit cycle instead. This implies that even learning algorithms designed to converge to rational behaviour do not necessarily come up with such a convergence, if the circumstances change due to the actions of the individuals. This contradicts the argument that individuals have to learn in a way that converges to rational behaviour because such a learning process is superior to all other learning processes. It simply may not be possible to find such a learning algorithm, because the change of behaviour according to the learning process may have an interactive effect on the environment.

Bayesian learning, the Robbins-Monro algorithm and least square learning have much in common. Their predictions about behaviour are all deterministic. According to the information collected, the individuals

come up with one well-defined decision. Furthermore, all these algorithms require a high mathematical understanding by the individuals;
they all look very much like elaborated numeric algorithms to find the
optimal behaviour. Therefore it is to no surprise that Sargent states,
"Learning algorithms and equilibrium computation algorithms look like
each other" (Sargent 1993, p. 106). However it is doubtful whether
people really learn in such a way.

3.3   MODELS OF ROUTINE-BASED LEARNING

In contrast to non-cognitive learning, there are no general features of
routine-based learning. Routine-based learning runs in accordance with
rules that individuals believe to be adequate, or the rules that individuals
once believed to be adequate and which have become automatically, non-
cognitively used. The beliefs about adequate learning rules can be various
and context-dependent. It might even be that individuals reflect the
situation and realise that to behave according to the normative rules
above would be the best thing to do. In such a case, learning can be
described by the models discussed in the previous section.

In general, however, the ways of behaviour discussed above are too
complicated to be realistic. Individuals generally choose routines that
are far simpler and often not so well adapted to the situation. Some
routines can be found that are applied by many people in many different
situations. In the literature these routines have been used repeatedly to
model learning.

There is an enormous number of such learning routines in the economic literature. Some authors tried to find a general description of
what they called *adaptive learning*, which will be described first. Others
focused on different aspects like imitation, choosing what was best in the
past, or correcting choice. In addition, there are very specific models,
like the mark-up pricing found by Cyert and March (1963) which is used
by individuals only in one specific situation.

Neglecting the specific learning models, there are four features that
occur repeatedly within learning models: the imitation of others; the
consideration of past experience; some kind of vanishing noise or *trial-
and-error* behaviour; and satisficing.

However, while the other three aspects can be seen as learning processes on their own, *satisficing* is no routine of learning but rather a
motivational aspect of learning. Satisficing can be interpreted in two
ways. One may claim that individuals follow a rule stating that they

should continue to behave in the same way if satisfied with their performance and that they should change their behaviour if dissatisfied. One may also claim that individuals switch between non-cognitive learning and routine-based learning according to their satisfaction. If they are satisfied with their performance, they withdraw their cognitive attention from the situation. Subsequently they learn non-cognitively. If they are dissatisfied, cognitive attention is attracted by the situation and they apply the learning rule they believe to be adequate.

The concept of satisficing can be found in many learning models in the literature. It was first proposed by Simon (1957) . Since this time many models have been proposed that describe learning on the basis of the *satisficing principle* (for a detailed description of the satisficing principle see Simon 1987). Examples are the models of Day (1967), Day and Tinney (1968), Witt (1986b), March (1988), Binmore and Samuelson (1994), and Dixon (1995). Each of these models, however, is based on one of the routine-based learning processes. Satisficing is only an additional aspect but does not constitute a learning process itself.

Some of the basic routine-based learning processes will be introduced in the following pages, namely general adaptive learning models, imitation, fictitious play, evolutionary algorithms and the learning direction theory.

3.3.1 Adaptive Learning

In recent years, increasing numbers of economists have come to use the expression *adaptation* in the context of learning. They understand learning as the process by which individuals try to adapt their behaviour to the situations they face. The principle motivation of this kind of learning is to find an adequate or satisfactory behaviour under given circumstances. Such a concept is adequate if we assume that individuals have only limited knowledge about the world they live in and try to make the best use of their limited knowledge. From this perspective the concept of adaptive learning has something in common with the concept of *bounded rationality* (cf. Sargent 1993). The assumption of omniscience, characterising most of the economic literature, is abandoned. Instead individuals are assumed to have only partial knowledge about their situation and to have to learn which behaviour serves their goals best.

There are several ways in which such an adaptive learning process is modelled in the literature. Some of them have been described in the previous section while others are described in the following. Besides these specific models of learning there can be also found general formulations of *adaptive learning*, for example by J. G. Cross (c.f. Cross 1983) . The model of Cross is described below.

Cross describes the decision process as a *stochastic choice* between sets of alternatives. He assumes that individuals assign a probability $p(a, t)$ to each possible action a ($a \in \mathcal{A}$, $\mathcal{A}$ is the set of possible actions) at time t. This means that the individuals choose alternative a with probability $p(a, t)$ at time t. Consequently, the behaviour of an individual is described by the vector $\mathbf{p}(t)$ $(= (p(a, t))_{a \in \mathcal{A}})$ at each time t. This probability distribution is altered after each action according to the individual observations which include their own action, denoted by $a(t)$, and the obtained payoff, denoted by $\Pi(t)$. The updating of the probability distribution can be written in a general form as

$$p(a, t + 1) - p(a, t) = L_a(\mathbf{p}, a(t), \Pi(t)) . \tag{3.22}$$

This formulation of an adaptive process, although it is intended to be a fairly general formulation, contains some assumptions about adaptive learning. First of all, equation (3.22) requires that people behave stochastically, meaning that they make their decisions according to a probability distribution given by $\mathbf{p}(t)$ at each time t. The question of whether individuals are able to make stochastic decisions according to a probability distribution is still unanswered and therefore controversially discussed.

Furthermore, the probability vector $\mathbf{p}(t)$ is the only state variable that characterises the state of the individuals. The adaptive learning process given by equation (3.22) is a *Markov process*. A Markov process has no memory. This means an event has no further influence on behaviour at any later point in time. A memory of events and a later reflection of this information is excluded in Cross's adaptive model. The next state in a time-discrete process, or the actual change of the state in a time-continuous process, depends only on the actual state. In the case of adaptive learning this means that the distribution $\mathbf{p}(t+1)$ of behaviours depends only on the current distribution $\mathbf{p}(t)$, the current behaviour, and its outcome. Former learning is included in the current distribution $\mathbf{p}(t)$. The influence of any one piece of information is transmitted from one moment in time to the next. However it is more and more concealed by each new piece of information.

Finally, adaptive learning excludes any cognitive creativity of the individuals. Individuals are assumed to choose from a given set of alternatives. After each decision they adapt their behaviour to new information about the situation. The creation of new alternatives, that is, the cognitive development of strategies, is not considered by adaptive learning models in the literature. One example of a learning model that is a special case of Cross's formulation is the Bush-Mosteller model which satisfies all the assumptions made here (cf. Cross 1983).

In addition to Cross's definition, other general definitions of adaptive learning exist in the literature. Some authors define adaptive learning by its results, the observable sequence of behaviours. In the context of games, for example P. Milgrom and J. Roberts (1991) defined adaptive learning as a process that leads the individual to a non-dominated strategy when time goes to infinity. During the adaptive learning process, they assume, dominated strategies are successively eliminated. Other authors define adaptive learning as a process that successively improves the performance of the individuals (cf. e. g. Marimon 1993).

All these general formulations of learning have one disadvantage in common. Since they include only a minimal set of assumptions, implications are few and rarely exceed the assumptions they are based upon. Therefore Cross specifies his learning model whenever he applies it to an economic context (cf. Cross 1983).

3.3.2 Imitation

The process of *imitation* is often used to describe learning processes in the context of economics. Yet no general model exists that describes imitation. Each author who considers imitation as an important aspect makes her/his own assumptions about the process. From the literature two crucially different levels of imitation have to be distinguished. In the context of *diffusion*, imitation is studied on the population or firm's level. Some assumptions are made about the ability of a firm or a group of firms (e. g. a country) to catch up technologically dependent on the technological difference (cf. the huge literature about technological spill-overs). Since I am more concerned here with individual learning processes, I neglect technological imitation.

In the context of individual decision processes, imitation is often seen as a helpful process for gathering information about the adequate behaviour in a repeated situation. Most models of imitation found in the literature assume that the individuals are able to observe the actions of other individuals and the resulting outcomes. They are said to choose the action which leads to the most preferred outcome. In some models it is claimed that individuals observe a number of others' action and calculate the average utility of each action on the basis of these observations. Subsequently the individuals realise the action that has given rise to the highest utility (cf. Eshel, Samuelson & Shaked 1996). Other authors claim that individuals imitate the one who has obtained the highest utility of all individuals observed (cf. Nowak & May 1993, Kirchkamp 1995, and Hegselmann 1996). In some models the imitative process is modelled stochastically. In this case the individuals are more likely to imitate other individuals who have performed comparatively better in the last occasion (cf. Schlag 1998 and Witt 1996).

Besides the performance of the individuals who are to be imitated, the probability that an action is imitated may depend on the number of individuals who already realised this action, and on their social status, especially if the actual utility derived from an action can not be observed error-free (cf. Latané 1981, where the imitation of behaviours not related to a utility is studied). These aspects are generally neglected in modelling imitation in an economic context. The dependency of imitation on the number of individuals is studied in the literature concerning the diffusion of innovations (cf. e. g. Rogers 1995). However in the context of diffusion, imitation is modelled on the level of populations.

To sum up, imitation is modelled in two principle ways in the literature; on the level of the individuals and on the level of populations. Most of the models on the level of the individuals neglect the aspect that imitation is more probable the more other individuals commit the action. Instead, the probability of imitation is generally assumed to depend on the performance of the individual or the individuals that are to be imitated. The influence of the number of individuals who commit an action is considered in the literature about diffusion of innovations.

3.3.3 Fictitious Play and Myopic Learning

The fictitious play model was developed within the context of *games*. When J. F. Nash presented his concept, which is today known as the concept of *Nash equilibrium* (cf. Nash 1950) the question arose of how the respective behaviour evolves. G. W. Brown (1951) proposed the fictitious play model of learning that was proved to converge to a Nash equilibrium under certain conditions by J. Robinson (Robinson 1951). Later, L. S. Shapley showed that this kind of learning does not always lead to a Nash-equilibrium-like behaviour (cf. Shapley 1964). It may also converge to a limit cycle. However, the fictitious play model of Brown was first accepted as an explanation for the evolution of behaviour according to the concept of Nash equilibria. Most game theorists are still claiming that behaviours according to Nash equilibria are the result of learning processes where this claim is supported by the application of Bayesian learning (cf. Osborne & Rubinstein 1994).

The fictitious play model (see Brown 1951) assumes that individuals in a game record all previous moves of their opponents. Let us denote each move of their opponents by the vector $\mathbf{a}_{i_-}(t)$ and their own action by $a_i(t)$. The individuals are assumed to memorise all previous behaviours of the other individuals. Thus they are able to calculate the frequency of occurrence for each action profile $\mathbf{a}_{i_-}$. They assume that their actions will occur with the same probability in the future. Consequently, the expected probability $p(\mathbf{a}_{i_-}, t)$ for each action profile $\mathbf{a}_{i_-}$ realised by the other individuals is given by

$$E\left(p(\mathbf{a}_{i_-}, t)\right) = \frac{1}{t} \sum_{\tau=0}^{t-1} \delta(\mathbf{a}_{i_-}(\tau) = \mathbf{a}_{i_-}) \qquad (3.23)$$

where

$$\delta(\mathbf{a}_{i_-}(\tau) = \mathbf{a}_{i_-}) = \begin{cases} 1 & \text{for} \quad \mathbf{a}_{i_-}(\tau) = \mathbf{a}_{i_-} \\ 0 & \text{for} \quad \mathbf{a}_{i_-}(\tau) \neq \mathbf{a}_{i_-} \end{cases} . \qquad (3.24)$$

Furthermore, the individuals have complete knowledge about their payoffs $\Pi_i(a_i, \mathbf{a}_{i_-})$ of each action profile $(a_i, \mathbf{a}_{i_-})$. So they are able to calculate the *best response* to the expected behaviours of their opponents. To this end, they calculate the expected average payoff

$$E\left(\Pi_i(a_i, t)\right) = \sum_{\mathbf{a}_{i_-}} \Pi_i(a_i, \mathbf{a}_{i_-}) \cdot E\left(p(\mathbf{a}_{i_-}, t)\right) \qquad (3.25)$$

for each action a_i they are able to realise. Then they choose the action a_i with the highest expected average payoff $E\left(\Pi_i(a_i, t)\right)$. This action is called the *best response* to the expectation given by $E\left(p(\mathbf{a}_{i_-}, t)\right)$.

Individuals behaving according to the fictitious play model can be interpreted as those who learn by collecting information about the behaviour of the others. After each action they receive information about the actions of others and update their expectations. The hypotheses they have about the behaviour of the others are quite simple. According to this interpretation, the individuals believe that the behaviour of all others follows a constant probability distribution over the possible actions. Hence all they have to do is to approximate this probability distribution by collecting more and more information. Since the probability is assumed to be constant, it is best estimated by the average of all previous moves. This is done in equation (3.23). If the behaviour of the other individuals changes, the fictitious play model allows only a very slow adaptation to the new circumstances. Nevertheless in the long run, the individuals manage to play the best response to the changed behaviour of the others. If the behaviour of the others changes continually, the fictitious play model is, of course, a rather inadequate learning process.

Moreover the fictitious play model, as it is described above, requires an enormous *cognitive capacity* because previous experience has to be stored in the memory and the best response has to be calculated. It is doubtful whether individuals are able to do so, especially in games allowing for many alternative actions.

In recent years, some modifications of the fictitious play model have been presented. These modifications reduce the requirements for the individual cognitive capacity. A small change has been proposed by P. Young (1993). He modelled individuals who are only able to remember the last k plays. They play the best response based on the average behaviour of the others in these k plays. By doing so the individuals adapt faster to changing circumstances. However they still have to be able to calculate the best response on the basis of the available information.

If k is reduced to one in Young's model, the model of *myopic learning* is obtained. The myopia hypothesis claims that individuals realise the *best response* to the actual distribution of behaviours in the population of other players (cf. e. g. Ellison 1993). Hence it assumes that the individuals are able to recognise the behaviour of other individuals in the last play, or at least identify the action that would have served them best. Subsequently, they assume that the behaviour of the others is unchanged in the next play and realise the best response based on behaviours in the last play. Therefore myopic learning does not require any memorising of previous plays.

Myopic learning is a very short-sighted process often leading to cyclic behaviour within a period of two time steps. There is some evidence that people sometimes behave quite short-sightedly and believe in unchanging adequate behaviours. Nevertheless a simple orientation on the last play lacks the ability to identify continuous changes. Furthermore the question remains whether individuals are really able to identify the best response. In addition, there is lack of experimental findings supporting the myopia hypothesis.

Some authors have modified the concept of myopic learning by the introduction of errors and occasional adaptation to the best response (cf. Samuelson 1994) or by the introduction of gradual convergence to the best response behaviour (cf. Crawford 1995). However, their models are still subject to the same objections that have been put forward above, namely the question of identification of the best response.

3.3.4 Evolutionary Algorithms

Evolutionary algorithms have become increasingly popular for modelling learning processes in the recent economic literature. To assist in gaining an idea of how these models work, it is helpful to understand the biological dynamics of evolution which evolutionary algorithms are based on. The concept of neo-Darwinism receives wide acceptance in biology. According to this view, the predispositions of organisms are determined by genes which are carried and recombined through sexual reproduction by succeeding generations. Through the struggle for survival of competing organisms, the fittest organisms are selected. Originally Darwin defined the fitness of an individual organism as its ability to survive and reproduce. From a neo-Darwinian perspective, however, fitness is defined as the ability of a genotype (the genetic constitution of an individual) to appear in the gene pool of the next generation.

Selection is, therefore, on the level of "competing" genotypes or even particular gene assemblies within a genotype, and evolution is the result of selection for superior genotypes and gene assemblies. The resulting change in the make-up of the gene pool constitutes evolution. However, because of the limited number of genotypes in an original population, natural selection forces could only alter a gene pool to a certain point and evolution would effectively end if the selective forces remained steady. For evolution to continue indefinitely, there must be the possibility of new genotypes emerging in a population. There are two processes which make this possible: *"crossing over"* and *mutation*. "Crossing over" is the exchange of genes between the chromosome of the mother and "partner" chromosome of the father, creating a genotype based on a gene assembly not possible before. Mutation is a pure "mistake" in the replication of the genetic code, resulting in a completely new or altered gene. The details of the mechanisms of crossing over and mutations are still not completely understood.

In the 1970s, some scientists realised the usefulness of the *biological concept of evolution* in solving optimisation problems. As a consequence Rechenberg (1973) and Holland (1975) developed the concepts of evolutionary strategies and genetic algorithms, respectively. Although they differ in many details, they and all their deviates are subsumed under the general term *evolutionary algorithms*. The study, advancement and application of evolutionary algorithms has become a major subject in mathematics, computer science, and the like. Evolutionary algorithms are one of the main tools for solving optimisation problems.

In the 1980s, evolutionary algorithms found their way into economics through *evolutionary game theory* (cf. Maynard Smith 1982 and Weibull 1995). However evolutionary game theory is not based directly on evolutionary algorithms as they have been proposed by Rechenberg and Holland. In addition to the modelling of biological evolution by algorithms, a second kind of modelling was established in the 1970s which is sometimes regarded as the aggregation of evolutionary algorithms at the *population level*. This second line of modelling formalised the evolutionary mechanism on the basis of equations of motion. By assuming that the population is sufficiently large, $x(i, t)$ is defined as the share of individuals within the population belonging to the genetic variant i $(i \in \mathcal{I})$ at time t. Subsequently it is assumed that the dynamics of evolution can be described by differential equations for the shares $x(i, t)$. In general, two processes are considered by these differential equations, the process of *mutation* and the one of *reproduction* and *selection*. The resulting equation is called *mutation-selection-equation* (cf. Eigen 1971) and can be written as (cf. Helbing 1995)

$$
\begin{aligned}
\frac{dx(i,t)}{dt} &= \sum_{j \in \mathcal{I}} \left[\omega(i|j, t) \cdot x(j, t) - \omega(j|i, t) \cdot x(i, t) \right] \\
&\quad + \nu(t) \cdot x(i, t) \left[\Pi(i, t) - \langle \Pi(t) \rangle \right] .
\end{aligned}
\tag{3.26}
$$

The first term on the right-hand side of equation (3.26) represents the mutation processes. $\omega(i|j, t)$ is the mutation matrix which defines the probability of a mutation from genetic variant j to genetic variant i. The mutation matrix has to be chosen according to the biological probabilities of crossovers, mutations and other similar processes. Some scientists neglect the process of mutation. In this case, the evolutionary dynamics are given by

$$
\frac{dx(i, t)}{dt} = \nu(t) \cdot x(i, t) \left[\Pi(i, t) - \langle \Pi(t) \rangle \right] .
\tag{3.27}
$$

The remaining term on the right-hand side represents the selection process. $\nu(t)$ is the *selection pressure*, meaning the velocity of the elimination of less fit species. $\Pi(i, t)$ is the *fitness* of the species i and $\langle \Pi(t) \rangle$ is the average fitness of the whole population at time t. The process described by equation (3.27) is also known as the *replicator dynamics* (cf. Hofbauer & Sigmund 1984).

The evolutionary algorithms of Rechenberg and Holland are not described exactly by equation (3.26) even on the population level. However they can be approximated by replicator dynamics (cf. Brenner 1998a for a more detailed discussion). I omit a presentation of the evolutionary algorithms here and suggest the original works of Rechenberg and Holland to the interested reader (Rechenberg 1973 and Holland 1975).

Stimulated by increasing acceptance of evolutionary game theory in economics in the last years, economists have increasingly directed their attention towards evolutionary algorithms. It has become common to model learning processes with the help of evolutionary algorithms (cf. e. g. Holland & Miller 1991, Dekel & Scotchmer 1992, Bullard & Duffy 1994b, Gale, Binmore & Samuelson 1995 and Dawid 1996). This is justified by a claim of analogy between the important aspects of both processes, *social/cultural evolution* or learning processes, and *biological evolution*. In evolutionary algorithms describing biological evolution, the main aspects are replication, mutation and selection. These can be compared to the main aspects of social evolution, namely imitation, variation and selection by abandonment (cf. Dawid 1996). If the analogy holds, the use of evolutionary algorithms is attractive for two reasons. First, knowledge about evolutionary algorithms is well-developed because the concept is frequently used in other sciences. When utilising evolutionary algorithms, one can take advantage of the store of knowledge about their features that has already been collected. Second, if one accepts the analogy, evolutionary algorithms contain the aspects of imitation, variation and selection, they are far more comprehensive than any of the other learning models used in economics.

However, the analogy between biological and social evolution is controversially discussed in the literature (cf. e. g. Maynard Smith 1982, Hallpike 1986, Witt 1991a, and Ramstad 1994). In this discussion some crucial differences between biological and social evolution have been identified. A comprehensive comparison of learning processes and evolutionary algorithms, on the basis of the analogy described above, can be found in Brenner 1998a. Three major differences have been identified in that study. First, evolutionary algorithms are unable to consider the past. The dynamics of evolutionary algorithms depends only on the current state of the system, whereas individuals who learn will remember earlier experiences and include this knowledge in their decision making. Second, in evolutionary algorithms the fitness is objectively given, whereas in learning processes individuals evaluate outcomes subjectively, and therefore often quite differently. Third, in evolutionary algorithms, strategies are eliminated by selection only due to the performance they lead to. In learning processes, individual motivations play an important role. Motivation may be a result of the history of an individual so that behaviours may be eliminated although they currently perform well. As a consequence of these three differences, it is claimed in Brenner 1998a that evolutionary algorithms have at least to be modified before they can be used to describe learning processes.

At the same time it is also repeatedly claimed that *replicator dynamics* is an adequate tool for describing the dynamics of learning. Especially in the context of *evolutionary game theory*, the dynamics, which are in fact replicator dynamics, are frequently interpreted as the dynamics of learning. This claim has been supported by some studies which have proved that reinforcement learning is well approximated by replicator dynamics, at least if the payoffs are positive (Börgers & Sarin 1993 have shown that the Bush-Mosteller model leads to replicator dynamics under certain circumstances. This claim has been re-examined in the context of games in Brenner 1997, a similar analysis has been done by Brenner & Witt 1997, in the context of games for the melioration principle).

To sum up, the enormous propagation of evolutionary algorithms in economics for modelling learning processes seems to be rather misguided. As long as economists use standard evolutionary algorithms in an unreflected way, the results represent the dynamics of learning only by chance. More detailed studies have shown that only reinforcement learning under certain circumstances can be described by replicator dynamics (cf. Börgers & Sarin 1993, Börgers 1996, and Brenner & Witt 1997). In the case of social evolution with imitation and variation, the evolutionary algorithms have to be modified if they are to represent learning processes. Thus, there exist cases in which evolutionary algorithms are adequate to describe learning, but before we begin to praise the dynamics of evolutionary algorithms we should prove their adequacy, which has rarely been done in the literature. Another way would be a modification of evolutionary algorithms. T. Brenner shows that evolutionary algorithms may be defined such that most differences between learning and evolutionary algorithms vanish (Brenner 1998a). Whether the knowledge, accumulated by the use of evolutionary algorithms in the context of optimisation, can be utilised for the description of learning, has to be left open for future research.

3.3.5   Learning Direction Theory

Learning direction theory was proposed by R. Selten in 1986 (cf. Selten & Stoecker 1986). It was inspired by experiments and so the principal advantage of the learning direction theory is its experimental robustness. Since its proposal by R. Selten, it has frequently been tested in different game settings and was strongly confirmed in most of the cases.

Learning direction theory can only be applied if individuals are confined to choosing from a set of alternatives that can be ordered in a meaningful way, or if, at least, individuals are able to separate the alternatives that increase performance from those which decrease performance each time. For example, if individuals have to decide how much of a given amount they want to offer to the other player in an *ultimatum game* (see Güth 1995 for a detailed description of the game), the possible actions can be ordered according to the amount of money that they offer to one other. Moreover, learning direction theory assumes that individuals are able to identify whether their last action was pitched too high or too low in this order of possible actions. Given these assumptions, learning direction theory states that individuals will change their behaviour in the direction in which they expect their own performance to increase, or stay with the same behaviour. Such a learning procedure has some similarities with gradient method used in optimisation problems, although in the case of the learning direction theory there does not necessarily have to be something like a potential function. In the example of an ultimatum game, if the share of the gain offered to the other player was accepted, the offer will most likely not be increased, and alternatively, if the share was refused, the offer will most likely not be decreased.

In other words, learning direction theory states that individuals change their behaviour in a way that increases their payoff more often than in a way that decreases it. As long as the situation is easy to understand, such a statement is straightforward. So it is no surprise that the theory has been confirmed in many experiments. Consequently, the implications of learning direction theory are rather weak. To describe the complex dynamics of learning requires more than the basic statement of the learning direction theory.

3.4 GENERAL MODEL OF ROUTINE-BASED LEARNING

In the previous section it was found that four aspects of learning are repeatedly used within the modelling of routine-based learning. T. Brenner developed a model, the *Variation-Imitation-Decision model* (VID model) that includes all four aspects (cf. Brenner 1994 and 1996a). In this book, the VID model will be used in some of the applications of learning. Moreover, it will be elaborated further with respect to several details. Therefore it seems worthwhile to explain the model to some extent below.

The VID model is an *adaptive learning* algorithm that includes the most frequently occurring aspects of routine-based learning, without claiming to be able to explain every kind of routine-based learning. It assumes that the outcomes of actions are evaluated according to a cardinal utility function. Individuals are assumed to adapt their behaviour according to their performance and the information from others, considering the aspects of imitation, information collection, satisficing and deviations from the "optimal" choice.

3.4.1 Basic Concept of the VID Model

In the VID model, the learning process is modelled as a dynamic decision process. Each decision is seen as the result of previous decisions and their outcomes. This means that the decision-makers learn from the previous outcomes and make their new choice according to this knowledge. The VID model is based on the assumption that people react on the knowledge they have collected in the past, and that they believe the past to be a good approximation of the future. The indirect causal relation "previous outcomes → rational expectations → new decision", used in rational expectation models, is replaced by the direct relation "previous outcomes → new decision", used in most of the other learning algorithms as well. To develop this direct causal relation, knowledge from psychology is utilised. The basic ideas of causality between the previous outcomes and the new decision are shown in the figure below.

The model's fundamental assumption is that people tend to make the same decision again and again. This tendency has been experimentally shown in Brenner 1995. An assumption that agents stay with the same choice in a repeated decision situation most of the time, provokes two questions: what causes individuals to decide to behave differently, and if they behave differently how will they behave?

To answer the first question I follow the causal line on the left-hand side of the diagram above. In the VID model, it is assumed that individuals need to be *motivated* before they change their decision or their behaviour, respectively. According to motivation theories in psychology, there may be two explanations for such motivation in this context: the theory of *optimal arousal* (cf. Hebb 1955) and theories about *aspirations*.

Another way psychologists explain motivation is by the dissonance theory. The dissonance theory analyses cognitive relations and their interactions, something that can not be included in the VID model. Thus, the dissonance theory does not offer an explanation for behavioural changes in the present context.

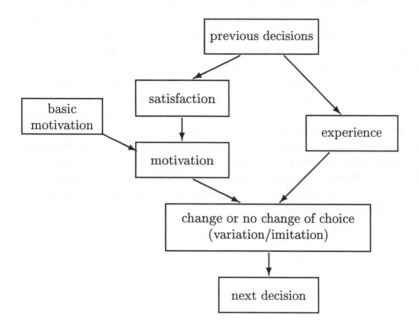

Figure 3.1: *Structure of the VID model*

The VID model is based on the theory of optimal arousal and the assumption of an *aspiration level* (both are discussed in more detail in the next section). The theory of optimal arousal states that there is always a desire to try something different from time to time, simply because people become bored by the repetition of events. The assumption of an aspiration level states that motivation is caused by *dissatisfaction*. Dissatisfaction itself may result from the outcomes of previous decisions. In this sense, the causal line starts from previous decisions that lead to a certain degree of satisfaction. Dissatisfaction in turn leads to motivation for change. There is also the *basic motivation* that is caused by the desire for alternation according to the theory of optimal arousal. The basic motivation is influenced by the overall situation of the individual, that is, by the overall feeling of a need for change. For convenience I assume that basic motivation randomly leads to behavioural changes. Both effects together determine how much the individual is motivated and therefore the overall probability of a change in the individual's behaviour.

If individuals decide to change their behaviour, there are two ways of doing so. They may either try a different behaviour by chance (*variation*) or imitate another individual (*imitation*). The question of which behaviour to change, and whether to imitate or to try a variation, depends on various influences. First of all, individuals do not forget their former *experiences*. Each decision or behaviour in the past has resulted in an outcome and it is assumed that this outcome was evaluated. In addition, individuals may have received information about the behaviours of others and the resulting payoffs. All this leads, theoretically, to an overall familiarity with the effect of each possible behaviour. When searching for a different behaviour, the individual is aware of these experiences. Thus the change is determined by the experience, independently of whether the individuals change their behaviour by variation or imitation. Furthermore, the new behaviour chosen depends on the overall preparedness to imitate or vary and, in the case of imitation, on the observation of others and the information about them.

Generally, it is assumed in the VID model that it is impossible to make deterministic statements about the behaviour of people. Therefore the only acceptable way to model human behaviour, like learning processes, is the description of probabilities for the occurrence of actions. Consequently, the VID model is designed in such a way that a probability for variation and imitation is defined, dependent on the influences mentioned above. By this, the model is able to describe the structures of learning behaviour, but it is not able to predict the dynamics of a single individual, except in a stochastic manner.

3.4.2 Characteristics of the Situation

As mentioned above, learning only takes place if the same situation, or at least similar ones, occur again and again. In addition, the use of the VID model requires some further assumptions about such a repeating situation:

First, it has to be assumed that a fixed number A of alternative behaviours or choices, respectively, exist. These alternatives have to be available at each occasion. Thus the model is based on the existence of a set $\mathcal{A}$ of alternative actions a $(a = 1, 2, ..., A)$. The alternatives stay the same over time, no new alternatives evolve, and no old ones disappear.

Second, it is assumed that N individuals exist that are able to interact through the exchange of information and through imitation. Individuals are labelled by i $(i = 1, 2, ..., N)$. At each time t the current action of individual i is given by $a_i(t)$.

Third, the outcome of each action is assumed to be measurable in terms of a real value. This value depends on the moment in time t, action a, and individual i and is denoted by $u_i(a, t)$. It reflects the subjective *utility* that individual i depicts by choosing alternative a at time t. It has to be emphasised that the utility $u_i(a, t)$ action a gives rise to is not necessarily constant in time. At the same time $u_i(a, t)$ is assumed to be well-defined and to be the only relevant information the outcome of choice $a_i(t)$ contains for individual i.

Fourth, time in the VID model is discrete. It is assumed that the situation repeats again and again. The time between one occasion and the next is seen as one time step. These time steps are assumed to be sufficiently similar to be considered as equal.

3.4.3 Experience

In the VID model, the variable $\eta_i(a, t)$, named *experience*, reflects the *knowledge* that individual i has about alternative a at time t. It is the weighted average of the utility of former outcomes, caused by action a, that has been recognised by the individual. In other words, the experience reflects the answer an individual would give to the question: What is your estimation of the utility that action a has given rise to in the past? Of course such a value differs between individuals. It depends on the information about this action collected by the individual. At each point in time, individuals gather new information in the form of the utility evoked by their own actions, as well as in form of transmitted information from other individuals. In addition, they still remember the information they have obtained so far.

Thus, the experience $\eta_i(a, t + 1)$ at each point in time $(t + 1)$ is the weighted sum of two parts, the former experience $\eta_i(a, t)$ and the new information obtained at time t (see Figure 3.2). Starting with the analysis of the first part, which is reflected by the current value of $\eta_i(a, t)$, the memory of information decays with time (cf. Ebbinghaus 1913). Thus, if individuals do not receive any information about an alternative a they loose the memory of former experiences. Such a process can be modelled with the help of a neutral value of the experience $\eta_{i,0}$. It is assumed that the experience $\eta_i(a, t)$, meaning the estimated utility of action a converges to $\eta_{i,0}$ if no new information about this action is obtained. This is modelled by the addition of $\eta_{i,0}$ multiplied by $\varsigma_{i,e}$ (the index e marks that $\varsigma_{i,e}$ determines the process of forgetting in the context of experience) to the respectively reduced old experience $\eta_i(a,t)$ (compare the right-hand side of Figure 3.2). In addition to the decay

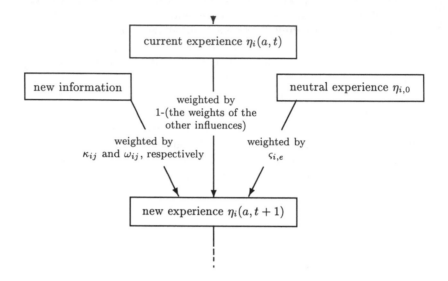

Figure 3.2: *Composition of the variable experience*

of memory, a second effect causes the influence of former information to decrease: the receipt of new information about the results of an action. In the VID model, the weight of the newest piece of information is constant in time. The influence of information gathered in the past, instead, is reduced at each time step. By this, information carries more weight the more recently it has been acquired. Therefore new information about an alternative is seen as replacing the old.

New information to be used in choosing a behaviour can be collected in three ways: (1) Each time individuals choose an alternative action they obtain an outcome, which they evaluate for its utility by $u_i(a,t)$ (the influence of this piece of information on experience is weighted by ω_i). (2) Individuals may watch the choice of another individual j and the corresponding outcome. Subsequently they evaluate this outcome and receive the information that alternative $a_j(t)$, chosen by individual j at time t, has given rise to the utility $u_i(a_j(t),t)$. The evaluations of others' success is made by the persons themselves so that the information is based on their own preferences. This kind of information gathering is only possible if individual i is able to watch individual j. In general such an observation experience is limited. Assume that individual i is able to recognise a proportion ω_{ij} of the actions and consequences connected with individual j. (3) Each individual j obtains the utility $u_j(a_j(t), t)$ at each time t. Individuals are able to hand this information over to other individuals. By this, the individual i may receive the information that the alternative $a_j(t)$ has given rise to the utility $u_j(a_j(t), t)$. In contrast to the second way of information gathering, the individual obtains this information by *communication* with the other individual. The evaluation of the outcome is done by the other individual. Individuals cannot be sure whether the evaluation of the other individual is similar to their own. Nevertheless, it may be helpful to make use of this information. Therefore the flux of information in this way is restricted by the willingness of individuals to share their own information and the reservation of individuals to use it. The proportion of information that is transmitted in such a way from individual j to individual i is denoted by κ_{ij}.

Most of the time, an individual receives information from many other individuals synchronously. The question arises whether the individual sums up this information or uses another algorithm for evaluation. B. Latané (1981) found that the influence of N other individuals on the individual's behaviour increases like N^β ($0 < \beta < 1$) with the number of individuals. Generally speaking, it can be stated that two individuals showing the same behaviour have between one and two times the effect on the individual observing. This means, the impact of each observed individual decreases with the total number of simultaneously observed individuals. Whether it decreases slowly or rather rapidly, depends on the subject that individuals learn about, or, to be more precise, on the belief of the individual whether the information units are independent of each other or not. For mathematical convenience I assume that the information units can simply be summed up. However it is easy to expand the model to a more adequate handling of information if it is necessary.

According to figure 3.2 the dynamics of $\eta_i(a,t)$ are given by

$$
\begin{aligned}
\eta_i(a,t+1) \;=\; & \left(1 - \varsigma_{i,e} - \sum_{\substack{j=1 \\ j \neq i}}^{N} \delta(a = a_j(t)) \cdot (\omega_{ij} + \kappa_{ij}) \right. \\
& \left. -\delta(a = a_i(t)) \cdot \omega_i \right) \cdot \eta_i(a,t) - \varsigma_{e,i} \cdot \eta_{i,0} \\
& +\omega_i \cdot \delta(a = a_i(t)) \cdot u_i(a,t) \sum_{\substack{j=1 \\ j \neq i}}^{N} \delta(a = a_j(t)) \\
& \cdot \left(\omega_{ij} \cdot u_i(a,t) + \kappa_{ij} \cdot u_j(a,t)\right)
\end{aligned}
$$

(3.28)

with

$$
\delta(a = a_j(t)) = \left\{ \begin{array}{ll} 1 & \text{for} \quad a = a_j(t) \\ 0 & \text{for} \quad a \neq a_j(t) \end{array} \right. .
$$

(3.29)

Therein, as shown in Figure 3.2, $\varsigma_{i,e}$, ω_i, κ_{ij} and ω_{ij} are parameters that determine the strength of the influence of the sources of information on the experience $\eta_i(a,t)$. The factor for the old experience $\left(1 - \varsigma_{i,e} - \sum_{\substack{j=1 \\ j \neq i}}^{N} \delta(a = a_j(t))(\omega_{ij} + \kappa_{ij}) - \delta(a = a_i(t)) \cdot \omega_i\right)$ is chosen in such a way that the sum of all weights is one. Consequently $\eta_i(a,t+1)$ is always the weighted average of the values $\eta_i(a,t)$, $\eta_{i,0}$, $u_j(a,t)$ and $u_i(a,t)$, i.e. the weighted average of the old experience, the neutral value of experience, and the new information that was received after the last decision.

New information can be obtained from every individual that the considered individual stays in contact with. Therefore I take the sum over all individuals in the population. However, only individuals j who have chosen alternative a in the last decision ($a = a_j(t)$) are relevant for $\eta_i(a,t)$ because only these individuals are able to create information about alternative a. To this end, the function $\delta(a = a_j(t))$ is used in equation (3.28).

The weights of this new information are given by ω_{ij} and κ_{ij}. These parameters together with $\varsigma_{i,e}$ and ω_i have to be chosen in such a way that $\varsigma_{i,e} + \sum_{j=1}^{N} \delta(a = a_j(t))(\omega_{ij} + \kappa_{ij}) + \omega_i \leq 1$ is always fulfilled. If the parameters ω_i, ω_{ij} and κ_{ij} are large, then new information influences experience more strongly. This means that individuals orient themselves mainly by looking at the latest outcomes. Small values of ω_i, ω_{ij} and κ_{ij} mean that individuals memorise all former outcomes and weight them almost identically.

The parameter $\varsigma_{i,e}$ reflects the loss of memory or destruction of information. This can easily be seen if we assume that no new information about alternative a is obtained. The last two terms on the right-hand side of equation (3.28) vanish in this case. Subsequently the new experience $\eta_i(a, t + 1)$ is the weighted average of the old experience $\eta_i(a, t)$ and the neutral experience $\eta_{i,0}$. In this case the experience converges to $\eta_{i,0}$. In the VID model the neutral experience can be seen in two ways. First, if individuals are not able to gather new information about an alternative, they may treat this alternative like one for which they never got any information. This means that they evaluate the alternative in a neutral way, by a value that is approximately the average outcome of all alternatives. Second, it may be interesting for individuals occasionally to try alternatives that they have neglected for a long time, alternatives for which they have no actual information. Since the evaluation $\eta_i(a, t)$ directs the behaviour of the individuals, the test of long-neglected alternatives can be modelled by a high value of $\eta_{i,0}$. If $\eta_{i,0}$ is large compared to the average utility that other alternatives give rise to, the experience $\eta_i(a, t)$ increases for neglected alternatives. By this, individuals are more likely to choose an alternative the longer they have obtained no information about it. Experience no longer reflects the memorised evaluation of an alternative in such a modelling. Instead it offers a simultaneous modelling of memorised evaluation and the desire to keep informed about alternative actions.

In general the parameter $\varsigma_{i,e}$ is small compared with ω_{ij} and κ_{ij} so that as long as new information is obtained about an alternative, the loss of memory has no relevant impact on the value of $\eta_i(a, t)$. This aspect becomes relevant only if no new information is obtained.

3.4.4 Aspiration Level

One of the basic elements of the VID model is the *satisficing* principle (see subsection 2.1.10 or Simon 1987 for a detailed description). In the VID model it is assumed that, except for some rare occasions, individuals change their behaviour only if they are dissatisfied. Dissatisfaction occurs if the consequences of one's behaviour are worse than the *aspiration level*. Thus, the aspiration level is a crucial element of the VID model.

The *aspiration level* $z_i(t)$ of individual i at time t in the VID model is the result of three influences:

1) Outcomes of the individual's own behaviour. These experiences are considered more seriously the more recent they are in correspondence to the fading of memory (cf. Thibaut and Kelley 1959).

2) Performances of others (cf. Festinger 1942) upon which individuals also base themselves. Here again the influence of outcomes decreases with

increasing time.

3) The loss of *memory*. According to Ebbinghaus' experimental findings, the memory of facts vanishes over time (Ebbinghaus 1913). This
aspect is also included in the ideas of Thibaut and Kelley, that facts
remembered from former outcomes have less influence on the level of
comparison the further in the past they have occurred.

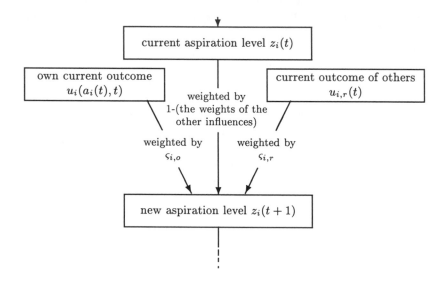

Figure 3.3: *Composition of the variable aspiration*

To aid consideration of these above four influences, I define the new
aspiration level $z_i(t+1)$ at time $(t+1)$ as the weighted sum of the
personal current performance $u_i(a_i(t), t)$, the recognised performance of
others $u_{i,r}(t)$, and the old aspiration level $z_i(t)$ as shown in figure 3.3.
The aspiration level adapts gradually to the new information. The old
value of the aspiration level makes up a proportion of $(1 - \varsigma_{i,o} - \varsigma_{i,r})$ of
the new value. The aspiration level is a weighted average of all outcomes
with a stronger weight on outcomes that occurred more recently (see also
the discussion within the definition of experience).

At the same time, the use of $(1 - \varsigma_{i,o} - \varsigma_{i,r})$ secures that the sum
of all weights is one. Consequently the new aspiration level is always a
weighted average of the several influences. A new aspiration level below
the smallest or above the highest value of $z_i(t)$, $u_i(a_i(t), t)$ and $u_{i,r}(t)$ is
impossible.

The utility $u_i(a_i(t), t)$ that individuals experience personally is weighted by $\varsigma_{i,o}$. The higher $\varsigma_{i,o}$ is, the faster the aspiration level adapts to the influences of the latest outcomes experienced by the individual. A comparison of the different parameters $\varsigma_{i,o}$ and $\varsigma_{i,r}$ shows which values are important. If the weight $\varsigma_{i,o}$ of the personal outcome is high compared to the other parameters, individuals build their aspirations according to their own experiences and more or less neglect other influences.

Individuals with a high parameter $\varsigma_{i,r}$ compared to the other parameters, intend to be at least as successful as others. In this case the aspiration level follows foremost the value $u_{i,r}(t)$. Festinger (1942) has shown the importance of the observed performance of others for the aspiration level. However, it is important to know how individuals have learnt of others' performance; through direct observation or through speaking with others. The utility function $u_i(a, t)$ is assumed to be subjective. A problem arises, similar to the one discussed in the last section. I assume that individuals gather information about the performance of others mainly by their own observation. Furthermore for simplicity, I assume that all other individuals can be observed by each individual or that at least the average performance is common knowledge in the population. $u_{i,r}$ is then given by

$$u_{i,r}(t) = \frac{1}{N} \cdot \sum_{j=1}^{N} u_i(a_j(t), t) . \tag{3.30}$$

Nevertheless other definitions of $u_{i,r}(t)$ can be used within the VID model as well.

The dynamics of the *aspiration level* are given by

$$z_i(t+1) = \left(1 - \varsigma_{i,o} - \varsigma_{i,r} - \varsigma_{i,k}\right) z_i(t) + \varsigma_{i,o} u_i(a_i(t), t) + \varsigma_{i,r} u_{i,r}(t) . \tag{3.31}$$

3.4.5 Satisfaction

In accordance with the *satisficing* theory (cf. Simon 1987), the VID model includes the idea that satisfaction with the current performance influences decision-making, leading to an occasional lack of motivation to change behaviour. Satisfaction is represented in the VID model by the variable $s_i(t)$. Each time individuals obtain an outcome, they compare this outcome with their aspiration level. An outcome above the aspiration level is satisfying while an outcome below the aspiration level is dissatisfying. The satisfaction $s_i(t)$ is defined in such a way that it is positive for outcomes above the aspiration level and negative for outcomes below. An obvious definition also used in the literature (cf. e.g. Day 1967, Witt 1986a and Binmore & Samuelson 1994) is

$$s_i(t) = u_i(a_i(t), t) - z_i(t) \; . \tag{3.32}$$

Satisfaction is a momentary feeling about a situation, therefore it is not assigned to any action a.

3.4.6 Motivation

Thibaut and Kelley (1959) found, in their experiments, that outcomes below the aspiration level (level of comparison in their terminology) motivate individuals to react. In the present context individuals are able to act only in the sense of changing their behaviour, that means choosing another alternative out of the set of possible actions $\mathcal{A}$. I denote the *motivation* of individual i to change behaviour at time t by $m_i(t)$.

Two reasons for motivation may be relevant in the VID model. One is given by the theory of optimal arousal (cf. Hebb 1955). According to this theory, individuals need some changes in their life from time to time. This may also be seen as a desire for alternation or novelty (cf. e.g. Witt 1987a). I assume that this basic desire for change can be modelled by a constant contribution to the motivation, the *basic motivation* $m_{i,0}$.

The second reason for motivation is the fact that dissatisfaction motivates behavioural changes. In this context, the motivation caused by dissatisfaction is greater the smaller the value of $s_i(t)$ is. However, the motivation at time t does not necessarily depend only on the satisfaction $s_i(t)$ with the utility obtained at that time t. Individuals generally do not change their behaviour as a reaction to disappointment with a single event. I assume that some weighted average is composed of the satisfaction with the present action in the past. Outcomes that were recently experienced are more important than outcomes that occurred long ago. To consider this aspect I define the *remembered satisfaction* using a recursive formula, similar to the ones of experience and the aspiration level:

$$\hat{s}_i(t+1) = \left(1 - \varsigma_{i,s}\right) \cdot \hat{s}_i(t) + \varsigma_{i,s} \cdot s_i(t) \; . \tag{3.33}$$

$\varsigma_{i,s}$ is an individual parameter that represents the speed with which the remembered satisfaction is adapted to recent experiences. The higher $\varsigma_{i,s}$ is, the more strongly the remembered satisfaction correlates with the actual satisfaction. In the case of $\varsigma_{i,s} = 1$ the remembered satisfaction equals satisfaction. If $\varsigma_{i,s}$ is very small, individuals consider all experiences almost equally.

However, not all events in the past are considered by individuals when they figure out whether their current behaviour gives rise to reasonable outcomes. Naturally only the outcomes that resulted from the current behaviour are considered. To this end, the remembered satisfaction $\hat{s}_i(t)$ depends only on the values of satisfaction $s_i(\tau)$ for all times τ at which the current action $a_i(t)$ has been chosen. If, furthermore, the set of considered values of satisfaction $s_i(\tau)$ is restricted to the period of time since behaviour changed last, the recursive definition (3.33) of $\hat{s}_i(t)$ can be still used. Then with each change of behaviour, the remembered satisfaction $\hat{s}_i(t)$ has to be redefined. I assume that $\hat{s}_i(t)$ is set to $s_{i,0}$ by that time. $s_{i,0}$ is positive if the individual is initially less critical towards new choices and zero if the individual expects satisfaction right from the beginning. Starting from this value, the remembered satisfaction evolves according to equation (3.33) as long as the behaviour stays the same.

Because the dynamics of experience, aspiration level, and remembered satisfaction look very much the same, it is important to state some crucial differences. Experience and aspiration level, in contrast to remembered satisfaction, change gradually. Consequently the related parameters ω_{ij}, κ_{ij}, $\varsigma_{i,e}$, $\varsigma_{i,o}$, $\varsigma_{i,k}$ and $\varsigma_{i,r}$ are small, much smaller than the parameter $\varsigma_{i,s}$. Experience and aspiration level can be seen as something like knowledge, which is built over a long period of time. Remembered satisfaction, instead, is a feeling that adapts very quickly to new outcomes. Furthermore, remembered satisfaction is related to one behaviour and is reset each time the behaviour changes. Experience $\eta_i(a,t)$ is related to one behaviour a as well, but through time its value changes undisturbed by behavioural changes. In addition, experience also depends on the outcomes of others. The aspiration level, in contrast, is not related to any behaviour. It depends on all outcomes, including those of other individuals, and evolves to an overall observed average outcome. The three variables together represent three crucially different estimations of average outcomes.

With the help of the remembered satisfaction, motivation can be written as

$$m_i(t) = \begin{cases} m_{i,0} & \text{if} \quad \hat{s}_i(t) \geq 0 \\ m_{i,0} - \varsigma_{i,m}\hat{s}_i(t) & \text{if} \quad \hat{s}_i(t) < 0 \end{cases} . \qquad (3.34)$$

The parameter $\varsigma_{i,m}$ describes how much individuals are motivated by dissatisfaction.

Individuals who are motivated to change their behaviour search for alternatives to their current behaviour. The VID model is a stochastic one so that a motivation does not necessarily lead to a change in behaviour. The more the individuals are motivated, however, the more likely they are to change their behaviour. In the following sections I will define the probabilities for such a change. Two kinds of changes are possible: the individuals either switch to another behaviour utilising only their own knowledge, or they imitate another individual. Both ways, *variation* and *imitation*, are described separately in the following.

3.4.7   Variation

I define *variation* as the process in which individuals look for another choice through self reflection. This search for another, more adequate action is somehow similar to a trial and error procedure. However, the individuals do not randomly try different actions. During the past they have gathered information about the various alternative actions. This knowledge represented by the variable $\eta_i(a, t)$ helps them to choose their next behaviour.

Two variables influence the probability of variation. One is motivation. Less motivated individuals are less likely to change their behaviour. The other influence is the value of the experience $\eta_i(\tilde{a}, t)$ related to other actions $\tilde{a}$. The higher the value $\eta_i(\tilde{a}, t)$, related to another alternative $\tilde{a}$, the more likely individual i will choose this very alternative. Consequently, the probability $r_{i,V}(a, t)$ changing from the current alternative $\tilde{a}$ to alternative a can be written as

$$r_{i,V}(a, t) = \nu_{i,V} \cdot m_i(t) \cdot \Psi(\eta_i(a, t)) \, . \tag{3.35}$$

$\nu_{i,V}$ is the *variation factor* and represents the overall preparedness of individual i to vary its behaviour. This factor is especially important in relation to imitation. The greater the variation factor is in comparison to the imitation factor (defined below), the more variation dominates the learning process.

The remaining two factors on the right-hand side of equation (3.35) can be seen as *push* and *pull factors*. $m_i(t)$ is the push factor; it represents the pressure on individuals to abandon their actual behaviour. $\Psi(\eta_i(a, t))$ is the pull factor; for each alternative a it characterises the attraction of this alternative. The pull factor is determined by the experience $\eta_i(a, t)$. A natural way to define the influence of experience on variation would be a linear dependence. However, in an experiment to evaluate stochastic models of decision-making, two other functions have proved to be more adequate (cf. Brenner 1995): an exponential function and a fermi-like function. Therefore I have used either a general function $\Psi(\eta_i(a,t))$ or one of these two functions that will be described below. In general $\Psi(\eta_i(a,t))$ has to be a monotonously increasing function. Furthermore I demand that

$$\sum_{a\in\mathcal{A}} \Psi(\eta_i(a,t)) = 1 \qquad (3.36)$$

which is important for simulations. It guarantees that $\nu_{i,V} \cdot m_i(t)$ is the probability that a variation takes place, while $\Psi(\eta_i(a,t))$ distributes this probability between the possible new choices.

For simulations it is most convenient to use the *fermi-like function*

$$\Psi(\eta) = \frac{C}{1 + \exp[-\beta_i \cdot (\eta - \gamma_i)]} . \qquad (3.37)$$

β_i $(\beta_i > 0)$ and γ_i are the parameters that characterise this function while C is determined by condition (3.36). The fermi-like function equals $\frac{C}{2}$ at $\eta = \gamma_i$ and its slope is most steep at that point. The derivative of $\Psi(\eta)$ converges to zero for $\eta \to -\infty$ and to c for $\eta \to \infty$. All values of $\Psi(\eta)$ are between zero and c. For two very large values of η the fermi-like function is nearly identical. This means, in the context of the VID model, that two alternatives with very high values $\eta_i(a,t)$ representing experience are chosen with nearly the same probability, although they may differ significantly with respect to $\eta_i(a,t)$.

Unfortunately the fermi-like function is mathematically cumbersome. Therefore I use an exponential function for analytical studies. Since both functions, the fermi-like and the exponential, predicted the experimental results well (cf. Brenner 1995), it seems acceptable to use the exponential function in mathematical applications for convenience (in simulations the exponential function is inconvenient because it causes the values of $\Psi(\eta_i(a,t))$ to range from very small to very high numbers). It is given by

$$\Psi(\eta) = C \cdot \exp[\beta_i\eta] . \qquad (3.38)$$

Again C is determined by condition (3.36). β_i $(\beta_i > 0)$ is the only parameter that shapes the exponential function in this case. The exponential function is positive and monotonously increasing but it is not bounded. The larger the value of η the larger is the derivative of the exponential function. In the context of the VID model, the exponential function implies that alternatives with a very high experience $\eta_i(a,t)$ dominate the variation process.

So far I have assumed that individuals are able and willing to change from each behaviour to every other behaviour. In some applications, however, this is not the case. It may be that, although the alternatives are fixed, the individuals are not aware of all of them. Furthermore although individuals know all the alternatives, they may not be willing to attempt or adapt certain behaviours. For example, if some behaviours are similar to each other, switching from one to another of them occurs more probably than between very different behaviours. This aspect can be modelled by the introduction of a *distance function*. The distance function is denoted by $d(a, \tilde{a})$ and represents the differences between action a and action $\tilde{a}$. The more similar the two alternatives are, the smaller is $d(a, \tilde{a})$. Accordingly the probability $r_{i,V}(a, t)$ can be written as

$$r_{i,V}(a, t) = \nu_{i,V} \cdot m_i(t) \cdot \Psi(\eta_i(a, t)) \cdot \exp[-d(a, a_i(t))] . \qquad (3.39)$$

The exponential function is chosen arbitrarily. Any relation can be expressed by this exponential function if the distance function $d(a, \tilde{a})$ is chosen respectively. The exponential function only assures that the probability $r_{i,V}(a, t)$ is always positive.

3.4.8   Imitation

I define *imitation* as the search for better behaviours by watching or asking others. This aspect of the VID model is based on the psychological knowledge about imitative learning (cf. e.g. Bandura 1977). In the psychological literature several factors can be found that influence the imitation of behaviour.

First, actions are imitated only if they lead to outcomes that are positively evaluated by the imitating individual. Consequently the evaluation of actions plays an important role. Such an evaluation might be obtained in different ways. Individuals may trust other individuals and/or their evaluation and simply ask them about it. In this case, I have to use the utility function $u_j(a_j(t), t)$ or the satisfaction $s_j(t)$ of the asked individual j, dependent on what they tell the individual who asked. The other alternative is that individuals may be able to watch others and evaluate the outcomes obtained by them. In this case, I have to use the utility function $u_i(a_j(t), t)$ of the imitating individual i. The influences of this evaluation on the probability of imitation can be manifold. To consider this effect in the VID model, I define a general function $\Phi_i(j, t)$ that has to be specified for each application separately. I will discuss this function in more detail below.

Second, the imitation depends on the status of the imitated individual and the relationship between the two individuals. It is more likely that an imitation occurs if the observed individual has a respected character or if the individuals are similar to each other. Therefore I have to define an imitation matrix φ_{ij} that represents the likelihood that individual i imitates individual j.

Third, imitation occurs only if the individual is motivated to watch or ask other individuals, that is, if the individual is motivated to look for alternative actions. This motivation to imitate is captured by the variable $m_i(t)$.

In addition, individuals do not imitate a behaviour if they have been dissatisfied by this behaviour in the past. In other words, while imitating, individuals consider their own experience or knowledge $\eta_i(a_j(t), t)$ of the action committed by the other individual j. The greater $\eta_i(a_j(t), t)$, the more likely it is that they imitate the behaviour $a_j(t)$ of individual j.

Considering all these influences, the probability for individual i to imitate individual j at time t reads

$$r_{i,I}(j,t) = \nu_{i,I} \cdot m_i(t) \cdot \varphi_{ij} \cdot \Phi_i(j,t) \cdot \Psi(\eta_i(a_j(t),t)) . \qquad (3.40)$$

$\nu_{i,I}$ is the *imitation factor* and represents the overall preparedness of the individual i to imitate. $\Psi(\eta)$ is again defined by equation (3.37) or (3.38). In contrast to variation, the distance function rarely has an impact on imitation. The reasoning that individuals are only aware of nearby alternatives does not hold for imitation. Furthermore, the reluctance to make substantial changes in behaviour diminishes if the individuals are able to watch others who behave in another fashion. Nevertheless, the possibility that the distance function influences imitation cannot be excluded completely. In such a case, the term $\exp[-d(a, a_j(t))]$ has to be added in equation (3.40).

Function $\Phi_i(j,t)$ that describes the influence of the performance of individual j on the likelihood of an imitation of individual j by individual i, cannot be defined generally. It depends very much on the situation. Therefore it can only be defined in the context of an application. Nevertheless I will give some examples here.

The first example is that of when individuals are able to watch the behaviour of others and the resulting outcomes, and they evaluate these outcomes using their own utility function $u_i(a_j(t), t)$. The more positive this evaluation (the higher the value of $u_i(a_j(t), t)$), the more likely it is that they imitate the behaviour of individual j. Subsequently $\Phi_i(j,t)$ is a monotonically increasing, positive function of $u_i(a_j(t), t)$.

One may use the fermi-like function or the exponential function given in equations (3.37) and (3.38), respectively. One may also use a function $\phi(u_i(a_j(t), t))$ that is defined by

$$\phi(u_i(a_j(t), t) - z_i(t)) = \begin{cases} u_i(a_j(t), t) - z_i(t) & \text{if} \quad u_i(a_j(t), t) \geq z_i(t) \\ 0 & \text{if} \quad u_i(a_j(t), t) < z_i(t) \end{cases}$$

(3.41)

Table 3.1: *Different situations and their implications for the evaluation of actions that may be imitated*

ability to watch others	information received from others	reliability of infor-mation	$\Psi(x)$ given by equation	basis for the evaluation	threshold for imitation
yes	-	yes	(3.42)	$u_i(a_j(t), t)$	$u_i(a_i(t), t)$ or $z_i(t)$
		no	(3.37) or (3.38)	$u_i(a_j(t), t)$	$u_i(a_i(t), t)$ or $z_i(t)$
no	$u_j(a_j(t), t)$	yes	(3.42)	$u_j(a_j(t), t)$	$u_i(a_i(t), t)$ or $z_i(t)$
		no	(3.37) or (3.38)	$u_j(a_j(t), t)$	$u_i(a_i(t), t)$ or $z_i(t)$
	$s_j(t)$	yes	(3.42)	$s_j(t)$	$s_i(t)$
		no	(3.37) or (3.38)	$s_j(t)$	$s_i(t)$

A definition of $\Phi_i(j, t)$ according to equation (3.41) implies the existence of a threshold (in equation (3.41) the threshold is the aspiration level $z_i(t)$). If the evaluation of action $a_j(t)$ is below that threshold, individual i is not certain to imitate individual j. Evaluations above the threshold, however, lead to an imitation with a probability that increases linearly with the evaluation. Three thresholds exist that seem to be reasonable: the aspiration level $z_i(t)$, the personal outcome $u_i(a_i(t), t)$ and the personal satisfaction $s_i(t)$ (if the satisfaction of the imitated individual is used for evaluation). In the first case $\Phi_i(j, t)$ would be given by

$$\Phi_i(j, t) = \phi(u_i(a_j(t), t) - z_i(t)) .$$

(3.42)

Equation (3.42) presents one example of a specification of $\Phi_i(j, t)$. Other specifications can be obtained by the replacement of $u_i(a_j(t), t)$ by

$u_j(a_j(t), t)$ or $s_j(t)$, and $z_i(t)$ by $u_i(a_i(t), t)$ or $s_i(t)$, respectively. For the specification of $\Phi_i(j, t)$ we may follow the systematics given in Table 3.1.

3.4.9 Advantages and Disadvantages

The VID model is one of the most complex mathematical models of learning used in economics. It contains many of the features of learning that are known in psychology (cf. Section 2.3). These are operant conditioning, the reinforcing aspect of imitative learning, the motivational aspects of the theory of optimal arousal, the aspiration level and the level of comparison that are considered by the variables satisfaction and motivation, the theory of social impact and the decay of memory. For these reasons it is a helpful tool for studying various learning processes.

Furthermore, since the VID model is firmly based on psychological knowledge about learning, it seems to be an appropriate tool for a positive theory. With the VID algorithm we are able to study the typical features of learning processes by simulations. In addition, we may use the VID algorithm in the context of economic situations to investigate the implication of learning on economic structures, as is done in this book.

Nevertheless the VID model also dispenses with some of the familiar facts of learning. The notion of learning as the development of associations between memory traces and of cognitive structures, is neglected in the VID model. Most of the recently developed cognitive theories about learning are based on this notion. Associations and cognitive structures are important, especially in situations where difficult problems have to be solved, where the ability to see things in their context influences the learning process, or where cognitive structures interfere with the learning process. In such situations the VID model is a rather crude approximation and the results have to be treated with caution.

Moreover, the VID model covers too many features. As a consequence, only simplifications of the model can be analysed mathematically. In most cases these simplifications are more adequate than the VID model as a whole because many features that are considered in the VID model are not actually relevant.

3.5 ASSOCIATIVE LEARNING

Associative learning is the process that shapes *cognitive models*. Various schematic models exist that describe the structure of cognitive models in the brain. However the features of this structure are controversially discussed. Some authors claim that the structure is hierarchically organised, while others believe in a structure similar to a network. Furthermore little is known about the learning process itself. It is sometimes claimed that the learning process of cognitive models follows principles that are similar to the principles of reinforcement learning (cf. e.g. Kandel & Schwartz 1982). At the same time, however, experimental evidence implies that only one cognitive model of a particular subject exists each time (cf. Köhler 1925). Thus individuals do not choose cognitive models with certain probabilities, as they would choose behaviours in the context of reinforcement learning. Nevertheless, cognitive models are stabilised by reinforcing results and destabilised by punishing outcomes. What the new cognitive model will look like if the old one is abandoned is a question that cannot be answered satisfactorily.

In most cases changes of the cognitive model are minor. A new aspect is added, an old element is eliminated, or parts of the cognitive model are replaced or rearranged. Nevertheless, even these minor changes are not understood comprehensively. Due to its complexity, associative learning has rarely been approached in mathematical models. In psychology many schematic models exist (cf. section 2.3). However, these are quite inprecise formulations of the principles of associative learning. In economics some recent works have referred to these psychological theories (cf. e.g. Denzau & North 1994, Gößling 1996 or Kubon-Gilke 1997).

Some economic studies contain elements of associative learning although the authors did not intend to describe cognitive learning processes. Learning of strategic behaviour in economics, for instance, is a cognitive associative learning process although it is usually not referred to as such. It is often modelled in the context of games. Since the study of Axelrod (cf. Axelrod 1987) it has become usual to talk of *conditional strategies*, like tit-for-tat, in the context of some specific games. Strategic behaviour implies that individuals are aware of their influence on the behaviour of their opponents, at least if the strategic behaviour is the result of a learning process (if conditional strategies are assumed to be genetically fixed, however, no cognitive processes interfere). Most approaches in the literature, however, neglect that aspect. Considering the psychological findings, we should assume that individuals establish hypotheses about their influence on the behaviour of their opponents. Such an approach is rarely made in the literature (see Glance & Huberman 1993 for an example of such an approach).

Knowledge of cognitive learning suggests that it can be modelled as follows. First, the possible cognitive models or the possible features of the relevant parts of the cognitive models have to be defined. In this context it is not necessary to define the structure of the cognitive models. It seems more practical to define the beliefs caused by the cognitive models. Subsequently if the set of possible cognitive models or beliefs is defined, the individuals start with an initial belief. Each belief or cognitive model implies a certain learning behaviour. As long as this learning behaviour leads to satisfactory results, the individuals have no incentive to revise their beliefs. However, if the events resulting from their behaviour contradict their beliefs or are dissatisfying, they may react in two ways. They may ignore these events or they may change their cognitive model. A cognitive model is more likely to be maintained, even though the observed events may contradict the model or the individual's performance is dissatisfying, the longer ago it was confirmed. If the cognitive model is to be changed, two processes can be assumed to occur. First, it might be assumed that several cognitive models compete, similar to the competition of several behaviours in reinforcement learning. Contrary to reinforcement learning, however, these cognitive models are not utilised randomly according to their strength. Instead, the cognitive model with the highest influence is the one that presents most strongly to the individual. Models are strengthened by confirming or reinforcing results and weakened by contradictory or punishing results. If the relevant part of the cognitive structure is strongly associated with other parts, the individuals may only be able to abandon both parts together. Thus some parts of the cognitive structure can stabilise others. Second, it might be assumed that if certain cognitive models are refuted by reality, individuals will change them in such a way that they predict also the deviation from the old cognitive model. According to this kind of modelling, individuals adapt their cognitive models directly to new information.

The way of modelling associative learning outlined above may or may not prove to be adequate, since cognitive learning is still not comprehensively understood. We have to proceed using a little trial and error with different kinds of modelling and find out whether they are helpful and realistic.

3.6 SUMMARY

This chapter gives a review of the learning models that can be found in the economic literature with respect to the distinction of learning processes made in Chapter 2. Besides the description of several models, some comments are made on the usefulness of each of the models and proposals are made about how each kind of learning can be modelled adequately. A summary of this categorisation of the learning models and the proposals is given in Table 3.2.

Table 3.2: *Categorisation of economic learning models with respect to the kind of learning*

	non-cognitive learning	routine-based learning	associative learning
models in the literature	Bush-Mosteller model melioration learning	Bayesian learning Robbins-Monro algorithm least squares learning imitation models fictitious play evolutionary algorithms learning direction theory	-
proposed models	Bush-Mosteller model (melioration learning)	VID model	-

Chapter 4

Mathematical Prerequisites for Modelling Learning

I have previously claimed the consideration of learning to be fruitful in the context of economic processes. This claim is justified by the findings that economic processes are path-dependent, that learning does not always lead to optimal behaviour, and that economic processes rarely occur in an environment remaining constant long enough for the processes to converge to a stable state. Consequently, the dynamics of learning play an important role in economic processes although it has often been neglected in the literature. Furthermore, learning is rarely a deterministic process. Most learning models assume learning processes to be stochastic or consider random errors. The features of a *stochastic process* differ crucially from the one of a deterministic process, and different mathematical tools are necessary to describe both processes. The general mathematical implications of dynamic and stochastic processes will be analysed below.

The first section presents some general thoughts about the dynamic process of learning in the context of economics. In the second, several concepts for approaching stochastic systems mathematically are described and discussed. The third section contains a discussion of path dependence based on learning processes.

4.1   LEARNING AND ECONOMIC DYNAMICS

The economic literature is dominated by the assumption that economic systems adapt so fast to changing circumstances that it is sufficient to study the *equilibrium* they converge to. However such an approach is only partly adequate. Changes in the behaviour of agents result in changes of the whole economic system. Everybody who takes learning seriously should also take dynamics into account, because learning results in a change of behaviour. Therefore learning and economic dynamics go together.

Economic dynamics can only be approached in two ways. First, the features of economic dynamics can be studied phenomenologically. On the basis of empirical observations, models can be proposed describing the dynamics adequately. Second, the features of economic dynamics can be deduced from the dynamics on the individual level. To this end, an adequate understanding of the dynamics of individual behaviour, that is, of learning processes, is necessary. With the help of such an understanding of learning processes, the economic dynamics may be deduced theoretically. This approach utilises the relation between learning and economic dynamics.

A glance through the economic literature shows that this fact has been widely neglected. Not only have most economists neglected the relevance of learning at all, but those who have written about learning have neglected the relevance of its dynamics. It is argued that the dynamics of learning is relevant only if an individual faces a new situation. After some time the individual will adapt to the situation and behave rationally, or whatever behaviour learning converges to. Therefore most of the works about learning use learning models only for retaining the behaviour learning converges to. In recent years, many theoretical papers have proved that learning converges to the rational equilibrium, especially in *game theory* (cf. e. g. Blume & Easley 1982, Marcet & Sargent 1989, Jordan 1991, Kalai & Lehrer 1993 and Marimon 1993). At the same time, many theoretical papers have proved the opposite (cf. e. g. Witt 1986b, Dekel & Scotchmer 1992, Bullard & Duffy 1994a and Brenner 1997). This implies that it depends on the learning process and the situation whether learning converges to the equilibrium predicted by a rational approach or not.

However, it may also be claimed that a stationary behaviour is an exception rather than the normal case. There are three reasons that support this claim. First, individuals rarely face the same situation for long. Our surroundings are changing continually so that we are constantly learning. As a consequence, the behaviour of economic agents is continually changing as well, and a stationary state is hardly ever reached. The assumption of an equilibrium is contra-intuitive in such a case. Second, economic behaviour depends on the past. This means that individuals behave differently in the same situation due to their different histories. Consequently the behaviour in a situation is not solely determined by the characteristics of that situation. A static analysis, however, can only be based on these characteristics and fails to capture the important aspect of path dependency. Third, an economic state is never really stable. In the real world, fluctuations occur all the time. These fluctuations, exogenous shocks as well as endogenous changes caused by individuals, are accompanied by a dynamic process that takes the system back to the previous state, or leads it away if a critical amount of fluctuation has brought the system too far from the stable state. The likelihood of such an abandonment of a stable state depends on the dynamics of the system.

Consequently, it is much more important to understand the dynamics of a process than to be able to calculate potential final states. The dynamics not only determines which of the stable states is reached in the long run, it also determine the degree of stability and the time the system needs to reach the stable state. In the context of economic behaviour, the dynamics are described on the individual level by learning processes.

Learning processes are often claimed to be adaptive. They are believed to improve the performance of individuals in a new situation successively, so that they only describe the path from the previously optimal behaviour to the currently optimal behaviour. The fact that learning might include more than this, like satisficing or the change of behaviour with the intention to creatively change the surrounding, is often neglected. Furthermore, the fact is often ignored that learning is a stochastic process. However the *fluctuations* in learning, caused by errors, curiosity, purposes of information gathering and imagination, are a crucial reason for learning processes not to settle down and behaviour not to become constant. Thus the fluctuations of learning processes have to be investigated in more detail.

The models and theories of learning make different statements about the fluctuations of learning processes. If we consider the learning models based on experimental knowledge about learning (namely the Bush-Mosteller model, melioration learning, imitative learning, and the learning direction theory), they all treat learning as a stochastic process. There is strong experimental evidence that learning can be described in a stochastic manner only. In addition to experimental evidence, various reasons can be stated in favour of a stochastic modelling of learning. It might be claimed that we still have only an incomplete understanding of learning, so that we may only hope for stochastic statements about reality. One may also claim that learning is influenced by too many circumstances that cannot all be considered adequately. A model considering only some of the relevant circumstances, in turn, describes real processes only on the average (if the neglected aspects have no impact on average). Finally, it might be claimed that learning is intrinsically stochastic, as some learning models claim.

The fact that learning has to be modelled stochastically has, reasons apart, important implications for mathematical analysis. These implications depend on the characteristics of the fluctuations that occur during the learning process. Therefore I will discuss the assumptions about fluctuations separately for each of the three learning processes outlined above. In the case of *non-cognitive learning*, that is, reinforcement learning, it is assumed that individuals begin by choosing all possible actions with similar probabilities, or according to a given probability distribution. Then the probabilities change according to the outcomes that are experienced. According to the *Bush-Mosteller model*, none of the probabilities ever decreases to zero during the learning process. The Bush-Mosteller model is based on evidence of experiments in which only one behaviour is studied which is assumed never to become extinct although it may become very rare. In this case, fluctuations never disappear (Roth and Erév 1995 expanded the Bush-Mosteller model in a way that allows behaviours to disappear from the set of behaviours used). In the concept of *melioration*, instead, two alternative actions are compared by the individual according to their results. The extinction of one of the two actions is not excluded if this action always results in less preferred outcomes. However, whether less successful actions disappear depends on the mathematical formulation of melioration learning. According to the *matching law* of Herrnstein (1961), fluctuations within individual behaviours should vanish. According to the formulation of melioration learning given in Brenner & Witt 1997, fluctuations never vanish but may become very unlikely.

Routine-based learning can, again, not be analysed generally because the routines may have various features. Trial and error processes, or the active imitation of other individuals, are examples of routine-based learning. During trial and error learning, individuals experiment extensively in the beginning so that their behaviour changes frequently. As time elapses they gather information about possible actions, and fluctuations should decrease. One may argue that the fluctuations should finally disappear but one may also argue that individuals retry alternatives from time to time, to check whether anything has changed. In the latter case, the fluctuations never vanish, while the former claim implies that fluctuations finally disappear. In the case of imitation, fluctuations are caused by the possibility of imitation one of various individuals behaving differently. As soon as all individuals behave identically, none of them can change her/his behaviour by imitation, so that the fluctuations disappear. As long as the individuals behave differently, fluctuations remain.

Associative learning processes are not understood as well as the other two learning processes. Thus one can only speculate about fluctuations in this context. If we follow the claim of neo-behaviourism that cognitive models are learnt by reinforcement, the comments about non-cognitive learning also hold for associative learning. Consequently, associative cognitive learning might be accompanied by vanishing fluctuations as well as persistent fluctuations.

To sum up, three aspects of learning cause a pure calculation of the stable states of learning to be inappropriate. First, the circumstances may change so that the learning process never reaches a stable state. Second, learning processes may be accompanied by fluctuations that never vanish. Third, the learning processes may converge to different, and not necessarily optimal, behaviours dependent on the features of the learning process and the circumstances. These aspects will occur repeatedly in the applications of learning to several economic topics in Chapters 6, 7, 8, 9 and 10. The second and the third aspects are analysed in more detail in the following sections.

4.2 STATIONARY STATES AND LEARNING

According to the discussion above, most learning processes are accompanied by fluctuations, which may or may not vanish over time. The persistence or disappearance of fluctuations is important for the existence of stationary states. Generally, stationary states for stochastic dynamics are defined as follows.

> DEFINITION 4.1 (STATIONARY STATES): *A state x̌ is a stationary state with respect to a stochastic dynamic if, and only if, the system, once the state of the system is x̌, changes its state with probability zero according to the stochastic dynamics.*

Thus, no stationary states exist if the dynamics are stochastic, as long as fluctuations do not vanish over time. As soon as they vanish, the system becomes deterministic. Nevertheless a system that remains stochastic may, in the long run, show features similar to stationary states or limit cycles. Therefore it is important to find tools to describe such a stability-like behaviour of stochastic systems.

To this end, it is helpful to define a stochastic process mathematically. Two approaches can be used. First, the definition of a stochastic process may be based on a deterministic process. Let me assume the state of the system to be given by a vector $\mathbf{x}(t)$ at each time t. The dynamics of a deterministic process are given either in a time-continuous form by

$$\frac{d\mathbf{x}(t)}{dt} = \mathbf{L}(\mathbf{x}(t)) \tag{4.1}$$

or in a time-discrete form by

$$\mathbf{x}(t+1) = \mathbf{x}(t) + \mathbf{L}(\mathbf{x}(t)) \tag{4.2}$$

where $\mathbf{L}(\mathbf{x}(t))$ determines the dynamics of the process. Analogously a stochastic process can be formulated by

$$\frac{d\mathbf{x}(t)}{dt} = \mathbf{L}(\mathbf{x}(t)) + \Gamma(t) \tag{4.3}$$

or

$$\mathbf{x}(t+1) = \mathbf{x}(t) + \mathbf{L}(\mathbf{x}(t)) + \Gamma(t) \tag{4.4}$$

where $\Gamma(t)$ is a stochastic vector. The probability distribution is denoted by $f(\Gamma, t)$, i. e. $\Gamma(t) = \Gamma$ occurs with the probability $f(\Gamma, t)$. Furthermore, the expected value of $\Gamma(t)$ is zero, i. e.

$$E(\Gamma(t)) = \int_{-\infty}^{\infty} f(\Gamma, t) \cdot \Gamma \, d\Gamma = 0 \tag{4.5}$$

and $\Gamma(t)$ is not inter-temporally correlated, i. e.

$$\int_{-\infty}^{\infty} \int_{-\infty}^{\infty} f(\Gamma, t) \cdot \Gamma \cdot f(\tilde{\Gamma}, \tau) \cdot \tilde{\Gamma} \, d\Gamma \, d\tilde{\Gamma} = 0 \qquad \forall \tau \neq t \,. \tag{4.6}$$

This way of describing a stochastic process is oriented on the corresponding deterministic process. It is especially helpful if the fluctuations are small and the dynamics of the deterministic process approximate the dynamics of the stochastic process, on average, quite well.

Second, a stochastic process may be defined by the formulation of *transition rates*. Again the state of the system is given by a vector $\mathbf{x}(t)$ ($\in \mathcal{X}$) at each time t. Based on the set of states $\mathcal{X}$ a probability distribution is defined that assigns to each state $\mathbf{x}$ the probability $f(\mathbf{x}, t)$ that this state is realised at time t. The dynamics of the system is given by probabilities or rates $r(\mathbf{x} \to \tilde{\mathbf{x}}, t)$ that define the probability per unit of time of the systems to change from state $\mathbf{x}$ to state $\tilde{\mathbf{x}}$ at time t. Again the dynamics can be described in a time-continuous and a time-discrete form. In the time-continuous case $r(\mathbf{x} \to \tilde{\mathbf{x}}, t)$ describes a *transition rate*, that is the probability per unit of time of the system to change from state $\mathbf{x}$ to state $\tilde{\mathbf{x}}$ at time t. The dynamics are given by the master equation (cf. Weidlich 1991)

$$\frac{df(\mathbf{x}, t)}{dt} = \sum_{\tilde{\mathbf{x}} \in \mathcal{X}} \left[r(\tilde{\mathbf{x}} \to \mathbf{x}, t) \cdot f(\tilde{\mathbf{x}}, t) - r(\mathbf{x} \to \tilde{\mathbf{x}}, t) \cdot f(\mathbf{x}, t) \right] . \qquad (4.7)$$

Equation (4.7) describes a time-continuous *Markov process*.

In the time-discrete case $r(\mathbf{x} \to \tilde{\mathbf{x}}, t)$ describes a *transition probability*, the probability of the system to change from state $\mathbf{x}$ to state $\tilde{\mathbf{x}}$ at time t. The dynamics of the system are given by the time-discrete master equation (cf. Haken 1983)

$$f(\mathbf{x}, t+1) = \sum_{\tilde{\mathbf{x}} \in \mathcal{X}} \left[r(\tilde{\mathbf{x}} \to \mathbf{x}, t) \cdot f(\tilde{\mathbf{x}}, t) - r(\mathbf{x} \to \tilde{\mathbf{x}}, t) \cdot f(\mathbf{x}, t) \right] \qquad (4.8)$$

if $r(\mathbf{x} \to \mathbf{x}, t)$ is defined as the probability of the system to remain in state $\mathbf{x}$ at time t. A process described by equation (4.7) or (4.8) is called a *Markov chain*. This way of describing a stochastic process works on the level of probabilities of the possible states. On this level, the stochastic process can be described by a deterministic equation (cf. equations (4.7) and (4.8) which are deterministic).

Both concepts to deal with stochastic dynamics mathematically can be transformed into one another. Depending on the application, one of the two is more convenient.

Most of the learning models described in section 2.1 use the second formulation given by equations (4.7) and (4.8); these are the Bush-Mosteller model, melioration learning, the learning direction theory and the VID model. Imitation learning is modelled in both ways in the literature.

Similar to a deterministic process, a stochastic process shows persistent patterns in the long run. In other words, the stochastic process converges to a dynamic that has some persistent characteristics, although it is still stochastic in most cases. There are some stability-like dynamics.

In the literature, four different ways of describing the long-run behaviour of stochastic systems can be found. All four can be applied to learning processes, and each of these four concepts reveals another aspect of the stability-like dynamics that we have to expect in the context of learning. Therefore I will discuss each of these concepts in detail below.

4.2.1   Analysis of the Corresponding Deterministic Dynamics

Very often in the economic literature, the stochastic aspect of learning is simply neglected. It is assumed that a study of the average behaviour is sufficient to understand the features or results of the learning process described. To this end, stochastic dynamics on each occasion are replaced by average dynamics at this time. If the stochastic dynamics are given by a formulation like the one in equation (4.3) or (4.4), the average dynamics are given by equation (4.1) or (4.2), respectively. If the stochastic dynamics are given in the form of (4.7) or (4.8), the average dynamics are defined by (cf. Weidlich 1991)

$$\frac{d\mathbf{x}(t)}{dt} = \sum_{\tilde{\mathbf{x}} \in \mathcal{X}} \left(\tilde{\mathbf{x}} - \mathbf{x} \right) \cdot r(\mathbf{x} \to \tilde{\mathbf{x}}, t) \qquad (4.9)$$

or

$$\mathbf{x}(t+1) = \sum_{\tilde{\mathbf{x}} \in \mathcal{X}} \tilde{\mathbf{x}} \cdot r(\mathbf{x} \to \tilde{\mathbf{x}}, t) \ . \qquad (4.10)$$

The resulting dynamics describe the *quasi-mean values* (this expression originates from W. Weidlich, a comprehensive discussion can be found in Weidlich 1991) of the variables that characterise the state of the system. Quasi-mean values are not equal to the mean values of the variables that can be deduced from the stochastic dynamics. Nevertheless, quasi-mean values are a good tool in the study of the stochastic dynamics. Their dynamics represent the average dynamics of the system. To make this point clearer, let me consider a one-dimensional dynamic that is given by the potential function $\phi(x)$ depicted in Figure 4.1 and equation

$$\frac{dx(t)}{dt} = -\frac{d\phi(x)}{dx} + \Gamma(t) \ . \qquad (4.11)$$

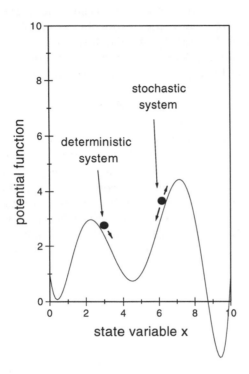

Figure 4.1: *Arbitrarily chosen potential function for illustration*

This equation implies that the motion of $x(t)$ can be described by a downhill movement in the potential landscape plus a stochastic deviation. Consequently, the deterministic system always moves downhill while the stochastic system may move in both directions. Nevertheless a downhill movement is more likely in the stochastic process. The deterministic process converges to one of the three valleys in Figure 4.1, dependent on the initial state. The stochastic system is able to reach any state at any time, though it will be found most probably in one of the valleys as well. This means that the deterministic process, that is, the dynamics of the quasi-mean values, represents the most likely behaviour of the stochastic process. Thus the study of quasi-mean values offers some insights into the features of the learning process. In certain circumstances the stable states of the dynamics of the quasi-mean values are identical with the local maxima in the stationary probability distribution over the state space (cf. Weidlich 1991). This means that the stable states of the corresponding deterministic dynamics are equal to the states that are locally most probable (as in the example of the potential function in Figure 4.1). Although this statement holds exactly only if certain requirements are fulfilled by the system, the stable states of the deterministic dynamics are often a good approximation of the most probable states of the stochastic system.

But an analysis of the corresponding deterministic dynamics tells only half of the story. The set of deterministically stable states represents a good approximation of the set of states in which the system can be found, most probably only if the fluctuations are small enough and if the attraction of these states is strong enough. Both these conditions, however, are not analysed in the context of deterministic stability. Therefore a deterministic approach misses some important features of stochastic dynamics, especially the amount of fluctuation. Thus, a deterministic analysis offers no insights into the probability of the system deviating from the most probable states, and the probability to switch between such states.

4.2.2   Stochastically Stable Equilibrium

Some authors claim that the fluctuations of learning processes should vanish with time (cf. e.g. Foster & Young 1990 or Samuelson 1994). While individuals gather more information about a situation and its outcomes, they should become more certain about the adequate behaviour. Such an assumption is in line with the statements that have been made about trial and error learning, above. As a consequence, in such a case long-run behaviour can be obtained as the stable state to which the learning process converges, if the strength of fluctuations tends to zero for time going to infinity. Realistically, a learning process takes only a finite period of time, so that fluctuations do not vanish completely.

Nevertheless, it is helpful to analyse the state that would result if the learning process continued long enough for the fluctuations to vanish. D. Foster and P. Young (1990) firstly proposed the consideration of such a state and called it *stochastically stable equilibrium* (SSE). It is defined as the state for which it holds that *"it is nearly certain that the system lies within every small neighborhood of P [the SSE state] as the noise tends slowly to zero"*. Foster and Young claimed that the condition for a SSE is a global criterion, while the condition for a stable state in the corresponding deterministic dynamics is a local criterion. This difference has important implications for stochastic dynamics.

In the context of a local stability analysis for a deterministic system each state is studied only with respect to its immediate neighbourhood. A state is stable if the system converges from each state within a small neighbourhood to this very state. By this, many states may be stable without competing with each other. To make this point more obvious, let me consider a system with one continuous state variable. The dynamics of the system shall be given by a *potential function* (see Figure 4.1). The motion of the system is then the same as the motion of a ball on the sphere of the potential function. If the potential function has several valleys, that is minima, each valley attracts the ball whenever it has crossed the edge of the surrounding hills. In other words, each of the valleys, that is, each of the stable states, possesses its own area from where the system converges to this stable state. The final state depends on the initial state of the system.

In the case of a stochastic system, things are different. The fluctuations within such a system push the ball around randomly. By this, the ball may cross some hills and reach a different valley from the one it started in. If in such a stochastic process the fluctuations vanish with time, the ball ends up in one of the valleys. From the literature on *simulated annealing* we know that the system converges to the lowest valley with probability one (cf. van Laarhoven & Aarts 1987, pp. 17). The stochastic process selects one of the deterministically stable states in this case. This state is the only stochastically stable equilibrium (SSE). However not every system can be treated as described above. The proof by van Laarhoven and Aarts holds only for irreducible and aperiodic Markov chains (cf. van Laarhoven & Aarts 1987, pp. 18).

To sum up, if a learning process contains fluctuations that vanish with time, it may converge to a set of states that is called stochastically stable equilibria (SSE). Since the fluctuations enable the system to reach any state independent of the initial state, these SSEs are the result of a global selection process. In other words, stochastic learning processes are able to explore the whole set of possible behaviours and converge, if fluctuations vanish and certain conditions are satisfied (cf. van Laarhoven & Aarts 1987), to the behaviour that is globally most successful. In realistic cases, however, the likelihood that a learning process takes place long enough for the fluctuations to vanish and the process to settle down, is rather small and the argumentation above only holds if time goes to infinity.

4.2.3   Stationary Probability Distribution

In contrast to the above argumentation, it can also be assumed that the fluctuations stay the same during the whole learning process. In this case the SSE is an inappropriate concept. The stable states of the corresponding deterministic dynamics may approximate the most frequently occurring states in the stochastic dynamics, but they offer no information about the magnitude of these frequencies.

An alternative approach is based on the definition of a probability measure $f(\mathbf{x}, t)$ on the state space and the use of equations of motion for this probability measure (4.7) and (4.8). Once the equations of motion have been set up for the probabilities $f(\mathbf{x}, t)$, the stationary values of these probabilities can be calculated. The dynamics of the probabilities $f(\mathbf{x}, t)$ is deterministic so that the usual tools for deterministic dynamic systems can be applied. If the equations of motion for the probabilities $f(\mathbf{x}, t)$ are independent of time, and if the system moves from any state to any other state with a probability greater than zero in a finite period of time, that is, if the stochastic dynamics are *irreducible* (cf. van Laarhoven & Aarts 1987), one, and only one, stationary set of probabilities $f_{st}(\mathbf{x})$ exists (cf. Helbing 1995). This set of probabilities $f_{st}(\mathbf{x})$ is called the *stationary probability distribution*.

The stationary probability distribution is not only useful for the analysis of a concrete learning process. Its existence and uniqueness also have general implications for learning processes. Before these implications are discussed, however, the conditions for the validity of such an approach should be recalled; the learning process should be irreducible. If this condition is fulfilled, the learning process converges to the stable probability distribution. This leads to three important implications:

1) The stable probability distribution is unique if the stochastic dynamics are irreducible. Thus, the probability distribution converges to the same distribution independent of the initial state, and therefore also independent of any intermediate state. In other words, independent of the current state, each other state $\mathbf{x}$ is reached after a time. Consequently no stationary state $\check{\mathbf{x}}$ can exist. Every state $\mathbf{x}$ can be reached independent of the system's past. The probability of finding the state $\mathbf{x}$ after a certain infinite long period of time, is given by $f_{st}(\mathbf{x})$ independent of the past.

2) If the stochastic dynamics are reducible, at least one subset of states has to exist, such that the probability of the system to leave this subset is zero. Such a subset of states is called an *absorbing set of states* because it absorbs the whole probability with time, if it is the only

absorbing set of states. If there are several absorbing sets of states, they together absorb the whole probability. The final probability distribution on the absorbing sets of states depends on the initial state. If the initial state lies within one absorbing set of states, none of the other absorbing sets of states can be reached. After an infinitely long time, the system can only be found in states that belong to absorbing sets of states, if at least one absorbing set of states exists. Nevertheless after any finite period of time, the probability that the system has reached an absorbing set of states may be small. Thus the existence of absorbing sets of states does not necessarily imply that the system approaches these absorbing sets of states in realistic periods of time (cf. the discussion about the extinction of a population in Weidlich & Haag 1983, pp.112-122).

An absorbing set of states may consist of only one state. In this case, the corresponding state is stationary in the sense that it is never left once it is reached. However the existence of such a state implies that the fluctuations vanish in this state. This means that, in contrast to the notion of a SSE, the fluctuations vanish not over time but dependent on the state of the system. Such a behaviour occurs, for example, if individuals imitate others by chance. Although this process is stochastic, the fluctuations vanish as soon as all individuals behave in the same way. Such a state is absorbing.

3) Even if there are no absorbing sets of states, we may claim that a state is stationary or at least nearly stationary. Let us, for example, assume that the stable probability distribution has several sharp peaks. This means that several well distinguishable states exist which are reached quite probably. All other states are rarely approached by the system. In such a case, the system moves quickly from one of the quite probable states to the next, and remains in each of these states for a certain period of time according to the probability. The question arises of how long the system will remain in one of these states. There are mathematical formulae to calculate the average time that the system does this (cf. Helbing 1995). The result might be a time that is too long to have any meaning for a process in real time. We may then regard the corresponding state as nearly stationary, or *meta-stable*, although there is a very small probability that this state is abandoned by the system.

4.2.4 Stability on the Level of Populations

In recent years, it has become increasingly common in economics to analyse *populations* instead of single or representative individuals. In such an approach, individuals are considered to be different with respect to their history and therefore their behaviour. Moreover, it is sometimes claimed that individuals are also different with respect to the rule that describes their behaviour, for example, with respect to their individual learning behaviour. Most of the time, however, they are assumed to behave according to the same rules. Fluctuations occur if either the behavioural rules cause random behaviour or the circumstances cause random outcomes. As a consequence, the individuals have different histories even if they behave according to the same rules.

To obtain a description of the behaviour on the level of populations, one has to understand the processes on the level of individuals first. This means that the starting point is still the description of the behaviour of each individual, which means a description of the individual learning processes. The learning processes are assumed to be stochastic and given by one of the equations (4.3), (4.4), (4.7) or (4.8). Two ways exist of aggregating the dynamics on the level of individuals and obtaining dynamics on the level of populations. Let me assume that the behaviour of an individual i is given by a variable $a_i(t)$ ($\in \mathcal{A}$) at time t. Furthermore for convenience, the learning process is assumed to be continuous in time (a time-discrete learning process can be studied similarily). Thus, two kinds of equations can be used to formalise the dynamics of learning on the level of individuals. Either the changes of the behaviour $da_i(t)/dt$ are given by a stochastic equation (cf. equation (4.3))

$$\frac{da_i(t)}{dt} = L_i(a_i(t)) + \Gamma(t) \tag{4.12}$$

or the dynamics of the probability $f_i(a,t)$ of individual i to perform action a at time t are presented by an equation (cf. equation (4.7)

$$\frac{df_i(a,t)}{dt} = \sum_{\tilde{a} \in \mathcal{A}} \left[r_i(\tilde{a} \to a, t) \cdot f_i(\tilde{a}, t) - r_i(a \to \tilde{a}, t) \cdot f_i(a, t) \right]. \tag{4.13}$$

Both formulations can be transformed into one another. In the latter case the change $df_i(a,t)/dt$ of the probabilities is deterministically given (cf. the discussion in the last paragraph). $L_i(a_i(t))$ and $r_i(\tilde{a} \to a, t)$ may depend on the actions of other individuals.

On the level of populations (the number of individuals in the population is denoted by N) we are generally interested either in the average behaviour of the individuals which is given by

$$\bar{a}(t) = \frac{1}{N} \sum_{i=1}^{N} a_i(t) \tag{4.14}$$

or in the shares $x(a,t)$ of individuals who realise action a at time t which are given by

$$x(a,t) = \frac{1}{N} \sum_{i=1}^{N} \delta(a_i(t) = a) \qquad (4.15)$$

where

$$\delta(a_i(t) = a) = \begin{cases} 1 & \text{for} \quad a = a_i(t) \\ 0 & \text{for} \quad a \neq a_i(t) \end{cases}. \qquad (4.16)$$

Both values, the average behaviour $\bar{a}(t)$ and the shares $x(a,t)$, are defined as the sum of stochastic values. Thus they are themselves only stochastically given. The same holds for their equations of motion, namely

$$\frac{d\bar{a}(t)}{dt} = \frac{1}{N} \sum_{i=1}^{N} \frac{da_i(t)}{dt} \qquad (4.17)$$

and

$$\frac{dx(a,t)}{dt} = \frac{1}{N} \sum_{i=1}^{N} \left[\delta(a_i(t) \to a) - \delta(a_i(t) = a) \right] \qquad (4.18)$$

where $\delta(a_i(t) \to a) = 1$ if the individual i changes her/his behaviour to behaviour a at time t and $\delta(a_i(t) \to a) = 0$ otherwise. $\delta(a_i(t) \to a) = 1$ also holds if the individual continues to realise action a at time t. $\delta(a_i(t) = a)$ is given in equation (4.16).

Equations (4.17) and (4.18) describe the dynamics on the level of populations. They are still stochastic. However, they become deterministic if one crucial assumption is made. This assumption is typical for almost all approaches that identify stable states on the level of populations.

It is assumed that the number of individuals is infinite. If this assumption is not made, an analysis on the level of populations can still be carried through but the concept of stability that is presented in the following cannot be used. Thus without this assumption, an analysis on the level of populations relies on the concepts of stability described above. The crucial advantage of population thinking, however, is that deterministic equations of motion are obtained although the dynamics is stochastic on the level of individuals. This only holds if the assumption of an infinitely large population is satisfied.

Given the assumption of infinitely large populations, the law of great numbers applies. As a consequence, every sum over the whole population of any stochastic characteristic is normally distributed with the average given by the sum of the average characteristics of each individual and a variance of zero. Thus the equations (4.14) and (4.15) can be rewritten:

$$\bar{a}(t) = \frac{1}{N} \sum_{i=1}^{N} \bar{a}_i(t) \tag{4.19}$$

and

$$x(a, t) = \frac{1}{N} \sum_{i=1}^{N} f_i(a, t) \tag{4.20}$$

where $\bar{a}_i(t)$ is the average behaviour of individual i given by

$$\bar{a}_i(t) = \sum_{\tilde{a} \in \mathcal{A}} \tilde{a} \cdot f_i(\tilde{a}, t) . \tag{4.21}$$

Both equations, (4.19) and (4.20), depend on the individual probabilities $f_i(a, t)$ only. The change $df_i(a, t)/dt$ of these probabilities with time is deterministically defined on the individual level. As a consequence, the changes of $\bar{a}(t)$ and $x(a, t)$ are described by deterministic equations of motion. Their stable states can be analysed with the help of all tools developed for deterministic systems. The equations of motion on the population level read

$$\frac{d\bar{a}(t)}{dt} = \frac{1}{N} \sum_{i=1}^{N} \sum_{\tilde{a} \in \mathcal{A}} \tilde{a} \cdot \frac{df_i(\tilde{a}, t)}{dt} \tag{4.22}$$

and

$$\frac{dx(a, t)}{dt} = \frac{1}{N} \sum_{i=1}^{N} \frac{df_i(a, t)}{dt} . \tag{4.23}$$

The dynamics on the level of individuals, represented by $df_i(a, t)/dt$, may depend on all actions of all individuals before time t. However, most learning models describe learning as a *Markov process*. As a consequence, $df_i(a, t)/dt$ is a function of the actions of all individuals at time t. This means that, in general, equations (4.22) and (4.23) cannot be analysed without studying the dynamics on the level of individuals. Hence, in general nothing is gained by switching to the level of populations. Nevertheless there are some cases in which closed equations of motion are obtained on the level of populations. This occurs whenever $df_i(a, t)/dt$ can be written as a linear function in $f_i(a, t)$, i.e.

$$\frac{df_i(a, t)}{dt} = \beta(x(a, t)) \cdot f_i(a, t) + \gamma(x(a, t)) \tag{4.24}$$

where $\beta(x(a,t))$ and $\gamma(x(a,t))$ may depend on $x(a,t)$. Condition (4.24) is satisfied in a number of cases, for example in the case of imitation. In all those cases, equations (4.22) and (4.23) are deterministic and can be analysed accordingly. To show this equation (4.24) is inserted into equation (4.23). It results that

$$
\begin{aligned}
\frac{dx(a,t)}{dt} &= \frac{1}{N} \sum_{i=1}^{N} \beta(x(a,t)) \cdot f_i(a,t) + \gamma(x(a,t)) \\
&= \beta(x(a,t)) \cdot x(a,t) + \gamma(x(a,t)) \, .
\end{aligned}
\tag{4.25}
$$

In general, however, no closed system of equations results.

To sum up, under the assumption of an infinitely large population and given condition (4.24), a closed set of deterministic equations can be derived from the stochastic equations that describe the dynamics on the individual level. These equations on the population level can be analysed much more easily. However, the assumption of an infinitely large population is never exactly true. Without this assumption, the equations of motion on the population level remain stochastic. Consequently, stability is reached only if it also occurs on the individual level. Thus, deterministic equations on the population level are obtained through a mathematical trick but do not represent reality. Nevertheless with an increasing number of individuals, it is more and more unlikely for the population to leave the states that are stable for an infinite population.

4.3 PATH DEPENDENCE

The importance of *path dependence* for economic processes has been pointed out frequently during the last years (cf. David 1985 and 1997, Arthur 1992 and Witt 1997). In general, path dependence means that the current state of a system does not only depend on the underlying rules, but also on the initial state and/or the path of states that the process took in the past. David (1997) defines a path dependent stochastic process as a process *"whose asymptotic distribution evolves as a consequence (function of) the process' own history"* (David 1997, p. 14).

The concept of path dependence showed up in the context of externalities, where it was claimed that due to increasing returns of scale a multiplicity of equilibrium solutions may occur and that, as a consequence, one equilibrium solution is reached by chance and stays forever (cf. David 1985 and Arthur 1989). The crucial aspect of path dependence according to David and Arthur, is the existence of a period of time during which the movement of the system determines the behaviour for the future. However, although nobody doubts the fact that economic processes are path dependent, in the sense that history influences the current state of a system, there is controversy about the definition of path dependence.

Let me consider a stochastic dynamics, as analysed in the previous section, to clarify this point. Assuming the situation given in Figure 4.1, with a system that is in the state given by the right ball in this figure at time t_0, the question of how the system behaves will be discussed to show what path dependence means. For the immediate future, it is possible to predict that the state of the system is unlikely to differ much from the current one. Such a dependence occurs whenever there is some continuity in the dynamics of the system. It would not be wise to call such a dependence "path dependence". In addition, it can be predicted that the system is very likely to be found near the state belonging to the minimum in the middle of Figure 4.1, in the medium run. This prediction holds if the fluctuations are sufficiently small that system moves downhill with a great probability and remains at the minimum for a long period of time, on average. I call such a behaviour *weak path dependent* if other states exist with the same property (otherwise the system will probably always converge to the same state, so that the current state has no influence on the medium-run behaviour). However, this definition of path dependence differs from what David and Arthur describe. It does not imply that the system remains in the state belonging to the minimum forever. According to the definition of David (1997), a process is *path dependent* if the final distribution, the stationary probability distribution that is reached in the long run, depends on the history of the system. I call this *strong path dependence*. In the example taken here, this would mean that the system is not able to reach all states as a condition of the initial state, for example, because the ball is not able to cross the hills. If the fluctuations are even zero, the ball will move downhill and rest at the bottom of the valley it started in. In such a case, we talk about a *lock-in* (cf. e.g. Arthur 1989 and Witt 1997). The difference between a lock-in and path dependence is that a lock-in requires that the dynamics of a system are restricted to one state dependent on the history of the system, while the dynamics of a path dependent system are restricted to a subset of all states from a certain point in time onwards. Thus, lock-ins require path dependence while path dependence does not necessarily lead to a lock-in.

From the analysis above, we know that if a system is irreducible, that means if it is ergotic, it is able to transform from any state to any other state in a finite period of time, although some transitions may be very unlikely. In such a system, no absorbing set of states exists and no strong path dependence occurs (cf. the definition of David 1997, p.13). Weak path dependence, instead, can be also found in irreducible systems. It is sufficient that several states or set of states exist that are unlikely to be left. The concept of weak path dependence, as proposed above, is a vague concept. It cannot be formulated strictly in a mathematical manner. It is similar to the concept of meta-stable states and only requires that certain states or sets of states are unlikely to be left, without the expression "unlikely" clearly defined. Nevertheless the concept of weak path dependence is meaningful for realistic systems. If a system is observed without the knowledge of the mathematical formulations, it may be possible to state whether the dynamics are path dependent or not, but it is never possible to distinguish between weak and strong path dependent dynamics. Only if the mathematical laws of the dynamics are known, is it possible to distinguish these two characteristics. I will come back to this point below, while discussing path dependence in the context of learning.

Learning processes are stochastic processes. Consequently the above considerations apply. If at least two absorbing sets of states exist, that is, if the system is reducible, the dynamics shows strong path dependence combined with the possibility of lock-ins. If only one absorbing set of states exists, the system will enter this absorbing set of states at some time and remain inside of it. We may talk of *temporal path dependence* in this case because the system can reach any state as long as it has not entered the absorbing set of states, while it can only reach the states belonging to this absorbing set of states once it has entered the absorbing set of states. Nevertheless, every process enters the absorbing set of states in the long run, so that with respect to the final state (for $t \to \infty$) no path dependence exists. If no absorbing set of states exists, any state can be reached from any other state in finite time, so that the system is able to get to any state in the state space, independent of the history. In this case, the dynamics are not strongly path dependent.

Thus we only have to analyse the existence of absorbing sets of states to know whether a learning process may show lock-ins and strong path dependence. No absorbing set of states exists whenever the fluctuations of the system never vanish, neither with time nor in specific states. Fluctuations in a learning process are caused by the stochastic behaviour of the individuals. Therefore, the fluctuations vanish if each individual realises one behaviour with certainty and the probabilities for any changes in behaviour are zero. According to the Bush-Mosteller model, individuals never choose one behaviour with certainty during reinforcement learning. Melioration learning, in its original formulation, allows for such a behaviour. The same holds for imitative learning, where fluctuations disappear if all individuals behave identically. In most of the adaptive learning routines, like Bayesian learning, least squares learning or myopic learning, fluctuations vanish as well. However other models, like the VID model or trial and error learning, suggest that fluctuations in behaviour remain. Hence no clear statement can be deduced from the knowledge of these types of learning models.

Whenever fluctuations vanish over time or under certain circumstances, which are not only given for one state, lock-ins and strong path dependence occur. If, instead, the behaviour of individuals contains unpredictable changes, lock-ins and strong path dependence does not occur. However, the dynamics may be weakly path dependent and the system may remain in a set of state for a very long time, although any other state can be still reached with a probability greater than zero. Thus, a system that shows weak path dependence may look like a system subject to strong path dependence. Although weak and strong path dependence are well distinguished mathematically, both types cannot be distinguished in reality because their implications are definitely different only in the case of time going to infinity. Let me consider a population where people shake hands whenever they meet, to show the difference between weak and strong path dependence (also cf. Witt 1997 who distinguishes between lock-ins and critical mass phenomenon). The individuals have two ways of shaking hands: They may either shake with their right hands or their left. One of them taking the right and the other taking the left will be uncomfortable. They learn by reinforcement which hand they should take. Each time they use the same hand as the person they meet, this action is reinforced. Reinforcement learning can be modelled in two ways: the Bush-Mosteller model assumes that the individuals never give up using either hand at least with a very small positive probability, while according to the melioration principle one behaviour may vanish completely. Given that shaking right hands has been established in the population, according to the melioration principle shaking with the left hand becomes extinct. Once shaking left hands has disappeared, the individuals will never alter their behaviour. This is a case of lock-in implying strong path dependence. If the individuals do not completely abolish the alternative behaviour of shaking left hands as assumed by the Bush-Mosteller model, each of the individuals will occasionally use the left hand. In general they will meet an individual who uses the right hand and switch back to the earlier behaviour immediately. Only if by chance a sufficiently large portion of the population changes its behaviour at the same time, the custom of using the right hand may be reversed. Such an event is very unlikely but in principle possible. In this case the dynamics are weakly path dependent. Which of the two is the correct description of what takes place in our society cannot be induced from watching individuals shaking with the right hand.

Assuming that a small amount of fluctuations is maintained on the individual level, strong path dependence never occurs. However, especially if individuals interact, weak path dependence may occur. As described above, a population of individuals may realise the same behaviour for a very long time because too many fluctuations in the same direction have to occur at the same time before the behaviour is permanently changed. The dividing line between path dependence and no path dependence, however, can only be drawn mathematically. Observing a system, it is fairly impossible to decide between strong and weak path dependence.

To sum up, I claim that learning always goes with fluctuations. Consequently a behaviour never disappears completely although it may come about very seldom. This implies that a dynamic system in which the dynamics are caused by individual learning processes, is able to transform from each state to any other state in a finite period of time. Strong path dependence does not exist in such a case. However weak path dependence may exist, in the sense that certain sets of states are very unlikely to be left again once they have been reached. In an observation of real processes these may look like lock-ins.

Part II

Learning in Diverse Economic Contexts

Chapter 5

Learning of Preferences

In Chapter 2, a categorisation of learning processes in three different classes has been proposed; non-cognitive learning, routine-based learning and associative learning. However, one learning process exists that cannot be classified unambiguously within this system although it is a learning process of crucial importance in economics; it is the evolution of preferences.

Traditionally preferences of individuals have been assumed to be constant in economics. Only in recent years have economists become interested in the evolution of preferences (cf. Witt 1991b and Güth & Yaari 1992). According to the utility theory, the understanding of decisions is based on the concept of preferences. Therefore an analysis of the evolution of preferences seem to be of crucial importance for economic research; it is rather surprising that not more approaches to this topic can be found in the literature. In the following pages, the evolution of preferences will be studied on the basis of learning processes.

The explanation of economic decisions is not the only purpose of the study of preferences. In relation to learning, preferences have two meanings. They are both objects of the learning process, meaning that they are what is learnt, and crucial elements of the learning process, meaning that they influence learning. Both aspects are studied in this chapter.

In the first section, the usual definition of preferences in economics is discussed. Subsequently an alternative definition is developed in the second. The changes of preferences over time are studied in the third. Finally, the meaning of preferences for learning processes is analysed in the fourth section.

5.1   PREFERENCES, AN ECONOMIC CONSTRUCT

When C. Menger wrote about the value of a good, he argued that the necessity of one specific good for the satisfaction of human desires causes this value (cf. Menger 1968). C. Menger defined the subjective value of a good only with respect to its significance for individual well-being.

Nowadays the subjective value of a good is defined by the utility that this good gives rise to. The utility of a decision or good is regarded to be a relative variable that can only be measured by observing the economic actions of individuals. Most economists believe that individual motives are too complex to be understood adequately. Therefore it is seen as more adequate to deduce the likes and dislikes of people from their observable economic action. For example, the subjective value of a good, the preference people have for it, is deduced from consumer behaviour.

Economic actions are interpreted as an individual's choice between different possible actions. In daily life individuals must always be making decisions. Each decision made reveals that the individual prefers the chosen action or bundle of goods to all other alternatives. Consequently if an individual is observed for a longer time, a preference order can be set up containing all the preferences of the observed individual (this only works if preferences are constant, a common assumption in economics). Mathematically, the decision behaviour of the individual can either be described by an ordinal preference order or a cardinal utility function (see e. g. Fishburn 1970 for a comprehensive discussion of both concepts).

Preference orders and utility functions are descriptive tools. They do not offer any explanation of economic behaviour (as long as no additional assumptions are made). However if individual preferences are constant, as is generally assumed in economics, they can easily be deduced from behaviour. Subsequently the following decisions are made according to the same preferences. The origin of the preferences need not be understood. They are the result of an analysis of previous decisions and, with the help of these preferences, economists are able to predict the observed individual's behaviour in future situations.

In this context, preferences need not have any psychological meaning. They are accumulated by observation, with each choice revealing some paired preferences. A statement going beyond a mere collection of paired preferences, can only be made by using some general assumptions. In economics some basic assumptions are commonly made, such as completeness, reflexivity and transitivity of preference orders. Besides these assumptions, however, the use of preference orders has no substance;

it is just a mechanism for handling information about the choice of an individual. However, it is a convincing concept because once a complete preference order is found for an individual, all her/his actions can be predicted by this preference order. Two conditions are required for the above reasoning to hold, however, and these basic requirements, the consistency of decision making and constancy of preferences, are not generally fulfilled. This has been shown for the consistency of decision making in several experiments (cf. e.g. Hogarth 1980 or Seidl & Traub 1995). The change of preferences is analysed in the following. To this end, preferences first have to be redefined.

5.2 DEFINITION OF PREFERENCES

Preferences, as they are understood in economics, are a mathematical reflection of the choices made by an individual, which are supposed to express tastes. Thus they contain no empirically testable propositions. For each history of actions committed, the corresponding preference order can be found. Preference orders gain predictive power only if it is assumed that preferences are constant. Under this assumption, preferences that can be observed in one situation also determine the behaviour in another.

If preferences change, then, the concept of a preference order or utility function is of no help. To deduce preferences, choices have to be observed. If preferences change, the change of choices has to be observed to learn about the change of preferences. Thus the dynamics of preferences can be only deduced from changes of behaviour, which means ex post. The concept of preferences looses its predictive power. Since this chapter focuses on the analysis of the evolution of preferences, a different notion of preferences is needed.

5.2.1 Mathematical Redefinition

In economics a preference order describes a subjective comparison of whole bundles of goods or states of affairs. Sometimes, especially in utility theory, utilities are assigned to single goods or specific characteristics of goods. For example, in the case of a *risk preference function*, utilities are assigned to the average payoffs and to the variance of the payoffs for each possible action. The utility that an action gives rise to, in this case a choice of assets, is given by the addition of these utilities. This means that different assets are valuated by the comparison of their characteristics, namely their average net yields and the variance of these yields. The evaluation of goods or events according to their characteristics is advantageous only if the evaluation of a good or event is the sum of the evaluations of the different characteristics. This condition is called the *separability of preferences*. Furthermore, in order to formulate the utility that a good or event gives rise to as the sum of the evaluations of its characteristics, a *cardinal utility function* has to be assumed. The use of ordinal utility functions versus cardinal utility functions has frequently been discussed in the economic literature (cf. e. g. Fishburn 1970). I do not intend to add to this endless debate. In the present context, it is claimed that the study of the evolution of preferences is meaningful only if the preferences are separable. The separability of preferences, in turn, can in a meaningful way be formulated only in terms of a cardinal utility function.

The separability of preferences is important for the analysis of the evolution of preferences. If preferences are separable, changes of preferences can be explained by changes in the evaluation of different characteristics. The set of characteristics is denoted by C. Mathematically, this implies that each event or good g ($g \in \mathcal{G}$ where $\mathcal{G}$ is the set of available goods) can be described completely by its attributes $\mathbf{b}(g)$ ($\mathbf{b} = (b)_{c \in C}$). $b_c(g)$ is the extent to which good g has characteristic c. The utility that a good or event gives rise to for individual i, is given by

$$u_i(g) = \sum_{c \in C} u_{i,c}(b_{i,c}(g)) \, . \tag{5.1}$$

$u_{i,c}(b)$ is the utility that an extent b of characteristic c gives rise to for individual i. This utility may be defined and observed as done in standard utility theory by the choices of individuals.

Above, the separability of the utility function is assumed; this is not generally given. The utility that one of these characteristics gives rise to depends on the presence of other characteristics. How the characteristics are defined determines whether the utility function is separable. If the set of characteristics C is defined such that the individual consequences of the characteristics neither depend on each other nor overlap with each other, the utility of a good or event can be written according to equation (5.1) and the utility function is separable.

Since the set of characteristics has to be defined with respect to the consequences for the individuals who receive the good, the characteristics are similar to Lancaster's *service characteristics* (cf. Lancaster 1966). The set of characteristics C_i, as well as the extent $b_{i,c}(g)$ to which a good or event g serves a certain characteristic c, may be perceived by each individual i differently. Both are subjective measures.

Below, it is assumed that a set C_i of characteristics has been defined that do not interfere with each other. Each individual is able to assign, at least after the consumption of a good g, a utility to this good or event which is given by

$$u_i(g,t) = \sum_{c \in C_i} u_{i,c}(b_{i,c}(g), t) \,. \tag{5.2}$$

The following assumptions are made in this context. The attribute $b_{i,c}(g)$ is a subjective measure. Nevertheless it is assumed to be constant in time. If individuals learn about the characteristics of goods, $b_{i,c}(g)$ has to be defined time-dependent. For the analysis of preferences, this aspect is neglected for convenience. Each characteristic c gives rise to a certain utility for each individual i. This utility is denoted by the utility function $u_{i,c}(b,t)$. A characteristic's utility function depends on the individual, on the extent $b_{i,c}(g)$ to which a characteristic is represented by a good or event, and on time t. I call $u_{i,c}(b,t)$ the *preferences* of an individual i because these utility functions directly reflect the attitude of the individual towards each characteristic c. The more $u_{c,i}(b,t)$ increases with b the stronger is the favour of individual i for characteristic c.

The *evolution of preferences* is described by the time-dependency of $u_{i,c}(b_{i,c}(g),t)$. In other words, I assume that the utility function assigned to a characteristic c changes with time. The explanation of these changes is the subject of the present section.

5.2.2   Two Kinds of Preferences

In the above formulation, preferences have been defined on the basis of the characteristics of goods. However, the definition was made only in a mathematical manner. The theoretical definition of the set of characteristics is addressed in the next paragraph. To this end, there is a need to clarify how preferences are used to describe behaviour.

In economics, individuals are generally assumed to choose the action that leads to the highest utility according to their preferences. This means that they predict the attributes $b_{i,c}(g)$ of each good g and evaluate the good according to their preferences $u_{i,c}(b_{i,c}(g),t)$. Subsequently they choose the good that leads to the highest utility given by equation (5.2). Such an approach implies that the preferences $u_{i,c}(b_{i,c}(g),t)$ used for this maximisation are the preferences expected by the individuals. The individuals anticipate both the attributes of the goods and the subjective utility caused by the various characteristics; they may know these from past experience. This implies that individuals have reflected upon their feelings after the consumption of goods, and know which characteristics make them feel good and which characteristics are undesirable. According to this standard definition from economics, preferences are known cognitively. I call such cognitively known preferences, in accord with U. Witt (cf. Witt 1989), *explicit preferences*.

In addition to explicit preferences, there is also another explanation for individuals' preferring one good over another and therefore receiving a higher utility. It is often claimed that utility maximisation is only a theoretical construct to describe decision making. In reality individuals learn how to behave through learning processes. If individuals learn their behaviour, they do not have to anticipate their own preferences. In such a case, individuals are not necessarily able to articulate their preferences. I call these preferences, again in accord with U. Witt (cf. Witt 1989), *implicit preferences*.

5.2.3   A Psychological Definition

In the psychological literature the expression "preference" rarely occurs. Psychologists either speak of *needs* or of *reinforcers*. However the distinction between explicit and implicit desires is common in psychology, although this terminology is not used. Psychologists speak often of needs as being the driving forces of action. People are motivated to satisfy their needs (cf. e.g. the field theory of Lewin 1963). To this end, individuals at least must have expectations of the consequences of their actions and choose a consequence to fit their needs. In addition, psychologists assume individuals sometimes commit actions by chance. If such an action leads to a positively evaluated outcome, the corresponding action is reinforced (cf. the literature about reinforcement learning, e.g. Skinner 1938). After that the action is realised more frequently. In such a case the satisfaction caused by the action has not been anticipated. Instead, the satisfaction felt after an action influences future actions. So choices are results of satisfying needs and include both conscious and subconscious activities

Owing to the evidence for a strong interplay between conscious and subconscious choices, and to include the different learning processes playing a role in economic actions, two kinds of preferences are distinguished; *implicit preferences* and *explicit preferences*. According to their definition above, implicit preferences are not cognitively known by the individual. They can only be observed indirectly through the change of behaviour which they cause. Explicit preferences, instead, are well-known by the individual. Individuals, for example, know their need to drink liquids. A strong preference for something to drink occurs whenever this need is not sufficiently satisfied. People are able to articulate this preference and are generally aware of opportunities to satisfy it. However not every basic need is well understood by individuals. Many people are lonely, that is, their need for social contact is not satisfied sufficiently. Nevertheless they are often not able to find a way to satisfy this need. Sometimes they even do not recognise what they lack.

Explicit Preferences
Preferences are explicit, that is, known by the individuals, for two reasons. First, people learn about their own preferences through conscious reflection. Second, there are some basic needs which are obviously physiologically indispensable so that they are recognised as such. There are other basic needs which are more subtle, which fall into the category of implicit preferences discussed in the next subsection.

Explicit preferences evoked by a clear basic need do not require much discussion. They occur whenever something physiologically necessary is not satisfied and are determined by human biology, so after early childhood they do not change over time. Furthermore the related basic needs can be satisfied by different goods (the need to drink liquids is satisfied by an enormous variety of beverages nowadays). Thus explicit preferences evoked by unsatisfied basic needs relate to certain characteristics of goods or events.

The explicit preferences people are aware of through cognitive reflection, however, do not necessarily relate to characteristics of goods or events. These preferences may be defined on different levels. In the case of goods, explicit preferences can be defined on the level of sets of goods (that is on bundles of goods, as is usually done in consumer theory), on goods themselves, or on the level of characteristics of goods. To find out on which level explicit preferences should be defined, we may take into account that they are determined by cognitive reflection about desires of individuals. From my point of view, individuals rarely reflect on their need for bundles of goods. Instead they generally know their preferences, at least those for characteristics related to goods they have consumed in the past. Consequently explicit preferences, if they are based on cognitive reflection, should be defined on the basis of goods or the characteristics of goods. Both levels may be adequate depending on the situation. Some people consciously know only that they prefer the colour red to the colour white while others may know that they prefer the colour red to white because they generally prefer warm colours to cold. The complexity of the understanding depends on the cognitive models that individuals develop.

However it can also be claimed that cognitive reflection about preferences is intended to identify implicit preferences, which cause reinforcement, to make the struggle for reinforcement easier or more efficient. In this case, the set of cognitively understood explicit preferences is a subjective picture of the set of implicit preferences. This picture, consisting of various cognitive models of personal preferences, is usually incomplete, partly erroneous, and represents a simplification (like a reduction of preferences to the level of goods). Nevertheless individuals often act according to the explicit preferences they believe in, so that the cognitive models of preferences can not be neglected in an analysis of preferences.

Implicit preferences

Implicit preferences primarily determine the feelings of individuals after they decide upon a good. Consequently they influence whether an action is realised more or less frequently in the future. This fits in with the concept of *reinforcement learning*. Psychologists have comprehensively studied the characteristics of goods or events leading to reinforcement, so that the level on which preferences can be defined is well established. The reinforcing characteristics of goods or events are called *reinforcers* in the psychological literature. Psychology distinguishes between *primary* and *secondary reinforcers*. Primary reinforcers are innate and common to all people. Secondary reinforcers evolve during the life of an individual. They develop by the process of *classical conditioning*; therefore they depend on the history of the individuals. Many characteristics of goods and events can become secondary reinforcers.

Primary and secondary reinforcers together influence whether an action is realised more or less frequently in the future. Hence reinforcers seem to be an adequate set of characteristics upon which to base a definition of preferences. This means that goods and events have to be divided into those aspects which are negatively or positively reinforcing. Then the preference for a good or event is given by the accumulation of these reinforcing aspects. Therefore two concepts, namely reinforcement learning and the concept of preferences, are combined (cf. a similar combination of these concepts in Alhadeff 1982 and Witt 1987b, whereas in Wilkie 1994, p.267 the use of classical conditioning is discussed in the context of marketing).

A use of reinforcers, as the basis for the definition of preference functions according to equation (5.2), requires that the impacts of reinforcers are additive, that the degree of a reinforcing character contained in a good or event is measurable, and that a utility can be assigned to each reinforcing strength. The first requirement, namely the additivity of reinforcers, is crucial for the validity of the present approach. Psychological research provides no evidence regarding the additivity of reinforcers. However the effectiveness of the psychological treatment method called behaviour therapy implies that positive and negative reinforcers may balance each other. There seems to be something like additivity of reinforcers although a mathematical formulation of this additivity, without further experimentation, may be a crude approximation. Nevertheless the outlined concept of preferences proves to be helpful in understanding how preferences come to be, and how they change over time.

5.2.4 Final Definition

To sum up, preferences are assumed to be separable. Thus each good or event can be treated as a sum of its characteristics. The characteristics are aspects of goods or events that are positive or negative reinforcers, or that are believed to be reinforcers according to the cognitive models of individuals. The set of characteristics and the amount to which a good or event offers a certain characteristic are subjective measures. The preference order of goods and events can be written in the form of a cardinal utility function, where the utility assigned to a good or event is the sum of the utilities assigned to its characteristics. For each characteristic c, that is, for each reinforcer, and each individual i an utility function $u_{i,c}(b,t)$ is defined which may change over time. These utility functions based on the characteristics of goods define the preferences of an individual.

5.3 EVOLUTION AND CHANGE OF PREFERENCES

Goods are characterised above by their reinforcing characteristics. Preferences are based on the set of these characteristics. Consequently a theory about the evolution and change of preferences, as they are used here, has to explain why, how, and when characteristics become important or less important to an individual.

Derived from the discussion above, there are three reasons for a characteristic to be desired or not: a characteristic may be a primary reinforcer, a secondary reinforcer or believed to be a reinforcer.

5.3.1   Primary Reinforcers

Primary reinforcers are innate reinforcers that are the same for everyone, only varying in degree from person to person. Thus they represent fixed preferences. Primary reinforcers are aspects necessary for the survival of individuals or, in the case of negative reinforcing characteristics, aspects that can endanger existence. Examples of necessary primary reinforcers are food, water and social contact; and examples of negative primary reinforcers are extreme heat or cold and excessive behaviours endangering health. Since primary reinforcers are inherited from birth and change very little, they represent the stable core of preferences. Primary reinforcers are early-life implicit preferences but many of them become understood by the individuals early on in life so that they also become explicit preferences.

5.3.2   Secondary Reinforcers

Secondary reinforcers emerge during a lifetime. According to the psychological theories, learning secondary reinforcers requires conditioning (cf. Hergenhahn & Olson 1997). Preferences based on secondary reinforcers emerge according to the principles of *classical conditioning* (cf. a similar argumentation in Witt 1987b). Classical conditioning is a non-cognitive process so that individuals are generally not aware of it and the resulting preferences are implicit. However when the resulting stimulus-response connection is cognitively understood, then the resulting preferences also can become explicit preferences.

Psychologists have shown that neutral stimuli can be conditioned such that they evoke, for example, the feeling of fear in individuals (cf. Watson & Rayner 1920). A stimulus that causes a positive feeling is a positive reinforcer, so individuals have a preference for this stimulus. A stimulus that causes a negative feeling, instead, is a negative reinforcer, so individuals dislike this stimulus or have a negative preference for it. They avoid goods or events that contain or cause such a stimulus (cf. Witt 1987b for a more detailed discussion).

In general every characteristic may be conditioned. This means that individuals are able to develop preferences for any characteristic of goods. Nevertheless psychologists have shown that not every neutral stimulus-response association can be classically conditioned by every existing stimulus-response association (cf. e.g. Garcia, McGowan, Ervin & Koelling 1968). These exceptions are, however, not clearly understood. Therefore it cannot be stated which characteristics individuals will be likely to develop preferences for. Let me ignore these exceptions and assume that all characteristics can become preferred. According to the psychological knowledge about classical conditioning, a preference evolves whenever a neutral characteristic of a good or event is experienced simultaneously, or shortly before, an already preferred characteristic. A typical example is the act of buying. Some people have developed a preference for this act. They feel satisfied after buying something, independent of the value of the commodity itself. Such a preference can be explained by classical conditioning. The act of buying a good is generally followed by the process of consumption, which causes satisfaction. After some time the act of buying a good is satisfying in and of itself.

Classical conditioning plays its strongest role in shaping preferences during childhood and is especially important in the context of social interaction. A detailed study of this can be found in Witt 1987b and to some extent in Witt 1991b.

From the knowledge of classical conditioning we also know that a stimulus should not be analysed in isolation. Whenever a stimulus is conditioned, there are similar stimuli that are affected as well. In the same way, preferences for one characteristic of a good never develop independently of preferences for similar characteristics of other goods.

To sum up, classical conditioning plays an important role in the evolution and change of preferences. There are some restrictions on the capability of different characteristics to become preferred. However these restrictions are not well understood. Besides these restrictions, preferences for certain characteristics evolve whenever the occurrence of these characteristics repeatedly coincides with a desired characteristic. Since individuals have different histories, they also have different preferences. However they also share many preferences. Two reasons can be found for the evolution of common preferences among a population or social group. First, individuals face similar conditioning situations (for example, the receipt of money is generally followed by the ability to purchase a preferred good, so that the preference for money is shared by virtually all individuals). Second, the social feedback connected to characteristics of goods or actions may condition a preference for these characteristics. If others reward the possession of goods having characteristics that they prefer themselves, preferences spread through a population for goods with certain characteristics, by means of classical conditioning from person to person. As a consequence common preferences are established. Classical conditioning leads primarily to implicit preferences, but, when accompanied by cognitive understanding, may become explicit as well.

5.3.3   Cognitive Models of Preferences

In addition to the non-cognitive processes of conditioning, individuals have the ability to reflect on which characteristics of goods are desirable and which are not. Through this they develop cognitive models that describe their own preferences. This enables them to avoid the time-consuming process of testing different goods or actions and evaluating them afterwards.

Cognitive models are learnt associatively. They are either confirmed by experience or reality forces individuals to reconsider their cognitive models. However, individuals do not necessarily react to discrepancies between their cognitive models and reality with an adaptation of their cognitive models. Other cognitive models or the scarcity of cognitive attention may hinder the abandonment of inadequate explicit preferences. Thus the explicit preferences may differ from the implicit ones.

It is difficult to make statements about these differences between explicit and implicit preferences. Associative learning is a complex process and, in particular, the resistance of the cognitive structure against changes is not adequately understood. All that might be stated is that cognitive models react with some delay to changes of reality, due to the scarcity of cognitive attention.

5.4   PREFERENCES IN THE CONTEXT OF LEARNING

Preferences not only develop due to learning processes, they also influence learning processes, and so the relation between preferences and learning is also complex. This influence will be analysed separately for each kind of learning described below.

5.4.1   Non-cognitive Learning

Non-cognitive learning is directed by reinforcement. Individuals realise those actions more frequently in the future that have reinforcing consequences. Whether the consequences are more or less reinforcing, or not reinforcing at all, depends on the amount of positive reinforcers that are added to the state of affairs, and on the amount of negative reinforcers that are removed. Thus the set of primary and secondary reinforcers resulting from an action determines which actions are realised and which are avoided. Above reinforcers, primary and secondary, are identified as one important source of preferences. These kinds of preferences determine the changes in non-cognitive learning processes. If non-cognitive learning processes have enough time to converge, they often lead to a behaviour that maximises an individual's payoff (cf. discussions and the analysis of necessary conditions in Börgers & Sarin 1993, Börgers 1996, Brenner & Witt 1997 and Brenner 1997). The payoffs are given by the reinforcers, that is, by the preferences. Thus non-cognitive learning leads to an adaptation of behaviour to the current preferences at each point in time, while the preferences are slowly changing according to the processes outlined above.

5.4.2 Routine-based Learning

In the case of routine-based learning, individuals base behaviour on some cognitive models of the situation. These cognitive models imply using certain learning rules such as imitation, trial and error and so on. Furthermore the cognitive models also determine the way in which the personal performance is evaluated. Thus the cognitive models of preferences play a role in the context of routine-based learning. A learning rule is regarded to be adequate if it leads to outcomes that are perceived to be preferred. The behaviour of individuals is directed by their belief about the desirable outcomes.

Whether these outcomes really make them feel better depends both on chance and the correctness of their cognitive models, that is, on the associative learning processes that took place beforehand.

5.4.3 Associative Learning

According to the assumptions that have been made about associative learning in the third chapter, cognitive associations develop and change due to reinforcement learning. Thus in the case of associative learning, reinforcers, and ultimately the preferences based on reinforcers, direct the learning processes.

Furthermore, associative learning is the connection between preferences as reinforcers, involving implicit preferences, and the cognitive models of preferences, involving explicit preferences. Associative learning is directed by reinforcers but it also determines the cognitive models of preferences. Thus associative learning should force cognitive models of preferences to adapt to implicit preferences. Whether both kinds of preferences assimilate, however, depends on the cognitive processes. The business of reweaving the whole cognitive structure may hinder single cognitive models in adapting to reality, causing associative learning often to lag behind the perceived changes in reality.

Chapter 6

Reinforcement Learning in Games

Interactions between individuals have become an increasingly important topic in economic research in the last decades. Situations of interaction are theoretically described in the form of *games* where the individuals are faced with different possibilities to act, and the utility they obtain is determined by the actions of all individuals. Behaviour in such a game is usually described by the rational assumption of utility maximisation. More recently evolutionary algorithms, or at least the behaviour they converge to, it is claimed, describe the behaviour in games well. However these concepts do not entirely describe real learning processes although they may approximate them. In the present chapter, the implications of reinforcement learning in the context of economic interactions will be studied. Reinforcement learning, as I have outlined, requires that interacting individuals are cognitively unaware of the situation, that is, in a game situation they do not realise that they interact with other individuals. They only adapt in a non-cognitive way to the payoffs that they receive.

In recent years, models of reinforcement learning have been applied in a game theoretic context in various approaches to repeated games (cf. Roth & Erév 1995, Börgers & Sarin 1997, Brenner & Witt 1997 and Brenner 1997). In repeated games individuals learn, either non-cognitively or cognitively, depending on the attention they pay to the situation. Non-cognitive learning processes take place if the interaction does not attract the attention of the individuals, that is, if the situation is regarded to be of less importance by the individuals. Examples are various unimportant interactions with other people at the work place and in private life. Unimportant interactions, with respect to the evaluation of the interacting individuals, are, for example, the action of greeting colleagues or the way in which colleagues from different departments communicate with each other. Normally nobody reflects on the detailed aspects of such interactions, they are mostly non-cognitively learnt. Nevertheless they may be important for the functioning of an organisation. If some new colleagues enter an organisation they may demonstrate different ways of communicating. Suddenly interactions may become unpleasant and/or ineffective without people understanding why.

The behaviour that reinforcement learning converges to will be analysed below. In the first section, the notation used is presented and some conditions for the approach to be adequate are discussed. Subsequently two models of reinforcement learning, namely the *Bush-Mosteller model* and the model of *melioration learning* are applied. Section 2 is devoted to the principle of melioration, while in Section 3 the Bush-Mosteller model is analysed.

6.1   GAME THEORY AND LEARNING

6.1.1   Notation

In the following section I will analyse reinforcement learning in a normal form game. The mathematical features and notations used are the following (cf. e.g. Osborne & Rubinstein 1994). N players are assumed to interact. Interaction in the context of games means that the payoff of one individual depends on the behaviour of the other individuals. Each player i ($i \in \mathcal{I} = \{1, ..., N\}$) is able to choose for a set of actions $\mathcal{A}_i$ ($i = 1, 2, ..., N$). The number of possible actions for each player i is A_i. The action of each player i at time t is denoted by $a_i(t)$ ($a_i(t) \in \mathcal{A}_i$). The action profile $\mathbf{a}(t) = (a_i(t))_{i \in \mathcal{I}}$ ($= (a_1(t), ..., a_N(t))$) represents the behaviour of all players in the game at time t. The set of all possible action profiles is denoted by $\mathbf{A}$. The outcome of the game is solely determined by the action profile $\mathbf{a}(t)$. It is evaluated subjectively by each individual. Usually there is a so-called *payoff function* $\Pi_i(\mathbf{a})$ defined on the set of outcomes. $\Pi_i(\mathbf{a})$ is the payoff obtained by player i if the actions of all interacting players are given by $\mathbf{a}$. The payoff function is usually interpreted as the utility an outcome gives rise to. In the present analysis, however, the payoff function describes the reinforcement strength of outcomes.

Using game theory and the concept of payoff matrices to describe interactions between individuals, however, includes some conceptual assumptions. First, the payoffs of different outcomes have to be measurable in a mathematical sense. This means that the players have to be able to assign a real value (the payoff $\Pi_i(\mathbf{a})$) to each possible outcome $\mathbf{a}$ that represents the reinforcement strength of this outcome. Second, the payoff $\Pi_i(\mathbf{a})$ has to contain the complete information relevant for the decision. In a real learning context this condition is not always satisfied. Outcomes of the interaction may reveal something besides the pure utility they give rise to. Learning processes in general depend not only on the past obtained payoffs but also on the knowledge of the other individuals' previous behaviour. Therefore, learning in the context of games is often modelled dependent on the whole history of behaviours.

Game theory is primarily used to study the structural implications of interactions between individuals, how they affect each others' decision making. Many typical situations in which people interact can easily be reproduced by a stylised payoff matrix. H. H. Kelley and J. W. Thibaut presented a comprehensive classification of theoretical situations, represented by simple games in their book (1978). The most simple games are the ones where two players interact and both of them have two alternative actions to choose from. Such games are characterised by a payoff matrix given in Table 6.1.

		column-player	
		action 1	action 2
row-player	action 1	$\Pi_2(1,1)$ $\Pi_1(1,1)$	$\Pi_2(1,2)$ $\Pi_1(1,2)$
	action 2	$\Pi_2(2,1)$ $\Pi_1(2,1)$	$\Pi_2(2,2)$ $\Pi_1(2,2)$

Table 6.1: *Payoff matrix in a general 2×2 game*

These 2×2 games, such as the *prisoner's dilemma*, the *coordination game*, the *chicken game* and others (see e.g. Rapoport & Guyer 1966) already represent a wide spectrum of different situations. One may, of course, also think of more complex cases, where each player has more than two options or where more than two players interact.

Two concepts are used in economics to deal with games with only a few exceptions: the rational game theory and the *evolutionary game theory* (cf. e. g. Osborne & Rubinstein 1994 and Weibull 1995). In addition to rational and evolutionary game theory, a third concept has been frequently used in recent years. More and more authors realise that learning may present a concept that is able to fill the gap left open where game theories leave off. In games where the individuals are restricted by *bounded rationality* or imperfect information, or where rational considerations lead to ambiguous results, rational game theory fails (cf. Krebs 1990). Osborne and Rubinstein stated in their book (1994, 6) that '*When we talk in real life about games we often focus on the asymmetry between individuals in their abilities... These differences, which are so critical in life, are missing from game theory in its current form... Modelling asymmetries in abilities and in perceptions of a situation by different players is a fascinating challenge for future research, which models of "bounded rationality" have begun to tackle*'. In such cases it is worth the effort to use the complex algorithms of learning to describe game behaviour.

However learning itself is restricted to a certain set of game situations as well. Learning occurs only if a situation is repeated, or at least only if situations can be linked due to their similarity. Thus learning is particularly attractive in the study of repeated games. Strategic games where the players choose their plan of action once and for all cannot be studied using a learning concept. Furthermore we have to exclude all games where the players behave rationally, have perfect information, and are able to draw unique conclusions about the behaviour of their opponents. In such cases there is nothing to learn. However it is unlikely in real life situations that the "players" have full information about the "game" and their "opponents" right from the beginning.

Although game behaviour is nearly stationary in many simple applications, it has been evolved or learnt once. Consequently, many recent works have addressed the question whether learning converges to a Nash equilibrium or not. Most of the results of these studies have been in favour of the rational concept. It has been proven for the Cross version of the Bush-Mosteller model (Börgers & Sarin 1997), for Bayesian learning (Jordan 1991, Kalai & Lehrer 1993, Eichberger, Haller & Milne 1993 and Jordan 1995), for imitation learning (Schlag 1998) and for melioration learning (Brenner & Witt 1997) that they converge to a Nash equilibrium, at least under certain circumstances (e. g. the constancy of the payoffs in time in the case of melioration learning) or if certain requirements are fulfilled by the initial state (e. g. in the case of Cross's version of the Bush-Mosteller model). At the same time, other authors have claimed or shown that learning does not always converge to a Nash equilibrium (cf. e. g. the general discussion in Börgers 1996 and the analysis of the general Bush-Mosteller model in Brenner 1997). Whether or not a learning process converges to a Nash equilibrium, seems to depend on the characteristics of the learning process. Furthermore, learning processes often do not have enough time to converge (cf. Roth & Erév 1995). In such cases rational game theory or the concept of *evolutionary stable strategies*, the stable state in evolutionary game theory, fail to describe real behaviour.

Therefore I claim that rational game theory and learning in games are complements (cf. the discussion in T. Börgers 1996). In some cases the games are transparent and the players have sufficient information. Although such games may be analysed using learning algorithms, it is much more convenient to use rational game theory, because the results are a good approximation of reality and the effort for the analysis is comparatively small. In other cases, learning algorithms may be the more appropriate tool to describe phenomena.

According to the categorisation of learning given in Chapter 3, for their functioning, the three kinds of learning processes each require certain circumstances. Furthermore there are situations in which the individuals act rationally. Rational behaviour has been sufficiently analysed in the context of games in the literature. The three learning processes, however, have been widely neglected. Therefore I will study at least two of them in this book (for a study of routine-based learning in games see Brenner 1997c). Associative learning processes are analysed in Chapter 8. In the following section, reinforcement learning in games will be studied.

6.1.2 Requirements for Reinforcement Learning in Games

In daily life, a shortage of cognitive capacity is a common feature because there are just too many things for individuals to think about. In experiments, however, the subjects generally have enough time to think their decisions over. Hence in experiments, reinforcement learning should be observed only if the subjects face a severe time constraint, or if the experiment is embedded in daily life so that the subjects have to allocate their cognitive attention either to the experiment or the other tasks they face. In such cases, some individuals regard the experiment as unimportant compared to their everyday tasks while others engage more in the experiment and devote a lot of cognitive capacity to it (cf. Brenner 1995 where such an experiment is analysed). In most experiments reported in the literature, however, the subjects have enough time, so that reinforcement learning should at least not be the only learning process that occurs.

Nevertheless Herrnstein and Prelec (1991) as well as Roth and Erév (1995) claimed that their subjects acted according to the principle of reinforcement learning, although they were instructed about the logic of the game and had enough time to reflect their decisions. Since the process of routine-based learning, especially if imitation is not possible, has some similarities with reinforcement learning, it can also be claimed that the subjects learnt according to a certain routine that mimics reinforcement learning. A more detailed study of the experimental data would be needed to decide whether learning without the scarcity of cognitive attention can still be described approximately by reinforcement learning models. I doubt it; thus I claim that reinforcement learning does not predominate in typical game experiments with human beings. Nevertheless reinforcement learning plays an important role in real-life situations.

Reinforcement learning can be described by two models: the generalised *Bush-Mosteller model* and the *melioration principle*. They make different assumptions about the learning of individuals, especially with respect to the characteristics of the situation. Consequently their implications for the behaviour in games are different as well (cf. Brenner & Witt 1997 and Brenner 1997).

The melioration principle is based on the assumption that individuals compare the average payoffs of different actions in the past, and increase the frequency of behaviours that have resulted in higher average payoffs. The modified Bush-Mosteller model, instead, describes a situation in which the individuals may choose whether they realise an action or not. It is still an open question which of these two models is more adequate under what circumstances.

To sum up, if the individuals are not cognitively aware of the situation, they either learn according to the melioration principle or according to the generalised Bush-Mosteller model. Both of them will be analysed in the context of games in the following section.

6.2   MELIORATION LEARNING IN GAMES

Herrnstein and Prelec (1991) suggested that melioration learning converges to an *evolutionary stable strategy* (ESS) in games. Brenner and Witt (1997) proved this suggestion in the case of a 2×2 game played by an infinite number of players that are matched randomly. Furthermore, they proved that the dynamics of melioration learning can be described approximately by the *replicator dynamics*, as long as the payoffs are constant in time. Below I will analyse games having constant payoffs in general. The restrictions of two players and two alternative actions are abolished. A population of randomly matched individuals and a game with two repeatedly interacting players are studied. In the case of the randomly matched population, it will be proved that the dynamics of melioration learning can be described approximately by the replicator dynamics. The case of repeatedly interacting individuals is studied as for a general 2×2 game.

6.2.1 A Population of Randomly Interacting Individuals

An infinite number of individuals (N is increased to infinity later in the analysis) is assumed to interact in an asymmetric n-player *game*. Each individual always takes the same position within the game so that the population is classified in n groups. N_i individuals exist of each type i ($i \in \{1, 2, ..., n\}$) in the whole population. For each game one individual is chosen at random from each group. This means that each game is played between randomly matched individuals of certain types (the types are entirely given and cannot be changed by the individual; examples are the sex of individuals or the types, seller or buyer, of market participants). The individuals are assumed to learn according to the melioration principle. The behaviour of one individual is analysed in the following section, and on the basis of this analysis the behaviour on the level of populations can be analysed.

Dynamics on the individual level

Let me consider an individual who holds position i in the game. The respective payoffs are given by $\Pi_i(\mathbf{a})$ where $\mathbf{a}$ denotes the *action profile* of all individuals interacting in the considered game. Each player of type i has to choose one of A_i alternative actions (the set of alternative actions is denoted by $\mathcal{A}_i$) at each time t. The choice is denoted by $a_i(t)$. The choice of all players who interact with this individual at that time is denoted by the vector $\mathbf{a}_{i_-}(t)$. Since the opponents in the game are randomly chosen each time, their behaviour is given by a probability distribution $p(\mathbf{a}_{-i}, t)$ at time t. The behaviour of the considered individual is given by the probability distribution $p_i(a, t)$ ($a \in \mathcal{A}_i$) that changes according to melioration learning given by equation (3.14).

I assume that individual i remembers the payoffs of the last $k_{i,a}(t)$ occasions in which (s)he realised action a. Generally, individual i has not realised action a the last $k_{i,a}(t)$ rounds of the game successively. The $k_{i,a}(t)$ points in time which are remembered by individual i, and at which individual i realised action a, are denoted by the set of times $\mathcal{T}_{i,a}(t)$. Consequently the remembered payoff $\hat{\Pi}_i(a,t)$ for action a is

$$\hat{\Pi}_i(a,t) = \frac{1}{k_{i,a}(t)} \cdot \sum_{\tau \in \mathcal{T}_{i,a}(t)} \Pi_i(a, \mathbf{a}_{i_-}(\tau)) \qquad (6.1)$$

where each possible action profile $\mathbf{a}_{i_-}(\tau)$ of the opponents at time τ occurs with probability $p(\mathbf{a}_{i_-}(\tau), \tau)$. Thus the combination of action profiles $(\mathbf{a}_{i_-}(\tau))_{\tau \in \mathcal{T}_{i,a}(t)}$ occurs with the probability

$$\prod_{\tau \in \mathcal{T}_{i,a}(t)} p(\mathbf{a}_{i_-}(\tau), \tau) . \qquad (6.2)$$

The change of $p_i(a,t)$ according to melioration learning, is given in a time-continuous manner by

$$\frac{dp_i(a,t)}{dt} = \nu_m \cdot p_i(a,t) \cdot \left[\hat{\Pi}_i(a,t) - \sum_{\tilde{a} \in \mathcal{A}_i} \hat{\Pi}_i(\tilde{a},t) \cdot p_i(\tilde{a},t) \right] . \qquad (6.3)$$

Dynamics on the level of populations

To analyse the dynamics on the level of populations, the share $x_i(a,t)$ is defined as the number of individuals of type i who realise action a at time t divided by the total number N_i of individuals of type i. The changes of these shares are studied below. To this end, the relation between the individual level and the level of populations has to be defined. $x_i(a,t)$ is generally given by (cf. Chapter 4)

$$x_i(a,t) = \frac{1}{N_i} \cdot \sum_{j=1}^{N_i} \delta(a_i^{(j)}(t) = a) \qquad (6.4)$$

where $a_i^{(j)}(t)$ is the action chosen by individual j of type i at time t and $\delta(a_i^{(j)}(t) = a)$ is defined by

$$\delta(a_i^{(j)}(t) = a) = \begin{cases} 1 & \text{if } a_i^{(j)}(t) = a \\ 0 & \text{if } a_i^{(j)}(t) \neq a \end{cases} . \qquad (6.5)$$

The actions are taken by chance by the individuals. If the number N_i of a type of individuals is very large (or infinite) the law of great numbers applies. This means that the stochastic influences on the action of each individual balance each other and the sum over all individuals who choose action a at time t equals the sum over the probabilities of all individuals to choose action a approximately. Then for $N_i \to \infty$ $x_i(a,t)$ converges to

$$x_i(a,t) = \frac{1}{N_i} \sum_{j=1}^{N_i} p_i^{(j)}(a,t) \ . \tag{6.6}$$

This will be used as an approximation for $x_i(a,t)$ below. As a next step, the analysis of the individual behaviour is replaced by an analysis on the population level. To this end, the probabilities

$$p_i^{(j)}(a,t)$$

of an individual j of type i to realise action a at time t are condensed to a vector

$$\mathbf{p}_i^{(j)}(t) = \left(p_i^{(j)}(a,t) \right)_{a \in \mathcal{A}_i} .$$

This vector represents the probability distribution of actions for individual j of type i at time t. The proportion of all individuals of type i behaving according to the probability distribution $\mathbf{p}_i$ at time t, is denoted by $f_i(\mathbf{p}_i, t)$. Since each individual of type i is identical, the behaviour of these individuals is sufficiently described by the share $f_i(\mathbf{p}_i, t)$ of individuals who act according to the probability distribution $\mathbf{p}_i$ at each time. As a consequence $x_i(a,t)$ is given by

$$x_i(a,t) = \int_0^1 \cdots \int_0^1 p_i(a) \cdot f_i(\mathbf{p}_i, t) \, d\mathbf{p}_i \tag{6.7}$$

where $d\mathbf{p}_i$ is the abbreviation of $\prod_{a \in \mathcal{A}_i} dp_i(a) = dp_i(1) \cdot \ldots \cdot dp_i(A_i)$. Furthermore the correlation between $p_i(a,t)$ and $p_i(\tilde{a},t)$ is defined by

$$C(p_i(a,t), p_i(\tilde{a},t))$$
$$= \int_0^1 \cdots \int_0^1 \left(p_i(a) - x_i(a,t) \right) \cdot \left(p_i(\tilde{a}) - x_i(\tilde{a},t) \right) \cdot f_i(\mathbf{p}_i,t) \, d\mathbf{p}_i \tag{6.8}$$

which plays a role later in the analysis. The change of the shares $x_i(a,t)$ over time are given by

$$\frac{dx_i(a,t)}{dt} = \int_0^1 \cdots \int_0^1 \frac{dp_i(a)}{dt} \cdot f_i(\mathbf{p}_i, t) \, d\mathbf{p}_i \tag{6.9}$$

Each individual of type i is identical. Furthermore (s)he is randomly matched with the individuals of the other types. Thus the average payoff for an individual of type i is given by

$$\bar{\Pi}_i(a, t) = \sum_{\mathbf{a}_{i_-}} \Pi_i(a, \mathbf{a}_{i_-}) \cdot p(\mathbf{a}_{i_-}, t) . \tag{6.10}$$

if the opponents realise action profile $\mathbf{a}_{i_-}$ with the probability $p(\mathbf{a}_{i_-}, t)$ at time t. If the distribution of behaviours in the population of opponents changes slowly, the average remembered payoff $\hat{\Pi}_i(a, t)$ equals the average payoff given by equation (6.10). Again, the law of great numbers can be used, so that the average payoff can be used in equation (6.3) instead of the individual payoff. Inserting equation (6.3) into equation (6.9) results in

$$
\begin{aligned}
\frac{dx_i(a,t)}{dt} \;=\;& \nu_m \int_0^1 \cdots \int_0^1 \Bigg[p_i(a) \cdot \Big(\bar{\Pi}_i(a, t) \\
&- \sum_{\tilde{a} \in \mathcal{A}_i} \bar{\Pi}_i(\tilde{a}, t) \cdot p_i(\tilde{a}) \Big) \Bigg] \cdot f_i(\mathbf{p}_i, t)\, d\mathbf{p}_i .
\end{aligned}
\tag{6.11}
$$

The average payoff $\bar{\Pi}_i(a, t)$ does not depend on the variable of integration $\mathbf{p}_i$ in equation (6.11) so that equation (6.11) can be written as

$$
\begin{aligned}
\frac{dx_i(a, t)}{dt} \;=\;& \nu_m \cdot \bar{\Pi}_i(a, t) \int_0^1 \cdots \int_0^1 p_i(a) \cdot f_i(\mathbf{p}_i, t)\, d\mathbf{p}_i \\
&- \nu_m \cdot \sum_{\tilde{a} \in \mathcal{A}_i} \bar{\Pi}_i(\tilde{a}, t) \int_0^1 \cdots \int_0^1 \Big[p_i(a) \cdot p_i(\tilde{a}) \Big] \cdot f_i(\mathbf{p}_i, t)\, d\mathbf{p}_i .
\end{aligned}
\tag{6.12}
$$

With the help of the equation $p_i(a, t) \cdot p_i(\tilde{a}, t) = \big(p_i(a, t) - x_i(a, t) + x_i(a, t) \big) \big(p_i(\tilde{a}, t) - x_i(\tilde{a}, t) + x_i(\tilde{a}, t) \big)$ one obtains

$$
\begin{aligned}
\frac{dx_i(a, t)}{dt} \;=\;& \nu_m \cdot x_i(a, t) \cdot \Bigg[\bar{\Pi}_i(a, t) - \sum_{\tilde{a} \in \mathcal{A}_i} \bar{\Pi}_i(\tilde{a}, t) \cdot x_i(\tilde{a}, t) \\
&- \sum_{\tilde{a} \in \mathcal{A}_i} \bar{\Pi}_i(\tilde{a}, t) \cdot \frac{C(p_i(a,t), p_i(\tilde{a},t))}{x_i(a,t)} \Bigg] .
\end{aligned}
\tag{6.13}
$$

The system of differential equations (6.13) is not closed because the dynamics of the shares $x_i(a, t)$ do not only depend on the shares themselves but also on the correlation function $C(p_i(a, t), p_i(\tilde{a}, t))$. A calculation of $C(p_i(a, t), p_i(\tilde{a}, t))$ requires the knowledge of $f_i(\mathbf{p}_i, t)$. Alternatively the dynamics of $C(p_i(a, t), p_i(\tilde{a}, t))$ can be obtained in the same way the dynamics of $x_i(a, t)$ have been obtained above. However, the resulting equations of motion would depend on the third moments of $f_i(\mathbf{p}_i, t)$, and the equations of motion for the third moments would depend on the fourth moments. Hence, a description of dynamics on the population level that does not depend on the state on the individual level, comprises an infinite number of differential equations. Thus for practical reasons, a description on the population level has to depend on the distribution of behaviours $f_i(\mathbf{p}_i, t)$. It should be noted at this point that such a differential equation cannot be solved.

Melioration dynamics and replicator dynamics

A comparison with *replicator dynamics* which is comprehensively discussed in section 3.3.4 has to fail because replicator dynamics describes a system entirely on the population level. The replicator dynamics in the present context is given by

$$\frac{dx_i(a, t)}{dt} = \nu \cdot x_i(a, t) \cdot \left[\bar{\Pi}_i(a, t) - \sum_{\tilde{a} \in \mathcal{A}_i} \bar{\Pi}_i(\tilde{a}, t) \cdot x_i(\tilde{a}, t) \right]. \qquad (6.14)$$

A comparison with equation (6.13), however, reveals only one difference: In the replicator dynamics the term dependent on the correlation function $C(p_i(a, t), p_i(\tilde{a}, t))$ is missing. Consequently the replicator dynamics is a good approximation of the dynamics of melioration learning whenever the term

$$\sum_{\tilde{a} \in \mathcal{A}_i} \bar{\Pi}_i(\tilde{a}, t) \cdot \frac{C(p_i(a, t), p_i(\tilde{a}, t))}{x_i(a, t)} \qquad (6.15)$$

is small. The correlation function depends on the probability distribution $f_i(\mathbf{p}_i, t)$ (cf. equation (6.8)). If $f_i(\mathbf{p}_i, t) = 1$ for one $\mathbf{p}_i$, i. e., if all individuals behave according to the same probability distribution, all correlation values vanish. In this case melioration learning can be described on the population level by replicator dynamics. In general the correlation values are small if the probability distribution $f_i(\mathbf{p}_i, t)$ is single-peaked and sharp. Since the individuals of one type are assumed to be identical, the sharpness of the distribution $f_i(\mathbf{p}_i, t)$ depends only on the fluctuations in behaviour on the individual level. Fluctuations in behaviour are caused by the fluctuations of the remembered payoffs. Each payoff realised in the past was stochastically determined according to the distribution of the possible actions of the opponents and the characteristics of the game. These fluctuations of the payoffs lead to fluctuations of the remembered payoffs.

Therefore the remembered payoffs fluctuate more the fewer rounds of the game individuals remember. A large memory reduces fluctuations of the remembered payoffs $\hat{\Pi}_i(a,t)$. The remembered payoffs determine the changes in the probability distributions $p_i^{(j)}(a,t)$. Consequently the probability distributions fluctuate less the slower the individuals learn and the more rounds of the game individuals remember. Thus the replicator dynamics offers a good approximation of melioration learning on the population level, whenever individuals have a large memory and learn slowly.

Stationary states

In addition to the similarity of the dynamics both dynamics have the same stationary states.

> LEMMA 6.1: *Every stationary state of the replicator dynamics is also a stationary state of the melioration learning process on the population level.*

Proof: A stationary state of the replicator dynamics (6.14) satisfies the condition

$$\bar{\Pi}_i(a,t) = \frac{1}{A_i} \sum_{\tilde{a} \in \mathcal{A}_i} \bar{\Pi}_i(\tilde{a},t) \cdot x_i(\tilde{a},t) \ . \tag{6.16}$$

Consequently every action a is either chosen with probability zero, i.e., $x_i(a,t) = 0$ or leads to the same average payoff $\bar{\Pi}_i(a,t) = \bar{\Pi}$ that all other actions $\tilde{a}$ with $x_i(\tilde{a},t) > 0$ give rise to. Let me first analyse the actions $a \in \tilde{\mathcal{A}}_i$ that satisfy $x_i(a,t) = 0$. $x_i(a,t) = 0$ implies that none of the individuals realise action a with a probability greater than zero ($p_i^{(j)}(a,t) = 0$ for all individuals j). Consequently $f_i(\mathbf{p}_i,t)$ is zero for all $\mathbf{p}_i$ with $p_i(a) > 0$. Inserting this result into the definition (6.8) of the correlation function results in $C(p_i(\tilde{a},t),p_i(a,t)) = 0$ for all $a \in \tilde{\mathcal{A}}_i$. Analysing the term (6.15) it remains

$$\sum_{\tilde{a} \in \mathcal{A}_i \setminus \tilde{\mathcal{A}}_i} \bar{\Pi}_i(\tilde{a},t) \cdot \frac{C(p_i(a,t),p_i(\tilde{a},t))}{x_i(a,t)} \tag{6.17}$$

According to the above consideration $\bar{\Pi}_i(a,t) = \bar{\Pi}$ for all $a \notin \tilde{\mathcal{A}}_i$. Thus the term (6.17) can be written as

$$\frac{\bar{\Pi}}{x_i(a,t)} \cdot \sum_{\tilde{a} \in \mathcal{A}_i \setminus \tilde{\mathcal{A}}_i} C(p_i(a,t),p_i(\tilde{a},t)) \tag{6.18}$$

Inserting equation (6.8) into equation (6.18) results in

$$\frac{\bar{\Pi}}{x_i(a,t)} \int_0^1 \cdots \int_0^1 \Big(p_i(a)-x_i(a,t)\Big) \cdot \sum_{\tilde{a}\in\mathcal{A}_i} \Big(p_i(\tilde{a},t)-x_i(\tilde{a},t)\Big) \cdot f_i(\mathbf{p}_i,t)\, d\mathbf{p}_i \ .$$

(6.19)

If we insert $\sum_{\tilde{a}\in\mathcal{A}_i} p_i(\tilde{a},t) = 1$ and $\sum_{\tilde{a}\in\mathcal{A}_i} x_i(\tilde{a},t) = 1$ into the term (6.19) the result is zero. Thus in every stationary state of the replicator dynamics (6.14) the dynamics of melioration learning on the population level are the same as the replicator dynamics. ∎

> LEMMA 6.2: *The change of a share $x_i(a,t)$ is positive or zero for the action a that leads to the highest average payoff. It is zero only if no action leading to a smaller average payoff is chosen with a probability greater than zero. Similarly the change of a share $x_i(a,t)$ is negative or zero for the action a that leads to the lowest average payoff.*

Proof: Let me consider equation (6.11)

$$\frac{dx_i(a,t)}{dt} = \nu_m \int_0^1 \cdots \int_0^1 \Big[\bar{\Pi}_i(a,t) - \sum_{\tilde{a}\in\mathcal{A}_i} \bar{\Pi}_i(\tilde{a},t)\cdot p_i(\tilde{a})\Big]$$
$$\cdot p_i(a) \cdot f_i(\mathbf{p}_i,t)\, d\mathbf{p}_i \ .$$

(6.20)

The term $\sum_{\tilde{a}\in\mathcal{A}_i} \bar{\Pi}_i(\tilde{a},t)\cdot p_i(\tilde{a})$ represents a weighted average of the average payoffs $\bar{\Pi}_i(\tilde{a},t)$. A weighted average can never be greater (smaller) than the highest (smallest) of these values. Thus the change of $x_i(a,t)$ can never be negative (positive) if action a leads to the highest (smallest) average payoff. It is zero only if the weighted average $\sum_{\tilde{a}\in\mathcal{A}_i} \bar{\Pi}_i(\tilde{a},t)\cdot p_i(\tilde{a})$ is equal to $\bar{\Pi}_i(a,t)$, i.e., if no action leading to a smaller (larger) average payoff is chosen with a probability greater than zero. ∎

> LEMMA 6.3: *All stationary states of melioration learning are also stationary states of the replicator dynamics.*

Proof: Whenever actions are chosen that lead to different average payoffs, one or several actions can be identified leading to the highest average payoff. According to Lemma 6.2 the shares $x_i(a,t)$ of these actions increase over time. Thus a state can only be stationary if all realised actions lead to the same average payoff. All these states are stationary states of the replicator dynamics. ∎

> THEOREM 6.1: *The stationary states of melioration learning on the population level are identical to the stationary states of the replicator dynamics.*

Proof: Lemma 6.1 and 6.3 state that for states being stationary with respect to the replicator dynamics is a sufficient (Lemma 6.1) and necessary (Lemma 6.3) condition for being stationary with respect to melioration learning. ∎

Stability of pure states

In general, it can only be proved that the stationary states of melioration learning and replicator dynamics are identical. A similar proof for the stability is not possible. However one important class of states can be analysed further; the class of *pure states*. I define pure states in analogy to the definition of pure strategies in evolutionary game theory. I call a state a pure state if all individuals of one type i choose the same action a exclusively in this state. If a pure state is stable the analogy between melioration learning and replicator dynamics holds:

> THEOREM 6.2: *A pure stationary state of melioration learning is stable if, and only if, it is an evolutionary stable strategy.*

Proof: Let me assume that almost all individuals of type i realise action a_i with probability one. This assumption applies to all types of individuals (**a** is the corresponding vector of actions). The average payoff for any individual of type i realising action a_i is then approximately given by $\bar{\Pi}_i(a, t) = \Pi(\mathbf{a})$. In the infinitesimally small neighbourhood of a pure evolutionary stable strategy given by **a**, the payoff $\Pi(\mathbf{a})$ is greater than all other payoffs that an individual of type i is able to obtain if almost all individuals of the other types behave according to **a**. According to Lemma 6.2 the share of a_i increases in such a case. Consequently the behaviour a_i is stable under melioration learning. If there is an alternative action resulting in a payoff higher than $\Pi(\mathbf{a})$ the stationary state is not evolutionary stable. Lemma 6.2 implies that the share of the behaviour leading to a higher average payoff increases, so that the stationary state is also not stable under melioration learning. ∎

   To sum up, the dynamics of melioration learning on the population level are given approximately by replicator dynamics. This approximation becomes better the more rounds of the game the individuals remember and the slower they learn. The stationary states of melioration learning, however, are given by the evolutionary stationary strategies of the game, independent of the circumstances. For pure states, the stability of these states is given by evolutionary stability. Nevertheless, all this only applies to the population level for an infinitely large population.

6.2.2 Melioration Learning in a Repeated 2×2 Game

A totally different situation occurs if two individuals repeatedly interact with each other. Replicator dynamics requires a population of an infinite number of individuals. Thus the similarity between the dynamics of melioration learning and the replicator dynamics only holds for a large number of individuals who are randomly matched. Economic interaction, however, often takes place between the same individuals again and again. If the individuals do not reflect on the situation, they learn according to the melioration principle. In the following section, a 2×2 game will be studied.

Dynamics in repeated two-player games

The behaviours of the players in two-player games are given by the probabilities $p_1(t)$, the probability that individual 1 realises action 1 at time t, and $p_2(t)$, the probability that individual 2 realises action 1 at this time. The dynamics of $p_1(t)$ and $p_2(t)$ are given in a time-continuous way by (according to equation (3.14))

$$\frac{dp_i(t)}{dt} = \nu_m \cdot p_i(t) \cdot (1 - p_i(t)) \cdot \left[\hat{\Pi}_i(1,t) - \hat{\Pi}_i(2,t) \right] \qquad (6.21)$$

where $\hat{\Pi}_i(a,t)$ is the average remembered payoff for action a by individual i. If player i remembers the last $k_{i,a}(t)$ occasions in which (s)he realised action a and if in $k_{i,a}(\tilde{a},t)$ of these occasions the other player realised action $\tilde{a}$, $\hat{\Pi}_i(a,t)$ is given by

$$\hat{\Pi}_i(a,t) = \frac{k_{i,a}(1,t)}{k_{i,a}(t)} \Pi_i(a,1) + \frac{k_{i,a}(2,t)}{k_{i,a}(t)} \Pi_i(a,2) . \qquad (6.22)$$

where $\Pi_i(a,\tilde{a})$ denotes the payoff of individual i if (s)he chooses action a while the opponent chooses action $\tilde{a}$. The numbers $k_{i,a}(1,t)$ and $k_{i,a}(2,t)$ are stochastic values. They are Bernoulli distributed if the probability distribution of the opponent has been constant in the time period remembered by individual i. Consequently $\hat{\Pi}_i(a,t)$ also is a stochastic value. Therefore the dynamics of $p_i(t)$ contain a deterministic and a stochastic aspect. Since the stochastic influence is neither normally distributed nor constant in time, the dynamics can only be analysed approximately or by simulations.

Stationary states

However four cases exist in which the fluctuations disappear. These are the cases with $p_1(t) = 0$ or $p_1(t) = 1$ and with $p_2(t) = 0$ or $p_2(t) = 1$.

If these values of $p_1(t)$ and $p_2(t)$ sustain for some time, $k_{i,a}(1,t)$ and $k_{i,a}(2,t)$ are given deterministically, i.e., they are either 0 or $k_{i,a}(t)$. Consequently the dynamics of $p_i(t)$ are deterministically given. In other words, the state in which both players use a pure strategy is the only state that might be stable under melioration learning. For all other states, some fluctuations remain so that the state cannot be stable (cf. the discussion about the stability in stochastic systems in section 4.1). Thus a mixed strategy cannot be stable. In the following section, the stability of these four possible stable states will be studied. The four states emerge from each other by a change of indices for the alternative actions. Thus it is sufficient to study one of these states. The state $p_1(t) = p_2(t) = 1$ is chosen in the following example.

> LEMMA 6.4: $p_1 = p_2 = 1$ *is a stationary state of the dynamics of melioration learning given by equation (6.21).*

Proof: Once the state given by $p_1 = p_2 = 1$ is reached, the fluctuations disappear. The remembered payoffs are then given by

$$\hat{\Pi}_i(a,t) = \Pi_i(a,1) \qquad (6.23)$$

with probability one. In this case the dynamics are given by

$$\frac{dp_i(t)}{dt} = \nu_m \cdot p_i(t) \cdot (1 - p_i(t)) \cdot \left[\hat{\Pi}_i(1,1) - \hat{\Pi}_i(2,1)\right]. \qquad (6.24)$$

Inserting $p_1(t) = p_2(t) = 1$ we obtain $\frac{dp_i(t)}{dt} = 0$. ∎

Stable states
To analyse the stability of the stationary states, I define what I call *complete dominance*, which will prove to be helpful in the following case.

> DEFINITION 6.1 (COMPLETE DOMINANCE): *An action a completely dominates action $\tilde{a}$ with respect to individual i if and only if*
>
> $$\Pi_i(a,\hat{a}) \geq \Pi_i(\tilde{a},\bar{a}) \qquad \forall_{i,\hat{a},\bar{a}\in\{1,2\}} \qquad (6.25)$$

Condition (6.25) includes the condition for *strict dominance* ($\Pi_i(a,\hat{a}) \geq \Pi_i(\tilde{a},\hat{a}) \; \forall_{i,\hat{a}\in\{1,2\}}$). However it requires more than strict dominance. Strict dominance means that for every action of the opponent, the payoff for one action is at least as high as the payoff for the other. Here it is required that all payoffs that one action can lead to are at least as high as the highest payoff that can result from the other action. Complete dominance implies strict dominance but not *vise versa*.

LEMMA 6.5: $p_1 = p_2 = 1$ *is stable if action 1 results in at least a payoff as high as the highest payoff that action 2 may result in (complete dominance of action 2 by action 1) for both players and if at least one payoff that action 1 may result in is higher than one of the payoffs that action 2 results in, i. e.*

$$\exists_{a,\tilde{a} \in \{1,2\}} : \Pi_i(1,a) > \Pi_i(2,\tilde{a}) \qquad \forall_{i \in \{1,2\}} . \qquad (6.26)$$

Proof: As long as $p_1, p_2 \neq 0, 1$ (the stationary states are never reached in real time if they are not the initial situation, because the speed of learning converges to zero if the stationary states are approached) the remembered average payoffs are given by equation (6.22). Thus $\hat{\Pi}_i(a,t)$ ranges between $\Pi_i(a,1)$ and $\Pi_i(a,2)$. The complete dominance of action 2 by action 1 and condition (6.26) imply that $\hat{\Pi}_i(1,t) \geq \hat{\Pi}_i(2,t)$ is always satisfied. Inserting this into equation (6.21) we obtain that $dp_i(t)/dt \geq 0$. Furthermore the condition that $\Pi_i(1,a) > \Pi_i(2,\tilde{a})$ for at least one combination of a and $\tilde{a}$ for every $i \in \{1,2\}$ implies that an occasion occurs with probability greater than zero in which $\hat{\Pi}_i(1,t) > \hat{\Pi}_i(2,t)$ holds. Thus $dp_i(t)/dt > 0$ at least sometimes. A dynamic that fulfils $dp_i(t)/dt \geq 0$ always and $dp_i(t)/dt > 0$ at least sometimes for every $p_i(t) < 1$ and is bounded by $p_i(t) = 1$ converges to $p_i(t) = 1$ with a probability of one. ∎

LEMMA 6.6: $p_1 = p_2 = 1$ *is unstable if action 2 can cause at least one payoff $\Pi_i(2,\hat{a})$ that is higher than the smallest payoff $\Pi_i(1,\tilde{a})$ caused by action 1 for one of the individuals.*

Proof: Let me denote the individual for whom $\Pi_i(2,\hat{a}) > \Pi_i(1,\tilde{a})$ by i and the opponent by j. For any state $p_1(t) = 1 - \epsilon_1$ and $p_2(t) = 1 - \epsilon_2$ there is a probability greater than zero that player j has chosen action $\hat{a}$ whenever player i chose action 2, and action $\tilde{a}$ whenever player i chose action 1 (the probability for such an event may be very small but not zero). In this case the remembered payoff $\hat{\Pi}_i(1,t)$ is smaller than $\hat{\Pi}_i(2,t)$ and the dynamics given by equation (6.21) departs from the stationary state $p_1 = p_2 = 1$. ∎

THEOREM 6.3 *A state in which both players realise a pure strategy given by a_1 and a_2 in a 2×2 game, is stable if, and only if, action a_1 completely dominates the alternative action of individual 1, and a_2 completely dominates the alternative action of individual 2.*

Proof: According to Lemma 6.4 all states in which both players realise a pure strategy are stationary states. Lemma 6.5 states that they are stable if equations (6.25) is satisfied and the payoffs for each individual are not all the same (cf. equation (6.26)) while Lemma 6.6 states that they are unstable if equation (6.25) is not satisfied. The case that all payoffs are the same for one of the players, is ignored because in such a case there is no real interaction between the players.   ∎

If none of the actions completely dominates the other one, at least for one of the players, there is no stable state at all. The behaviour of the players fluctuates continually and every state can be reached after some time, independent of the state where the dynamics start. Nevertheless once a stationary state is almost reached, the probability that the dynamics depart from the neighbourhood of this stationary state may become very small (although it is always positive). Thus it may be very unlikely that the neighbourhood of the stationary state is left again. In such a case it seems inappropriate to talk about an unstable state; therefore I define such a state as *convergingly stable*.

> DEFINITION 6.2 (CONVERGING STABILITY): *A state is convergingly stable if the probability of the system to move from the edge of the neighbourhood of this state into the inside of this neighbourhood converges to one if the size of the neighbourhood converges to zero.*

Converging stability requires that the probability of leaving the neighbourhood of an convergingly stable state decreases with the distance between the actual state and this state. Therefore the focus will next be on the probability of moves away from a state.

> LEMMA 6.7: *A mixed strategy cannot be convergingly stable.*

Proof: Let me consider a state given by $p_1(t)$ and $p_2(t)$ with $p_i(t) \neq 0, 1$ for at least one $i \in \{1, 2\}$. Furthermore action a_j shall be the action that is more likely to be realised by the other individual j. Thus the payoffs $\Pi_i(1, a_j)$ and $\Pi_i(2, a_j)$ are both realised in any small neighbourhood of this state with a probability greater than zero. Consequently the dynamics of melioration learning are given by

$$\frac{dp_i(t)}{dt} = \nu_m \cdot p_i(t) \cdot (1 - p_i(t)) \cdot \left[\Pi_i(1, a_j) - \Pi_i(2, a_j) \right] \qquad (6.27)$$

with a probability greater than zero. The probability of $p_i(t)$ to move in the direction given by equation (6.27) does not converge to zero if the neighbourhood becomes infinitesimally small. As a consequence either for $p_i(t) = p_i + \epsilon$ or for $p_i(t) = p_i - \epsilon$, melioration learning does not guarantee $p_i(t)$ to move towards the inner domain of the neighbourhood if $\epsilon \to 0$. ∎

LEMMA 6.8: $p_1 = p_2 = 1$ *is convergingly stable if* $\Pi_i(1,1) >$ $\Pi_i(2,1)$ *for both players* $i \in \{1,2\}$.

Proof: The dynamics of the probabilities $p_i(t)$ for $p_i(t) = 1 - \epsilon_i$ are given by equation (6.21) where $\hat{\Pi}_i(a,t)$ is

$$\hat{\Pi}_i(a,t) = \Pi_i(a,1) \tag{6.28}$$

with probability $(1 - \epsilon_j)^{k_{i,a}(t)}$ (j is 1 if $i = 2$ and 2 if $i = 1$) and

$$\Pi_i(a,t) = \frac{k_{i,a}(t) - 1}{k_{i,a}(t)} \cdot \Pi_i(a,1) + \frac{1}{k_{i,a}(t)} \cdot \Pi_i(a,2) \tag{6.29}$$

with probability $k_{i,a}(t) \cdot \epsilon_j \cdot (1 - \epsilon_j)^{k_{i,a}(t)-1}$. In addition all other values given by equation (6.22) may occur. However the probability for remembered payoffs, other than the one presented in equation (6.28) and (6.29), is at least quadratic in ϵ_i. Consequently these cases can be neglected for $\epsilon_i \to 0$. Even the probability of a payoff given by equation (6.29) converges to zero for $\epsilon_i \to 0$. Thus the payoffs are given by equation (6.28) with probability one for $\epsilon_i \to 0$. Inserting equation (6.28) into equation (6.21) results in

$$\frac{dp_i(t)}{dt} = \nu_m \cdot p_i(t) \cdot (1 - p_i(t)) \cdot \left[\Pi_i(1,1) - \Pi_i(2,1)\right]. \tag{6.30}$$

The state $p_1 = p_2 = 1$ is convergingly stable if the change of $p_i(t)$ given by equation (6.30) is positive for both $i \in \{1,2\}$. ∎

THEOREM 6.4: *The behaviours of both players are convergingly stable if, and only if, both individuals play a pure strategy and would lower their payoff if they changed their behaviour.*

Proof: According to Lemma 6.7 a mixed strategy cannot be convergingly stable. Four states exist in which both players realise a pure strategy. One is given by $p_1 = p_2 = 1$. This is convergingly stable if $\Pi_i(1,1) > \Pi_i(2,1)$ for both $i \in \{1,2\}$ (cf. Lemma 6.8), that is, if both players would decrease their payoff by changing their behaviour. The other three cases result from this case by an exchange of the indices. Thus the same holds in all four cases in which only pure strategies are realised.   ∎

According to Definition 6.2, converging stability of a state implies that the nearer the system comes to this state the more likely it is to converge further towards this state. In other words, convergingly stable states will more probably be sustained the nearer the system approaches it. Once the system has come infinitesimally close to the convergingly stable state, the probability of converging further to this state becomes approximately one. Nevertheless there is always a probability greater than zero that the system leaves the neighbourhood of a convergingly stable state again. However, convergingly stable states may hold for a very long time.

The condition in Theorem 6.4 is sufficient but not necessary for a *Nash equilibrium* and an *evolutionary stable strategy*. Thus *converging stability* implies *evolutionary stability* but not vice versa. The differences between both concepts, however, should not to be overstated. The main difference between the two is that mixed strategies may be evolutionary stable but can never be convergingly stable.

6.2.3 Melioration Learning and Evolutionary Game Theory

It is often claimed in the literature that learning can be described by evolutionary algorithms (cf. e. g. Holland & Miller 1991 and Dawid 1996). This is seen as a justification for using evolutionary game theory to describe the behaviour of economic agents. Above, it has been shown that the *replicator dynamics* can indeed be used as an approximation for the dynamics of a population that learns according to the melioration principle. Moreover all ESSs are also stable under melioration learning in a randomly matched, large population. As long as melioration learning is studied on the population level and the individuals are matched randomly, the claim of an analogy between learning and evolutionary processes is justified, although the dynamics of learning can be represented only approximately by replicator dynamics.

Even in the case of two interacting players, most pure ESSs are convergingly stable (the definition of an asymptotically stable state in Theorem 6.4 corresponds to the definition of an ESS, except in the case in which the payoff of one player remains constant if (s)he changes behaviour). Nevertheless there are some crucial differences between the stability achievable with melioration learning and the evolutionary stability, if only two individuals interact. Stability, as it is usually understood, occurs only if the behaviours of all interacting individuals remain the same permanently once a stable state is reached. In the case of melioration learning, this only holds for the pure behaviours that completely dominate all other behaviours. Pure ESSs are, in general, only convergingly stable. This means that they may be abandoned again with a probability greater than zero, although this probability may tend to zero the closer the ESS is approached. Mixed ESS are never stable under melioration learning if two individuals interact repeatedly.

Finally, it has to be stated that the analogy between biological evolution and learning processes only holds in the case of melioration learning. Below we will see that other learning processes lead to completely different results. Melioration learning only occurs under the specific circumstances stated above. Only if these circumstances are given, are the concepts of biological evolution transferable to learning processes.

6.3 BUSH-MOSTELLER MODEL IN GAMES

In addition to the melioration principle, the Bush-Mosteller model was repeatedly proposed for the description of reinforcement learning processes (cf. Bush & Mosteller 1955, Cross 1973 and Roth & Erév 1995). In the context of games, three approaches have to be mentioned: T. Börgers and R. Sarin (1997) show that Cross's version of the Bush-Mosteller model leads to learning dynamics similar to the *replicator dynamics*, at least for an infinite number of interacting individuals. A. Roth and I. Erév (1995) analyse Cross's version of the Bush-Mosteller model in the context of games, and compare the results with experimental data. They use three different modifications of the model and focus on the dynamics of the process. By doing so, they have been able to explain the results of several experiments. A comprehensive study of the Bush-Mosteller model, in the context of a 2×2 game, is conducted in Brenner 1997. There the Bush-Mosteller model is modified, so that it is a combination of the original version and Cross's version (cf. Section 3.1.1). In the following the model proposed in Brenner 1997 will be used to deduce the conditions for stable states, in a general game played by a randomly matched population of individuals.

6.3.1 Stability on the Level of Populations

Notation and learning dynamics
The notation introduced in Section 6.2 is adopted here. The following is an analysis of the behaviour of a homogeneous population of N

individuals who repeatedly interact in a *symmetric n-player game* ($n <$ N so that always a randomly chosen part of the population interacts in each game). Since the game is symmetric, all players have the same options and receive payoffs given by the same payoff matrix. In contrast to the above approach, the population is not divided into subgroups. The payoff for each individual i is given by $\Pi(\mathbf{a}(t)) = \Pi(a_i(t), \mathbf{a}_{i_-}(t))$ if (s)he realises action $a_i(t)$ and the action profile $\mathbf{a}_{i_-}(t)$ is realised by the group of individuals who interact with individual i at the considered time t. The vector $\mathbf{a(t)}$ denotes the action profile of all individuals who interact with each other in the symmetric n-player game at time t. The action profile is not ordered, in the sense that the actions of each individual occur at a certain place in the vector. Since the game is symmetric, the outcome of the game depends only on the frequency of each action chosen by the interacting individuals. The payoff of each individual depends on the personal action $a_i(t)$ and the frequencies of actions chosen by the other players $\mathbf{a}_{i_-}(t)$. Thus the payoff $\Pi(a_i(t), \mathbf{a}_{i_-}(t))$ of individual i is denoted as a function of the personal action $a_i(t)$ and the unordered action profile $\mathbf{a}_{i_-}(t)$ of the other players with whom individual i interacts at time t.

The individuals have to choose one of A alternative actions denoted by $a \in \mathcal{A}$ at each time t ($\mathcal{A}$ denotes the set of possible actions while A denotes the number of possible actions). The number of individuals is assumed to be infinitely large ($N \to \infty$). Moreover the individuals are assumed to be randomly matched each time.

According to the Bush-Mosteller model, individuals behave stochastically. The behaviour of individual i is given by the probability distribution $p_i(a, t)$ of actions at time t. $p_i(a, t) = p$ states that individual i chooses action a with a probability p at time t. The probability for individual i to face the action profile $\mathbf{a}_{i_-}$ of the opponents is denoted by $p(\mathbf{a}_{i_-}, t)$. This probability depends on the current behaviour of all individuals because the opponents of individual i are randomly chosen each time.

The individuals are assumed to learn according to the modified Bush-Mosteller model, so that the dynamics of $p_i(a, t)$ are given by equation (3.7) that means by

$$p_i(a, t+1) = p_i(a, t) + \begin{cases} \alpha \cdot \Pi(\mathbf{a}(t)) \cdot (1 - p_i(a, t)) \\ \quad \text{if} \quad a = a_i(t) \wedge \Pi(\mathbf{a}(t)) \geq 0 \\[1em] \alpha \cdot \Pi(\mathbf{a}(t)) \cdot p_i(a, t) \\ \quad \text{if} \quad a = a_i(t) \wedge \Pi(\mathbf{a}(t)) < 0 \\[1em] -\alpha \cdot \Pi(\mathbf{a}(t)) \cdot p_i(a, t) \\ \quad \text{if} \quad a \neq a_i(t) \wedge \Pi(\mathbf{a}(t)) \geq 0 \\[1em] -\alpha \cdot \Pi(\mathbf{a}(t)) \cdot \frac{p_i(a_i(t), t) \cdot p_i(a, t)}{1 - p_i(a_i(t), t)} \\ \quad \text{if} \quad a \neq a_i(t) \wedge \Pi(\mathbf{a}(t)) < 0 \end{cases} \qquad (6.31)$$

where α is the parameter of the modified Bush-Mosteller model that describes the speed of learning.

Stochastic dynamics of individual behaviour

Equation (6.31) describes the learning process of one individual. In the following text, however, the dynamics expanded to the level of populations are analysed, concentrating on the stable states. In order to do this, two steps have to be taken. First, the behaviour of the individual has to be described in relation to the behaviour on the level of populations. Second, the dynamics of behaviour on the level of populations has to be deduced from the dynamics on the individual level.

The dynamics of the behaviour of individual i given by equation (6.31). This dynamics depends on the action profile $\mathbf{a}(t)$, which itself is a stochastic variable. Thus not only is the behaviour of individual i given by a probability distribution $\mathbf{p}_i(t) = (p_i(a))_{a \in A}$ meaning that $\mathbf{p}_i(t)$ is the vector containing all probabilities $p_i(a, t)$ of individual i to commit each action a at time t, but also the dynamics of $\mathbf{p}_i(t)$ are determined stochastically. Therefore, theoretically, it is only possible to calculate the probability that the behaviour of individual i is given by the probability distribution $\mathbf{p}_i(t) = \mathbf{p}$ at time t. Moreover, $\mathbf{p}$ is a continuous A-dimensional variable. Thus a probability can only be defined for a certain subspace in the A-dimensional state space. For each state $\mathbf{p}$ only a probability density can be defined. This probability density is denoted by $f_i(\mathbf{p}, t)$ in the following. This means that the behaviour of individual i is given approximately by $\tilde{\mathbf{p}}$ at time t with the probability

$$\int_{\tilde{p}(1)-\Delta}^{\tilde{p}(1)+\Delta} \cdots \int_{\tilde{p}(A)-\Delta}^{\tilde{p}(A)+\Delta} f_i(\mathbf{p},t) \, d\mathbf{p} \qquad (6.32)$$

where $d\mathbf{p} = \prod_{a\in\mathcal{A}} dp(a)$ (or $d\mathbf{p} = dp(1)\cdot \ldots \cdot dp(A)$ if the actions are described by natural numbers from 1 to A), and Δ is the range of deviation, so we still use the expression "approximately".

Let me assume that the initial behaviour of all individuals is the same. Subsequently, their histories may differ due to the random matching with others and the stochastic behaviour they exhibit themselves (remember the action of an individual is determined stochastically according to $\mathbf{p}_i(t)$). Nevertheless, the probability of facing a certain history is the same for all individuals (the population is assumed to be homogeneous), so that the probability density $f_i(\mathbf{p},t)$ of the behaviour of individual i to be given by a certain probability distribution $\mathbf{p}$ ($\mathbf{p}_i(t) = \mathbf{p}$) is the same for all individuals. Hence the index i can be dropped, and the probability of meeting an individual with a behaviour given by $\mathbf{p}$ at time t, is denoted by $f(\mathbf{p},t)$. The probability that a randomly chosen individual chooses action a at time t is given by

$$x(a,t) = \int_0^1 \cdots \int_0^1 p(a) \cdot f(\mathbf{p},t) \, d\mathbf{p} \ . \qquad (6.33)$$

The probabilities $x(a,t)$ are important in the present analysis for two reasons. On the one hand, they denote the share of individuals who commit action a at time t. They therefore describe the behaviour on the level of populations sufficiently. Thus the principle aim of the present section is to go through the calculation of the stable values of $x(a,t)$, that is, the frequency with which action a is taken in the population in the long run (if a stationary state exists on the population level). On the other hand, $x(a,t)$ describes the action of the opponents of an individual i sufficiently, because the opponents of individual i are randomly chosen from the whole population at each time t, so that $x(a,t)$ denotes the probability that their randomly chosen opponent commits action a. Consequently $x(a,t)$ determines the dynamics of $f(\mathbf{p},t)$.

$f(\mathbf{p},t)$ changes according to the individual learning processes. Individuals change their behaviour according to equation (6.31). This change depends on the probability distribution $\mathbf{p}(t)$ and the action profile $\mathbf{a}(t)$ realised at time t. In other words, the probability distribution $\mathbf{p}_i(t+1)$ at time $(t+1)$ depends on the probability distribution $\mathbf{p}_i(t)$ at time t and the actions $\mathbf{a}(t)$ chosen by the interacting individuals at time t. Although the learning process and therefore the probability densities $f(\mathbf{p}, t)$ are the same for all individuals, a number still has to be assigned to the individual to denote the realisations of actions at certain times. In other words, the probability that the behaviour of an individual is given by $\mathbf{p}$ at time t is the same for all individuals, but the real behaviour of individual i at time t is given by $\mathbf{p}_i(t)$. Thus each time a realisation is considered, below, an index is used (for the considered individual $i = 1$). Each action profile $\mathbf{a}(t) = \mathbf{a} = (a_1, a_2, ..., a_n)$ occurs with the probability

$$p_1(a_1, t) \prod_{j=2}^{n} x(a_j, t) \ . \tag{6.34}$$

$x(a_j, t)$ describes the actions of the opponents adequately because they are randomly chosen from the whole population.

Equation (6.31) describes the dependence of the behaviour at time $(t + 1)$ on the behaviour at time t. For the following calculation, the opposite dependence is needed; the dependence of the behaviour at time t on the behaviour at time $(t+1)$. Given the action profile $\mathbf{a}(t)$ it results from equation (6.31):

$$p_1(a, t) = \begin{cases} \frac{p_1(a, t+1) - \alpha \cdot \Pi(\mathbf{a}(t))}{1 - \alpha \cdot \Pi(\mathbf{a}(t))} & \text{if} \quad a = a_1(t) \wedge \Pi(\mathbf{a}(t)) \geq 0 \\[2mm] \frac{p_1(a, t+1)}{1 + \alpha \cdot \Pi(\mathbf{a}(t))} & \text{if} \quad a = a_1(t) \wedge \Pi(\mathbf{a}(t)) < 0 \\[2mm] \frac{p_1(a, t+1)}{1 - \alpha \cdot \Pi(\mathbf{a}(t))} & \text{if} \quad a \neq a_1(t) \wedge \Pi(\mathbf{a}(t)) \geq 0 \\[2mm] \frac{p_1(a, t+1)}{1 - \alpha \cdot \Pi(\mathbf{a}(t)) \cdot \frac{p(a_i(t), t)}{1 - p(a_i(t), t)}} & \text{if} \quad a \neq a_1(t) \wedge \Pi(\mathbf{a}(t)) < 0 \end{cases} . \tag{6.35}$$

Equation (6.35) defines $p_1(a, t)$ dependent on $p_1(a, t + 1)$ and $\mathbf{a}(t)$, i.e. according to equation (6.35) the distribution of actions of an individual at time t can be calculated knowing the current distribution of actions at time $(t+1)$, the action taken at time t and the payoff received at that time. This dependence is crucial for the following mathematical analysis so that this dependence is denoted explicitly by using $p_1(a, t, p_i(a, t + 1), \mathbf{a}(t))$ and $\mathbf{p}_1(t, \mathbf{p}_1(t + 1), \mathbf{a}(t))$.

With the help of these definitions it is possible to approach the dynamics of $f(\mathbf{p}, t)$. Since $f(\mathbf{p}, t)$ is the same for all individuals, it is sufficient to analyse the dynamics of $f(\mathbf{p}, t)$ for one specific individual. Individual 1 is chosen arbitrarily. To analyse the dynamics of $f_1(\mathbf{p}, t)$, $f_1(\mathbf{p}, t + 1)$ is calculated dependent on $f_1(\mathbf{p}, t)$. To this end, a certain behaviour $\tilde{\mathbf{p}}$ is considered and the probability density $f_1(\tilde{\mathbf{p}}, t + 1)$ is calculated. The action profile relevant for individual 1 at time t is given by $\mathbf{a}(t) = \hat{\mathbf{a}}$. Consequently, the behaviour of individual 1 is given by $\tilde{\mathbf{p}}$ at time $(t + 1)$ only if her/his behaviour was given by $\mathbf{p}_i(t) = \hat{\mathbf{p}}(t, \tilde{\mathbf{p}}, \hat{\mathbf{a}})$ according to equation (6.35). In other words, if the behaviour of individual 1 was given by $\hat{\mathbf{p}}(t, \tilde{\mathbf{p}}, \hat{\mathbf{a}})$ at time t with the relevant actions profile is $\hat{\mathbf{a}}$, it is given by $\tilde{\mathbf{p}}$ at time $(t + 1)$. The probability of an action profile $\mathbf{a}$ occurring is given by (6.34). Thus if the behaviour of individual 1 was given by $\hat{\mathbf{p}}(t, \tilde{\mathbf{p}}, \hat{\mathbf{a}})$ at time t, it is given by $\tilde{\mathbf{p}}$ at time $(t + 1)$ with a probability

$$\hat{p}(\hat{a}_1, t) \prod_{j=2}^{n} x(\hat{a}_j, t) \,. \tag{6.36}$$

This holds for any action profile $\hat{\mathbf{a}}$ so that the probability density $f_1(\tilde{\mathbf{p}}, t + 1)$ is given by (to make understanding easier ~ is used for all values related to time $(t + 1)$ and ^ is used for all values related to time t)

$$f_1(\tilde{\mathbf{p}}, t+1) = \sum_{\hat{\mathbf{a}}} \left(\hat{p}(\hat{a}_1, t, \tilde{\mathbf{p}}, \hat{\mathbf{a}}) \cdot \prod_{j=2}^{n} x(\hat{a}_j, t) \right) \cdot f_1(\hat{\mathbf{p}}(t, \tilde{\mathbf{p}}, \hat{\mathbf{a}}), t) \cdot \det(\mathbf{H}(\tilde{\mathbf{p}}, \hat{\mathbf{a}}))$$
$$\tag{6.37}$$

where the elements of matrix $\mathbf{H}(\tilde{\mathbf{p}}, \hat{\mathbf{a}})$ are given by

$$H_{a\bar{a}}(\tilde{\mathbf{p}}, \hat{\mathbf{a}}) = \frac{d\hat{p}(a, t, \tilde{\mathbf{p}}, \hat{\mathbf{a}})}{d\tilde{p}(\bar{a})} \,. \tag{6.38}$$

The factor $\det(\mathbf{H}(\tilde{\mathbf{p}}, \hat{\mathbf{a}}))$ in equation (6.37) is necessary because $f_1(\mathbf{p}, t)$ is a probability density and not a probability.

Dynamics on the level of populations

With the help of the equations above, it is possible to approach the reinforcement learning processes on the level of populations. To this end, the changes of the shares $x(a, t + 1)$ have to be studied. These are given by (replace t in equation (6.33) by $(t + 1)$ and remember that $f_1(\mathbf{p}, t) = f(\mathbf{p}, t)$)

$$x(a, t + 1) = \int_0^1 \dots \int_0^1 \tilde{p}(a) \cdot f_1(\tilde{\mathbf{p}}, t + 1) \, d\tilde{\mathbf{p}} \,. \tag{6.39}$$

Inserting equation (6.37) into equation (6.39) results in (still ~ relates to time $(t + 1)$ and ^ to time t)

$$x(a, t+1) \;=\; \int_0^1 \cdots \int_0^1 \tilde{p}(a) \cdot \left[\sum_{\hat{\mathbf{a}}} \left(\hat{p}(\hat{a}_1, t, \tilde{\mathbf{p}}, \hat{\mathbf{a}}) \cdot \prod_{j=2}^n x(\hat{a}_j, t) \right) \right.$$
$$\left. \cdot \; f_1(\hat{\mathbf{p}}(t, \tilde{\mathbf{p}}, \hat{\mathbf{a}}), t) \cdot \det(\mathbf{H}(\tilde{\mathbf{p}}, \hat{\mathbf{a}})) \right] d\tilde{\mathbf{p}} \;.$$

$$(6.40)$$

Some mathematical transformations lead to

$$x(a, t+1) \;=\; \sum_{\hat{\mathbf{a}}} \left(\prod_{j=2}^n x(\hat{a}_j, t) \right) \int_0^1 \cdots \int_0^1 \tilde{p}(a) \cdot \hat{p}(\hat{a}_1, t, \tilde{\mathbf{p}}, \hat{\mathbf{a}})$$
$$\cdot \; f_1(\hat{\mathbf{p}}(t, \tilde{\mathbf{p}}, \hat{\mathbf{a}}), t) \cdot \det(\mathbf{H}(\tilde{\mathbf{p}}, \hat{\mathbf{a}})) \, d\tilde{\mathbf{p}} \;.$$

$$(6.41)$$

The integral in equation (6.41) can be further simplified by the substitution of the integration variable $\tilde{\mathbf{p}}$ by $\hat{\mathbf{p}}$ because $\det(\mathbf{H}(\tilde{\mathbf{p}}, \hat{\mathbf{a}})) \, d\tilde{\mathbf{p}} = d\hat{\mathbf{p}}$. One obtains

$$x(a, t+1) = \sum_{\hat{\mathbf{a}}} \left(\prod_{j=2}^n x(\hat{a}_j, t) \right) \int_0^1 \cdots \int_0^1 \tilde{p}(a, t+1, \hat{\mathbf{p}}, \hat{\mathbf{a}}) \cdot \hat{p}(\hat{a}_1) \cdot f_1(\hat{\mathbf{p}}, t) \, d\hat{\mathbf{p}}$$

$$(6.42)$$

where $\tilde{p}(a, t+1)$ has to be written dependent on $\hat{\mathbf{p}}$ and $\hat{\mathbf{a}}$, and is given by equation (6.31). Equation (6.31) consists of two terms; one that is always $p_i(a, t)$ and one that depends on action $a_i(t)$ and the payoff obtained. Therefore inserting equation (6.31) into equation (6.42) two terms result. The first one reads

$$\sum_{\hat{\mathbf{a}}} \left(\prod_{j=2}^n x(\hat{a}_j, t) \right) \int_0^1 \cdots \int_0^1 \hat{p}(a) \cdot \hat{p}(\hat{a}_1) \cdot f_1(\hat{\mathbf{p}}, t) \, d\hat{\mathbf{p}} \;. \qquad (6.43)$$

In this term only $\hat{p}(\hat{a}_1)$ depends on $\hat{a}_1$ so that summing the whole term (6.43) over $\hat{a}_1$ means summing $\hat{p}(\hat{a}_1)$ over $\hat{a}_1$ which results in one. Similarly only $x(\hat{a}_j, t)$ depends on $\hat{a}_j$ so that the term given by (6.43) finally reads

$$\int_0^1 \cdots \int_0^1 \hat{p}(a) \cdot f_1(\hat{\mathbf{p}}, t) \, d\hat{\mathbf{p}} = x(a, t) \;. \qquad (6.44)$$

The second case-dependent term in equation (6.31) is more complex. The abbreviations

$$C(p(a), p(\tilde{a}), t) = \int_0^1 \cdots \int_0^1 p(a) \cdot p(\tilde{a}) \cdot f_1(\mathbf{p}, t) \, d\mathbf{p} \qquad (6.45)$$

and

$$C'(p(a), p(\tilde{a}), t) = \int_0^1 \cdots \int_0^1 \frac{p(a) \cdot p(\tilde{a})}{1 - p(\tilde{a})} \cdot f_1(\mathbf{p}, t) \, d\mathbf{p} \ . \qquad (6.46)$$

are used so that the whole equation (6.42) can be written as

$$x(a, t+1) \ = \ x(a, t) + \alpha \cdot \sum_{\hat{\mathbf{a}}} \left(\prod_{j=2}^n x(\hat{a}_j, t) \right) \cdot \Pi(\hat{\mathbf{a}})$$

$$\cdot \ \begin{cases} \left[x(\hat{a}_1, t) - C(\hat{p}(a), \hat{p}(\hat{a}_1), t) \right] & \text{if} \quad a = \hat{a}_1 \wedge \Pi(\hat{\mathbf{a}}) \geq 0 \\ C(\hat{p}(a), \hat{p}(\hat{a}_1), t) & \text{if} \quad a = \hat{a}_1 \wedge \Pi(\hat{\mathbf{a}}) < 0 \\ -C(\hat{p}(a), \hat{p}(\hat{a}_1), t) & \text{if} \quad a \neq \hat{a}_1 \wedge \Pi(\hat{\mathbf{a}}) \geq 0 \\ -C'(\hat{p}(a), \hat{p}(\hat{a}_1), t) & \text{if} \quad a \neq \hat{a}_1 \wedge \Pi(\hat{\mathbf{a}}) < 0 \end{cases}$$

$$(6.47)$$

Equation (6.47) describes the dynamics of the generalised Bush-Mosteller model on the level of populations. It is not a closed set of differential equations because the functions $C(\hat{p}(a), \hat{p}(\tilde{a}), t)$ and $C'(\hat{p}(a), \hat{p}(\tilde{a}), t)$ depend on the distribution of behaviour on the individual level. Therefore the dynamics can not be analysed mathematically in general. However, the stability of pure behavioural states (called *pure states* in the following), meaning states in which all individuals choose the same action for certain, can be analysed mathematically. This will be done below.

6.3.2   Mathematical Conditions for a Reinforcably Stable State

In this section, the conditions for the stability of a pure state are analysed. A stable pure state is called a *reinforcably stable state* (RSS) (cf. Brenner 1997 where the requirements for such a state are deduced for a 2×2 game). In the following section I will deduce the requirements for a reinforcably stable state, in the case of a general symmetric normal form game where the players are matched randomly. A reinforcably stable state is defined as follows.

> DEFINITION 6.3 (STABILITY ON THE POPULATION LEVEL: *A state of the population given by* $\check{\mathbf{x}} = (\check{x}(a))_{a \in \mathcal{A}}$ *is called reinforcably stable if for every state* $\mathbf{x}(\mathbf{t})$ *in the infinitesimally small surrounding of* $\check{\mathbf{x}}$, *the dynamics of learning does not take the system away from* $\check{\mathbf{x}}$.

Stationarity of pure states

Below, the stability of a state is analysed in which action $\breve{a}$ is exclusively chosen by all individuals, i.e. $x(a,t) = 0$ holds for every $a \neq \breve{a}$ while $x(\breve{a}, t) = 1$. Thus the probability density $f(\mathbf{p}, t)$ is the δ-distribution (a δ-distribution is a probability density that is zero for all values of the variable it depends on except one, while the integral of this distribution over all possible states of the respective variable is one) defined by

$$\int_0^1 \cdots \int_0^1 F(p(1), ..., p(\breve{a} - 1), p(\breve{a}), p(\breve{a} + 1), ..., p(A)) \cdot f(\mathbf{p}, t) \, d\mathbf{p}$$
$$= F(0, ..., 0, 1, 0, ..., 0)$$

(6.48)

where $F(p(1), ..., p(\breve{a} - 1), p(\breve{a}), p(\breve{a} + 1), ..., p(A))$ is any function in the probabilities $p(1)$ to $p(A)$ if the actions are numbered by 1 to A.

The analysis is started by studying the dynamics once a pure state is reached. A pure state can only be reinforcably stable if it is a stationary state, that is, if reinforcement learning leads to no behavioural changes once the pure state is reached. Therefore equation (6.47) is analysed for the situation given by equation (6.48). To this end, an action profile where all players realise action $\breve{a}$ is denoted by $\breve{\mathbf{a}}$, and the corresponding distribution of behaviours in the population is denoted by $\breve{\mathbf{x}}$ given by $\breve{x}(a) = 0$ for all $a \neq \breve{a}$ and $\breve{x}(\breve{a}) = 1$. Equation (6.48) implies that $\mathbf{a}(t) = \breve{\mathbf{a}}$ with probability one. Inserting this into equation (6.47) results in

$$x(a, t+1) \quad = \quad x(a,t) + \alpha \cdot \Pi(\breve{\mathbf{a}})$$
$$\cdot \begin{cases} \left[x(\breve{a},t) - C(p(a), p(\breve{a}), t)\right] & \text{if} \quad a = \breve{a} \wedge \Pi(\breve{\mathbf{a}}) \geq 0 \\ C(p(a), p(\breve{a}), t) & \text{if} \quad a = \breve{a} \wedge \Pi(\breve{\mathbf{a}}) < 0 \\ -C(p(a), p(\breve{a}), t) & \text{if} \quad a \neq \breve{a} \wedge \Pi(\breve{\mathbf{a}}) \geq 0 \\ -C'(p(a), p(\breve{a}), t) & \text{if} \quad a \neq \breve{a} \wedge \Pi(\breve{\mathbf{a}}) < 0 \end{cases}$$

(6.49)

Furthermore equation (6.48) inserted into equation (6.45) leads to

$$C(p(a), p(\tilde{a}), t) = \begin{cases} 1 & \text{if} \quad a = \breve{a} \wedge \tilde{a} = \breve{a} \\ 0 & \text{else} \end{cases}$$

(6.50)

while inserting equation (6.48) into equation (6.46) results in

$$C'(p(a), p(\tilde{a}), t) = \begin{cases} \text{not defined} & \text{if} \quad \tilde{a} = \breve{a} \wedge a = \breve{a} \\ \frac{1}{A-1} & \text{if} \quad \tilde{a} = \breve{a} \wedge a \neq \breve{a} \\ 0 & \text{else} \end{cases} \quad . \quad (6.51)$$

Finally inserting equations (6.50) and (6.51) into equation (6.49) the dynamics of reinforcement learning is given by

$$x(\breve{a}, t+1) = \begin{cases} x(\breve{a}, t) & \text{if} \quad \Pi(\breve{a}) \geq 0 \\ x(\breve{a}, t) + \alpha \cdot \Pi(\breve{a}) & \text{if} \quad \Pi(\breve{a}) < 0 \end{cases} \quad (6.52)$$

and

$$x(a, t+1) = \begin{cases} x(a, t) & \text{if} \quad \Pi(\breve{a}) \geq 0 \\ x(a, t) - \alpha \cdot \Pi(\breve{a}) & \text{if} \quad \Pi(\breve{a}) < 0 \end{cases} \quad . \quad (6.53)$$

for all $a \neq \breve{a}$.

This leads to the first necessary condition for a reinforcably stable behaviour:

LEMMA 6.9 (CONDITION RSS-1): *A pure state* $\breve{\mathbf{x}}$ *can be reinforcably stable only if*

$$\Pi(\breve{a}, ..., \breve{a}) \geq 0$$

Proof: The pure state $\breve{a}$ is only stable within a population if it is a stationary state. This means that no behavioural changes are allowed to occur if all individuals commit action $\breve{a}$ for certain. According to equations (6.52) and (6.53) this is the case only if $\Pi(\breve{a}) \geq 0$. ∎

Dynamics in the infinitesimally small neighbourhood of a pure state

If the above condition RSS-1 (Lemma 6.9) is satisfied, action $\breve{a}$ is a stationary behaviour. However for $\breve{a}$ also to be a stable behaviour according to Definition 6.3, behaviour should not diverge further from $\breve{a}$ whenever an infinitesimally small part of the population deviates from this behaviour for external reasons. A state in the infinitesimally small neighbourhood of $\breve{\mathbf{x}}$ is given by an infinitesimally small number of individuals, denoted by $N \cdot \epsilon$, who choose action $\hat{a}$ instead of action $\breve{a}$. Above, the population has been defined as homogeneous. As a consequence, the probability density $f(\mathbf{p}, t)$ has to be the same for all individuals. $f(\mathbf{p}, t)$ is given by a δ-distribution that is defined by (cf. equation (6.48))

$$\int_0^1 \ldots \int_0^1 F(p(1), \ldots, p(\breve{a} - 1), p(\breve{a}), p(\breve{a} + 1), \ldots$$

$$, p(\hat{a} - 1), p(\hat{a}), p(\hat{a} + 1), \ldots, p(A)) \cdot f(\mathbf{p}, t) \, d\mathbf{p} \qquad (6.54)$$

$$= F(0, \ldots, 0, (1 - \epsilon), 0, \ldots, 0, \epsilon, 0, \ldots, 0) \,.$$

On the level of populations, this state is given by $x(a, t) = 0$ for all $a \neq \breve{a}$ and $a \neq \hat{a}$, $x(\hat{a}, t) = \epsilon$, and $x(\breve{a}, t) = 1 - \epsilon$. By this, the state to be analysed is sufficiently defined and can be studied by the same procedure used above.

First, the probability for each action profile to occur has to be calculated. Let me start with the action profile $\mathbf{a}_{i_-}$ of the opponents of a considered individual i. This action profile is given by a binomial distribution. Each of the opponents commits action $\breve{a}$ with probability $(1 - \epsilon)$ and action $\hat{a}$ with probability ϵ. Thus the probability that l opponents realise action $\breve{a}$, and $(n - l - 1)$ opponents realise action $\hat{a}$, is given by

$$\binom{n - 1}{l} \cdot (1 - \epsilon)^l \cdot \epsilon^{n-1-l} \,. \qquad (6.55)$$

ϵ is defined as an infinitesimally small value. Thus all action profiles $\mathbf{a}_{i_-}$ that occur with a probability quadratic in ϵ, are neglected (this neglect is justified as long as not all influences on the learning dynamics depending linearly on ϵ, disappear). Consequently only two action profiles $\mathbf{a}_{i_-}$ are considered; all opponents committing action $\breve{a}$, denoted by $\breve{\mathbf{a}}_{i_-}$, and all opponents committing action $\breve{a}$, except one who realises action $\hat{a}$, denoted by $\hat{\mathbf{a}}_{i_-}$. The first case occurs with probability $(1 - \epsilon)^{n-1}$, the second case with probability $(n - 1) \cdot \epsilon \cdot (1 - \epsilon)^{n-2}$ (cf. equation (6.55)). Furthermore the action of individual i is for a randomly chosen individual $\breve{a}$ with a probability of $(1 - \epsilon)$ and $\hat{a}$ with a probability of ϵ. Inserting the above considerations into equation (6.47), four cases have to be considered. First, individual i realises action $\breve{a}$ and the opponents $\breve{\mathbf{a}}_{i_-}$. Second, individual i realises action $\breve{a}$ and the opponents $\hat{\mathbf{a}}_{i_-}$. Third, individual i realises action $\hat{a}$ and the opponents $\breve{\mathbf{a}}_{i_-}$. Fourth, individual i realises action $\hat{a}$ and the opponents $\hat{\mathbf{a}}_{i_-}$. It results

$$x(a, t+1) - x(a, t)$$

$$= \alpha \cdot (1-\epsilon)^{n-1} \cdot \Pi(\breve{a}, \breve{\mathbf{a}}_{i_-})$$

$$\cdot \begin{cases} \left[1 - \epsilon - C(p(a), p(\breve{a}), t) \right] & \text{if} \quad a = \breve{a} \wedge \Pi(\breve{a}, \breve{\mathbf{a}}_{i_-}) \geq 0 \\ C(p(a), p(\breve{a}), t) & \text{if} \quad a = \breve{a} \wedge \Pi(\breve{a}, \breve{\mathbf{a}}_{i_-}) < 0 \\ -C(p(a), p(\breve{a}), t) & \text{if} \quad a \neq \breve{a} \wedge \Pi(\breve{a}, \breve{\mathbf{a}}_{i_-}) \geq 0 \\ -C'(p(a), p(\breve{a}), t) & \text{if} \quad a \neq \breve{a} \wedge \Pi(\breve{a}, \breve{\mathbf{a}}_{i_-}) < 0 \end{cases}$$

$$+ \alpha \cdot \epsilon \cdot (1-\epsilon)^{n-2} \cdot \Pi(\breve{a}, \hat{\mathbf{a}}_{i_-})$$

$$\cdot \begin{cases} \left[1 - \epsilon - C(p(a), p(\breve{a}), t) \right] & \text{if} \quad a = \breve{a} \wedge \Pi(\breve{a}, \hat{\mathbf{a}}_{i_-}) \geq 0 \\ C(p(a), p(\breve{a}), t) & \text{if} \quad a = \breve{a} \wedge \Pi(\breve{a}, \hat{\mathbf{a}}_{i_-}) < 0 \\ -C(p(a), p(\breve{a}), t) & \text{if} \quad a \neq \breve{a} \wedge \Pi(\breve{a}, \hat{\mathbf{a}}_{i_-}) \geq 0 \\ -C'(p(a), p(\breve{a}), t) & \text{if} \quad a \neq \breve{a} \wedge \Pi(\breve{a}, \hat{\mathbf{a}}_{i_-}) < 0 \end{cases}$$

$$+ \alpha \cdot (1-\epsilon)^{n-1} \cdot \Pi(\hat{a}, \breve{\mathbf{a}}_{i_-})$$

$$\cdot \begin{cases} \left[\epsilon - C(p(a), p(\hat{a}), t) \right] & \text{if} \quad a = \hat{a} \wedge \Pi(\hat{a}, \breve{\mathbf{a}}_{i_-}) \geq 0 \\ C(p(a), p(\hat{a}), t) & \text{if} \quad a = \hat{a} \wedge \Pi(\hat{a}, \breve{\mathbf{a}}_{i_-}) < 0 \\ -C(p(a), p(\hat{a}), t) & \text{if} \quad a \neq \hat{a} \wedge \Pi(\hat{a}, \breve{\mathbf{a}}_{i_-}) \geq 0 \\ -C'(p(a), p(\hat{a}), t) & \text{if} \quad a \neq \hat{a} \wedge \Pi(\hat{a}, \breve{\mathbf{a}}_{i_-}) < 0 \end{cases}$$

$$+ \alpha \cdot \epsilon \cdot (1-\epsilon)^{n-2} \cdot \Pi(\hat{a}, \hat{\mathbf{a}}_{i_-})$$

$$\cdot \begin{cases} \left[\epsilon - C(p(a), p(\hat{a}), t) \right] & \text{if} \quad a = \hat{a} \wedge \Pi(\hat{a}, \hat{\mathbf{a}}_{i_-}) \geq 0 \\ C(p(a), p(\hat{a}), t) & \text{if} \quad a = \hat{a} \wedge \Pi(\hat{a}, \hat{\mathbf{a}}_{i_-}) < 0 \\ -C(p(a), p(\hat{a}), t) & \text{if} \quad a \neq \hat{a} \wedge \Pi(\hat{a}, \hat{\mathbf{a}}_{i_-}) \geq 0 \\ -C'(p(a), p(\hat{a}), t) & \text{if} \quad a \neq \hat{a} \wedge \Pi(\hat{a}, \hat{\mathbf{a}}_{i_-}) < 0 \end{cases}$$

$$(6.56)$$

Again, the next step is to calculate the values of $C(p(a), p(\tilde{a}), t)$ and $C'(p(a), p(\tilde{a}), t)$. Inserting equation (6.54) into equations (6.45) and (6.46) results in

$$C(p(a), p(\tilde{a}), t) = \begin{cases} (1-\epsilon)^2 & \text{if} \quad a = \breve{a} \wedge \tilde{a} = \breve{a} \\ \epsilon \cdot (1-\epsilon) & \text{if} \quad a = \breve{a} \wedge \tilde{a} = \hat{a} \\ \epsilon \cdot (1-\epsilon) & \text{if} \quad a = \hat{a} \wedge \tilde{a} = \breve{a} \\ \epsilon^2 & \text{if} \quad a = \hat{a} \wedge \tilde{a} = \hat{a} \\ 0 & \text{else} \end{cases} \qquad (6.57)$$

and

$$C'(p(a), p(\tilde{a}), t) = \begin{cases} \frac{(1-\epsilon)^3}{\epsilon^2} & \text{if} \quad a = \breve{a} \wedge \tilde{a} = \breve{a} \\ \frac{\epsilon}{\epsilon^2} & \text{if} \quad a = \breve{a} \wedge \tilde{a} = \hat{a} \\ (1-\epsilon)^2 & \text{if} \quad a = \hat{a} \wedge \tilde{a} = \breve{a} \\ \frac{\epsilon^3}{1-\epsilon} & \text{if} \quad a = \hat{a} \wedge \tilde{a} = \hat{a} \\ 0 & \text{else} \end{cases} \tag{6.58}$$

Equations (6.57) and (6.58) can be inserted into equation (6.56). The result is presented most helpfully for each action a separately. In this context, three actions should be distinguished; $\breve{a}$, $\hat{a}$, and any action a with $a \neq \breve{a}$ and $a \neq \hat{a}$. Furthermore, condition RSS-1 is assumed to be satisfied because additional conditions for reinforcably stable states need to be found, i.e., $\Pi(\breve{a}, \breve{\mathbf{a}}_{i_-}) \geq 0$. Moreover all terms that are quadratic in ϵ, or even of higher order in ϵ, are neglected. Then

$$\begin{aligned} x(\breve{a}, t+1) \quad = \quad & x(\breve{a}, t) \\ & + \alpha \cdot \Pi(\breve{a}, \breve{\mathbf{a}}_{i_-}) \cdot \epsilon \\ & + \alpha \cdot \Pi(\breve{a}, \hat{\mathbf{a}}_{i_-}) \cdot \epsilon \cdot \begin{cases} 0 & \text{if} \quad \Pi(\breve{a}, \hat{\mathbf{a}}_{i_-}) \geq 0 \\ 1 & \text{if} \quad \Pi(\breve{a}, \hat{\mathbf{a}}_{i_-}) < 0 \end{cases} \\ & + \alpha \cdot \Pi(\hat{a}, \breve{\mathbf{a}}_{i_-}) \cdot \epsilon \cdot \begin{cases} -1 & \text{if} \quad \Pi(\hat{a}, \breve{\mathbf{a}}_{i_-}) \geq 0 \\ 0 & \text{if} \quad \Pi(\hat{a}, \breve{\mathbf{a}}_{i_-}) < 0 \end{cases} \end{aligned} \tag{6.59}$$

holds for the stationary behaviour $\breve{a}$,

$$\begin{aligned} x(\hat{a}, t+1) \quad = \quad & x(\hat{a}, t) \\ & - \alpha \cdot \Pi(\breve{a}, \breve{\mathbf{a}}_{i_-}) \cdot \epsilon \\ & + \alpha \cdot \Pi(\breve{a}, \hat{\mathbf{a}}_{i_-}) \cdot \epsilon \cdot \begin{cases} 0 & \text{if} \quad \Pi(\breve{a}, \hat{\mathbf{a}}_{i_-}) \geq 0 \\ -1 & \text{if} \quad \Pi(\breve{a}, \hat{\mathbf{a}}_{i_-}) < 0 \end{cases} \\ & + \alpha \cdot \Pi(\hat{a}, \breve{\mathbf{a}}_{i_-}) \cdot \epsilon \cdot \begin{cases} 1 & \text{if} \quad \Pi(\hat{a}, \breve{\mathbf{a}}_{i_-}) \geq 0 \\ 0 & \text{if} \quad \Pi(\hat{a}, \breve{\mathbf{a}}_{i_-}) < 0 \end{cases} \end{aligned} \tag{6.60}$$

for the behaviour $\hat{a}$ that occurred occasionally, and

$$x(a, t+1) = x(a, t) \tag{6.61}$$

for all actions a with $a \neq \breve{a}$ and $a \neq \hat{a}$.

The dynamics of learning in an infinitesimally small neighbourhood of a pure state $\breve{a}$, is given by the equations (6.59), (6.60) and (6.61) if not all terms in these equations vanish (if all terms vanish, the terms quadratic in ϵ have to be considered). Equation (6.61) states that the frequency of an action a in the population does not change as long as no individuals commit this action. Consequently, it is sufficient to study the changes of the share $x(\hat{a}, t)$ of action $\hat{a}$ that has arisen due to the small deviation from the pure state, and the changes of the share $x(\breve{a}, t)$ of action $\breve{a}$ realised most frequently in the population. Only these two shares change over time in the considered state. The sum of all shares, $\sum_{a \in \mathcal{A}} x(a, t)$, has to equal one, so that each increase of $x(\breve{a}, t)$ has to be accompanied by a decrease of $x(\hat{a}, t)$ by the same value. It is sufficient to analyse only one of the two equations (6.59) and (6.60) because the other equation is given by the condition $x(\breve{a}, t) + x(\hat{a}, t) = 1$. Equation (6.59) is studied in the following.

Further conditions for the stability of pure states
Equation (6.59) describes the change of the share $x(\breve{a}, t)$ in the neighbourhood of the pure state in which all individuals choose action $\breve{a}$ for certain. A pure state is reinforcably stable according to Definition 6.3, if the dynamics in every infinitesimally small neighbourhood of the pure state is such that the system does not move further from the pure state. The dynamics in the neighbourhood of a pure state is given by equation (6.59). It does not diverge from the pure state, in which all individuals only choose action $\breve{a}$ if the share $x(\breve{a}, t)$ increases or remains constant. Three further conditions for the stability of a pure state result from these considerations.

> LEMMA 6.10 (CONDITION RSS-2): *A pure state* $\breve{\mathbf{x}}$ *can be reinforcably stable only if*

$$\Pi(\breve{a}, \breve{\mathbf{a}}_{i_-}) \geq \Pi(\hat{a}, \breve{\mathbf{a}}_{i_-}) \qquad \forall \hat{a} \neq \breve{a}$$

Proof: To prove the necessity of condition RSS-2, I assume the opposite and prove that this leads to instability. $\Pi(\breve{a}, \breve{\mathbf{a}}_{i_-}) < \Pi(\hat{a}, \breve{\mathbf{a}}_{i_-})$ implies that $\Pi(\hat{a}, \breve{\mathbf{a}}_{i_-}) > 0$ because $\Pi(\breve{a}, \breve{\mathbf{a}}_{i_-}) > 0$ according to condition RSS-1. Thus from equation (6.59) it results:

$$
\begin{aligned}
x(\breve{a}, t+1) \;=\; & x(\breve{a}, t) \\
& + \alpha \cdot \epsilon \cdot \left[\Pi(\breve{a}, \breve{\mathbf{a}}_{i_-}) - \Pi(\hat{a}, \breve{\mathbf{a}}_{i_-}) \right] \\
& + \alpha \cdot \epsilon \cdot \Pi(\breve{a}, \hat{\mathbf{a}}_{i_-}) \cdot \begin{cases} 0 & \text{if } \Pi(\breve{a}, \hat{\mathbf{a}}_{i_-}) \geq 0 \\ 1 & \text{if } \Pi(\breve{a}, \hat{\mathbf{a}}_{i_-}) < 0 \end{cases}
\end{aligned}
\tag{6.62}
$$

The last term of the right-hand side of equation (6.62) is either zero or negative. Given the assumption that $\Pi(\breve{a}, \breve{\mathbf{a}}_{i_-}) < \Pi(\hat{a}, \breve{\mathbf{a}}_{i_-})$, the second term of the right-hand side of equation (6.62) is negative. Thus the share $x(\breve{a}, t)$ decreases if condition RSS-2 is not fulfilled. ∎

Condition RSS-2 states that for an action $\breve{a}$ to be stable the payoff $\Pi(\breve{a}, \breve{\mathbf{a}}_{i_-})$ that this action gives rise to, if all others choose the same action $\breve{a}$, has to be greater or equal to the payoff $\Pi(\hat{a}, \breve{\mathbf{a}}_{i_-})$ that any other action $\hat{a}$ gives rise to, again playing with individuals who all choose action $\breve{a}$. In other words, individuals must not be able to increase their payoff by switching to another behaviour.

> LEMMA 6.11 (CONDITION RSS-3): *A pure state* $\breve{\mathbf{x}}$ *can be reinforcably stable only if*
>
> $$\Pi(\breve{a}, \breve{\mathbf{a}}_{i_-}) + \Pi(\breve{a}, \hat{\mathbf{a}}_{i_-}) \geq 0 \qquad \forall \hat{a} \neq \breve{a}$$

Proof: Again, I prove the necessity of condition RSS-3 for the stability of a pure state by assuming that condition RSS-3 is not satisfied, that is, I assume $\Pi(\breve{a}, \breve{\mathbf{a}}_{i_-}) < -\Pi(\breve{a}, \hat{\mathbf{a}}_{i_-})$. This implies that $\Pi(\breve{a}, \hat{\mathbf{a}}_{i_-}) < 0$ because $\Pi(\breve{a}, \breve{\mathbf{a}}_{i_-}) > 0$ according to condition RSS-1. Consequently equation (6.59) reads

$$
\begin{aligned}
x(\breve{a}, t+1) \;=\; & x(\breve{a}, t) \\
& + \alpha \cdot \epsilon \cdot \left[\Pi(\breve{a}, \breve{\mathbf{a}}_{i_-}) + \Pi(\breve{a}, \hat{\mathbf{a}}_{i_-}) \right] \\
& + \alpha \cdot \Pi(\breve{a}, \breve{\mathbf{a}}_{i_-}) \cdot \begin{cases} -\epsilon & \text{if} \quad \Pi(\hat{a}, \breve{\mathbf{a}}_{i_-}) \geq 0 \\ 0 & \text{if} \quad \Pi(\hat{a}, \breve{a} - i_-) < 0 \end{cases}
\end{aligned}
\tag{6.63}
$$

Similar to the proof of RSS-2, the last term on the right-hand side of equation (6.63) is either zero or negative. The second term of the right-hand side of equation (6.63) is negative, given the assumption that $\Pi(\breve{a}, \breve{\mathbf{a}}_{i_-}) < -\Pi(\breve{a}, \hat{\mathbf{a}}_{i_-})$. Thus $x(\breve{a}, t)$ decreases if condition RSS-3 is not satisfied. ∎

Condition RSS-3 states that the payoff $\Pi(\breve{a}, \breve{\mathbf{a}}_{i_-})$, obtained if all players choose action $\breve{a}$, should be at least as high as the negative value of the payoff $\Pi(\breve{a}, \hat{\mathbf{a}}_{i_-})$ obtained by an individual choosing action $\breve{a}$, if all other players choose action $\breve{a}$ except one, who chooses action $\hat{a}$. In other words, the payoff in the pure state should balance a possibly negative payoff if one of the opponents deviates from the common action $\breve{a}$. This can be understood as follows: if the deviation of one individual from the common action $\breve{a}$ leads to a negative payoff for all other individuals, they are motivated to abandon their current behaviour. Thus negative payoffs, in the case of deviations from the common action by opponents, destabilise a pure state. Condition RSS-3 gives that, on average, this destabilisation is outweighed by a respectively high payoff for all players choosing action $\breve{a}$.

> LEMMA 6.12 (CONDITION RSS-4): *A pure state $\breve{x}$ can be reinforcably stable only if*
>
> $$\Pi(\breve{a}, \breve{a}_{i_-}) + \Pi(\breve{a}, \hat{a}_{i_-}) - \Pi(\hat{a}, \breve{a}_{i_-}) \geq 0 \qquad \forall \hat{a} \neq \breve{a}$$

Proof: As before, I prove condition RSS-4 by assuming the opposite; $\Pi(\breve{a}, \breve{a}_{i_-}) + \Pi(\breve{a}, \hat{a}_{i_-}) - \Pi(\hat{a}, \breve{a}_{i_-}) < 0$. Since $\Pi(\breve{a}, \breve{a}_{i_-}) > 0$ (condition RSS-1), this assumption can be satisfied only if $\Pi(\breve{a}, \hat{a}_{i_-}) < 0$ and/or $\Pi(\hat{a}, \breve{a}_{i_-}) > 0$. Let me assume that only the first of these inequalities is satisfied. In this case, the assumption that condition RSS-4 is not satisfied implies that $\Pi(\breve{a}, \breve{a}_{i_-}) + \Pi(\breve{a}, \hat{a}_{i_-}) < 0$. This contradicts stability according to condition RSS-3. Subsequently, let me assume that only the latter of the above inequalities is satisfied. In this case, the assumption that condition RSS-4 is not satisfied implies that $\Pi(\breve{a}, \breve{a}_{i_-}) - \Pi(\hat{a}, \breve{a}_{i_-}) < 0$, which contradicts stability according to condition RSS-2. Thus if the assumption $\Pi(\breve{a}, \breve{a}_{i_-}) + \Pi(\breve{a}, \hat{a}_{i_-}) - \Pi(\hat{a}, \breve{a}_{i_-}) < 0$ should lead to the stability of the pure state in which all individuals commit action $\breve{a}$ for certain, both inequalities $\Pi(\breve{a}, \hat{a}_{i_-}) < 0$ and $\Pi(\hat{a}, \breve{a}_{i_-}) > 0$ have to be satisfied. In this case, equation (6.59) reads

$$x(\breve{a}, t+1) = x(\breve{a}, t) + \alpha \cdot \epsilon \cdot \left[\Pi(\breve{a}, \breve{a}_{i_-}) + \Pi(\breve{a}, \hat{a}_{i_-}) - \Pi(\hat{a}, \breve{a}_{i_-}) \right] . \quad (6.64)$$

Again if condition RSS-4 is not satisfied, the share $x(\breve{a}, t)$ decreases. ∎

Condition RSS-4 states that the two destabilising aspects found in condition RSS-2 and condition RSS-3 add up, so that the positive payoff in the case of all individuals realising action $\breve{a}$, has to outweigh both of them simultaneously.

Sufficient conditions for reinforcably stable states

The conditions RSS-1 to RSS-4 are necessary for a pure state, with action $\breve{a}$ committed by all individuals, to be reinforcably stable. However, they have not been proven to be sufficient for a reinforcably stable state.

> THEOREM 6.4: *A pure state based on action $\breve{a}$ is reinforcably stable if the four conditions*

$$\Pi(\breve{a}, \breve{a}_{i_-}) > 0$$

$$\Pi(\breve{a}, \breve{a}_{i_-}) - \Pi(\hat{a}, \breve{a}_{i_-}) > 0 \qquad \forall \hat{a} \neq \breve{a}$$

$$\Pi(\breve{a}, \breve{a}_{i_-}) + \Pi(\breve{a}, \hat{a}_{i_-}) > 0 \qquad \forall \hat{a} \neq \breve{a}$$

$$\Pi(\breve{a}, \breve{a}_{i_-}) + \Pi(\breve{a}, \hat{a}_{i_-}) - \Pi(\hat{a}, \breve{a}_{i_-}) > 0 \qquad \forall \hat{a} \neq \breve{a}$$

$$(6.65)$$

are satisfied.

Proof: In equation (6.59) four cases are distinguished according to the signs of the payoffs $\Pi(\breve{a}, \hat{a}_{i_-})$ and $\Pi(\hat{a}, \breve{a}_{i_-})$. For each of these cases the difference $x(\breve{a}, t+1) - x(\breve{a}, t)$ can be calculated. For each of the cases a difference results that is positive according to one of the inequalities in condition (6.65). Thus the share $x(\breve{a}, t)$ increases in any infinitesimally small neighbourhood of the pure state related to action $\breve{a}$, if condition (6.65) is given. ∎

By conditions RSS-1 to RSS-4 and Theorem 6.4 the stability of all pure states is defined, except if none of the conditions RSS-1 to RSS-4 is violated and one of the following equations is fulfilled.

$$\Pi(\breve{a}, \breve{a}_{i_-}) = 0$$

$$\exists_{\hat{a} \neq \breve{a}} : \qquad \Pi(\breve{a}, \breve{a}_{i_-}) = \Pi(\hat{a}, \breve{a}_{i_-})$$

$$\exists_{\hat{a} \neq \breve{a}} : \qquad \Pi(\breve{a}, \breve{a}_{i_-}) + \Pi(\breve{a}, \hat{a}_{i_-}) = 0$$

$$(6.66)$$

$$\exists_{\hat{a} \neq \breve{a}} : \qquad \Pi(\breve{a}, \breve{a}_{i_-}) + \Pi(\breve{a}, \hat{a}_{i_-}) - \Pi(\hat{a}, \breve{a}_{i_-}) = 0$$

In this case, the terms quadratic in ϵ of equation (6.47) have to be analysed. This mathematical procedure is omitted here for convenience. It has no crucial impact on the interpretation of *reinforcably stable states* because it relates to only a negligible number of parameter sets.

6.3.3 Comments on Reinforcably Stable States

The concept of reinforcably stable states (RSS) can be seen as an alternative to the concepts of *Nash equilibria* or *evolutionary stable strategies*. Therefore, the characteristics of the RSSs and the differences between these concepts will be discussed next.

Condition RSS-2 is identical with the condition for a Nash equilibrium; thus, each RSS is also a Nash equilibrium. The condition for an ESS is slightly stronger than that for a Nash equilibrium, that is, than that given in RSS-2. However this difference relates only to the case of

$\Pi(\breve{a}, \breve{\mathbf{a}}_{i_-}) = \Pi(\hat{a}, \breve{\mathbf{a}}_{i_-})$, a case which is omitted from the above analysis. For a 2×2 game, it has been shown that a RSS always is also an ESS (cf. Brenner 1997). Nevertheless a Nash equilibrium or an ESS do not necessarily have to be a RSS. In addition to the condition for a Nash equilibrium or an ESS, respectively, a RSS also has to fulfil the conditions RSS-1, RSS-3, and RSS-4. The conditions for a RSS are much stronger than those for an ESS or a Nash equilibrium. Therefore the conditions for a RSS may serve as a selection criterion in the case of several Nash equilibria.

Moreover, the conditions for a RSS reveal some crucial new insights into game behaviour. Since RSSs are the result of a reinforcement learning process, they should describe game behaviour adequately whenever individuals repeatedly interact and do not reflect on their behaviour. In such cases, behaviour may deviate crucially from the prediction of traditional game theory. The conditions for a RSS imply that, in such a case a behaviour stabilises only if it leads to a positive payoff (see condition RSS-1). Behaviours resulting in negative payoffs, that is, in outcomes which are regarded to be punishing, are not adopted by individuals. For example, in a *prisoner's dilemma game*, only one Nash equilibrium exists: the defection by all individuals (cf. Osborne & Rubinstein 1994, p. 16). In the case of reinforcement learning, defection is stable only if it leads to a positive payoff for the individuals (see condition RSS-1). In this context, positive payoff means that the outcome is positively reinforcing. For example, receiving money is a positive reinforcer (cf. Alhadeff 1982). Hence if mutual defection always leads to a positive but smaller payoff compared with the payoff for mutual cooperation, then we have to expect individuals to defect if they are learning only by reinforcement. If the payoff for defection, however, is negative, defection is no RSS. Such a case occurs if the inability to establish a *public good* endangers survival. Nevertheless the concept of RSSs does not predict cooperation in such a case. If defection leads to a negative payoff, no RSS exists at all. Defection is not reinforcably stable because it violates condition RSS-1, and cooperation is not reinforcably stable because it violates condition RSS-2. Reinforcement learning leads to a continual change of behaviour in such a case.

A continual change in behaviour, however, may signify cognitive reflection. As soon as individuals are cognitively aware of the situation, the concept of RSS no longer holds, because it is based on the assumption that the individuals learn non-cognitively. To sum up, the concept of RSS states that individuals defect in a dilemma situation if the payoffs for defection are positive. If they are negative, the individuals will most probably engage in other learning processes described in the next sections (the prisoner's dilemma situation is studied in detail in Chapter 10).

In addition there is another important difference between RSSs, Nash equilibria and ESSs. The concept of Nash equilibrium is based on reflection at the individual level. Consequently, mixed strategies can only be interpreted as a stochastic behaviour of the individuals (cf. Osborne & Rubinstein 1994, p. 31). The condition for a *mixed strategy* to be stable, according to the concept of Nash equilibria, is the same as for a pure state. In the case of a mixed ESS, the conditions are also identical to the ones for pure ESSs. However, mixed ESSs can also be interpreted as situations in which part of the population plays only one strategy and part of it plays another (cf. Oechssler 1995). The RSSs are defined on the population level as well. Thus a mixed RSS can be interpreted as different individuals playing different pure states. Above, only the stability of *pure states* has been studied. In general, a stationary state of the dynamics of reinforcement learning given by equation (6.42) has to fulfil the condition

$$\sum_{\hat{\mathbf{a}}} \Big(\prod_{j=2}^{n} x(\hat{a}_j, t) \Big) \int_0^1 \cdots \int_0^1 \tilde{p}(a, t+1, \hat{\mathbf{p}}, \tilde{\mathbf{a}}) \cdot \hat{p}(\hat{a}_1) \cdot f_1(\hat{\mathbf{p}}, t) \, d\hat{\mathbf{p}} = 0 \quad (6.67)$$

$\forall_{a \in \mathcal{A}}$. Condition (6.67) can be satisfied by a mixed strategy. In such a case, the shares of behaviour $x(a, t)$ remain constant. The same holds for the probability density functions $f(\mathbf{p}, t)$. The behaviour of each player, however, does not stop changing. According to equation (6.31) reinforcement learning may lead to a stable behaviour on the individual level, only if the individuals realise a *pure state*. Thus a stable mixed strategy can only be reached on the level of populations. In contrast to the concepts of Nash equilibria or ESSs, such a stable mixed strategy can neither be interpreted as the aggregation of various pure states nor as the result of the realisation of each action with a fixed probability. The individuals change their probability distributions of actions continually if the dynamics on the level of populations converge to a mixed strategy. Therefore, I do not call a stable mixed strategy on the population level, a RSS. On the individual level, a stable mixed strategy cannot exist according to reinforcement learning because, if the behaviour of an individual does not converge to the repeated choice of the same action, the stochastic choice will cause payoffs to occur stochastically and behavioural probabilities to fluctuate.

Chapter 7

Reinforced Consumer Behaviour

One of the main topics in economics is *consumer behaviour*. In microeconomics the behaviour of individual consumers is described by the *utility theory*. Individuals are assumed to distribute their budget over a number of goods in such a way that it maximises their utility. Such a view requires that the individuals either calculate their optimal choice of goods or at least behave as if they optimise. In economics, it is often claimed that individuals learn by experience and that their behaviour converges to the optimal, becoming an observable phenomenon (cf. e.g. Sargent 1993). This statement will be investigated below.

To this end, the analysis is restricted to consumption that is directed by *reinforcement learning*. Obviously, goods exist which are chosen by taking a careful decision, goods with a high value (cars, flats and so on) or services which are important for life (insurance, education and so on). Nevertheless many things, especially those which are bought frequently, are chosen non-cognitively. The consumption of these goods is the result of a reinforcement learning process.

It is claimed here that, in most cases, the consumption of one good is not to be regarded as an alternative to the consumption of another. For example, if individuals decide to buy and read a book, they do not interpret this as a decision not to go to the cinema. Each act of consumption is to be regarded as an independent choice, although the whole *bundle of goods* that is consumed is restricted with respect to time and money. Again this assumption restricts the range of consumer behaviour that

171

can be explained. The present approach cannot be used to analyse the choice between brands or retailers because these decisions are choices between several alternatives. Furthermore, it is not possible to study the consumption of goods that are related with the present approach, although it would be possible to enlarge the approach respectively.

The assumption that consumer decisions are made for each good separately, allows one to analyse a single good separately. However, the consumption of other goods has an impact in so far as it influences the restriction of time and money. The decision itself is assumed to be made non-cognitively. The modified *Bush-Mosteller model* given by equation (3.7) is used to describe the dynamics of this behaviour (cf. e. g. Foxall 1990 for a more comprehensive discussion of reinforcement learning in consumer behaviour). One may also use the principle of melioration, since there is no reason for the exclusive use of the Bush-Mosteller model. However, an arbitrary choice has to be made in order not to duplicate the analysis.

The study of consumer behaviour, based on reinforcement processes incorporates the investigation of the time structure of consumption, a subject generally neglected in the literature. Furthermore, the focus of the present approach is entirely different from the traditional approach to consumer behaviour. Consumption is not regarded as distribution of the scarce resource of money between a set of goods, nor are individuals assumed to be aware of the opportunity costs of each act of consumption. Instead, consumers are assumed to react myopically to the experiences that they gather. Whether such an approach is realistic depends on the personal circumstances of the consumer, as well as the characteristics of the goods under consideration. A more detailed study, and a comparison with empirical data, would be needed to judge in what contexts the present approach is valuable. However, the present approach offers an interpretation of the utility function and therefore an explanation for various aspects of consumption, such as fashion. In the context of the whole book, the approach to consumer behaviour, based on reinforcement learning, is seen as one example of the inclusion of learning processes in studying different topics of economic activity. In my view, the ability of the present approach to attach a meaning to utility functions, and to predict fashion consumption on the basis of a reinforcer, seems to be promising enough to demonstrate that reinforcement learning may also aid in understanding other features of consumer behaviour.

In the first section of this chapter, a model of consumer behaviour, based on reinforcement learning, is discussed. The second section is devoted to the analysis of consumption patterns for fixed circumstances, such as, fixed prices, budgets and preferences. It is shown that the results of traditional consumer theory are an extreme case of the results obtained here. In the third section, the impact of interactions between individuals on consumer behaviour is studied.

7.1 MODELLING CONSUMPTION BEHAVIOUR

7.1.1 Definition of Goods

To analyse consumer behaviour the subject has first to be defined properly. A population of N individuals is assumed to exist where each individual is indexed by i ($i \in \mathcal{I}$, $\mathcal{I}$ may be defined as $\mathcal{I} = \{1, 2, ..., N\}$). All individuals face the same set of goods $\mathcal{G}$ which they may consume. Each good is denoted by g ($g \in \mathcal{G}$), and may be a product or a service. Commodities perceived by the consumers as substitutes are condensed to one good, while commodities that are independently chosen (apart from the dependence on the budget and time restriction) are regarded as different goods.

7.1.2 Reinforcement and Satiety

At each time t each individual i has to make the decision which good (s)he consumes. The decision is denoted by $g_i(t)$. $g_i(t) = g$ means that individual i consumes good g at time t. In contrast to the traditional consumer theory in which the choice of the whole bundle of goods is made simultaneously, the choice of goods is assumed to be made successively here. Again, this assumption is adequate only in situations where consumers decide at a certain point in time to consume a good, and where the consumption of the goods takes some time, although some may require only the time taken to purchase them.

The consumption of good g leads to a certain amount of reinforcement or punishment denoted by a value $\Pi_i(g)$ and which I call *reinforcement strength*. The value $\Pi_i(g)$ has a meaning somewhat similar to the term "utility", as used in traditional consumer theory. It represents the subjective evaluation of a good. However, in contrast to the utility function used as a theoretical construct to describe decisions, the reinforcement strength of a good is defined in a psychological sense. It reflects the reinforcing characteristics of a good. In general, reinforcing characteristics are difficult to analyse on a theoretical basis; however some are well known. These characteristics allow for a theoretical analysis of certain features of consumer behaviour. Other preferences may be obtained by empirical investigations. The changes of preference follow the features outlined in Chapter 5. The following analysis focuses on the implications of certain well-known reinforcing characteristics.

The reinforcement strength $\Pi_i(g)$ possessed by a good is a subjective measure, depending on the individual. Furthermore it depends on the individual's previous choices. In agreement with traditional consumer theory of marginal utilities, reinforcement strengths are assumed to decrease with the frequency of consumption per period of time. The more often a good has been consumed in the past, the less valuable is a repeated consumption of this good. This also corresponds with the psychological knowledge of reinforcement learning. Reinforcers are active only if individuals have been deprived of them in the past. This means that reinforcers are subject to satiation (temporary). The more satiation, the more they lose their reinforcing power. Furthermore, the consumption of other goods may also have an influence on the reinforcement strength $\Pi_i(g)$ of a good. A good generally contains several reinforcers (if the reinforcing characteristics of goods are regarded as their service characteristics, the claim for several reinforcing characteristics combined in one good is similar to the thoughts of Lancaster 1966). For example, a new dish simultaneously satisfies the need for food and the desire for novelty. Similarly, one and the same reinforcer may be contained in several goods. Consequently, the consumption of one good satisfying a certain desire, weakens the reinforcement character of the other good satisfying the same desire. In the traditional approach, this is considered by the definition of the utility function with respect to the whole bundle of goods. Here the goods are assumed to be consumed successively. Hence each consumption of a good g leads to a reinforcement strength $\Pi_i(g)$ on its own. To consider the aspects of satiation or substitution of different goods, $\Pi_i(g)$ has to be defined in a way dependent on previous choices. To this end, a variable called *satiety* is defined. It is denoted by $\mathbf{q}_i(t)$ $(= (q_i(g,t))_{g \in \mathcal{G}})$. For each good g it denotes the satiety $q_i(g,t)$ of individual i with this good at time t. Satiety with a good depends on its consumption in the past. The more a good is consumed, the higher is the satiety with this good. It is assumed here that the influence of the consumption of a good g on satiety $q_i(g,t)$ exponentially vanishes over time. Consequently $q_i(g,t)$ can be defined as

$$q_i(g, t+1) = \varsigma_s \cdot q_i(g,t) + (1 - \varsigma_s) \cdot \delta(g = g_i(t)) \qquad (7.1)$$

with

$$\delta(g = g_i(t)) = \begin{cases} 1 & \text{for} \quad g = g_i(t) \\ 0 & \text{for} \quad g \neq g_i(t) \end{cases} \tag{7.2}$$

where ς_s $(0 < \varsigma_s < 1)$ is the parameter that determines how quickly satiety vanishes if a good is not consumed. This definition is chosen arbitrarily. There may be other plausible definitions.

Reinforcement strength $\Pi_i(g)$ has to be redefined to include the aspect of satiety. In general, reinforcement strengths can be written as $\Pi_i(g, \mathbf{q}_i(t))$.

7.1.3 Temporal Structure of Consumption

Three fundamental differences exist between the present approach to consumer behaviour and traditional consumer theory. First, the utility that a good gives rise to is interpreted as the reinforcement strength of the good. In traditional consumer theory, the utility function is not interpreted; it only reflects the preference order revealed by consumption behaviour. This does not contradict an interpretation of utilities as reinforcement strength. Second, the present concept concerns frequencies and probabilities of consumption instead of the numbers of goods that are consumed. Frequencies and probabilities, however, can be transformed into numbers of goods by the definition of suitable chosen periods of time. Third, the present concept is a dynamic concept. This is the most important difference between this concept and traditional consumer theory. Therefore this will be discussed in more detail.

The consumption of goods is assumed to be a successive process. Each consumption of a good takes some time and the next consumption is considered when the current one has been achieved. The time necessary for each consumption differs between goods. Nevertheless let us assume, for the present approach, that all goods considered take the same amount of time to be consumed. Consequently the learning process can be adequately modelled with discrete time. One unit of time is assumed to be the period of time that is necessary for the consumption of one good. Thus an individual's consumption can be expressed in a diagram like Figure 7.1.

Figure 7.1 shows a possible successive consumption of four goods. Each is consumed with a certain frequency, although the period of time between the consumption of one and the same good varies over time. The time intervals between two acts of consumption of the same good are determined stochastically, and depend on the desire to consume other

good

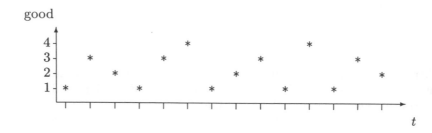

Figure 7.1: *Arbitrarily chosen example for the temporal course of the consumption of four different goods.*

goods in the meantime.

According to the theory of reinforcement learning, people choose actions stochastically. In the context of consumer behaviour, this means that the probability of consuming a good is always given by a probability distribution, here denoted by $\mathbf{p}_i(t)$. This probability distribution is determined by the learning process. The result is a stochastic behaviour, where a good is sometimes quite frequently consumed and at other times rarely. On average, however, the frequency of consumption corresponds to the probability distribution.

This may also be interpreted differently. With each consumption of a good, the satiety increases with respect to this good. According to the first of Gossen's laws, the utility or reinforcement strength of a good decreases with the frequency of its consumption. So each time a good is chosen for consumption, the desire for it decreases. During the period of time in which the good is not consumed, the desire for it increases. In this context, consumption can be seen as the choosing of the currently most desired good. After the act of consumption, the desire for this good decreases and another is chosen. In the present approach, however, the consumers are assumed to learn from their experience, and are not able to choose the good that is most rewarding.

Another important assumption of the present approach is that consumption cannot be aggregated in a meaningful way. The acts of consumption are seen as single events. Thus, no period of consumption and no bundle of goods are defined. Instead an endless process of successive acts is described. The consumption of each single good is seen as an independent process, related to other acts by the time constraint, the budget constraint and satiety. Furthermore, the assumption of a successive consumption of goods, as it is formalised here, implies that at each time t one good is consumed. This has the consequence that there is a maximum number of goods that individuals are able to consume. In contrast, traditional consumer theory neglects time so that consumers are simply regarded as able to consume as many goods as they can afford. In reality, however, time is an important factor of consumption, at least for the kinds of goods considered here. Time is scarce, so that there is pressure in many branches to reduce the time necessary for consumption. An upper limit on the goods that can be consumed is a realistic feature. Nevertheless, a comprehensive study of the implications of the time constraint would require abandoning the assumption that each good takes the same amount of time to consume.

7.1.4 Budget Constraints

Above, a good's reinforcement strength was discussed. At the same time each good also removes a reinforcer, namely money. Money is generally seen as a secondary reinforcer (cf. Alhadeff 1982). Consequently the whole impact of the consumption of a good g is the reinforcement strength caused by consumption minus the reinforcement strength removed by the loss of money.

In the following analysis, a fixed price $P_g(t)$ is assumed to exist for each good at each time t, which is the same for all consumers. Furthermore, each consumer i is assumed to have an average monetary budget of $B_i(t)$ per time available at each time t. In reality, consumers receive the money that they are able to spend, at certain points in time (e. g. a monthly salary). In the present theoretical approach, the monetary budget is assumed to be equally distributed over time. The monetary restriction, however, is not strict. Individuals are able to spend more money one time and less the next.

It is claimed here that individuals do not consider the budget restraint explicitly (remember that only non-cognitive consumption processes are considered). However, the receipt of money is reinforcing while the loss of money is punishing. Therefore money can be considered as a good, just like any other, with a positive reinforcing character. Thus a reinforcement strength can be assigned to money. This reinforcement strength is denoted by $\Pi_i(P, S_i(t))$ where P is the amount of money that is evaluated and $S_i(t)$ is, similar to $q_i(g, t)$, the experience of satiety from money (so far no assumption is made about the increase or decrease of the personal valuation of money, with increasing satiety from money). For example, the price $P_g(t)$ that has to be paid for good g gives rise to a reinforcement strength (in this case a punishment) of $\Pi_i(-P_g(t), S_i(t))$. $S_i(t)$ depends on the amount of money left from previous consumption. The more money is left, the more the individuals are saturated with money and the greater is the value $S_i(t)$. The reinforcement strength $\Pi_i(-P_g(t), S_i(t))$ decreases monotonously in $S_i(t)$. This means that spending money becomes more punishing the less money is left over from the past; this way the budget constraint implicitly directs consumption behaviour. If too much money is spent, individuals become unwilling to spend more. If, instead, money is left over, individuals are more generous. Satiety with respect to money is modelled in correspondence with equation (7.1) as

$$S_i(t+1) = \varsigma_m \cdot S_i(t) + (1 - \varsigma_m) \cdot \Big(B_i(t) - P_{g_i(t)}(t) \Big) \qquad (7.3)$$

where ς_m $(0 < \varsigma_m < 1)$ is the speed of the adaptation of satiety from money to the current flows of money. Since $B_i(t)$ is the budget available at time t and $P_{g_i(t)}(t)$ the price of the good consumed at this time, $B_i(t) - P_{g_i(t)}(t)$ is the spare money left after consumption. ς_m represents the speed of adaptation of satiety to the current amount of spare money.

To clarify the impact of the budget constraint on consumer behaviour in the present modelling, three different time horizons have to be considered. In the very short run, that is, for one single act of consumption, the budget constraint is irrelevant. Given a balanced budget in the past, goods are consumed if their positive reinforcement outweighs the negative reinforcement of their costs, independent of whether their costs exceed the budget constraint or not. In a medium-term perspective, however, the consumption of too-expensive goods, compared to the available budget, evokes a more frugal consumption behaviour afterwards. By this the budget is balanced. Nevertheless, the reinforcement strength of goods compared with the reinforcement strength of money may be too high or too low. In other words, individuals' behaviour with respect to the budget constraint is biased. Some individuals tend to save large amounts or are even unable to spend their money, while others are in debt persistently. These aspects change in the long run but are not considered in the present analysis.

7.1.5 Learning of Consumption Behaviour

Before beginning an analysis of consumer behaviour on the basis of reinforcement learning, the basic assumptions will be repeated. In the following section, consumers are assumed to choose at each time t a good to consume. The good chosen by consumer i is denoted by $g_i(t)$. This good gives rise to a reinforcement strength $\Pi_i(g_i(t), \mathbf{q}_i(t))$ where

$\mathbf{q}_i(t)$ represents the satiety of the consumer i from each good at time t. The dynamics of $\mathbf{q}_i(t)$ are given by equation (7.1). Furthermore, for each good a price has to be paid. A loss of money is assumed to be punishing, so that a second reinforcement is accompanied with each act of consumption. Both reinforcements together determine the reinforcement strength of the consumption of a good.

The following analysis focuses on the consumption of goods that are consumed frequently and are of minor importance for consumers, so that consumers are not motivated to engage in any cognitive reflection about their choice. This means that the consumers choose the goods according to the dynamics of reinforcement learning. The behaviour of consumer i is described in the form of a probability distribution $\mathbf{p}_i(t)$ $(= (p_i(g,t))_{g \in \mathcal{G}})$ at each time t. $p_i(g,t)$ denotes the probability that individual i consumes good g at time t. These probabilities change over time, due to the learning process.

To analyse the generalised Bush-Mosteller model, the reinforcing aspects involved have to be defined for each act of consumption. Two reinforcing aspects are considered. First, the good consumed reinforces individuals. The respective reinforcement strength is given by $\Pi_i(g_i(t), \mathbf{q}_i(t))$. Second, the consumer has to pay for the good; this implies a loss of money. Money is regarded as a secondary reinforcer so that a loss of money is punishing. The respective reinforcement strength is given by $\Pi_i(-P_{g_i(t)}(t), S_i(t))$. I assume that both parts add up to the reinforcement strength

$$\Pi_i(g_i(t), t) = \Pi_i(g_i(t), \mathbf{q}_i(t)) + \Pi_i(-P_{g_i(t)}(t), S_i(t)) \,. \qquad (7.4)$$

The learning process is given by the modified Bush-Mosteller model (cf. equation (3.7):

$$p_i(g, t+1) = p_i(g, t) + \begin{cases} \alpha \cdot \Pi_i(t) \cdot (1 - p_i(g, t)) \\ \quad \text{if} \quad g = g_i(t) \wedge \Pi_i(g_i(t), t) \geq 0 \\[1em] \alpha \cdot \Pi_i(t) \cdot p_i(g, t) \\ \quad \text{if} \quad g = g_i(t) \wedge \Pi_i(g_i(t), t) < 0 \\[1em] -\alpha \cdot \Pi_i(t) \cdot p_i(g, t) \\ \quad \text{if} \quad g \neq g_i(t) \wedge \Pi_i(g_i(t), t) \geq 0 \\[1em] -\alpha \cdot \Pi_i(t) \cdot \frac{p_i(g,t) \cdot p_i(g_i(t), t)}{1 - p_i(g_i(t), t))} \\ \quad \text{if} \quad g \neq g_i(t) \wedge \Pi_i(g_i(t), t) < 0 \end{cases} \qquad (7.5)$$

$\mathbf{p}_i(t)$ denotes the number of pieces of each good which, on average, is consumed at each time t. It is somewhat similar to the economic concept of a *bundle of goods* that individual i consumes at time t, although the goods are assumed to be consumed successively in the present approach. This bundle of goods changes over time according to reinforcement learning. In this context the bundle of goods is defined stochastically. Although the goods are consumed according to the ratio given by $\mathbf{p}_i(t)$ on average, occasions may occur in which one good is not consumed for a period of time, while others are consumed more frequently than usual.

7.2   STABLE CONSUMPTION BEHAVIOUR

7.2.1   Dynamics of Average Consumption

According to the considerations in Chapter 4, there are several alternative methods for analysing stable consumer behaviour although these methods reveal the behaviour only approximately. In the context of consumer behaviour, the focus usually is on the level of populations. Thus fluctuations in the behaviour of individual consumers balance each other out so that they can be ignored. Behaviour on the population level corresponds to the average behaviour of one consumer, which will be analysed below.

The average change of the probability distribution $\mathbf{p}_i(t)$ can be calculated as follows (notice that the dynamics of the quasi-mean values are used, cf. section 4.2.1). At time t one good $g_i(t)$ is consumed by consumer i. Each good $\tilde{g}$ is chosen with the probability $p_i(\tilde{g}, t)$. If good $\tilde{g}$ is chosen and the reinforcement strength $\Pi_i(\tilde{g}, t)$ obtained by consumer i, the probabilities $p_i(g, t)$ change according equation (7.5). These changes occur with a probability $p_i(\tilde{g}, t)$; the probability that good $\tilde{g}$ is chosen. Adding together these changes, multiplied by the probability $p_i(\tilde{g}, t)$ of their occurrences over all goods $\tilde{g}$, the average changes of $p_i(g, t)$ are obtained:

$$p_i(g, t+1) = p_i(g, t) + \alpha \cdot p_i(g, t) \cdot \sum_{\tilde{g} \in \mathcal{G}} h_i(g, \tilde{g}, \Pi_i(\tilde{g}, t)) \cdot \Pi_i(\tilde{g}, t) \cdot p_i(\tilde{g}, t)$$

(7.6)

where $\Pi_i(\tilde{g}, t)$ is the reinforcement strength obtained by consumer i consuming good $\tilde{g}$ at time t and where

$$h_i(g, \tilde{g}, \Pi_i(\tilde{g}, t)) = \begin{cases} \frac{1 - p_i(g,t)}{p_i(g,t)} & \text{if } \tilde{g} = g \wedge \Pi_i(\tilde{g}, t) \geq 0 \\ 1 & \text{if } \tilde{g} = g \wedge \Pi_i(\tilde{g}, t) < 0 \\ -1 & \text{if } \tilde{g} \neq g \wedge \Pi_i(\tilde{g}, t) \geq 0 \\ -\frac{p_i(\tilde{g},t)}{1 - p_i(\tilde{g},t)} & \text{if } \tilde{g} \neq g \wedge \Pi_i(\tilde{g}, t) < 0 \end{cases} .$$

(7.7)

$h_i(g, \tilde{g}, \Pi_i(\tilde{g}, t))$ is independent of g if $\tilde{g} \neq g$ ($h_i(g, \tilde{g}, \Pi_i(\tilde{g}, t))$ has no economic meaning and is only defined for mathematical convenience). Thus for $\tilde{g} \neq g$, a function $h_i(\tilde{g}, \Pi_i(\tilde{g}, t))$ can be defined by

$$h_i(\tilde{g}, \Pi_i(\tilde{g}, t)) = \begin{cases} -1 & \text{if } \Pi_i(\tilde{g}, t) \geq 0 \\ -\frac{p_i(\tilde{g},t)}{1 - p_i(\tilde{g},t)} & \text{if } \Pi_i(\tilde{g}, t) < 0 \end{cases} .$$

(7.8)

Furthermore, in the following equations the abbreviation $H_i(t)$ is used which is defined by

$$H_i(t) = - \sum_{\tilde{g} \in \mathcal{G}} h_i(\tilde{g}, \Pi_i(\tilde{g}, t)) \cdot \Pi_i(\tilde{g}, t) \cdot p_i(\tilde{g}, t) .$$

(7.9)

With the help of this variable, equation (7.6) can be written as

$$p_i(g, t+1) = p_i(g, t) + \alpha \cdot p_i(g, t) \cdot \left[-H_i(t) + p_i(g, t) \cdot \Pi_i(g, t) \right. $$
$$\left. \cdot \Big(h_i(g, g, \Pi_i(g, t)) - h_i(g, \Pi_i(g, t)) \Big) \right] .$$

(7.10)

Inserting equations (7.7) and (7.8) into equation (7.10) results in

$$p_i(g, t+1) = p_i(g, t) + \alpha \cdot p_i(g, t) \cdot \begin{cases} \Pi_i(g, t) - H_i(t) \\ \quad \text{if} \quad \Pi_i(g, t) \geq 0 \\ \Pi_i(g, t)\frac{p_i(g,t)}{1 - p_i(g,t)} - H_i(t) \\ \quad \text{if} \quad \Pi_i(g, t) < 0 \end{cases} \quad (7.11)$$

This equation can be further simplified if a transformed reinforcement strength is defined by

$$\tilde{\Pi}_i(g, t) = \begin{cases} \Pi_i(g, t) & \text{if} \quad \Pi_i(g, t) \geq 0 \\ \Pi_i(g, t)\frac{p_i(g,t)}{1 - p_i(g,t)} & \text{if} \quad \Pi_i(g, t) < 0 \end{cases} \quad (7.12)$$

Subsequently equation (7.11) can be written as

$$p_i(g, t+1) = p_i(g, t) + \alpha \cdot p_i(g, t) \cdot \left(\tilde{\Pi}_i(g, t) - H_i(t) \right). \quad (7.13)$$

This equation describes the dynamics of the quasi-average consumption behaviour (assuming reinforcement learning) in a convenient form and is the basis for the following stability analysis.

7.2.2   Stability of Consumption

In the following section, I analyse the stable consumption behaviour, given the assumption that all circumstances, namely prices, budgets and preferences, are constant. The dynamics of consumption are, on average, such that they converge towards this stable consumption. Thus, stable states of consumption are a good approximation of consumption behaviour in most cases (whenever the circumstances do not change too fast and only one consumption behaviour is stable).

> LEMMA 7.1: *In a stationary state, all goods consumed by individual i give rise to the same transformed reinforcement strength $\tilde{\Pi}_i(g, t) = H_i(t)$.*

Proof: A stationary state is defined by $p_i(g, t+1) = p_i(g, t)$. According to equation (7.13), this condition is satisfied if, and only if, for every good g either $\tilde{\Pi}_i(g, t) = H_i(t)$ or $p_i(g, t) = 0$ holds.   ∎

According to equation (7.4), the reinforcement strength that a good gives rise to depends on the satiety of individual i. The reinforcement strength $\Pi_i(g,t)$ is assumed to decrease with frequency $q_i(g,t)$ of consumption of good g (i.e. the consumption of a good is less reinforcing the more frequently it has been consumed in the past, which holds for most kinds of goods). For nearly each reinforcement strength, a frequency $q_i(g,t)$ can be found, such that the consumption of good g gives rise to this strength. Consequently Lemma 7.1 does not state that goods are only consumed that give rise to the same reinforcement strength. Rather, the goods are consumed to such an extent that they give rise to the same reinforcement strength. There may be some goods that are not able to give rise to a reinforcement strength equal to that of other goods. These goods are not consumed.

> LEMMA 7.2: *All goods that are consumed in a stable state give rise to a positive reinforcement.*

Proof: According to Lemma 7.1, all goods that are consumed in a stable state give rise to the same reinforcement strength. Hence they are either all reinforcing or all punishing. Let me assume that one good exists that is generally reinforcing but is free of charge. An example is the good "relaxation". Since it costs no money, it has only the reinforcing character that it brings about of itself. In addition to relaxing, there are many other activities that cost nothing. It is assumed that an individual is enjoying at least one of these free goods at any given time, though this always gives one reinforcing good for this individual. To help in proving Lemma 7.2, let me assume hypothetically that individual i only consumes goods that are punishing, that is, goods with $\tilde{\Pi}_i(g,t) < 0$, in a state that is supposed to be stable. An infinitesimally small deviation from this state leads to an occasional consumption of the always-reinforcing good. Since the reinforcement strength of this good is higher than those of all the other goods consumed, the probability of consuming this good increases. Consequently, the system departs from the supposedly stable state. Thus a state can be stable only if all goods consumed are reinforcing, when at least one good exists that is always reinforcing. ∎

Once all goods that give rise to a negative reinforcement strength are avoided, the dynamics of the bundle of goods $\mathbf{p}_i(t)$ are given by (cf. equation (7.11)

$$p_i(g, t+1) = p_i(g,t) + \alpha \cdot p_i(g,t) \cdot \left[\Pi_i(g,t) - H_i(t) \right] \qquad (7.14)$$

where $H_i(t)$ is the average reinforcing strength that individual i perceives by consuming the bundle of goods $\mathbf{p}_i(t)$:

$$H_i(t) = \sum_{\tilde{g} \in \mathcal{G}} \Pi_i(\tilde{g}, t) \cdot p_i(\tilde{g}, t) . \tag{7.15}$$

Inserting equation (7.15) into equation (7.14) results in

$$p_i(g, t+1) = p_i(g, t) + \alpha \cdot p_i(g, t) \cdot \left[\Pi_i(g, t) - \sum_{\tilde{g} \in \mathcal{G}} \Pi_i(\tilde{g}, t) \cdot p_i(\tilde{g}, t) \right] . \tag{7.16}$$

This equation is the time-discrete version of the *replicator dynamics*, which is generally given by (cf. e. g. Hofbauer & Sigmund 1984)

$$\frac{dx(g, t)}{dt} = \alpha \cdot x(g, t) \cdot \left[\Pi(g, t) - \sum_{\tilde{g} \in \mathcal{G}} \Pi(\tilde{g}, t) \cdot x(\tilde{g}, t) \right] . \tag{7.17}$$

Thus the dynamics of non-cognitive learning in the context of consumer behaviour, can be approximated by the replicator dynamics.

According to Lemma 7.1, a stationary state is given by $\tilde{\Pi}_i(g, t) = H_i(t)$. $\tilde{\Pi}_i(g, t)$ is given by equation (7.12) and equals $\Pi_i(g, t)$, if $\Pi_i(g, t) \geq 0$, which is given according to Lemma 7.2. Inserting equation (7.4) into $\Pi_i(g, t) = H_i(t)$ results in

$$\Pi_i(g, \mathbf{q}_i(t)) + \Pi_i(-P_g, S_i(t)) = H_i(t) \qquad \forall g \in \mathcal{G} . \tag{7.18}$$

Equation (7.18) has to be fulfilled by a stationary state. If such a state remains for a long period of time $\mathbf{q}_i(t)$ converges to $\mathbf{p}_i(t)$ $(= (p_i(g, t))_{g \in \mathcal{G}})$, which I denote by $\check{\mathbf{p}}_i$ in the case of a stable state. Similarly $S_i(t)$ converges to a constant value which is denoted by $\check{S}_i$ in the following. The same holds for $H_i(t)$, which converges to a value denoted by $\check{H}_i$. Thus for a stable state of consumption, the following holds:

> THEOREM 7.1: *In a stable situation individuals consume all goods in such amounts that they lead to the same reinforcement strength. Goods leading to a smaller reinforcement strength are not consumed. The probability distribution $\check{p}_i(g)$ of consumption is given by*
>
> $$\Pi_i(g, \check{\mathbf{p}}_i) + \Pi_i(-P_g, \check{S}_i) = \check{H}_i \qquad \forall g \in \mathcal{G} \tag{7.19}$$
>
> *where $\check{H}_i$ is a constant determined by $\sum_{g \in \mathcal{G}} \check{p}_i(g) = 1$.*

Proof: According to Lemmas 7.1 and 7.2, a stable state requires that all goods consumed have to give rise to the same positive reinforcement strength. This leads to equation (7.18) which has to be satisfied by a stationary state. Consequently equation (7.19) is a necessary condition for a stable state. Furthermore the reinforcement that a good gives rise to, decreases with the frequency of its consumption. Therefore it can be argued as in traditional consumer theory. A stationary consumption is given by equation (7.19). Assume that a consumer deviates from this consumption pattern by consuming one piece more of good g and one piece less of good $\tilde{g}$. Since both goods have given rise to the same reinforcement strength before, $\Pi_i(g, \breve{\mathbf{p}}_i) < \Pi_i(\tilde{g}, \breve{\mathbf{p}}_i)$ holds after this deviation. Consequently the dynamics of consumer behaviour tend towards the stationary state $\breve{\mathbf{p}}_i$ after such a deviation. Thus a stationary state $\breve{\mathbf{p}}_i$ is always stable. ∎

Equation (7.19) can be also written as

$$\Pi_i(g, \breve{\mathbf{p}}_i) = \breve{H}_i - \Pi_i(-P_g, \breve{S}_i) \ . \tag{7.20}$$

Assuming that $\Pi_i(P_g, \breve{S}_i)$ is linearly decreasing in P_g, it can be written as

$$\Pi_i(P_g, \breve{S}_i) = -\beta_i(\breve{S}_i) \cdot P_g \tag{7.21}$$

where $\beta_i(\breve{S}_i)$ is the evaluation of money by individual i. This evaluation decreases with the spare money $\breve{S}_i$. Inserting equation (7.21) into equation (7.20) it results

$$\frac{\Pi_i(g, \breve{\mathbf{p}}_i) - \breve{H}_i}{P_g} = \beta_i(\breve{S}_i) \ . \tag{7.22}$$

$\beta_i(\breve{S}_i)$ is the same for all goods. It depends on the spare money which, in turn, depends on the budget constraint. The higher the budget of a consumer, the smaller is $\beta_i(\breve{S}_i)$. It seems worth reminding the reader of the fact that equation (7.22) represents the stable state of consumption. The influence of the budget constraint on consumer behaviour is delayed in time. According to equation (7.3) $S_i(t)$ gradually increases after an increase of the monetary budget. This, in turn, leads to a gradual decrease of the evaluation of money $\beta_i(\breve{S}_i)$. Only if the value of $S_i(t)$ has adapted completely to the new budget, is consumer behaviour again stationary. In other words, according to the present consumer theory, individuals adapt their consumption slowly to changes in their budget. In the long run, the adapted behaviour is given by equation (7.22).

Equation (7.22) resembles what traditional consumer theory claims. Since $\beta_i(\breve{S}_i)$ is the same for all goods, the fraction $(\Pi_i(g, \breve{\mathbf{p}}_i) + \breve{H}_i)/P_g$ is the same for all goods as well. Thus for each two goods g and $\tilde{g}$ the following equation holds.

$$\frac{\Pi_i(g, \breve{\mathbf{p}}_i) - \breve{H}_i}{\Pi_i(\tilde{g}, \breve{\mathbf{p}}_i) - \breve{H}_i} = \frac{P_g}{P_{\tilde{g}}} \tag{7.23}$$

(7.23) restates the fundamental result of traditional consumer theory; if $\Pi_i(g, \breve{\mathbf{p}}_i) - \breve{H}_i$ is interpreted as the marginal utility of a good and therefore $\Pi_i(g, \breve{\mathbf{p}}_i) - \breve{H}_i$ divided by the price of the good, is the marginal utility that one unit of money gives rise to, if it is spent for purchasing this good, the marginal utilities per unit of money have to be the same for all goods. Since traditional consumer theory makes no claim about the psychological background of utilities, such an interpretation does not contradict traditional consumer theory. Nevertheless this interpretation of $\Pi_i(g, \breve{\mathbf{p}}_i) - \breve{H}_i$ reveals some interesting facts.

Above it was stated that $\Pi_i(g, \breve{\mathbf{p}}_i)$ is the reinforcement strength of a good and relates to its utility. Now this proves to be correct only if $\breve{H}_i = 0$. Hence $\breve{H}_i$ plays an important role. $H_i(t)$, which converges to $\breve{H}_i$ in the case of a stable consumer behaviour, is defined by equation (7.15). According to Lemma 7.1, $\breve{H}_i$ equals the reinforcement strength each good gives rise to, including the punishing aspect of its costs. Thus for goods in which consumption is based on reinforcement learning, the utility function used in economics represents the reinforcement strength of the good, excluding the aspect of its costs, minus the reinforcement strength from other alternative goods, including the punishing aspect of their costs.

$\breve{H}_i$ may be different for different consumers, although it is always greater than zero (cf. Lemma 7.2). If $\breve{H}_i$ is small, the consumption of a good is only slightly rewarding ($\breve{H}_i$ equals the reinforcement strength of each good including the punishing aspect of its cost). In this case the cost balances out most of the reinforcement obtained from a good. Thus, time has not a high value for a consumer i with a small value of $\breve{H}_i$. Some more time would enable this consumer to consume a little bit more but this consumption would be only slightly rewarding. Consequently the time constraint is not important for such consumers. The constraint that really limits their consumption is the budget constraint.

Consumers with a high value of $\breve{H}_i$, instead, are strongly reinforced by the consumption of goods. For them most of the goods represent a reward that is much more highly evaluated than the money they would have to pay. Thus they would like to consume more but they lack the time to do so. The consumption of these individuals is mainly restricted by the scarcity of time.

To reveal the difference in the consumption pattern displayed between these two kinds of consumers, let me consider two individuals; one with $\check{H}_i = 0$ and one with $\check{H}_i = 0.5$. Furthermore, a good $\tilde{g}$ is assumed to exist that costs $P_{\tilde{g}} = 1$ and gives rise to a reinforcement strength, excluding the aspect of its costs, of $\Pi_i(\tilde{g}, \mathbf{p}_i) = \Pi_j(\tilde{g}, \mathbf{p}_j) = 1$ for both individuals. Furthermore, good g is assumed to give rise to the same reinforcement strength of $\Pi_i(g, \mathbf{p}_i) = \Pi_j(g, \mathbf{p}_j) = \Pi$ for both consumers. Now the question of how much the consumers are willing to pay for the other goods in the stationary state can be answered. For consumer i ($\check{H}_i = 0$) results (cf. equation (7.23))

$$P_g^{(i)} = \Pi \,, \tag{7.24}$$

while for consumer j ($\check{H}_j = 0.5$) one obtains

$$P_g^{(j)} = 2 \cdot \Pi - 1 \,. \tag{7.25}$$

Thus consumer i is willing to pay higher prices than consumer j when $\Pi < 1$, while consumer j is willing to pay higher prices than consumer i when $\Pi > 1$. Hence, consumers that are mainly restricted by the scarcity of time (like consumer j) tend to buy more reinforcing goods for high prices, while consumers that are mainly restricted by the scarcity of money tend to buy less reinforcing goods for low prices. Since the scarcity of money depends on the available monetary budget, we may also state that an increase in the budget causes individuals to consume relatively more expensive goods. I derived this aspect of consumer behaviour without assuming a specific utility function (as is done in traditional consumer theory) but only by assuming that consumer behaviour is the result of reinforcement learning, and that the reinforcement strength of a good decreases with the frequency of its consumption.

7.3 SOCIAL INTERACTION AND CONSUMPTION

Fads and fashions are common features in consumer behaviour; they are caused by interactions between consumers. Nevertheless, they are rarely studied theoretically in the economic literature (exceptions are MacIntegre & Miller 1992, Adams & McCormick 1992, Bikhchandani, Hirshleifer & Welch 1992, Weise 1993 and Weidlich & Brenner 1995). In the present approach to consumer behaviour, fads and fashions are the natural consequences of two primary reinforcers: social appreciation and novelty. I will focus on the influence of social appreciation below.

7.3.1   Reinforcing Characters of a Good

To describe the evolution of fashion, the assumptions discussed above are made again; consumers learn by reinforcement and all goods give rise to a positive reinforcement strength ($\Pi_i(g,t) > 0$). Consequently the dynamics of consumption are given by equation (7.14). The reinforcement strength of a good is given by equation (7.4) where the dependence on the price of the good is assumed to be linear, that is, given by equation (7.21).

While studying one good g, it is assumed that this good is rarely consumed, so that $H_i(t)$ is nearly uninfluenced by its consumption. Hence $H_i(t)$ is constant over time and denoted by H_i (the consumption of the other goods is assumed to be constant). According to equations (7.13), (7.4), (7.21) and the assumptions made, the dynamics of the consumption of good g are given by

$$p_i(g,t+1) = p_i(g,t) + \alpha \cdot p_i(g,t) \cdot \Big(\Pi_i(g_i(t), \mathbf{q}_i(t)) - \beta_i \cdot P_g + H_i \Big) . \quad (7.26)$$

$\Pi_i(g, \mathbf{q}_i(t))$ is the reinforcement strength that good g gives rise to if the satiety of consumer i is given by $\mathbf{q}_i(t)$.

A good generally gives rise to reinforcement in several respects. The reinforcer to be studied here is *social appreciation*. Social appreciation is, for different reasons, caused by many goods. Examples are the extravagance of a good that evokes attention and often admiration, or the scarcity of a good. Below, the focus will be on the *group pressure* to *conform*. Group pressure is important for the evolution of fashions (cf. Venkatesan 1966). It occurs whenever individuals obtain social appreciation for conforming consumer behaviour and social disapproval for divergent consumer behaviour (cf. also Leibenstein 1976).

Therefore the good g is assumed to give rise to two kinds of reinforcers: one that is served by the good itself and one that is served if others consume that good as well. The first one is described by a reinforcement strength $\Pi_i^{(c)}(g, \mathbf{q}_i(t))$ that decreases with the frequency of the consumption of good g in the past. I assume that this reinforcement strength is given by

$$\Pi_i^{(c)}(g, \mathbf{q}_i(g,t)) = \frac{\gamma_{i,c}}{q_i(g,t) + l_i} \qquad (7.27)$$

where $\gamma_{i,c}$ and l_i are positive parameters that characterise the demand for good g and its dependence on satiety $q_i(g,t)$. Equation (7.27) is arbitrarily chosen (cf. Brenner 1995 for a detailed discussion of such a function). The influence of the consumption of other goods on $\Pi_i^{(c)}(g, \mathbf{q}_i(g,t))$ is neglected because the consumption of all other goods is assumed to be constant.

The second reinforcement character of good g is caused by social interaction, by group pressure to conform. The aspect of punishment for deviations from the common behaviour is neglected. The reinforcement strength for conformity depends on the consumer behaviour of the other individuals. The more a good g is consumed by the population, the stronger a single individual is reinforced for the consumption of this good. Average consumption of good g by the population is denoted by $Q(g,t)$. It is given by

$$Q(g,t) = \frac{1}{N} \cdot \sum_{j \in \mathcal{I}} p_j(g,t) . \tag{7.28}$$

For each consumer i only the consumption of the other consumers is relevant. This consumption is given by

$$Q_i(g,t) = \frac{N \cdot Q(g,t) - p_i(g,t)}{N-1} . \tag{7.29}$$

$Q_i(g,t)$ determines the pressure on individual i to consume good g. The higher $Q_i(g,t)$ is, the more reinforcing is the consumption of good g. However the reinforcement strength does not increase linearly with $Q_i(g,t)$. In accordance with the findings of Latané (1981) I assume that the reinforcement strength increases with $Q_i(g,t)^{\rho_i}$. Thus the second reinforcement character is given by

$$\Pi_i^{(s)}(Q_i(g,t)) = \gamma_{i,s} \cdot Q_i(g,t)^{\rho_i} \tag{7.30}$$

where $\gamma_{i,s} > 0$ and $0 < \rho_i \leq 1$.

Adding both reinforcing aspects, one obtains

$$\Pi_i(g, q_i(g,t), Q_i(g,t)) = \frac{\gamma_{i,c}}{q_i(g,t) + l_i} + \gamma_{i,s} \cdot Q_i(g,t)^{\rho_i} . \tag{7.31}$$

7.3.2 Dynamics of Consumption

If the consumption of all other goods is assumed to be constant, the dynamics of the consumption of good g by individual i, is given on average by (cf. equation (7.26))

$$
\begin{aligned}
p_i(g, t+1) &= p_i(g, t) + \alpha \cdot p_i(g, t) \cdot \left(\frac{\gamma_{i,c}}{q_i(g,t)+l_i} + \gamma_{i,s} \cdot Q_i(g,t)^{\rho_i} \right. \\
&\quad - \left. \beta_i(S_i(t)) \cdot P_g + H_i \right) .
\end{aligned}
$$

$$(7.32)$$

Furthermore, the dynamics of the satiety with respect to money is given by equation (7.3). The difference between the monetary budget and the costs of the average consumption of other goods is denoted by $S_{i,0}$. This value is assumed to be constant over time. In addition the consumption of good g reduces the budget by $p_i(g, t) \cdot P_g$ on average. Thus

$$
S_i(t+1) = \varsigma_m \cdot S_i(t) + (1 - \varsigma_m) \cdot \left(S_{i,0} - p_i(g, t) \cdot P_g \right) . \qquad (7.33)
$$

Finally, the function $\beta_i(S_i(t))$ has to be specified. $\beta_i(S_i(t))$ denotes the valuation of money. This valuation depends on the history of each individual; therefore it can hardly be analysed theoretically. It should be more easy to approach the preference for money empirically. Due to the lack of any empirical knowledge about the preference for money, an arbitrary assumption is made here: the valuation of money is rather low as long as there is plenty of money left after consumption and it increases rapidly if the spare money approaches zero. Such an valuation of money can be denoted mathematically by

$$
\beta_i(S_i(t)) = \frac{\gamma_{i,m}}{S_i(t)} . \qquad (7.34)
$$

Inserting equation (7.34) into equation (7.32) it results

$$
\begin{aligned}
p_i(g, t+1) &= p_i(g, t) + \alpha \cdot p_i(g, t) \cdot \left(\frac{\gamma_{i,c}}{q_i(g,t)+l_i} \right. \\
&\quad + \left. \gamma_{i,s} \cdot Q_i(g,t)^{\rho_i} - \frac{\gamma_{i,m} \cdot P_g}{S_i(t)} + H_i \right) .
\end{aligned}
$$

$$(7.35)$$

Equations (7.33) and (7.35) represent the dynamics of the average behaviour of individual i. They do not represent the real behaviour of individual i because that is subject to persistent fluctuations. However if individuals only slowly change their behaviour $p_i(g, t)$ and their satiety from money $S_i(t)$, these equations approximate the real consumption behaviour sufficiently well.

7.3.3 Stable Consumption by One Consumer

To analyse these dynamics the behaviour of all other consumers is first set as constant. Thus $Q_i(g,t)$ is constant. Stationary consumption behaviour $\breve{p}_i(g,t)$ has to fulfil

$$\frac{\gamma_{i,c}}{q_i(g,t)+l_i} - \frac{\gamma_{i,m}\cdot P_g}{S_i(t)} = H_i - \gamma_{i,s}\cdot Q_i(g,t)^{\rho_i} \qquad (7.36)$$

for all goods g with $p_i(g,t) > 0$ and

$$S_i(t) = S_{i,0} - p_i(g,t)\cdot P_g \qquad (7.37)$$

If a stationary behaviour is realised for some period of time, $q_i(g,t)$ converges to $p_i(g,t)$ (cf. equation (7.1)). Thus $q_i(g,t) = \breve{p}_i(g)$. If furthermore, equation (7.37) is inserted in equation (7.36) one obtains

$$\frac{\gamma_{i,c}}{\breve{p}_i(g)+l_i} - \frac{\gamma_{i,m}\cdot P_g}{S_{i,0}-\breve{p}_i(g)\cdot P_g} = H_i - \gamma_{i,s}\cdot Q_i(g,t)^{\rho_i}\ . \qquad (7.38)$$

The right-hand side of equation (7.38) is a constant under the given assumptions. The left-hand side is a monotonously decreasing function in $\breve{p}_i(g)$. Consequently at best, only one value of $\breve{p}_i(g)$ satisfies equation (7.38). The left-hand side of equation (7.38) ranges between $-\infty$ and $\frac{\gamma_{i,c}}{l_i} - \frac{\gamma_{i,m}\cdot P_g}{S_{i,0}}$. Thus one stationary state exists if

$$\frac{\gamma_{i,c}}{l_i} - \frac{\gamma_{i,m}\cdot P_g}{S_{i,0}} > H_i - \gamma_{i,s}\cdot Q_i(g,t)^{\rho_i}\ . \qquad (7.39)$$

If this condition is not fulfilled, the left-hand side of equation (7.38) is always less than the right-hand side. Consequently the dynamics given by equation (7.35) lead to a permanent decrease of $p_i(g,t)$. This means that the consumption of good g disappears if condition (7.39) is not satisfied. The price

$$\hat{P}_{i,g} = \frac{S_{i,0}}{\gamma_{i,m}}\cdot\left[H_i - \gamma_{i,s}\cdot Q_i(g,t)^{\rho_i} - \frac{\gamma_{i,c}}{l_i}\right] \qquad (7.40)$$

is usually called the *prohibitive price*. For all prices above the prohibitive price, good g is not consumed. In the present approach, this price depends on the average consumption $Q_i(g,t)$ of good g by the other consumers. This reflects the interaction between the consumers.

If condition (7.39) is satisfied, one stationary frequency $\breve{p}_i(g)$ of consumption of good g exists. Since the left-hand side of equation (7.38) decreases monotonously, for values of $p_i(g,t)$ less than $\breve{p}_i(g)$ it is greater than the right-hand side of equation (7.38). Consequently $p_i(g,t)$ increases for values less than $\breve{p}_i(g)$ according to equation (7.35). Similarly, $p_i(g,t)$ decreases for values greater than $\breve{p}_i(g)$. Thus whenever a stationary frequency $\breve{p}_i(g)$ exists, it is stable. The consumption of good g by individual i converges to $\breve{p}_i(g)$ independent of the initial state.

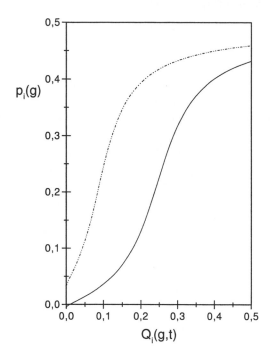

Figure 7.2: *Consumption $\breve{p}_i(g)$ of individual i dependent on the consumption $Q_i(g,t)$ of the other individuals in two arbitrary chosen cases ($\gamma_{i,c} = 5$, $\gamma_{i,m} = 5$, $\gamma_{i,s} = 1$, $\rho_i = 0.7$, $S_i = 0.5$, $P_g = 1$ and $l_{i,g} = 1$). The upper line presents a case in which the good is consumed even if all other individuals neglect the good ($H = 2.5$). The lower line presents a case in which the good would be neglected without social interaction ($H = 5$).*

The stable consumption $\breve{p}_i(g)$ increases with $Q_i(g,t)$. This can be shown by equation (7.38). The left-hand side of this equation decreases monotonously with $\breve{p}_i(g)$ while the right-hand side decreases monotonously with $Q_i(g,t)$. An example of the dependence of $\breve{p}_i(g)$ on $Q_i(g,t)$ is given in Figure 7.2.

7.3.4 Interaction in a Group of Homogeneous Consumers

The stable consumption of individual i is given by equation (7.38) if the consumption behaviour of all other individuals is constant. However if consumers interact, they change their behaviour simultaneously. For each consumer the dynamics of consumption are given by equation (7.35). If all consumers are identical, they consume the same average amount of good g at each time. Thus

$$Q_i(g,t) = p_i(g,t) \, . \tag{7.41}$$

Inserting equation (7.41) into equation (7.35) results in (since all individuals are identical, I omit the index i from now on)

$$
\begin{aligned}
p(g,t+1) \;=\; & p(g,t) + \alpha \cdot p(g,t) \cdot \left(\tfrac{\gamma_c}{q(g,t)+l} \right. \\
& \left. + \gamma_s \cdot p(g,t)^\rho - \tfrac{\gamma_m \cdot P_g}{S_0 - p(g,t) \cdot P_g} + H \right) .
\end{aligned}
\tag{7.42}
$$

The stationary states of these dynamics are given by $p(g,t) = 0$ or

$$\frac{\gamma_c}{q(g,t)+l_g} + \gamma_s \cdot p(g,t)^\rho - \frac{\gamma_m \cdot P_g}{S_0 - p(g,t) \cdot P_g} + H = 0 \, . \tag{7.43}$$

LEMMA 7.3: *There are not more than four stationary states of the learning dynamics given by (7.42).*

Proof: Differentiating the left hand side of equation (7.43) twice with respect to $p(g,t)$ the following term results:

$$\frac{2\gamma_c}{(q(g,t)+l_g)^3} + \rho \cdot (\rho - 1) \cdot \gamma_s \cdot p(g,t)^{\rho-2} - \frac{2\gamma_m \cdot P_g^3}{(S(t) - p(g,t) \cdot P_g)^3} \, . \tag{7.44}$$

This term is monotonously decreasing in $q(g,t)$ (remember that $0 < \rho \le 1$). Consequently it has one zero point at best. This implies that the derivative of the left-hand side of equation (7.43) has two zero points at the most. Finally, this implies that there are three solutions to condition (7.43) at most. In addition, $p(g,t) = 0$ is a stationary state as well. ∎

Between two stable stationary solutions of a one-dimensional differential equation, at least one unstable stationary solution has to exist. Consequently the learning dynamics (7.42) has not more than two stable states.

THEOREM 7.2: *The consumption of a good by a homogeneous population converges to zero, to a fixed value, or to one of two fixed values, if everything else is held constant.*

Proof: Lemma 7.3 implies that four cases have to be distinguished: (1) there is no solution to (7.43), (2) there is one solution, (3) there are two solutions, or (4) there are three solutions. In addition, $p(g,t)$ is bounded to

$$0 \le p(g,t) < \frac{S(t)}{P_g} .$$

If $p(g,t)$ approaches zero, the change of $p(g,t)$ (cf. equation (7.42)) converges to zero as well, so that $p(g,t) = 0$ represents a stationary state. If $p(g,t)$ approaches $\frac{S(t)}{P_g}$ the right-hand side of equation (7.42) becomes negative so that for

$$p(g,t) = \frac{S(t)}{P_g} - \epsilon$$

($\epsilon > 0$ and infinitesimally small) $p(g,t)$ decreases. Thus the state $p(g,t) = \frac{S(t)}{P_g}$ can be treated as an unstable state. The four cases identified above, lead to the following predictions with respect to the stability of the stationary states.

1) If there is no stationary solution for equation (7.43) satisfying

$$0 < p(g,t) \le \frac{S(t)}{P_g} ,$$

an unstable upper boundary implies that the dynamics converge to the lower boundary, in this case $p(g,t) = 0$.

2) If there is one stationary solution for

$$0 < p(g,t) \le \frac{S(t)}{P_g} ,$$

this has either to be stable or a saddle point, because an unstable state cannot be next to an unstable state in a one-dimensional dynamic system. A stochastic process is able to leave a saddle point although it may first converge to it. Thus, the dynamics of the system correspond to the ones for no stationary solution of (7.43) if the only stationary state is a saddle point (the cases with more than one stationary solution reduce similarly). Thus the possibility of saddle points is ignored below because they do not result in sufficiently different dynamics of the system. If the stationary state is stable, $p(g, t)$ converges to the respective value (in this case $p(g, t) = 0$ has to be unstable).

3) If two stationary states exist, one has to be stable and one unstable if they are not saddle points . Since the upper boundary is unstable, the stationary state with the higher value of $p(g, t)$ is stable, the one with the lower value of $p(g, t)$ is unstable, and the state $p(g, t) = 0$ is stable. Consequently, the consumption $p(g, t)$ either converges to the value given by the stable stationary solution or to zero. Between these two stable states an unstable state exists, which divides the range of $p(g, t)$ into the sets of initial states that converge to either of the stable states.

4) Three stationary states imply that two of them are stable while the other is unstable. Similar to the argumentation in case (3), the system converges to one of the stable states, while the unstable state divides the set of initial states with respect to their convergence. ∎

If there is one stable state of consumption, the learning dynamics is similar to the case with no interactions between the consumers. The interesting case is the one with two stable states; in this, the consumption behaviour is *path dependent*. Of these two stable states, one is related to a low consumption of the good and one to a high consumption. Thus they may be interpreted as two market states; a state in which the good is fashionable, and a state in which the good is out of fashion. Which of the two states consumption converges to depends on the initial state. Generally if a new good is introduced, the initial rate of consumption is zero. Subsequently, the consumption converges to the stable state with the lower rate of consumption. The good is not yet fashionable. According to the dynamics discussed above, the good would remain unfashionable forever. The question then arises, how a good becomes fashionable. The present approach offers several answers.

Fluctuations : The above calculations are based on the average behaviour of individuals. Reinforcement, however, leads to fluctuations in individual behaviour. Consequently the behaviour of the homogeneous population fluctuates as well. These fluctuations may cause the system to cross the dividing line between the sets of states that are attracted by either of the stable states. Since in one of these states the good is fashionable (consumed frequently) while in the other it is out of fashion (consumed less frequently), a good may become fashionable by chance. However, the more consumers interact, the less likely are the fluctuations to be large enough to cause a crossing of the dividing line.

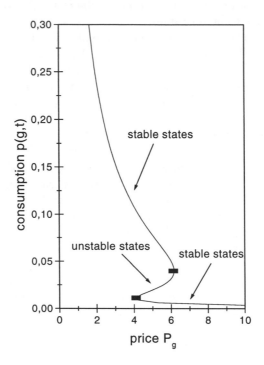

Figure 7.3: *Stable and unstable consumption dependent on the price of a good g ($\gamma_g = 0.1$, $\gamma_m = 1$, $\gamma_s = 7$, $S = 0.5$, $H = 15$, $N = 250$, $\rho = 0.7$ and $l_g = 0$). For an explanation of the meaning of such a bifurcation diagram, see Figure 7.4.*

Price reductions : An interesting result of the present approach is that goods can be made fashionable by a price reduction. For many parameter sets, the stable and unstable amounts of consumption $p(g, t)$ depend on the absolute price of the good, as shown in Figure 7.3.

There is a range of prices (in Figure 7.3 prices between around 4 and 6) for which two stable states exist, while for higher and lower prices only one amount of consumption is stable. Let me assume that the price the supplier charges lies within this range (e. g. $P_g = 5$ in Figure 7.3). Since the good is new on the market, the consumption will converge to the lower stable state (in the case of Figure 7.3 this implies a consumption of less than 0.01 pieces per person and unit of time, while about 0.08 pieces per person and unit of time would be consumed in the other stable state). There is the following way out of the lower stable state: if the price is reduced below the range where two stable states exist (below $P_g = 4$ in figure 7.3), the consumption converges to the only stable state, that is, a state with a high rate of consumption.

After some time, the good has become fashionable, that is, consumption has converged. Then the price can be raised again. The consumption converges from above to the stable state with higher consumption. This means that the good remains fashionable as long as the price is not increased above the range within two stable states. This way, price reductions during the introductory phase of a good may increase later sales. However, a range of prices within two stable states does not exist for all sets of parameters. Only certain goods can become fashionable or unfashionable.

Quality : A similar picture to Figure 7.3 is obtained in many cases for the dependence of $p(g,t)$ on the reinforcement factor γ_c for a good (cf. Figure 7.4). γ_c denotes the experienced reinforcement of the good itself, except the aspects of satiety and social appreciation. Suppliers are able to increase the reinforcement strength of a good by an increase in quality. With the help of fashion, it might be sufficient for a supplier to increase the quality of the product only for a certain period of time. During this period of time, consumption converges to the only stable state with a high consumption. The good becomes fashionable and remains fashionable even if the quality is later reduced, as long as it is not reduced too much.

Desire for novelty : According to the considerations in the context of advertisement, goods become fashionable if their evaluation by consumers is sufficiently increased at the beginning and there are two stable states for the long-run evaluation. Novelty is a primary reinforcer; therefore the evaluation of new goods is generally increased because they satisfy the desire for novelty. This may be sufficient to make the good fashionable. If most of the value of a good is caused by the satisfaction of the desire for novelty, the evaluation of the good decreases permanently. Finally, the stable state with a high consumption of the good disappears and the good is abandoned. This explains the successive occurrence of new fashions.

7.4 SUMMARY

The above studies have shown that an analysis of consumption on the basis of reinforcement learning, offers various new insights into consumer behaviour. Different aspects of goods, such as, their ability to satisfy desires for social appreciation or novelty, can easily be analysed by this approach. Furthermore the dynamics of consumption, generally neglected in the economic literature, can be studied. For example, a process that leads to the change of fashions is outlined above. Moreover in addition to the budget constraint, the time constraint and its influence on consumption can be studied.

In combination with the concept of preferences proposed in Chapter 5 the reinforcing characteristics of goods can be identified in more detail. Subsequently the choice between different goods, brands or retailers may be studied, as well as the changes of preferences and their impact on consumption behaviour, but this is left for further studies.

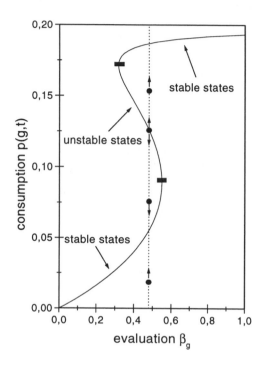

Figure 7.4: *Stable and unstable states dependent on the reinforcement factor* γ_c *(* $\gamma_m = 0.04$, $\gamma_s = 1$, $S = 1$, $H = 15$, $N = 250$, $\rho = 0.7$, $P_g = 5$ *and* $l = 0$*). The logic of this bifurcation diagram can be explained with the help of the dotted line. For an evaluation of* $\gamma_c = 0.48$*, two stable states and one unstable state exist (the three points where the curve and the dotted line intersect). The evaluation was assumed to be constant. Thus the dynamics are restricted to the dotted line. The system always converges to a stable state without crossing an unstable state (see the dots and arrows).*

Chapter 8

Routine-based Choices of Assets

Routine-based learning processes are the most frequently studied learning processes in economics. Economists generally assume that people reflect their actions and try to behave in a way that serves their aims best. Furthermore, they assume that individuals understand the logic of the situation and are able to apply an appropriate learning rule; this rule is determined by the characteristics of the situation. Several rules can be found in the literature (e. g. Bayesian learning, least square learning and the Robbins-Monro algorithm). The assumed rules are designed such that, under certain conditions, they lead to optimal behaviour, at least in the long run.

Learning routines have many different features (cf. the discussion in Sections 3.2 and 3.3). They occur whenever individuals have enough time and cognitive capacity to reason about behaviours and their results. *Cognitive models*, that is, ideas as to how the situation can be best dealt with, determine the features of these learning routines.

Routine-based learning models are an appropriate tool to describe learning whenever cognitive models remain constant over time, that is, if the routines are well established, and whenever there is an incentive to follow these routines due to the importance of the situation. A typical example is the mark-up pricing rule described by R. M. Cyert and J. G. March (1963). Furthermore, there are many routines for dealing with situations which are not that explicitly formulated. Examples are imitations in situations where individuals lack knowledge, or believe that others have more knowledge (relevant for the adoption of new goods, technologies and organisational features), trial and error behaviour in situations where the circumstances remain constant, or routines to handle information if the outcomes are stochastic.

Two examples of routine-based learning will be given here. The first one, concerning the investment behaviour of small savers, will be studied in this chapter and the second one, the diffusion of innovations, in the next. Both approaches should be regarded, first of all, as examples to demonstrate the implications of routine-based learning. In this context of investment behaviour, the approach is restricted to one specific kind of behaviour which, I believe, can frequently be found in the case of small investors, or as I refer to them "small" savers. All other investors have to be excluded from the present analysis.

In the first section of the present chapter, the learning situation and the assumptions are presented. Section 2 is devoted to the analysis of the behaviour of an isolated saver, and lays the mathematical groundwork for the following analyses. In Section 3 savers who exchange information and imitate each other, are analysed. Section 4 presents the theoretical study of investment behaviour in the case of changing interest rates at the financial market. The chapter closes with a short summary.

8.1   BEHAVIOUR OF SMALL SAVERS

8.1.1   Assumptions About the Savers' Behaviour

There is a large amount of literature describing how investors should choose their portfolios when facing a set of capital assets A (cf. e.g. Markowitz 1959 and Lintner 1965). These studies all start with a given preference function, usually a *risk preference function*, and answer the question of how individuals should behave in order to maximise their expected utility in terms of their preference function. In the present approach, the focus is on the real behaviour of small savers and not on the actions we might advise them to take.

According to the categorisation in Chapter 3, three kinds of learning can be distinguished: non-cognitive learning; routine-based learning; and associative learning. The investment of money may lead to high losses and high gains, therefore, it is unlikely for savers to invest their money non-cognitively. As a consequence, two kinds of investors can be distinguished; those with a fixed cognitive model who invest according to a routine, and those who adapt their cognitive model in order to gain a better understanding of the processes of the financial market, and then act accordingly. Examples of the second kind of investors are individuals who develop cognitive models of the dynamics of the assets' prices at the stock market (e. g. *fundamentalists* and *chartists*). These investors will be omitted in the present approach.

> ASSUMPTION 8.1: *Savers, as modelled in the following, believe that they are not able to understand the complex dynamics of assets and search for a satisficing way to invest their spare money on the basis of their experience and information from others (which includes reading the newspapers and using other similar sources of information).*

To model the savers' behaviour, I use a modified version of the VID-model which describes *routine-based* learning.

8.1.2 Distinction Between Routine-based and Associative Learning

In the context of capital investment, the difficulty of distinguishing between *routine-based* and *associative* learning processes becomes obvious. All three kinds of investors, fundamentalists, chartists and adaptive savers, who invest according to experience, have a theory about the regularities of price movements at the stock market. This means that all three of them have a cognitive model that directs their learning processes.

Even adaptive savers have a cognitive model of financial markets. They believe that, apart from certain fluctuations, the future net yields of assets can fairly well be approximated by the past net yields, or they at least assume that they perform well if they stick to assets that have been satisfying in the past. These common beliefs are learnt associatively and may change. However in the present approach, they are taken to remain constant during the considered period of time. It is assumed that the associative learning process leading to this belief took place in the past and does not interfere with the current routine-based learning process, although the cognitive model, that is, the result of the associative learning, determines the features of the learning routine. This also holds for the fundamentalists and chartists.

The principal difference between adaptive savers and fundamentalists or chartists is that adaptive savers act according to a cognitive model (a model that advises them to imitate individuals who were successful in the past) which is helpful under various circumstances, while fundamentalists and chartists have developed specific cognitive models that are relevant to financial markets only. Thus, the learning routines of adaptive savers are much easier to identify than the routines of fundamentalists or chartists, because they can be observed in various situations. Furthermore the learning routines of adaptive savers are generally not the results of experience with financial markets. Whereas the specific cognitive models of fundamentalists or chartists develop while the investors act on, or watch, the stock market (or by the adoption of other individuals' cognitive models). Thus in their case, associative and routine-based learning processes are much more interwoven.

8.1.3   Set of Capital Assets

Before the choice of assets can be modelled, the situation has to be defined in more detail. Each saver is to have a certain amount of spare money each time that (s)he invests in one capital asset (throughout the whole chapter the amount of money the savers invest is ignored, only the assets that they choose are analysed). Thus the savers have to choose each time, one asset of an available set of *capital assets*, denoted by $\mathcal{A}$. The net return that asset a ($a \in \mathcal{A}$) yields at time t is denoted by $\Pi(a, t)$; it is the same for all investors. However the net returns of assets are not given deterministically. They are assumed to be normally distributed every time. The probability that asset a gives rise to a net return of Π at time t, is given by (this assumption is familiar in the theory of *portfolio selection* cf. e. g. Markowitz 1991).

$$P(\Pi|a, t) = \frac{1}{\sqrt{\pi\sigma}} \cdot \exp\left[-\frac{(\Pi - \Pi_0(a, t))^2}{\sigma(a, t)} \right] \qquad (8.1)$$

where $\Pi_0(a, t)$ is the average net return of asset a at time t and $\sigma(a, t)$ the variance of this net return. In Section 8.2 and 8.3 $\Pi_0(a, t)$ and $\sigma(a, t)$ are assumed to be constant:

> ASSUMPTION 8.2: *The probability distribution of the net returns of each asset is constant, i. e.* $\Pi_0(a, t) = \Pi_0(a)$ *and* $\sigma(a, t) = \sigma(a)$.

In Section 8.4 assumption 8.2 will be given up.

8.1.4   Behaviour of Adaptive Savers

According to definition, adaptive savers are those who apply routines that have proved to be generally helpful whenever they have no understanding of the situation faced. The *VID model* has several features that satisfy this requirement; therefore it is used to describe adaptive savers' learning processes. To this end, the VID model is modified slightly to reduce its complexity and adapt it to the present application.

There is a population of N individuals where the set of individuals is denoted by $\mathcal{I}$ and the index i $(i \in \mathcal{I})$ marks all variables belonging to individual i. The action of individual i at time t is given by $a_i(t)$. For convenience, individuals are assumed to invest all their money in one capital asset. If savers are able to split their money, this can be considered by the assumption that each individual i represents one unit of money to be invested, instead of one saver. The main orientation for savers is the information gathered about each alternative asset. This information is represented by *experience* $\eta_i(a, t)$ in the VID model. The utility that assets give rise to is purely monetary, so that the problem of different evaluations by different individuals can be ignored. Thus information about the utility that different assets give rise to, can be exchanged easily. The influence of information about net returns from individual j on the experience of individual i, will be denoted by κ_{ij} (cf. the discussion in Section 3.4.3). Consequently the dynamics of the individuals' experiences is given by (cf. equation (3.28))

$$
\begin{aligned}
\eta_i(a, t+1) \;=\; & \left(1 - \sum_{j \in \mathcal{I}} \delta(a = a_j(t)) \cdot \kappa_{ij}\right) \cdot \eta_i(a, t) \\
+ \; & \sum_{j \in \mathcal{I}} \delta(a = a_j(t)) \cdot \kappa_{ij} \cdot \Pi(a, t)
\end{aligned}
\tag{8.2}
$$

with

$$
\delta(a = a_j(t)) = \left\{ \begin{array}{ll} 1 & \text{for} \quad a = a_j(t) \\ 0 & \text{for} \quad a \neq a_j(t) \end{array} \right. .
\tag{8.3}
$$

Equation (8.2) requires that $\sum_{j \in \mathcal{I}} \kappa_{ij} < 1$ so that the new experience is always a weighted average of the old experience and the new information about an asset a.

Furthermore it is assumed that the *motivation* to change investment behaviour plays a crucial role in the learning process. Individual i's *aspiration level* at time t is denoted by $z_i(t)$. $z_i(t)$ changes over time according to the personal experience and knowledge of other agents' performance. The average net return observed at time t is given by

$$
\left(1 - \sum_{\substack{j=1 \\ j \neq i}}^{N} \kappa_{ij}\right) \cdot \Pi(a_i(t), t) + \sum_{\substack{j=1 \\ j \neq i}}^{N} \kappa_{ij} \cdot \Pi(a_j(t), t) .
\tag{8.4}
$$

In addition, individuals have some tolerance towards a performance below average or a desire to perform better than in the past. This is considered by a value $\Delta\Pi_i$, which is added to the new information on possible net returns. If $\Delta\Pi_i > 0$, individual i intends to outperform the others and the previous results. $\Delta\Pi_i < 0$ implies that individual i is satisfied by a performance lower than the observed average. The dynamics of the aspiration level is given by (cf. equation (3.31) and the corresponding discussion)

$$
\begin{aligned}
z_i(t+1) &= \left(1 - \varsigma_{i,o}\right) z_i(t) + \varsigma_{i,o} \cdot \left((1 - \sum_{\substack{j=1 \\ j \neq i}}^{N} \kappa_{ij}) \cdot \Pi(a_i(t), t) \right. \\
&+ \left. \sum_{\substack{j=1 \\ j \neq i}}^{N} \kappa_{ij} \cdot \Pi(a_j(t), t) + \Delta\Pi_i \right).
\end{aligned}
$$

(8.5)

Remembered satisfaction with the actual behaviour, as defined in Chapter 2, is given by equation (3.32):

$$
\hat{s}_i(t+1) = \left(1 - \varsigma_{i,s}\right) \hat{s}_i(t) + \varsigma_{i,s} \left(\Pi(a_i(t), t) - z_i(t) \right).
$$

(8.6)

Moreover, remembered satisfaction is set to zero each time saver i changes behaviour, because satisfaction caused by the former choice has no influence on current satisfaction.

In the VID model, motivation is caused by dissatisfaction and by the basic desire to change behaviour from time to time. The second aspect is neglected here because it only plays a minor role, if any, in the context of capital investment. Motivation is given by (cf. equation (3.34)

$$
m_i(t) = \begin{cases} 0 & \text{for} \quad \hat{s}_i(t) \geq 0 \\ -\varsigma_{i,m}\hat{s}_i(t) & \text{for} \quad \hat{s}_i(t) < 0 \end{cases}.
$$

(8.7)

Motivation to change performance may lead to a variation of behaviour or an imitation of other individuals. Both processes are described by one equation. The probability of a saver i changing from current asset $a_i(t)$ to another asset $\tilde{a}$, is given by

$$
r_i(\tilde{a}, t) = m_i(t) \cdot \Psi(\eta_i(\tilde{a}, t)) \cdot \Phi(x_i(\tilde{a}, t))
$$

(8.8)

where $x_i(\tilde{a}, t)$ is the subjective knowledge of individual i about the proportion of savers who invest in asset $\tilde{a}$ at time t, i.e.,

$$
x_i(\tilde{a}, t) = \sum_{j=1}^{N} \kappa_{ij} \cdot \delta(a_j(t) = \tilde{a}),
$$

(8.9)

and $\Psi(..)$ and $\Phi(..)$ are monotonously increasing functions in $\eta_i(\tilde{a}, t)$ and $x_i(\tilde{a}, t)$, respectively.

In contrast to the original VID model (cf. Brenner 1996), imitation is not assumed to be more likely the better the observed individual performs (cf. equations (3.35) and (3.40)). Thus $\Phi(x_i(a,t))$ only represents the influence of the number of savers known by individual i to invest currently in asset a. This aspect is similar to the theory of *social impact* by B. Latané (1981). Thus $\Phi(x_i(a,t))$ may be assumed to increase with $x_i(a,t)$ similar to equation (2.4). However in the present context, a change to an asset not chosen by any individual known to individual i is possible as well. Thus

$$\Phi(x_i(a,t)) = \Phi_0 + \beta_i \cdot x_i(a,t)^{\gamma_i} . \qquad (8.10)$$

where $\beta_i > 0$ and $0 < \gamma_i < 1$.

It is important to mention that $r_i(\tilde{a},t)$ given by equation (8.8) depends only on the asset $\tilde{a}$ and not on the asset $a_i(t)$ currently invested in. Current choice has an influence on $r_i(\tilde{a},t)$ only in so far as it determines the motivation $m_i(t)$ to change investment behaviour.

8.2 AN ISOLATED SAVER

To understand the consequences of modelling savers' investment decisions as a boundedly rational learning process, the analysis is first conducted for one isolated small saver. An isolated saver has no possibility of learning from the experience of others or of imitating anyone; (s)he can only learn from her/his own experience. Such a saver seems to be unlikely to exist in a world where information about assets is offered by newspapers and other mass media. The analysis of such a saver is done only for theoretical reasons, to build a basis for further studies.

The rate of change in investment behaviour at time t from a to $\tilde{a}$ is given by (cf. equation(8.8))

$$r_i(\tilde{a},t) = m_i(t) \cdot \Psi(\eta_i(\tilde{a},t)) \cdot \Phi_0 . \qquad (8.11)$$

Equation (8.11) describes the dynamic investment behaviour of an isolated saver. Φ_0 is a constant that describes the overall preparedness to change investment behaviour. However, this constant Φ_0 only influences the speed of the learning process. $m_i(t)$ is a parameter restricted to values above zero and depends on the individual's recent experience. $\Psi(\eta_i(\tilde{a},t))$ is a positive value that represents the influence of the experience with asset $\tilde{a}$ in the past on the decision to choose this asset. $\eta_i(\tilde{a},t)$ considers a long period of time and adapts slowly to new experience. $\Psi(\eta_i(\tilde{a},t))$ is a monotonously increasing function in $\eta_i(\tilde{a},t)$. There may exist a value $\hat{\eta}_i$ such that for all $\eta_i(\tilde{a}, t) < \hat{\eta}_i$, $\Psi(\eta_i(\tilde{a}, t)) = 0$ holds. If such a value $\hat{\eta}_i$ exists, the individual does not choose any asset a that has led to an experience $\eta_i(a, t) < \hat{\eta}_i$. All other assets are chosen, if the individual is motivated to change investment behaviour, with a probability greater than zero. Thus $\hat{\eta}_i$ represents a threshold that determines whether an asset is worth testing.

8.2.1 Stable Behaviour of an Isolated Saver

> LEMMA 8.1 *An investment in asset a is stable if the asset*
> *never gives rise to dissatisfying net returns $(s_i(t) \geq 0)$*
> *or if all other assets lead to unacceptably low net returns*
> *$(\eta_i(\tilde{a}, t) < \hat{\eta}_i \ \forall \ \tilde{a} \neq a)$.*

Proof: An investment in a capital asset a is stable if, and only if, it is stationary. Stationarity of a behaviour requires that the behaviour remains unchanged once it is realised. This means that $r_i(\tilde{a}, t)$ given by equation (8.11) has to be zero for all $\tilde{a} \neq a$ if the saver invests in asset a. Since Φ_0 is a positive constant, either $m_i(t) = 0$ or $\Psi(\eta_i(\tilde{a}, t)) = 0$ for all $\tilde{a} \neq a$. The latter is given only if $\eta_i(\tilde{a}, t)) < \hat{\eta}_i$, that is, if the experience of saver i with asset $\tilde{a}$ is unacceptably bad. $m_i(t) = 0$ is given if $\hat{s}_i(t) \geq 0$ according to equation (8.7). ∎

The two alternative conditions for a stable state, given by Lemma 8.1, are investigated in the following. To analyse the condition $\eta_i(\tilde{a}, t) < \hat{\eta}_i$, the meaning of $\hat{\eta}_i$ has to be discussed. According to the assumptions made, $\Psi(\eta_i(a, t))$ is a monotonously increasing function, and a value $\hat{\eta}_i$ may exist such that $\Psi(\eta_i(a, t)) = 0$ for all $\eta_i(a, t) < \hat{\eta}_i$. The existence of such a value implies that saver i never starts to invest in an asset with $\eta_i(a, t) < \hat{\eta}_i$. Since an isolated saver can collect information about an asset only by investing in it, experience $\eta_i(a, t)$ with an asset a remains constant as long as the asset is not chosen. Thus an asset with $\eta_i(a, t) < \hat{\eta}_i$ has no chance to be chosen ever again. An isolated saver with an acceptance frontier $\hat{\eta}_i$ neglects all assets once they have fallen out of favour. Such a procedure is dangerous because it eliminates one asset after the other, and all assets with $\sigma(a, t) > 0$ sometimes cause an experience $\eta_i(a, t) < \hat{\eta}_i$. In this case, the saver would become more and more inflexible. Therefore, instead of assuming an acceptance frontier in the case of an isolated individual, the following assumption will be made.

> ASSUMPTION 8.3: *An isolated saver i considers every asset*
> *with a probability greater than zero when changing invest-*
> *ment behaviour $(\Psi(\eta_i(a, t))$ is strictly positive).*

Assumption 8.2 implies that investment behaviour can only be stable if $m_i(t) = 0$ (cf. Lemma 8.1). Motivation $m_i(t) = 0$ crucially depends on the aspiration level, which is given by equation (8.5). At a certain time t the following expression holds for $z_i(t)$ (the following equation results after recursively applying equation (8.5)):

$$z_i(t) = \varsigma_{i,o} \cdot \sum_{\tau \in [-\infty, t-1]} \Pi(a_i(\tau), \tau) \cdot \left(1 - \varsigma_{i,o}\right)^{t-\tau-1} + \Delta \Pi_i . \qquad (8.12)$$

To calculate satisfaction in a similar way, it has to be considered that $s_i(t)$ is set to zero whenever saver i changes her/his behaviour. Remembered satisfaction changes according to equation (8.6) only as long as the individual invests in the same asset. If the saver has started to invest in the currently chosen asset at time t_i ($\hat{s}_i(t_i) = 0$), inserting equation (8.12) into equation (8.6) results after some arrangements in

$$
\begin{aligned}
\hat{s}_i(t) \;=\; & \varsigma_{i,s} \cdot \sum_{\tau \in [t_i, t-1]} \Pi(a, \tau) \cdot \frac{\varsigma_{i,s}(1 - \varsigma_{i,s})^{t-\tau-1} - \varsigma_{i,o}(1 - \varsigma_{i,o})^{t-\tau-1}}{\varsigma_{i,s} - \varsigma_{i,o}} \\
& -\; z_i(t_i) \cdot \varsigma_{i,s} \cdot \frac{(1 - \varsigma_{i,s})^{t-t_i} - (1 - \varsigma_{i,o})^{t-t_i}}{\varsigma_{i,o} - \varsigma_{i,s}} \\
& -\; \Delta \Pi_i \cdot \Bigg[1 - (1 - \varsigma_{i,s})^{t-t_i} \\
& \qquad\qquad -\varsigma_{i,s} \cdot \frac{(1 - \varsigma_{i,s})^{t-t_i} - (1 - \varsigma_{i,o})^{t-t_i}}{\varsigma_{i,o} - \varsigma_{i,s}} \Bigg] .
\end{aligned}
$$

$$(8.13)$$

Since $\Pi(a, \tau)$ is distributed according to $P(\Pi|a, t)$ (cf. equation (8.1)), remembered satisfaction $\hat{s}_i(t)$ is a sum of normally distributed variables. Thus $\hat{s}_i(t)$ is normally distributed as well, and its average value is given by (considering Assumption 8.1)

$$
\begin{aligned}
\bar{s}_i(t) \;=\; & \varsigma_{i,s} \cdot \left(\Pi_0(a) - z_i(t_i)\right) \cdot \frac{(1 - \varsigma_{i,s})^{t-t_i} - (1 - \varsigma_{i,o})^{t-t_i}}{\varsigma_{i,o} - \varsigma_{i,s}} \\
& -\; \Delta \Pi_i \cdot \Bigg[1 - (1 - \varsigma_{i,s})^{t-t_i} \\
& \qquad\qquad -\varsigma_{i,s} \cdot \frac{(1 - \varsigma_{i,s})^{t-t_i} - (1 - \varsigma_{i,o})^{t-t_i}}{\varsigma_{i,o} - \varsigma_{i,s}} \Bigg] .
\end{aligned}
$$

$$(8.14)$$

The variance of the remembered satisfaction is given by

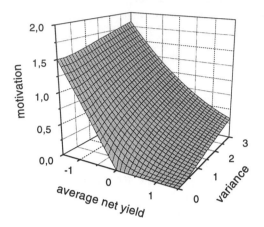

Figure 8.1: *Motivation to change investment behaviour dependent on the average net returns and their variance*

$$\sigma(\hat{s}_i(t)) = \varsigma_{i,s} \cdot \sigma(a)$$

$$\cdot \left[\sum_{\tau \in [t_i, t_0]} \sqrt{-\frac{\varsigma_{i,s}(1 - \varsigma_{i,s})^{t-\tau-1} - \varsigma_{i,o}(1 - \varsigma_{i,o})^{t-\tau-1}}{\varsigma_{i,s} - \varsigma_{i,o}}} \right.$$

$$+ \sum_{\tau \in [t_0, t-1]} \left. \sqrt{\frac{\varsigma_{i,s}(1 - \varsigma_{i,s})^{t-\tau-1} - \varsigma_{i,o}(1 - \varsigma_{i,o})^{t-\tau-1}}{\varsigma_{i,s} - \varsigma_{i,o}}} \right].$$

$$(8.15)$$

Given the history of investment $a_i(t)$ of individual i, remembered satisfaction is normally distributed with average remembered satisfaction and variance given by equations (8.14) and (8.15), respectively. With the help of this distribution, the average motivation to abandon asset

$a_i(t)$ can be calculated. It is given by

$$\bar{m}_i(t) = - \int_{-\infty}^{0} \frac{\varsigma_{i,m}}{\sqrt{\pi \cdot \sigma(s_i(t))}} \cdot s \cdot \exp\left[-\frac{(s - \bar{s}_i(t))^2}{\sigma(s_i(t))} \right] ds . \qquad (8.16)$$

Average motivation depends on average remembered satisfaction and its variance. This dependence is illustrated in Figure 8.1.

Lemma 8.1 in combination with Assumption 8.2 implies that an investment behaviour can only be stable if motivation $m_i(t)$ is zero ($m_i(t) \geq 0$ holds per definition, so that $m_i(t) = 0$ with certainty is equivalent to the condition $\bar{m}_i(t) = 0$). Consequently a saver continues to invest in one asset if the average motivation $\bar{m}_i(t)$ given by equation (8.16), equals zero for all future times. I call such behaviour a stable behaviour.

> DEFINITION 8.1 (STABILITY): *An investment behaviour is called stable if, and only if, a saver who realises this behaviour never changes behaviour in the future.*

An analysis of the stability of investment behaviour results in:

> THEOREM 8.1: *The investment in one asset a by an isolated saver is stable if, and only if, $\sigma(a,t) = 0$ (the asset is a fixed deposit), $\Delta\Pi_i \leq 0$ (the saver is not ambitious) and $z_i(t_i) \leq \Pi_0(a)$ (asset a has to be satisfying when saver i starts to invest in it).*

Proof: According to Lemma 8.1, Assumption 8.3 and Definition 8.1, an investment behaviour is stable if, and only if, it never causes a motivation greater than zero. Equation (8.16) implies that the variance of satisfaction has to be zero and the average satisfaction has to be greater than or equal to zero for the average motivation to vanish. According to equation (8.15), variance of satisfaction is zero if, and only if, $\sigma(a) = 0$. Average satisfaction is given by equation (8.14). It has to be greater or equal to zero for all times $t > t_i$, that is:

$$\varsigma_{i,s} \cdot \Big(\Pi_0(a) - z_i(t_i)\Big) \cdot \frac{(1 - \varsigma_{i,s})^{t-t_i} - (1 - \varsigma_{i,o})^{t-t_i}}{\varsigma_{i,o} - \varsigma_{i,s}}$$
$$-\Delta\Pi_i \cdot \left[1 - \frac{\varsigma_{i,o} \cdot (1 - \varsigma_{i,s})^{t-t_i} - \varsigma_{i,s} \cdot (1 - \varsigma_{i,o})^{t-t_i}}{\varsigma_{i,o} - \varsigma_{i,s}} \right] \geq 0 .$$
$$(8.17)$$

Inserting $t = t_i + 1$ into equation (8.17) one obtains $\Pi_0(a) \geq z_i(t_i)$. Thus,

$\Pi_0(a) \geq z_i(t_i)$ is a necessary condition. Inserting $t \to \infty$ into equation
(8.17) $-\Delta\Pi_i \geq 0$ results. Thus, $\Delta\Pi_i \leq 0$ is a necessary condition as well.
Furthermore $\varsigma_{i,o} < \varsigma_{i,s}$ holds because satisfaction adapts more quickly to
new experience than the aspiration level does (cf. Section 2.2). Thus
$\frac{(1-\varsigma_{i,s})^{t-t_i} - (1-\varsigma_{i,o})^{t-t_i}}{\varsigma_{i,o}-\varsigma_{i,s}} > 0$ and

$$0 < \frac{\varsigma_{i,o} \cdot (1-\varsigma_{i,s})^{t-t_i} - \varsigma_{i,s} \cdot (1-\varsigma_{i,o})^{t-t_i}}{\varsigma_{i,o} - \varsigma_{i,s}} < 1 \ . \qquad (8.18)$$

Consequently, assuming that both conditions, $\Pi_0(a) \geq z_i(t_i)$ and $\Delta\Pi_i \leq$
0, are satisfied, condition (8.17) is satisfied as well. The two conditions
are also sufficient.   ∎

Theorem 8.1 implies that only investment in fixed deposits can be
stable. Furthermore it implies that only investment of individuals with
$\Delta\Pi_i \leq 0$ can stabilise. Therefore two kinds of savers should be distinguished: ambitious and less ambitious.

8.2.2 Less Ambitious Savers

Savers with $\Delta\Pi_i \leq 0$ do not aim at permanently improving their investment behaviour. They are satisfied by net returns equal to the ones they
obtained before, or they may even accept slight decreases in net returns.
Once they are accustomed to low interest rates, they are satisfied with
these rates as long as they stay the same.

Theorem 8.1 states that investing in a fixed deposit with $\Pi_0(a) \geq$
$z_i(t)$ represents a stable investment behaviour for these savers at time
t. $z_i(t)$ is a stochastic variable as long as investing in one fixed deposit
has not stabilised. Thus for any $\Pi_0(a)$, the aspiration level $z_i(t)$ will at
some point in time, be satisfying $z_i(t) \leq \Pi_0(a)$. Consequently for less
ambitious savers, the investment in assets with varying interest rates
becomes unstable at some time. Investing in fixed deposits, on the other
hand, represents an absorbing state. This means that if these individuals
by chance invest their money in an asset with fixed interest rates while
$z_i(t) \leq \Pi_0(a)$, they never change their investment behaviour anymore.
In the long run, one of these absorbing states is reached although this
may take a long time (cf. Section 4.2).

This way, the large number of savers can be explained who only save
in the form of fixed deposits. According to the above considerations,
all less ambitious savers ($\Delta\Pi_i \leq 0$) will buy only fixed deposits in the
long run. However, two influences exist that modify this result. First,
individuals know of the performance of other individuals. As a consequence their aspiration level depends not only on their own experience,

as assumed in equation (8.12), but also on the net returns that other individuals have achieved. Second, the payoffs of different assets change over time, and not only due to fluctuations. For example, the interest rate for a fixed deposit depends on the current rates set by the central bank and on the situation in the financial market. Therefore average net returns of different capital assets change slowly over time. As a result, the shares of individuals who invest in a certain asset also change over time. These two aspects are analysed in Sections 8.3 and 8.4, respectively.

8.2.3 Ambitious Savers

Ambitious savers with $\Delta\Pi_i > 0$ aim at permanently improving their net returns; they always search for better alternatives. According to Theorem 8.1, no stable investment behaviour exists for ambitious savers. Therefore the investment of ambitious savers never stabilises. They are permanently switching from one asset to another in search of higher net returns. The time path of their investment behaviour is difficult to predict. However, the probability of finding such a saver investing in asset a at any randomly chosen point in time, under the assumptions made above, can be calculated.

To this end, changes in investment behaviour have to be analysed. To analyse the frequency of investment in asset a, the probability of starting to invest in asset a, as well as the probability of stopping, have to be studied. Equation (8.11) presents the probability per unit of time for a saver to change from the currently chosen asset a to asset $\tilde{a}$ ($\neq a$) at time t. Thus the probability of abandoning the currently chosen asset at any time t is given by the sum of these rates

$$r_i(a \to, t) = m_i(t) \cdot \Phi_0 \cdot \sum_{\tilde{a} \in \mathcal{A} \backslash \{a\}} \Psi(\eta_i(\tilde{a}, t)) . \qquad (8.19)$$

While savers invest in asset a, their experience $\eta_i(\tilde{a}, t)$ with all other assets $\tilde{a} \neq a$ remains constant. Motivation $m_i(t)$, however, changes according to equations (8.16), (8.14) and (8.15). Inserting equations (8.14) and (8.15) into equation (8.16) does not lead to any mathematical form that is easy to interpret. Thus I pass over the explicit mathematical description of $m_i(t)$. In general it can be stated that $m_i(t)$ decreases with $\Pi_0(a)$ and increases with $\sigma(a)$ and $\Delta\Pi_i$. The average period of time $T_i(a)$ that saver i remains investing in asset a, if (s)he started to do so at time t_i, is given by

$$T_i(a) = 1 + \sum_{\tau=1}^{\infty} \prod_{\tilde{\tau}=1}^{\tau} \left(1 - m_i(t_i + \tilde{\tau}) \cdot \Phi_0 \cdot \sum_{\tilde{a} \in \mathcal{A} \setminus \{a\}} \Psi(\eta_i(\tilde{a}, t_i + \tilde{\tau}))\right) . \quad (8.20)$$

$T_i(a)$ represents the first part of the analysis and answers the question of when the individual stops investing in asset a, which is, on average after a time of $T_i(a)$. This result has to be combined with the answer to the question of how often the individual starts to invest in asset a compared to the other alternative investments. The probability of changing investment behaviour at time t, and choosing capital asset a, is given by $r_i(a,t)$ in equation (8.11). If saver i changes behaviour at time t_i, the probability that (s)he invests in asset a is given by

$$\frac{m_i(t_i) \cdot \Psi(\eta_i(a, t_i)) \cdot \Phi_0}{\sum_{\tilde{a} \in \mathcal{A}} m_i(t_i) \cdot \Psi(\eta_i(\tilde{a}, t_i)) \cdot \Phi_0} . \quad (8.21)$$

Since $m_i(t_i)$ and Φ_0 are independent of $\tilde{a}$, the term (8.21) can be written as

$$\frac{\Psi(\eta_i(a, t_i))}{\sum_{\tilde{a} \in \mathcal{A}} \Psi(\eta_i(\tilde{a}, t_i))} . \quad (8.22)$$

The function $\Psi(\eta_i(\tilde{a}, t))$ has to satisfy $\sum_{\tilde{a} \in \mathcal{A}} \Psi(\eta_i(\tilde{a}, t)) = 1$. Thus the probability that asset a will be the new choice, results in $\Psi(\eta_i(a, t_i))$. The average long run value of $\Psi(\eta_i(a, t_i))$, is denoted by $\bar{\Psi}(\eta_i(a))$ which is the frequency with which the saver starts investing in asset a.

Combining both results leads to:

> THEOREM 8.2: *The average probability $\check{f}_i(a)$ for saver i to invest in asset a in the long run is given by*

$$\check{f}_i(a) = \frac{\bar{\Psi}(\eta_i(a)) \cdot T_i(a)}{\sum_{\tilde{a} \in \mathcal{A}} \bar{\Psi}(\eta_i(a)) \cdot T_i(a)} . \quad (8.23)$$

Proof: asset a is, on average, chosen with probability $\bar{\Psi}(\eta_i(a))$ after a change of investment behaviour. Then saver i stays with this asset for a period of time of $T_i(a)$, on average. Let me assume that saver i has changed her/his behaviour n times in the past. Then each asset has been chosen $n \cdot \bar{\Psi}(\eta_i(a))$ times and the total period of time elapsed is given by $\sum_{\tilde{a} \in \mathcal{A}} n \cdot \bar{\Psi}(\eta_i(\tilde{a})) \cdot T_i(\tilde{a})$. A period of time of $n \cdot \bar{\Psi}(\eta_i(a)) \cdot T_i(a)$ has been spent by saver i investing in asset a. Thus, the probability that saver i has chosen asset a at any time during the considered period of time is given by equation (8.23). ■

Theorem 8.2 has two crucial implications for the behaviour of an isolated saver.

First, isolated adaptive savers do not behave rationally in the sense that they maximise their net return. Nor do they behave rationally in the sense that they maximise their utility according to a risk preference function. The first would imply that they only invest in the capital asset with the highest average net return (according to their perception the asset with the highest value $\eta_i(a,t)$). The latter would imply that assets with the same average returns, but a higher variance of net returns than another asset, would not be chosen. Equation (8.23), however, assigns to each asset a positive share of the available money if $T_i(a) < \infty$ for all $a \in \mathcal{A}$, $\Psi(\eta_i(a,t)) > 0$ and $\Psi(\eta_i(a,t)) < \infty$. $T_i(a) = \infty$ only holds if $m_i(t) = 0$ for $t \to \infty$ (cf. equation (8.20)). $m_i(t) = 0$ cannot hold for an ambitious saver. $\Psi(\eta_i(a,t)) > 0$ holds according to Assumption 8.2. Finally, $\Psi(\eta_i(a,t)) < \infty$ holds because $\eta_i(a,t)$ is finite and $\Psi(..)$ is a monotonous function defined on $(-\infty, \infty)$. Thus every asset is chosen with a positive probability, although this probability may be very small.

Second, isolated savers show a particular form of risk aversion. In the literature individuals are defined as risk averse if they "strictly prefer a certainty consequence to any risky prospect whose mathematical expectation of consequences equals that certainty" (Hirshleifer & Riley 1992, p. 23). According to the traditional understanding, if individuals prefer one option to another, the other is definitely not chosen. In the present approach, however, every option is chosen with a certain probability. Thus a different notion of preferences is needed. The *nominal logit model* offers such an interpretation (cf. e.g. McFadden 1981). According to this model each alternative action a is realised with a probability

$$\frac{\exp(v(a))}{\sum_{\tilde{a} \in \mathcal{A}} \exp(v(\tilde{a}))} \tag{8.24}$$

where $u(a)$ denotes the evaluation of action a. Consequently if action a is preferred to action $\tilde{a}$, action a is chosen more frequently than action $\tilde{a}$ but both actions are chosen with a certain probability. Hence, to study whether savers are risk averse, the frequency of investment in a fixed deposit a has to be compared with the frequency of investment in an asset $\tilde{a}$ with the same average net return but $\sigma(\tilde{a}) > 0$. The same average net return implies that $\bar{\Psi}(\eta_i(a)) = \bar{\Psi}(\eta_i(\tilde{a}))$. Furthermore, the dynamics of average satisfaction, given by equation (8.14), is the same for both assets. However, the variance of satisfaction differs. While $\sigma(s_i(t)) = 0$ in the case of the fixed deposit, $\sigma(s_i(t)) > 0$ for asset $\tilde{a}$. This implies that $\bar{m}_i(t)$ is greater for asset $\tilde{a}$ than for asset a according to equation (8.16) (cf. Figure 8.1). As a consequence, $T_i(a) > T_i(\tilde{a})$ according to equation (8.20). Finally, this implies that asset a is chosen more frequently than asset $\tilde{a}$. Hence an ambitious isolated saver is found to behave as if being risk averse. This risk aversion is not the result of any arbitrarily chosen utility function. In the model used, no assumption has been made about the attitude of savers towards risk. Behaviour similar to risk aversion is found to be the natural result of learning processes described by the VID model, caused by the element of satisficing.

8.3   INTERACTION BETWEEN SAVERS

In reality, savers are able to communicate the experience gained with different capital assets (studies like Walker, Roberts, Burgoyne & Webley 1997 have shown that they really do exchange experience). To analyse the consequences of this exchange of information on investment behaviour, N savers are assumed to act in a financial market. The interaction is assumed to be without any structure. This means that each individual exchanges information with each other individual to the same degree given by κ, i. e., $\kappa_{ij} = \frac{\kappa}{N}$ for all $j \neq i$ in equations (8.2) and (8.5). As a consequence of communication, the variables $\eta_i(a, t)$ and $z_i(t)$ do not only depend on the individual's personal experience but also on the experience of other savers. The average value of $\eta_i(a, t)$ is not affected by information from other savers if they all evaluate net returns identically (which is a plausible assumption since net returns are an objective measure). It might even be assumed that experience $\eta_i(a, t)$ equals average net return $\Pi_0(a)$, because the individuals obtain so much information about the yields of an asset that the average net return is sufficiently precise (the average net return of each asset is constant according to Assumption 8.1). The aspiration level $z_i(t)$, by contrast, changes according to the situation of one saver, due to the exchange of information. In the case of a single saver, the aspiration level is the average net return that (s)he has obtained in the past. If several savers exchange information, the change of the aspiration level of individual i is given by (cf. equation (8.5))

$$z_i(t+1) = \left(1 - \varsigma_{i,o}\right)z_i(t) + \varsigma_{i,o} \cdot \Big((1-\kappa) \cdot \Pi(a_i(t),t)$$
$$+ \kappa \cdot \sum_{\tilde{a} \in \mathcal{A}} x_i(\tilde{a},t) \cdot \Pi(\tilde{a},t) + \Delta\Pi_i\Big) \tag{8.25}$$

where $x_i(a,t)$ is the share of all other individuals who invest in asset a at time t. Since the net return of each asset at time t is given by the normal distribution (8.1) $\sum_{\tilde{a} \in \mathcal{A}} x_i(\tilde{a},t) \cdot \Pi(\tilde{a},t)$ is a normally distributed stochastic value. The more assets that exist, the smaller the variance of this value, if the fluctuations of the net returns of different assets are not correlated. Assuming that there is a sufficient number of assets term (??) can be approximated by its average value. Thus, the dynamics of the aspiration level is given by

$$z_i(t+1) = \left(1 - \varsigma_{i,o}\right)z_i(t) + \varsigma_{i,o} \cdot \Big((1-\kappa) \cdot \Pi(a_i(t),t)$$
$$+ \kappa \cdot \sum_{\tilde{a} \in \mathcal{A}} x_i(\tilde{a},t) \cdot \Pi_0(\tilde{a}) + \Delta\Pi_i\Big) . \tag{8.26}$$

8.3.1 Population Level

According to the calculations from the previous section, most savers change their behaviour persistently. Nevertheless according to the considerations in Section 4.2, the behaviour of savers can be stable on the population level, if the population is infinitely large ($N = \infty$).

ASSUMPTION 8.4: *The number N of savers is sufficiently large so that investment behaviour can be described by assuming $N = \infty$.*

Given Assumption 8.4, a stable investment behaviour may exist on the level of populations. A study of this follows.

A stable investment behaviour on the population level means that the number of individuals who invest in one asset a remains constant, although each individual may change behaviour permanently. Let the share of savers who invest in asset a in the stable state be denoted by $\breve{x}(a)$. The average net return $\bar{\Pi}_0$ obtained by the population of savers is defined by

$$\bar{\Pi}_0 = \sum_{\tilde{a} \in \mathcal{A}} \breve{x}(\tilde{a}) \cdot \Pi_0(\tilde{a}) . \tag{8.27}$$

The dynamics of the aspiration level $z_i(t)$ is given by (cf. equation (8.26))

$$z_i(t+1) = \left(1 - \varsigma_{i,o}\right) z_i(t) + \varsigma_{i,o} \cdot \left((1-\kappa) \cdot \Pi(a_i(t), t) + \kappa \cdot \bar{\Pi}_0 + \Delta \Pi_i\right). \quad (8.28)$$

Similar to equation (8.13), remembered satisfaction is given by

$$
\begin{aligned}
\hat{s}_i(t) \;=\;& \varsigma_{i,s} \cdot \sum_{\tau \in [t_i, t-1]} \Pi(a, \tau) \cdot \frac{\varsigma_{i,s}(1 - \varsigma_{i,s})^{t-\tau-1} - \varsigma_{i,o}(1 - \varsigma_{i,o})^{t-\tau-1}}{\varsigma_{i,s} - \varsigma_{i,o}} \\
-\;& \varsigma_{i,s} \cdot \kappa \cdot \sum_{\tau \in [t_i, t-1]} \Pi(a, \tau) \\
&\cdot \frac{\varsigma_{i,o}(1 - \varsigma_{i,s})^{t-\tau-1} - \varsigma_{i,o}(1 - \varsigma_{i,o})^{t-\tau-1}}{\varsigma_{i,s} - \varsigma_{i,o}} \\
-\;& z_i(t_i) \cdot \varsigma_{i,s} \cdot \frac{(1 - \varsigma_{i,s})^{t-t_i} - (1 - \varsigma_{i,o})^{t-t_i}}{\varsigma_{i,o} - \varsigma_{i,s}} \\
-\;& \left(\kappa \cdot \bar{\Pi}_0 + \Delta \Pi_i\right) \cdot \left[1 - (1 - \varsigma_{i,s})^{t-t_i}\right. \\
-\;& \varsigma_{i,s} \cdot \left. \frac{(1 - \varsigma_{i,s})^{t-t_i} - (1 - \varsigma_{i,o})^{t-t_i}}{\varsigma_{i,o} - \varsigma_{i,s}}\right]
\end{aligned}
$$

$$(8.29)$$

and the average remembered satisfaction is given by (cf. equation (8.14))

$$
\begin{aligned}
\bar{s}_i(t) \;=\;& \varsigma_{i,s} \cdot \left(\Pi_0(a) - z_i(t_i)\right) \cdot \frac{(1 - \varsigma_{i,s})^{t-t_i} - (1 - \varsigma_{i,o})^{t-t_i}}{\varsigma_{i,o} - \varsigma_{i,s}} \\
+\;& \kappa \cdot \Pi_0(a) \left[1 - \frac{\varsigma_{i,o} \cdot (1 - \varsigma_{i,s})^{t-t_i} - \varsigma_{i,s} \cdot (1 - \varsigma_{i,o})^{t-t_i}}{\varsigma_{i,o} - \varsigma_{i,s}}\right] \\
-\;& \left(\kappa \cdot \bar{\Pi}_0 + \Delta \Pi_i\right) \cdot \left[1 - (1 - \varsigma_{i,s})^{t-t_i}\right. \\
-\;& \varsigma_{i,s} \cdot \left. \frac{(1 - \varsigma_{i,s})^{t-t_i} - (1 - \varsigma_{i,o})^{t-t_i}}{\varsigma_{i,o} - \varsigma_{i,s}}\right].
\end{aligned}
$$

$$(8.30)$$

The variance of remembered satisfaction is again a linear function in $\sigma(a)$ and average motivation is given by equation (8.16).

8.3.2   Stable Distribution of Investment

The stochastic behaviour of savers is still given by the considerations in Theorem 8.2, although Φ_0 has now to be replaced by $\Phi(\check{x}(a))$ so that equation (8.23) reads

$$\check{f}_i(a) = \frac{\bar{\Psi}(\eta_i(a)) \cdot \Phi(x(a))}{\sum_{\tilde{a} \in \mathcal{A}} \bar{\Psi}(\eta_i(\tilde{a})) \cdot \Phi(x(\tilde{a}))} \cdot T_i(a) . \tag{8.31}$$

Furthermore, the period of time $T_i(a)$ is not given by equation (8.20) if saver i is able to imitate other savers. $T_i(a)$ now reads

$$T_i(a) = 1 + \sum_{\tau=1}^{\infty} \prod_{\tilde{\tau}=1}^{\tau} \left(1 - m_i(t_i + \tilde{\tau}) \cdot \sum_{\tilde{a} \in \mathcal{A} \setminus \{a\}} \Phi(\check{x}(\tilde{a})) \cdot \Psi(\eta_i(\tilde{a}, t_i + \tilde{\tau})) \right) . \tag{8.32}$$

$m_i(t)$ is still given by equation (8.16) although satisfaction is given by equation (8.29). Thus $m_i(t)$ as well as $\Phi(\check{x}(\tilde{a}))$ depend on the stationary distribution $\check{\mathbf{x}}$ of investment in the population, so that $T_i(a)$ also depends on $\check{\mathbf{x}}$.

The stationary distribution results from addition of all individual distributions:

$$\check{x}(a) = \frac{1}{N} \cdot \sum_{i \in \mathcal{I}} \check{f}_i(a) . \tag{8.33}$$

This equation describes the stationary distribution of investment on the population level. However, some simplifying assumptions have to be made to obtain $f_i(a)$ in a mathematical form that allows for clear interpretation.

ASSUMPTION 8.5: *Savers very slowly ($\varsigma_{i,o} \approx 0$) adapt their aspiration level to new information. In addition, savers have enough information about each alternative asset so that their experience equals the average net return ($\eta_i(a,t) = \Pi_0(a)$). Furthermore, satisfaction is immediately adapted to the current net returns ($\varsigma_{i,s} \approx 1$). Finally, the probability of imitation follows the findings of B. Latané (1981) so that*

$$\Phi(\check{x}(a)) = \Phi_0 \cdot \check{x}(a)^{\beta} . \tag{8.34}$$

Given Assumption 8.5, the stationary behaviour on the individual level can be calculated:

LEMMA 8.2: *Given Assumptions 8.1, 8.2, 8.3, 8.4 and 8.5, the stationary distribution of investment over time of saver i is given by*

$$\check{f}_i(a) \approx C \cdot \frac{\check{x}(a)^{\beta} \cdot \Psi(\Pi_0(a))}{\bar{m}_i(a)} \tag{8.35}$$

where C is given by the condition

$$\sum_{a \in \mathcal{A}} f_i(a) = 1 .$$

(8.36)

Proof: The aspiration level of saver i, given by equation (8.28), can be transformed into the form

$$z_i(t) = \varsigma_{i,0} \cdot \sum_{\tau=-\infty}^{t-1} \left[(1-\kappa) \cdot \Pi(a_i(\tau), \tau) + \kappa \cdot \bar{\Pi}_0 + \Delta\Pi_i \right] \cdot \left(1 - \varsigma_{i,o} \right)^{t-\tau-1} .$$

(8.37)

Inserting $\varsigma_{i,o} \approx 0$ (Assumption 8.5) results in

$$\bar{z}_i \approx (1-\kappa) \cdot \bar{\Pi}_{i,0} + \kappa \cdot \bar{\Pi}_0 + \Delta\Pi_i$$

(8.38)

where $\bar{\Pi}_{i,0}$ is the average net return obtained by saver i in the past. It is given by

$$\bar{\Pi}_{i,0} = \sum_{a \in \mathcal{A}} \Pi_0(a) \cdot \check{f}_i(a)$$

(8.39)

if the stationary state $(\check{f}_i(a))_{a \in \mathcal{A}}$ has persisted for a sufficiently long period of time. Inserting $\varsigma_{i,s} \approx 1$ (Assumption 8.5) and equation (8.38) into equation (8.30) results in

$$\bar{s}_i(a) \approx \left(\Pi_0(a) - (1-\kappa) \cdot \bar{\Pi}_{i,0} - \kappa \cdot \bar{\Pi}_0 - \Delta\Pi_i \right)$$

(8.40)

where the use of $\bar{s}_i(a)$ instead of $\bar{s}_i(t)$ expresses that the average remembered satisfaction depends only on the current choice a and not on the time. The corresponding variance is given by

$$\sigma(s_i(a)) \approx \sigma(a)$$

(8.41)

and the corresponding motivation reads

$$\bar{m}_i(a) = - \int_{-\infty}^{0} \frac{\varsigma_{i,m}}{\sqrt{\pi \cdot \sigma(s_i(a))}} \cdot s \cdot \exp\left[-\frac{(s - \bar{s}_i(a))^2}{\sigma(s_i(a))} \right] ds .$$

(8.42)

Motivation influences the rate of changes of investment according to equation (8.8) in a linear manner. Hence, motivation is a stochastic variable influencing a probability per unit of time linearly. It is, furthermore, not correlated with the other influences on the rate of change $r_i(\tilde{a}, t)$. Thus motivation can be replaced by its average value in equation (8.8) and therefore also in all other equations in which it occurs.

The average motivation $\bar{m}_i(a)$ does not depend on time according to equation (8.42). Thus equation (8.32) holds ($\eta_i(a,t) = \Pi_0(a)$ according to Assumption 7.4 and $\Phi(\check{x}(a)) = \Phi_0 \cdot \check{x}(a)^\beta$ according to equation (8.34))

$$
\begin{aligned}
T_i(a) &= 1 + \sum_{\tau=1}^{\infty} \prod_{\tilde{\tau}=1}^{\tau} \Big(1 \\
&\qquad - \bar{m}_i(a) \cdot \sum_{\tilde{a} \in \mathcal{A} \setminus \{a\}} \Phi_0 \cdot x(\tilde{a})^\beta \cdot \Psi(\Phi_0(\tilde{a})) \Big) \\
&= 1 + \sum_{\tau=1}^{\infty} \Big(1 - \bar{m}_i(a) \cdot \sum_{\tilde{a} \in \mathcal{A} \setminus \{a\}} \Phi_0 \cdot x(\tilde{a})^\beta \cdot \Psi(\Phi_0(\tilde{a})) \Big)^\tau \\
&= \sum_{\tau=0}^{\infty} \Big(1 - \bar{m}_i(a) \cdot \sum_{\tilde{a} \in \mathcal{A} \setminus \{a\}} \Phi_0 \cdot x(\tilde{a})^\beta \cdot \Psi(\Phi_0(\tilde{a})) \Big)^\tau \\
&= \frac{1}{\bar{m}_i(a) \cdot \sum_{\tilde{a} \in \mathcal{A}} \Phi_0 \cdot \check{x}(\tilde{a})^\beta \cdot \Psi(\Pi_0(a))} \; .
\end{aligned}
\tag{8.43}
$$

Inserting equations (8.34) and (8.43) into equation (8.31) one obtains

$$
\check{f}_i(a) = \frac{\check{x}(a)^\beta \cdot \Psi(\Pi_0(a))}{\bar{m}_i(a) \cdot \Phi_0 \cdot \Big(\sum_{\tilde{a} \in \mathcal{A}} \Phi_0 \cdot \check{x}(\tilde{a})^\beta \cdot \Psi(\Pi_0(\tilde{a})) \Big)^2}
\tag{8.44}
$$

■

Thus the stationary distribution on the population level is given by:

THEOREM 8.3: *Given Assumptions 8.1, 8.2, 8.3, 8.4 and 8.5, the stationary behaviour of a population of savers is given by*

$$
\check{x}(a) = \left[\frac{C \cdot \Psi(\Pi_0(a))}{N} \cdot \sum_{i \in \mathcal{I}} \frac{1}{m_i(a)} \right]^{\frac{1}{1-\beta}} .
\tag{8.45}
$$

Proof: Inserting equation (8.44) into equation (8.33) results in

$$
\check{x}(a) = \frac{1}{N} \cdot \sum_{i \in \mathcal{I}} \frac{C \cdot \Psi(\Pi_0(a)) \cdot \check{x}(a)^\beta}{m_i(a)}
\tag{8.46}
$$

Some rearrangements lead to equation (8.45).   ■

It has to be pointed out that the share of individuals investing in asset a is not explicitly given by equation (8.45). Motivation $m_i(a)$ still depends on $\check{x}$ and $\check{f}_i(a)$, so that equation (8.45) represents an implicit equation for $\breve{x}(a)$. Nevertheless, equation (8.45) reveals some important aspects of the average investment behaviour of a population of savers.

A comparison with the results for a single saver helps to understand the influence of information exchange on investment behaviour. The behaviour of a single saver is given by Theorem 8.2. Given Assumption 8.5

$$\breve{f}_i(a) = \frac{C \cdot \Psi(\Pi_0(a))}{m_i(a)} \tag{8.47}$$

results from equations (8.20) and (8.23). This equation can be directly compared to equation (8.45). Three implications for investment behaviour on the population level will be mentioned.

First, investment in an asset a in both cases crucially depends on the preparedness $\Psi(\Pi_0(a))$ of individuals to invest in an asset with an average net return of $\Pi_0(a)$. The higher the average net return of an asset, the more likely it is that individuals will invest in it. Assets that give rise to higher net returns are preferred.

Second, investment in an asset a depends on the motivation to reconsider the current investment. Each asset a gives rise to a different average motivation. Average motivation $\bar{m}_i(a)$ depends on the variance $\sigma(\hat{s}_i(a)) = \sigma(a)$ and the average remembered satisfaction $\bar{s}_i(a)$. Average remembered satisfaction, in turn, depends on the average net return $\bar{\Pi}_0$ in the population, the average net return $\Pi_0(a)$ of asset a, and the individual ambition $\Delta\Pi_i$. This way, motivation depends on individual characteristics ($\Delta\Pi_i$), the performance of the whole population ($\bar{\Pi}_0$), and characteristics of the asset ($\Pi_0(a)$ and $\sigma(a)$).

Investment $\breve{x}(a)$ depends, according to equation (8.45), on the sum of individual motivations, so that the individual characteristics are somewhat levelled. The influences of the population's average net return $\bar{\Pi}_0$ and the asset's characteristics $\Pi_0(a)$ and $\sigma(a)$, remain. The latter dependence on $\Pi_0(a)$ and $\sigma(a)$ also occurred in the case of an isolated saver. The findings in the case of an isolated saver can be transferred to the present case, so that behaviour similar to risk aversion is obtained again. The dependence on the average net return $\bar{\Pi}_0$ of the population occurs only if savers interact. Similar to personal ambition, a high value of $\bar{\Pi}_0$ adds to the aspiration level, and decreases the probability of an investment in assets that give rise to lower average net returns. In other words, if others do better, savers become more ambitious for themselves, while if others do worse, they become less so.

Third, the crucial difference between equation (8.45) and equation (8.47) is that, in the case of a population of savers, the right-hand side of equation (8.45) is raised to the power of $\frac{1}{1-\beta}$. This leads to an exponential increase of $\breve{x}(a)$ with the value

$$\frac{C \cdot \Psi(\Pi_0(a))}{N} \cdot \sum_{i \in \mathcal{I}} \frac{1}{m_i(a)} . \qquad (8.48)$$

Term (8.48) represents the probability of a single saver investing in asset a given by equation (8.47). $\frac{1}{1-\beta} \geq 1$ because $0 \leq \beta < 1$. Thus the term is raised to a power higher than one. All values given by equation (8.48) have to be less than one, because according to equation (8.45) they represent $\breve{x}(a)^{1-\beta}$ with $\breve{x}(a)$ denoting a share which has to satisfy $0 \leq \breve{x}(a) \leq 1$. Therefore the values given by equation (8.48) decrease if they are raised to the power of $\frac{1}{1-\beta}$, whereby higher values are decreased less than smaller values (it is important to state that C is chosen in both cases such that the sum of all $\breve{x}(a)$ is one). Thus, interacting savers invest more frequently in assets with high values (8.48) and less frequently in assets with low values (8.48), compared to single savers. The higher the parameter β is, the more savers adopt what others do, and the more investment is focused on the assets that lead to the highest values of (8.48). For $\beta = 1$, only the asset with the highest value of (8.48) is chosen.

8.4   DYNAMICS IN THE FINANCIAL MARKET

In the above analysis, it was assumed that the characteristics of each asset a, namely the average net return $\Pi_0(a, t)$ and the variance of the net return $\sigma(a, t)$, are constant over time (cf. Assumption 8.1). In reality, however, these values change over time. Therefore in the following section, net returns are assumed to be time-dependent, especially the average net returns of assets. Assumption 8.1 does no longer hold.

As a consequence, the question arises how savers react to a change of the average net returns of one or several assets. If the average net return $\Pi_0(a, t)$ of only one asset a changes, the implications are easy to deduce. More interesting is the case in which the average net returns of several assets simultaneously change in the same direction; this will be analysed below.

To this end, it is assumed, for convenience, that the average net returns $\Pi_0(a, t)$ of all available assets change by the same amount Δ at time $t = 0$. Two kinds of effects can be distinguished: long-run effects and short-run effects.

8.4.1 Long-run Effects

In the long run, the aspiration levels of savers change by the same value Δ. The aspiration level is a weighted average of the net returns experienced personally and by others, plus an individual constant $\Delta\Pi_i$. If the net returns of all assets increase by Δ, any weighted average increases by Δ as well. Thus as soon as the experiences with the old net returns are sufficiently far in the past, the aspiration level is changed by Δ compared to the aspiration level before $t = 0$. As a consequence, the motivation each asset gives rise to is the same in the long run as it was before $t = 0$, because the satisfaction of individuals depends on the difference between the obtained net returns and the aspiration level (in this case both change by the same amount). Thus the behaviour of savers, given by equation (8.45), in the long run changes only due to the changes of $\Psi(\Pi_0(a))$. $\Psi(\Pi_0(a))$ represents the influence of the experience $\eta_i(a,t)$, here equal to the average net return $\Pi_0(a)$, on the choice of an asset if the previous investment is stopped and a new asset has to be chosen. This influence, in combination with the number of individuals who currently invest in asset a, determines the likelihood of saver i to choose asset a in relation to the likelihood of choosing another asset. It seems plausible to assume that if the average net returns $\Pi_0(a)$ of all assets change be the same amount, the relative probabilities of choosing one of them after the abandonment of the previous behaviour, should not change. This means that if $\Psi(\Pi_0(a)) = \gamma \cdot \Psi(\Pi_0(\tilde{a}))$ holds for two assets a and $\tilde{a}$ before the change of all net returns, this relation $\Psi(\Pi_0(a)) = \gamma \cdot \Psi(\Pi_0(\tilde{a}))$ should also hold after the change of the net returns. This persistence of the fraction $\frac{\Psi(\Pi_0(a))}{\Psi(\Pi_0(\tilde{a}))}$ towards equal changes of $\Pi_0(a)$ and $\Pi_0(\tilde{a})$ holds only if $\Psi(.)$ is an exponential function. Given that $\Psi(.)$ is an exponential function, an equal change of the net returns of several assets does not alter the relative attractiveness of these assets compared with each other. As a consequence, the distribution of investment should, in the long run, be the same as the distribution before $t = 0$. If, however, $\Psi(.)$ is not an exponential function, the distribution of investment changes according to the characteristics of function $\Psi(.)$. Such a case will not be further analysed here.

Nevertheless the distribution of investment may change in the long run, due to the fact that, for some savers, the stable distribution of investment $(\check{f}_i(a))_{a\in\mathcal{A}}$ is not unequivocally determined. Less ambitious savers are satisfied by several fixed deposits. As a consequence, investment in one of these fixed deposits represents a stationary behaviour for these savers. The fixed deposit chosen depends on historical contingencies. Let me assume that at time $t = 0$ all less ambitious savers, that is all savers for whom at least the investment in one fixed deposit is stationary, realise a stationary behaviour. If the net returns of all assets increase, the behaviours of less ambitious savers remain stationary. Consequently their behaviour does not change in the long run. If the net returns of all assets decrease, some of the less ambitious savers may be dissatisfied by their current choice, because their net returns decrease while their aspiration level does not react immediately. This is more likely to be the case for fixed deposits with smaller average net returns. As a consequence, these savers search for better ways to invest their money. During this search their aspiration level adapts to the new circumstances. Thus each investment in a fixed deposit that has been stationary before the change becomes stationary again. However, most of those individuals who have invested in the fixed deposits with lower net returns, have adverted their choice. After the change of net returns they choose one of the stationary investment behaviours at random so that an investment in fixed deposits with higher net returns become more likely. This way each decrease of all net returns increases the number of individuals who invest in fixed deposits with high returns, and decreases the number of individuals who invest in fixed deposits with low returns in the long run. Increases of all net returns do not change investment behaviour in the long run.

8.4.2   Short-run Effects

In the short run, a change of all net returns has an impact on the investment behaviour of all individuals. To analyse the changes of investment behaviour in the short run, the dynamics at time Δt with Δt infinitesimally small, is studied. Three variables characterise the state of an individual: experience $\eta_i(a,t)$; aspiration level $z_i(t)$; and remembered satisfaction $s_i(t)$. These three variables are modelled in a similar way to the VID model; their values change gradually according to new experience and information. Thus, if the circumstances change, all three variables adapt slowly to the new circumstances. However, the speed of this adaptation is not the same for the three variables. Satisfaction adapts more quickly to new circumstances compared with the two other variables (cf. discussion in Section 3.4) so it is the variable that first reacts perceptibly. The aspiration levels of the savers can be assumed to remain unchanged during the period of time from $t = 0$ to $t = \Delta t$, i. e.

$$z_i(\Delta t) \approx z_i(0) \ . \tag{8.49}$$

Similarly, the experience $\eta_i(a, t)$ with each asset, remains approximately constant for some time after the change of the net returns. Average satisfaction $\bar{s}_i(a)$, by contrast, increases or decreases by a value Δs_i proportional to Δ until time Δt. Therefore it increases if they increase and decreases if the net returns decrease. The variance of satisfaction remains unchanged, because only the average net returns have been changed and not their variances. Motivation at time $t = 0$ is given by equation (8.42), whereas motivation at time Δt reads (I write $\bar{m}_i(a, \Delta t)$ instead of $\bar{m}_i(a)$ because the motivation at time Δt is later compared with the motivation at time $t = 0$ denoted by $\bar{m}_i(a, 0)$, the average motivation changes due to the change of the net returns)

$$
\begin{aligned}
\bar{m}_i(a, \Delta t) &= -\int_{-\infty}^{0} s \cdot \frac{\varsigma_{i,m}}{\sqrt{\pi \cdot \sigma(\hat{s}_i(a))}} \cdot \exp\left[-\frac{(s - \bar{s}_i(a) - \Delta s_i)^2}{\sigma(\hat{s}_i(a))}\right] ds \\
&= -\int_{-\infty}^{0} s \cdot \frac{\varsigma_{i,m}}{\sqrt{\pi \cdot \sigma(\hat{s}_i(a))}} \cdot \exp\left[-\frac{(s - \bar{s}_i(a))^2}{\sigma(\hat{s}_i(a))}\right] ds \\
&\quad - \int_{-\infty}^{0} \Delta s_i \cdot \frac{\varsigma_{i,m}}{\sqrt{\pi \cdot \sigma(\hat{s}_i(a))}} \cdot \exp\left[-\frac{(s - \bar{s}_i(a))^2}{\sigma(\hat{s}_i(a))}\right] ds \\
&\quad - \int_{0}^{-\Delta s_i} \left(s + \Delta s_i\right) \cdot \frac{\varsigma_{i,m}}{\sqrt{\pi \cdot \sigma(\hat{s}_i(a))}} \\
&\quad \cdot \exp\left[-\frac{(s - \bar{s}_i(a))^2}{\sigma(\hat{s}_i(a))}\right] ds .
\end{aligned}
$$

$$(8.50)$$

With the help of equation (8.42) one obtains

$$
\begin{aligned}
\bar{m}_i(a, \Delta t) &= \bar{m}_i(a, 0) - \int_{-\infty}^{0} \Delta s_i \cdot \frac{\sigma_{i,m}}{\sqrt{\pi \cdot \sigma(\hat{s}_i(a))}} \cdot \exp\left[-\frac{(s - \bar{s}_i(a))^2}{\sigma(\hat{s}_i(a))}\right] ds \\
&\quad - \int_{0}^{-\Delta s_i} \left(s + \Delta s_i\right) \cdot \frac{\sigma_{i,m}}{\sqrt{\pi \cdot \sigma(\hat{s}_i(a))}} \cdot \exp\left[-\frac{(s - \bar{s}_i(a))^2}{\sigma(\hat{s}_i(a))}\right] ds .
\end{aligned}
$$

$$(8.51)$$

The probability that saver i changes from asset a to asset $\tilde{a}$ at time t is given by (cf. equation (8.8))

$$
r_i(a \to \tilde{a}, t) = \bar{m}_i(a, t) \cdot \Psi(\eta_i(\tilde{a}, t)) \cdot \Phi(x(\tilde{a}, t)) .
$$

$$(8.52)$$

Immediately after the change of all net returns, the experience of the savers is roughly unchanged. The same holds for the number $(N \cdot x(a, t))$ of savers who invest in asset a. The first variable that changes is the individuals' satisfaction and, consequently, also their motivation. To analyse the short run dynamics after a change of all net returns, it is sufficient to study the impact of these changes on investment behaviour. Switches from one investment to another have already been common before the change of all net returns. These switches have balanced each other, as long as the investment behaviour has been in a stationary state on the level of populations. The frequency of these switches changes at time $t = 0$ due to a change in the average motivation $\bar{m}_i(\Delta t)$ given by equation (8.51).

LEMMA 8.3: *The increase or decrease of investment in asset a after the change of all net returns is determined by the average motivation it caused before ($\bar{m}_i(a,0)$) and after ($\bar{m}_i(a, \Delta t)$) the change. It is proportional to*

$$\frac{\sum_{\tilde{a} \in \mathcal{A}} \bar{m}_i(\tilde{a}, \Delta t) \cdot f_i(\tilde{a}, 0)}{\sum_{\tilde{a} \in \mathcal{A}} \bar{m}_i(\tilde{a}, 0) \cdot f_i(\tilde{a}, 0)} - \frac{\bar{m}_i(a, \Delta t)}{\bar{m}_i(a, 0)} . \tag{8.53}$$

Proof: The change of the probability of saver i investing in asset a is given by the master equation (cf. Weidlich 1991)

$$\frac{df_i(a, t)}{dt} = \sum_{\tilde{a} \in \mathcal{A}} \left[r_i(\tilde{a} \to a, t) \cdot f_i(\tilde{a}, t) - r_i(a \to \tilde{a}, t) \cdot f_i(a, t) \right] . \tag{8.54}$$

If the probability distribution $(f_i(a,t))_{a \in \mathcal{A}}$ was in its stationary state before the change of all net returns, the change of the probabilities given by equation (8.54) is zero for time $t = 0$. Thus

$$\sum_{\tilde{a} \in \mathcal{A}} \left[r_i(\tilde{a} \to a, 0) \cdot f_i(\tilde{a}, 0) \right] = \sum_{\tilde{a} \in \mathcal{A}} \left[r_i(a \to \tilde{a}, 0) \cdot f_i(a, 0) \right] . \tag{8.55}$$

Inserting equation (8.52) into equation (8.55) results in

$$\sum_{\tilde{a} \in \mathcal{A}} \left[\bar{m}_i(\tilde{a}, 0) \cdot \Psi(\eta_i(a, 0)) \cdot \Phi(x(a, 0)) \cdot f_i(\tilde{a}, 0) \right]$$
$$= \sum_{\tilde{a} \in \mathcal{A}} \left[\bar{m}_i(a, 0) \cdot \Psi(\eta_i(\tilde{a}, 0)) \cdot \Phi(x(\tilde{a}, 0)) \cdot f_i(a, 0) \right] . \tag{8.56}$$

The change of $f_i(a, t)$ at time Δt is given by

$$\frac{df_i(a, \Delta t)}{dt} = \sum_{\tilde{a} \in \mathcal{A}} \left[\bar{m}_i(\tilde{a}, \Delta t) \cdot \Psi(\eta_i(a, 0)) \cdot \Phi(x(a, 0)) \cdot f_i(\tilde{a}, 0) \right.$$
$$\left. - \bar{m}_i(a, \Delta t) \cdot \Psi(\eta_i(\tilde{a}, 0)) \cdot \Phi(x(\tilde{a}, 0)) \cdot f_i(a, 0) \right] = 0 . \tag{8.57}$$

With the help of equations (8.51) and (8.56) one obtains

$$
\begin{aligned}
\frac{df_i(a, \Delta t)}{dt} &= \Psi(\eta_i(a,0)) \cdot \Phi(x(a,0)) \cdot \left[\sum_{\tilde{a} \in \mathcal{A}} \bar{m}_i(\tilde{a}, 0) \cdot f_i(\tilde{a}, 0) \right] \\
&\times \left[\frac{\sum_{\tilde{a} \in \mathcal{A}} \bar{m}_i(\tilde{a}, \Delta t) \cdot f_i(\tilde{a}, 0)}{\sum_{\tilde{a} \in \mathcal{A}} \bar{m}_i(\tilde{a}, 0) \cdot f_i(\tilde{a}, 0)} - \frac{\bar{m}_i(a, \Delta t)}{\bar{m}_i(a, 0)} \right] \cdot
\end{aligned}
$$

$$(8.58)$$

∎

Lemma 8.3 implies that the change of the share $x(a, \Delta t)$ of individuals investing in asset a immediately after the change of all average net returns, depends on the motivation caused by the asset, relative to the motivation caused by other assets. The first term of (8.53) is the same for all assets. Thus, the second term determines whether an asset is chosen more or less frequently after the change of the average net returns. This term is given according to equation (8.51) by

$$
\begin{aligned}
\frac{\bar{m}_i(a, \Delta t)}{\bar{m}_i(a, 0)} &= 1 - \frac{1}{\bar{m}_i(a, 0)} \cdot \int_{-\infty}^{0} \Delta s_i \cdot \frac{\sigma_{i,m}}{\sqrt{\pi} \cdot \sigma(\hat{s}_i(a))} \\
&\cdot \exp\left[-\frac{(s - \bar{s}_i(a))^2}{\sigma(\hat{s}_i(a))} \right] ds \\
&- \frac{1}{\bar{m}_i(a, 0)} \cdot \int_{0}^{-\Delta s_i} \left(s + \Delta s_i \right) \cdot \frac{\sigma_{i,m}}{\sqrt{\pi} \cdot \sigma(\hat{s}_i(a))} \\
&\cdot \exp\left[-\frac{(s - \bar{s}_i(a))^2}{\sigma(\hat{s}_i(a))} \right] ds \ .
\end{aligned}
$$

$$(8.59)$$

Since Δt is assumed to be infinitesimally small, Δs_i is infinitesimally small as well. Consequently, equation (8.59) can be approximated by

$$
\begin{aligned}
\frac{\bar{m}_i(a, \Delta t)}{\bar{m}_i(a, 0)} &\approx 1 - \frac{\Delta s_i \cdot \sigma_{i,m}}{\bar{m}_i(a, 0)} \cdot \int_{-\infty}^{0} \frac{1}{\sqrt{\pi} \cdot \sigma(\hat{s}_i(a))} \\
&\cdot \exp\left[-\frac{(s - \bar{s}_i(a))^2}{\sigma(\hat{s}_i(a))} \right] ds \ .
\end{aligned}
$$

$$(8.60)$$

The integral on the right-hand side of equation (8.60) is the probability that a choice of asset a leads to dissatisfaction for saver i at time $t = 0$ (this is the space in Figure 8.2 left of the vertical axis, limited by the

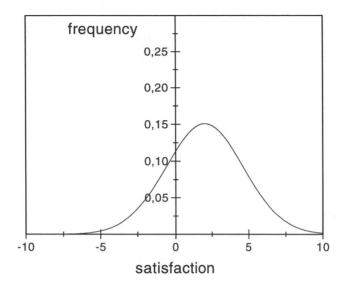

Figure 8.2: *Arbitrarily-chosen frequency distribution of satisfaction*

probability distribution and both axes). It is also the probability that saver i is motivated to stop investing in asset a. $\bar{m}_i(a, 0)$ is the average motivation of individual i investing in asset a. The average motivation divided by the probability to be motivated, results in the average motivation in the case of dissatisfaction (this means, in Figure 8.2, the curve on the left-hand side of the vertical axis is multiplied with such a constant that the integral of this curve equals one; subsequently, the average negative satisfaction given by the resulting distribution has to be calculated (see Figure 8.3)). This average motivation, in the case of dissatisfaction, does not depend on the probability of an asset to be dissatisfying; it only depends on the slope of the probability distribution, to the left of the vertical axis, in relation to the probability of $s_i(0) = 0$. The faster the frequency distribution decreases compared to its value left of the vertical axis, the smaller is the average motivation in the case of dissatisfaction (cf. Figure 8.3).

Remembered satisfaction is distributed normally (cf. Figure 8.3). Thus, remembered satisfaction decreases strongly for $\hat{s}_i(a) < 0$ if the normal distribution is sharp and the maximum of the normal distribution is not too near and not too far from $\hat{s}_i(a) = 0$. Consequently, the second term on the right-hand side of equation (8.60) is large for assets that lead to an average satisfaction $\bar{s}_i(a)$ slightly above zero, and that leads to net returns with a small variance.

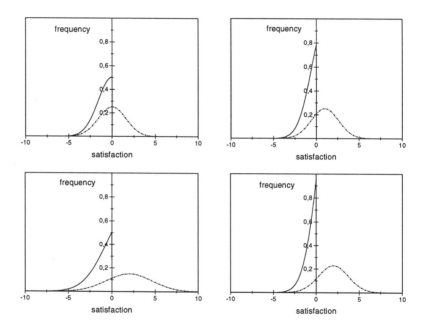

Figure 8.3: *Four arbitrarily-chosen frequency distributions of satisfaction (dotted lines), the consideration of the distributions if only the cases of dissatisfaction are considered (solid lines), and the average motivation in the case of dissatisfaction* ↑

If the net returns of all assets are decreasing ($\Delta s < 0$), a high value of this term causes a high value of $\frac{\bar{m}_i(a,\Delta t)}{\bar{m}_i(a,0)}$ according to equation (8.60). Thus, the investment in an asset a decreases for $t > 0$ if the second term on the right-hand side of equation (8.60) is large for asset a. Small values of this term mean that the corresponding asset is chosen more frequently after the change of the average net returns.

Combining the considerations of the two previous paragraphs, a decrease of net returns reduces investment in assets that cause a satisfaction slightly above $\bar{s}_i(a) = 0$, and that leads to a small variance in net returns.

Savers are different with respect to their aspiration level so that for each of them a certain average net return, different from the one of other savers, leads to a certain value above $\bar{s}_i(a) = 0$. Hence, no asset satisfies the condition that $\bar{s}_i(a)$ is slightly above zero with respect to all savers. Therefore, decreasing overall net returns lead to a less frequent investment in assets with small variances of the corresponding net returns. At the same time, investment in assets with a high variance of net returns becomes more frequent (the preparedness of savers to invest in more risky assets at times of decreasing interest rates, i. e. decreasing average net returns for all assets affected by interest rates, is a phenomenon also reported by bankers). Increasing overall net returns have the opposite effect.

8.5 SUMMARY

This chapter analyses the investment behaviour of small savers as an example of routine-based learning. To this end, some assumptions have been made about the behaviour of small savers in the financial market. Whether these assumption are realistic is not investigated within this work, but the results of the analysis suggest that the assumptions hold true, at least for some small savers. It is assumed that, for most small savers, investment in assets is too important to be made non-cognitively, but, it is also too complex to develop specific cognitive models about the net returns of assets and their temporal evolution. As a consequence, small savers apply general routines of learning as they are described, for example, by the VID model.

Four results of the detailed analysis of such behaviour are worth mentioning. First, a learning process described by the VID model converges to a behaviour that shows some kind of risk aversion. Thus risk-averse-like behaviour is shown not necessarily to be an innate characteristic of people, rather, it is a feature that results from learning under certain circumstances (a more detailed study can be found in Brenner 1995). Second, the large number of savers who prefer fixed deposits to risky assets, although the risky assets offer much higher average net returns, has been explained by the present approach. Whether individuals invest in fixed deposits or in risky assets depends crucially on their aspiration level, that is, their ambition to obtain high net returns. Less ambitious savers are satisfied by the smaller net returns of fixed deposits, and direct their scarce cognitive attention to other preoccupations of their lives. Third, imitation between savers leads to a stricter avoidance of less preferred assets. Thus, communication between savers makes it harder to sell assets that are not competitive. Fourth, if the average net returns of all available assets change simultaneously, investment behaviour changes at least in the short run. In financial markets, the average interest rates move up and down constantly so that investment behaviour is adequately described by its reaction to such changes in the short run. The above calculations imply that if net returns move upwards, savers increase their demand for assets with a small variance in net returns, whereas if interest rates move downwards, savers increase their demand for risky assets, in the short run. All these findings are in accordance with knowledge of the investment behaviour of savers, which confirms the claim that savers' behaviour can be adequately described by a boundedly rational learning algorithm, like the VID model.

Chapter 9

Learning and Diffusion

Another example of routine-based learning in an economic context is the diffusion of innovations, and the adoption of procedures by individuals if they are not able to anticipate the suitability of the procedures beforehand. Usually, individuals calculate or approximate the suitability of procedures through their cognitive models of the situation, that is, through their cognitive understanding. However, in many situations it is impossible to anticipate the utility of a procedure before it is applied. Particularly in the case of innovations, the suitability of an innovation cannot easily be anticipated. Furthermore, many organisational or technical procedures are difficult to evaluate and as a consequence, the individuals are only able to apply general learning routines, like the VID model. In this chapter, the diffusion of new procedures, meaning innovations, is analysed as a second example of routine-based learning.

The *diffusion* of *innovations*, especially in the context of technical innovation, is a research topic comprehensively studied in the last decades (cf. Rogers 1995 and references therein). Consequently, the features of diffusion on the macro level are well understood. However, on the micro level, new insights are obtainable if learning processes aiding diffusion are studied in a comprehensive way. In the literature, the adoption of innovations is modelled as a process of information-gathering and optimal decision-making. The aspect of bounded rationality and routine-based stochastic decision-making is usually neglected. The present approach, however, regards diffusion as a consequence of boundedly rational learning processes. Innovations which might be diffused are called *procedures* in the following section. A procedure might be a behaviour, a technology, or an organisational structure.

It is assumed that the individuals or groups of individuals have a strong interest in finding an adequate procedure, that is, a procedure that serves their goals. At the same time, however, the individuals are assumed to have no associative knowledge about the situation (firms often do not know when they implement an innovation whether it will be favourably accepted by the consumers). This means that people are only able to learn about a situation from their personal experience and the experiences of others. They are not able to anticipate the outcomes of a procedure by theoretical calculations, at least not precisely enough. Therefore individuals rely in their search for adequate procedures, on the information gathered in the past. Such a learning process can be modelled again by the *VID model*.

This chapter proceeds as follows. In the first section, the learning model is described. In the second section this model is used to study the dynamics and stationary states of the application of a given set of procedures, on the level of populations with the number of individuals assumed to be infinite. The third section is devoted to a similar analysis of behaviour in the case of a finite number of individuals. In the fourth section, the diffusion of an innovation is analysed. The fifth section contains a short summary.

9.1   MODELLING DIFFUSION

In the present approach, diffusion is modelled as the change of the aggregate of an individual's behaviour over time. Thus the analysis is based on a model of individual learning. The learning process is modelled by the VID model, which has been modified slightly to fit this situation. For example, the basic motivation is ignored here because, especially in the case of technological or organisational procedures, procedures are not changed merely due to boredom or the desire of managers for novelty. Thus, two reasons for a change of behaviour remain. One is that they are searching actively for other procedures, out of dissatisfaction with their present performance. The second reason is that they are influenced by the procedures that are applied by others. They have a tendency to imitate others even if they are satisfied with their current performance. This aspect is somehow similar to the notion of *social impact* (cf. Latané 1981). In this context, imitation is more likely the better the observed individual performs.

The model used has the following features. A population is considered of N individuals (each individual is indexed by $i \in \mathcal{I}$), who have to apply each time, one procedure a of a set of procedures $\mathcal{A}$ (the number of procedures is denoted by A). The procedure applied by individual i at time t is denoted by $a_i(t)$. The set of procedures is assumed to be exogenously given, although individuals do not necessarily know all of them at the beginning. The utility that a procedure gives rise to cannot be anticipated; individuals know about this utility only after they have applied the procedure. Furthermore, the utility is not the same each time for any one procedure. Instead, for each procedure, a fixed probability distribution over the space of utility is given. Let me assume an individual i who applies procedure $a_i(t)$ at time t. This leads to a utility of $u_i(t)$ for this individual. The utility arises by chance according to a probability distribution $P(u|a)$. Furthermore, the individual has an *aspiration level* $z_i(t)$. If the utility $u_i(t)$ is above this aspiration level, the individual is satisfied with the applied procedure $a_i(t)$. If the utility $u_i(t)$ is below $z_i(t)$, the individual is dissatisfied and motivated to change the procedure. *Motivation* is given by

$$m_i(t) = \begin{cases} 0 & \text{for} \quad u_i(t) > z_i(t) \\ z_i(t) - u_i(t) & \text{for} \quad u_i(t) < z_i(t) \end{cases} . \tag{9.1}$$

The individuals are assumed to act *myopically*; they do not memorise their experience. Their feeling of dissatisfaction and their motivation to change their behaviour depends only on the current performance and not on their past experience with the procedures. This simplification is done for mathematical convenience. In Brenner 1996b, the VID model with its originally more complex features is investigated by simulations. A comparison of the results shows that the present simplification does not alter the implications of the approach, on principle.

Individuals use two alternative ways to change the procedure they apply. They may attempt another procedure by chance or imitate other individuals. A trial of another procedure by chance, named *variation* according to the terminology of the VID model, occurs only if the individuals are motivated to search for a better procedure. Since the utilities of procedures cannot be anticipated, and knowledge obtained in the past is assumed not to be memorised, the trial of any procedure occurs with the same probability $r_{i,V}(a,t)$:

$$r_{i,V}(a,t) = \nu_{i,V} \cdot m_i(t) . \tag{9.2}$$

Imitation occurs for two reasons. First, for individuals who are dissatisfied and search for alternative procedures, it is most convenient to imitate others. Second, individuals, even if they are satisfied with their current procedure, have an inner tendency to imitate others, especially if the others are successful. In both cases, the imitation depends crucially on the performance $u_j(t)$ of the individual j observed. The higher $u_j(t)$ is, the more likely it is that this individual is imitated, at least if both individuals share the same preference order (see Section 2.2.8 for a comprehensive discussion of different evaluations of outcomes). This dependence of the imitation probability on the utility gained by the observed individual, is represented by function $\Psi(u_j(t))$. The probability that individual i imitates individual j is given by

$$r_{i,I}(j,t) = \left[\nu_{i,I} \cdot m_i(t) + \nu_{i,S}\right] \cdot \Psi_i(u_j(t)) . \qquad (9.3)$$

The first term on the right-hand side of equation (9.3) represents the imitation that is caused by an active search for alternative procedures. The second term on the right-hand side of equation (9.3) is caused by social impact. Generally $\nu_{I,i} > \nu_{S,i}$ holds.

The probability of an individual changing from the application of procedure a to the application of procedure $\tilde{a}$ at time t, is given by

$$
\begin{aligned}
r_i(a \rightarrow \tilde{a}, t) \quad = \quad & \nu_{i,V} \cdot m_i(t) + \left(\nu_{i,I} \cdot m_i(t) + \nu_{i,S}\right) \\
\cdot \quad & \tfrac{1}{N-1} \cdot \sum_{j \in \mathcal{I} \setminus \{i\}} \left[\Psi_i(u_j(t)) \cdot \delta(a_j(t) = \tilde{a})\right]
\end{aligned}
\qquad (9.4)
$$

where

$$\delta(a_j(t) = \tilde{a}) = \begin{cases} 1 & \text{for} \quad a_j(t) = \tilde{a} \\ 0 & \text{for} \quad a_j(t) \neq \tilde{a} \end{cases} . \qquad (9.5)$$

Equation (9.4) describes the adaptive behaviour of an individual under the present assumptions. This type of adaptive behaviour will be analysed below under different circumstances.

9.2   AN INFINITE NUMBER OF INDIVIDUALS

First, the behaviour of an infinite *population* of identical, adaptive individuals is analysed. The behaviour of each individual is given by equation (9.4). The parameters are the same for all individuals ($\nu_{i,V} = \nu_V$, $\nu_{i,I} = \nu_I$, and $\nu_{i,S} = \nu_S$). Furthermore, the population is sufficiently large, meaning that the behaviour of the population is the same as if the number of individuals were infinite (cf. Section 4.2.4).

9.2.1 Equations of Motion on the Level of Populations

The behaviour on the level of populations is adequately described at each time by the share $x(a,t)$ of the whole population that applies procedure a. The number of individuals who apply procedure a at time t is given by $N \cdot x(a,t)$. For $x(a,t) > 0$ this number is sufficiently large because N is assumed to be sufficiently large. Each of the individuals who applies procedure a obtains a utility u with the probability $P(u|a)$. Thus, each utility u occurs within the individuals who apply procedure a with a frequency of $N \cdot x(a,t) \cdot P(u|a)$. Hence

$$\sum_{j \in \mathcal{I}} \left[\Psi_i(u_j(t)) \cdot \delta(a_j(t) = \tilde{a}) \right] = N \cdot x(a,t) \cdot \int_{-\infty}^{\infty} \Psi_i(u) \cdot P(u|\tilde{a}) \, du \ . \quad (9.6)$$

Furthermore for a sufficiently large population holds:

$$\sum_{j \in \mathcal{I} \setminus \{i\}} \left[\Psi_i(u_j(t)) \cdot \delta(a_j(t) = \tilde{a}) \right] \approx \sum_{j \in \mathcal{I}} \left[\Psi_i(u_j(t)) \cdot \delta(a_j(t) = \tilde{a}) \right] \ . \quad (9.7)$$

Consequently, the probability of an individual changing from the application of procedure a to the application of procedure $\tilde{a}$, is given by (cf. equation (9.4))

$$r_i(a \to \tilde{a}, t) = \nu_V \cdot m_i(t) + \left(\nu_I \cdot m_i(t) + \nu_S \right) \bar{u}_{\to}(\tilde{a}) \cdot x(\tilde{a}, t) \quad (9.8)$$

where $m_i(t)$ is given by equation (9.1) and $\bar{u}_{\to}(\tilde{a})$ is called the *pull factor* of procedure $\tilde{a}$, which can be calculated by

$$\bar{u}_{\to}(\tilde{a}) = \int_{-\infty}^{\infty} \Psi_i(u) \cdot P(u|\tilde{a}) \, du \ . \quad (9.9)$$

The pull factor $\bar{u}_{\to}(\tilde{a})$ represents the average attractiveness of procedure $\tilde{a}$, caused by the utility distribution it gives rise to. The pull factor $\bar{u}_{\to}(\tilde{a})$ together with the share $x(\tilde{a}, t)$ determine the likelihood that individuals who change their behaviour through imitation, choose procedure $\tilde{a}$ in the next period of time.

Motivation $m_i(t)$ depends on the utility $u_i(t)$ and the aspiration level $z_i(t)$. The utility is a stochastic value. This means that two individuals may derive different utilities although they apply the same procedure a at the same time. Each value of utility is obtained by individual i with the probability $P(u|a_i(t))$ at time t. It is assumed that all individuals evaluate the outcomes of the procedures in the same way, so that the objective probability distribution $P(u|a)$ represents the subjective distribution of utilities for all individuals. Moreover, the aspiration level is assumed to be constant and to be the same for all individuals. It is denoted by z_0. Therefore the average motivation for an individual who currently applies procedure a, is given by

$$\bar{m}(a) = \int_{-\infty}^{z_0} \left(z_0 - u\right) \cdot P(u|a) \, du \, . \tag{9.10}$$

This motivation does not depend on the individual or time explicitly. It only depends on the procedure that is applied by the individual at the considered time.

On the level of populations, changes of the behaviour of a single individual are not relevant. Only the aggregated behaviour can be observed on the level of populations. Thus, instead of the individual probability per time to change behaviour given by equation (9.8), the average probability per time of changing from applying procedure a to applying procedure $\tilde{a}$, for all individuals utilising the same procedure a at a time t, is calculated, which results in

$$\bar{r}(a \to \tilde{a}, t) = \nu_V \cdot \bar{m}(a) + \left(\nu_I \cdot \bar{m}(a) + \nu_S\right) \cdot \bar{u}_{\to}(\tilde{a}) \cdot x(\tilde{a}, t) \, . \tag{9.11}$$

Equation (9.11) represents the average probability per time of an individual applying procedure a at time t to switch to procedure $\tilde{a}$ at this time. The total number of individuals switching from procedure a to $\tilde{a}$ at time t, is given by $\bar{r}(a \to \tilde{a}, t) \cdot N \cdot x(a, t)$. Thus, the total number per time of individuals who abandon procedure a at time t, is given by

$$\sum_{\tilde{a} \in \mathcal{A} \setminus \{a\}} \bar{r}(a \to \tilde{a}, t) \cdot N \cdot x(a, t) \tag{9.12}$$

Similarly the number per time of individuals who start to apply procedure a at time t is given by

$$\sum_{\tilde{a} \in \mathcal{A} \setminus \{a\}} \bar{r}(\tilde{a} \to a, t) \cdot N \cdot x(\tilde{a}, t) \tag{9.13}$$

The number given by (9.13) minus the number given by (9.12) is the overall change per time of the number of individuals applying procedure a at time t. Dividing this by N, the change of the share $x(a, t)$ results (cf. the *master equation* in Weidlich 1991):

$$\frac{dx(a, t)}{dt} = \sum_{\tilde{a} \in \mathcal{A}} \left(\bar{r}(\tilde{a} \to a, t) \cdot x(\tilde{a}, t) - \bar{r}(a \to \tilde{a}, t) \cdot x(a, t)\right) \, . \tag{9.14}$$

Inserting equation (9.11) into equation (9.14) one obtains

$$
\begin{aligned}
\frac{dx(a,t)}{dt} \;=\;& \nu_V \cdot \left[\sum_{\tilde{a} \in \mathcal{A}} \Big(\bar{m}(\tilde{a}) \cdot x(\tilde{a},t) \Big) - A \cdot \bar{m}(a) \cdot x(a,t) \right] \\
+\;& \nu_I \cdot \Big[\bar{u}_{\to}(a) \cdot \sum_{\tilde{a} \in \mathcal{A}} \Big(\bar{m}(\tilde{a}) \cdot x(\tilde{a},t) \Big) \\
-\;& \bar{m}(a) \cdot \sum_{\tilde{a} \in \mathcal{A}} \Big(\bar{u}_{\to}(\tilde{a}) \cdot x(\tilde{a},t) \Big) \Big] \cdot x(a,t) \\
+\;& \nu_S \cdot \Big[\bar{u}_{\to}(a) - \sum_{\tilde{a} \in \mathcal{A}} \Big(\bar{u}_{\to}(\tilde{a}) \cdot x(\tilde{a},t) \Big) \Big] \cdot x(a,t) \,.
\end{aligned}
$$
$$(9.15)$$

9.2.2 Stable Behaviour

In a stationary state $(\breve{x}(a))_{a \in \mathcal{A}}$ on the level of populations, the derivatives $\frac{dx(a,t)}{dt}$ given by equation (9.15) have to be zero:

$$
\begin{aligned}
0 \;=\;& \nu_V \cdot \left[\sum_{\tilde{a} \in \mathcal{A}} \Big(\bar{m}(\tilde{a}) \cdot \breve{x}(\tilde{a}) \Big) - A \cdot \bar{m}(a) \cdot \breve{x}(a) \right] \\
+\;& \nu_I \cdot \Big[\bar{u}_{\to}(a) \cdot \sum_{\tilde{a} \in \mathcal{A}} \Big(\bar{m}(\tilde{a}) \cdot \breve{x}(\tilde{a}) \Big) \\
-\;& \bar{m}(a) \cdot \sum_{\tilde{a} \in \mathcal{A}} \Big(\bar{u}_{\to}(\tilde{a}) \cdot \breve{x}(\tilde{a}) \Big) \Big] \cdot \breve{x}(a) \\
+\;& \nu_S \cdot \Big[\bar{u}_{\to}(a) - \sum_{\tilde{a} \in \mathcal{A}} \Big(\bar{u}_{\to}(\tilde{a}) \cdot \breve{x}(\tilde{a}) \Big) \Big] \cdot \breve{x}(a) \,.
\end{aligned}
$$
$$(9.16)$$

This equation facilitates calculation of stationary shares $\breve{x}(a)$. However, before approaching the stationary states in general, the question of whether a single behaviour conducted by all individuals can be stable, is addressed.

LEMMA 9.1 *The application of only one procedure a by the whole population is stationary if, and only if, it leads to an average motivation $\bar{m}(a) = 0$.*

Proof: A state is stationary if it satisfies condition (9.16). Inserting $x(a,t) = 1$ and $x(\tilde{a},t) = 0$ for all $\tilde{a} \neq a$ into equation (9.16) it results

$$ -\nu_V \cdot (A - 1) \cdot \bar{m}(a) = 0 \,. \tag{9.17} $$

This condition is only satisfied if, and only if, $\bar{m}(a) = 0$. ∎

Lemma 9.1 elucidates the importance of motivation $\bar{m}(a)$ for the prevailing of a procedure in a population to come to the fore. Motivation originates from dissatisfaction with present performance. Consequently, motivation disappears whenever the realised procedure always leads to outcomes that are better than the aspiration level.

Nevertheless, a stationary state is not necessarily stable. Stability of a stationary state defined by Lemma 9.1, requires that use of a different procedure by a small number of individuals disappears with time.

THEOREM 9.1: *The application of only one procedure a by the whole population, is stable if, and only if, it gives rise to $\bar{m}(a) = 0$ and satisfies*

$$\bar{u}_\rightarrow(a) > \frac{\nu_S \cdot \bar{u}_\rightarrow(\hat{a}) - \nu_V \cdot \bar{m}(\hat{a})}{\nu_S + \nu_I \cdot \bar{m}(\hat{a})} \qquad \forall \hat{a} \neq a . \qquad (9.18)$$

Proof: Stability of a state requires that this state is stationary. According to Lemma 9.1 the application of only one procedure by the whole population is stationary if, and only if, $\bar{m}(a) = 0$. Thus $\bar{m}(a) = 0$ is a necessary condition for stability. Furthermore, stability requires that for any small deviation from the stationary state ($\breve{x}(a) = 1$ and $\breve{x}(\tilde{a}) = 0$ for all $\tilde{a} \neq a$) the dynamics converge to the stationary state. The dynamics, generally given by equation (9.15), in a state given by $x(a, t) = 1 - \epsilon$, $x(\hat{a}, t) = \epsilon$ and $x(\tilde{a}, t) = 0$ for all $\tilde{a} \neq a, \hat{a}$ reads (using also $\bar{m}(a) = 0$)

$$\begin{aligned}
\frac{dx(a, t)}{dt} &= \nu_V \cdot \bar{m}(\hat{a}) \cdot \epsilon \\
&+ \nu_I \cdot \bar{u}_\rightarrow(a) \cdot \bar{m}(\hat{a}) \cdot \epsilon \cdot \left(1 - \epsilon\right) \qquad (9.19) \\
&+ \nu_S \cdot \left[\bar{u}_\rightarrow(a) - \bar{u}_\rightarrow(\hat{a})\right] \cdot \epsilon \cdot \left(1 - \epsilon\right) .
\end{aligned}$$

Since ϵ is infinitesimally small, all terms that are quadratic in ϵ can be ignored. The application of only procedure a is stable if the share $x(a, t)$ increases for every small deviation, i.e. if $\frac{dx(a,t)}{dt} > 0$. Thus condition (9.18) results. ∎

LEMMA 9.2: *A procedure a that is stable according to Theorem 9.1 prevails in a population, i. e. finally all individuals apply this procedure exclusively.*

Proof: Stability implies $\bar{m}(a) = 0$ (lemma 9.1). Inserting $\bar{m}(a) = 0$ into equation (9.15) results in

$$\frac{dx(a,t)}{dt} = \nu_V \cdot \sum_{\tilde{a} \in \mathcal{A}} \left(\bar{m}(\tilde{a}) \cdot x(\tilde{a},t) \right)$$
$$+ \nu_I \cdot \bar{u}_{\rightarrow}(a) \cdot \sum_{\tilde{a} \in \mathcal{A}} \left(\bar{m}(\tilde{a}) \cdot x(\tilde{a},t) \right) \cdot x(a,t)$$
$$+ \nu_S \cdot \left[\bar{u}_{\rightarrow}(a) - \sum_{\tilde{a} \in \mathcal{A}} \left(\bar{u}_{\rightarrow}(\tilde{a}) \cdot x(\tilde{a},t) \right) \right] \cdot x(a,t) .$$
$$(9.20)$$

Inserting equation (9.18) in equation (9.20) it results

$$\frac{dx(a,t)}{dt} \geq \nu_V \cdot \sum_{\tilde{a} \in \mathcal{A}} \left(\bar{m}(\tilde{a}) \cdot x(\tilde{a},t) \right)$$
$$- \nu_V \cdot x(a,t) \cdot \sum_{\tilde{a} \in \mathcal{A}} \left(\bar{m}(\tilde{a}) \cdot x(\tilde{a},t) \right) .$$
$$(9.21)$$

Consequently the share $x(a,t)$ increases as long as $x(a,t) < 1$. ∎

LEMMA 9.3: *If the procedure with the highest pull factor is always satisfying, it is stable according to Theorem 9.1 and prevails in the long run.*

Proof: For a procedure a with $\bar{u}_{\rightarrow}(a) > \bar{u}_{\rightarrow}(\tilde{a})$ for all $\tilde{a} \neq a$ condition (9.18) is satisfied. Furthermore $\bar{m}(a) = 0$ is assumed. Thus, the exclusive application of this procedure is a stable state (Theorem 9.1). According to Lemma 9.2, the dynamics converge to this stable state. ∎

Lemma 9.3 implies that, at least in the long run, all individuals adopt the procedure with the highest pull factor, if this procedure is always satisfying. If the procedure with the highest pull factor is not always satisfying, the application of this procedure by all individuals is not stable (Lemma 9.1). There is another procedure that prevails in the population if one of the procedures gives rise to an average motivation $\bar{m}(a) = 0$ and satisfies condition (9.18) (Theorem 9.1).

Thus, three different cases can be distinguished:

- No procedure exists that is always satisfying. In this case no procedure is able to prevail in the population (Lemma 9.1).

- The procedure a with the highest pull factor of all procedures $\tilde{a}$ with $\bar{m}(\tilde{a}) = 0$ satisfies condition (9.18). In this case, the dynamics converge to a state in which all individuals apply procedure a exclusively (Lemma 9.2).

- None of the procedures with $\bar{m}(a) = 0$ satisfies condition (9.18). Again no procedure is able to prevail in the population because no procedure is both stationary (implied by lemma 9.1 if $\bar{m}(a) > 0$) and stable at the same time (implied by Theorem 9.1, if the procedure does not satisfy condition (9.18)).

The second case is sufficiently described by Theorem 9.1 and Lemma 9.2. In the first and the third cases, the dynamics converge to a state characterised by a simultaneous use of all procedures.

LEMMA 9.4: *If no stable state exists according to Theorem 9.1, no procedure disappears.*

Proof: A procedure a with $\bar{u}_\rightarrow(a) > \bar{u}_\rightarrow(\tilde{a})$ for all $\tilde{a} \neq a$ satisfies condition (9.18) if $\bar{m}(a) = 0$. Such a procedure is stable. If no stable state exists, the procedure a with the highest pull factor $\bar{u}_\rightarrow(a)$ is not always satisfying ($\bar{m}(a) > 0$). Either there is no procedure that is always satisfying, or condition (9.18) is fulfilled by none of the procedures that are always satisfying. In both cases, a procedure that is not consistently satisfying exists and remains in use, because if only procedures that are satisfying exist, condition (9.18) is satisfied for one of them or some procedures lead to exactly the same pull factor (which is infinitesimally unlikely and disregarded here for convenience). For a procedure $\tilde{a}$ to disappear, $x(\tilde{a}, t) = 0$ has to be stable. Inserting $x(\tilde{a}, t) = 0$ into equation (9.15) the result is

$$\frac{dx(a,t)}{dt} = \nu_V \cdot \sum_{\tilde{a} \in \mathcal{A}} \left(\bar{m}(\tilde{a}) \cdot x(\tilde{a}, t) \right) \tag{9.22}$$

This derivative is zero only if all procedures that are used are satisfying; otherwise it is positive. Above, however, it is proved that at least one procedure that is not always satisfying remains in use. Thus $x(\tilde{a}, t) = 0$ is unstable for all procedures $\tilde{a}$. ∎

Lemma 9.4 implies that if no procedure prevails, each procedure is applied by some individuals at each time t. The individuals are occasionally dissatisfied by their procedure or they imitate other individuals. This results in permanent fluctuations on the individual level. On the level of populations, by contrast, the dynamics converge to a distribution of procedures, with fixed shares of the population applying each procedure. The stationary shares $\breve{x}(a)$ of the population that apply each procedure a are given as follows.

THEOREM 9.2: *If no application of only one procedure is stable, the behaviour on the level of populations converges* *to a state where each procedure is used by a share of $\breve{x}(a)$ of all individuals:*

$$\breve{x}(a) = \left(\nu_V \cdot \langle \bar{m} \rangle\right) \cdot \left(\nu_V \cdot A \cdot \bar{m}(a) + \nu_I \cdot \left[\bar{m}(a) \cdot \langle \bar{u}_\rightarrow \rangle \right.\right.$$
$$\left.\left. - \langle \bar{m} \rangle \cdot \bar{u}_\rightarrow(a)\right] + \nu_S \cdot \left[\langle \bar{u}_\rightarrow \rangle - \bar{u}_\rightarrow(a)\right]\right)^{-1}$$
$$\text{(9.23)}$$

where

$$\langle \bar{m} \rangle = \sum_{\tilde{a} \in \mathcal{A}} \bar{m}(\tilde{a}) \cdot \breve{x}(\tilde{a}) \qquad (9.24)$$

and

$$\langle \bar{u}_\rightarrow \rangle = \sum_{\tilde{a} \in \mathcal{A}} \bar{u}_\rightarrow(\tilde{a}) \cdot \breve{x}(\tilde{a}) . \qquad (9.25)$$

Proof: Equation (9.23) can be deduced from equation (9.16) by some conversions under the assumption that $\breve{x}(a) > 0$ for all a (Lemma 9.4). ∎

We may realise from equation (9.23) that a high pull factor $\bar{u}_\rightarrow(a)$ of a procedure leads to the frequent choice of this procedure. The same holds for a low average motivation $\bar{m}(a)$ that a procedure gives rise to. Nevertheless the population behaves heterogeneously, that is, different procedures are applied by different individuals each time. None of the procedures are avoided completely.

To sum up, in a homogeneous population, two cases may occur if individuals face a choice between different procedures. First, a procedure may exist representing a stable behaviour according to Theorem 9.1. This procedure prevails in the population in the long run. Second, maybe no procedure exists satisfying the conditions of Theorem 9.1. In this case the procedures are used by the population according to the distribution given in Theorem 9.2.

9.3 A FINITE NUMBER OF INDIVIDUALS

In the previous section, I claimed that the behaviour of a population of individuals either converges to the use of one procedure by all individuals (Theorem 9.1) or to a use of all procedures with a certain probability given by equation (9.23) (Theorem 9.2). These results have been obtained under the assumption that the number of individuals in the population is infinite, or at least sufficiently high that the dynamics is identical to the dynamics of an infinite population. In reality, however, the number of individuals in a population is finite, which has some important implications for the dynamics that will be shown. This does not only hold for the present analysis of diffusion but for all other mathematical analyses on the level of populations.

In a population with a finite number of individuals, stable and stationary states have a different meaning, because the dynamics remains stochastic on the population level (cf. Chapter 4). *Stationary states* are defined as states in which the dynamics of a system theoretically come to a halt. Once a stationary state is reached, it will never be abandoned again. However with some systems, the dynamics may never lead the system to such a stationary state, where the existence of the stationary state has no further impact on the dynamics. In this case, an additional concept is necessary to analyse the behaviour of dynamic processes. For deterministic dynamics, the concept of *stability* satisfies this need. A stationary state is stable if the dynamics of the system converge to that state once they have reached an infinitesimally small neighbourhood. In the case of stochastic dynamics, however, the concept of stability has to be replaced by the concept of absorbing sets of states. Therefore, the analysis of the learning dynamics for a population with a finite number of individuals, is started by an analysis of the stationary and absorbing states.

9.3.1   Stationary and Absorbing States

The dynamics of the individuals' behaviour is defined by probabilities of changing behaviour per unit time (equation (9.11) in the present approach). The fluctuations in the individuals' behaviour disappear only if all transition rates given by equation (9.11) are zero for every individual.

> THEOREM 9.3 *A distribution* $\breve{\mathbf{x}} = (\breve{x}(a))_{a \in \mathcal{A}}$ *of behaviours in a finite population is stationary if, and only if, all individuals apply the same procedure* $\breve{a}$ *(*$\breve{x}(\breve{a}) = 1$ *and* $\breve{x}(a) = 0$ *for all* $a \neq \breve{a}$*) and this procedure gives rise to an average motivation* $\bar{m}(\breve{a}) = 0$*.*

Proof: Let me consider an individual i applying procedure $\breve{a}$. This behaviour remains the same with probability one if $r(\breve{a} \to a, t) = 0$ for all $a \neq \breve{a}$, where $r(\breve{a} \to a, t)$ is given by equation (9.11):

$$r(\breve{a} \to a, t) = \nu_V \cdot \bar{m}(\breve{a}) + \left(\nu_I \cdot \bar{m}(\breve{a}) + \nu_S \right) \cdot \bar{u}_\to(a) \cdot \breve{x}(a, t) . \quad (9.26)$$

The parameters ν_V, ν_I and ν_S are positive per definition while $\bar{u}_\rightarrow(a)$ is positive because $\Psi_i(u)$ is defined to be always positive (cf. section 3.4 and equation (9.9)). Thus $r_i(\breve{a} \rightarrow a, t) = 0$ is satisfied if and only if $m(\breve{a}) = 0$ and $\breve{x}(a, t) = 0$ for all $a \neq \breve{a}$.   ∎

Once a stationary state given by Theorem 9.3 is reached, the system remains in this state indefinitely. In a state given by Theorem 9.3, every individual is satisfied by the results of the procedure currently applied, so that the individuals have no incentive to search for other alternatives. Furthermore there is no other individual who applies a different procedure, so that the individuals will not become aware of other alternatives by observation.

In contrast to a deterministic dynamics, where the stability of a stationary state determines whether this state is reached or not, stochastic dynamics can reach any state by chance, as long as fluctuations are present and not restricted. Thus the learning process presently studied may reach each of the stationary states by chance. Once such a state is reached, it is never abandoned again. The set of stationary states given by Theorem 9.3 constitutes the set of absorbing states.

These stationary states are the only absorbing sets of states associated with the present learning process. Consequently, if time goes to infinity, the system is sure to end in one of the stationary states.

9.3.2   Behaviour in the Short and in the Long Run

According to the previous considerations, the stability analysis conducted in the last section has no meaning for real behaviour in a finite population, in the long run. The individuals' behaviour is finally described by one of the absorbing states given by Theorem 9.3. Nevertheless the analysis of stable states (Theorems 9.1 and 9.2) helps to understand the dynamics in the short run.

To make this point clear, let me assume the simple case of two alternative procedures, where one procedure a_s is always satisfying ($\bar{m}(a_s) = 0$) and the other procedure a_u has the higher pull factor ($\bar{u}_\rightarrow(a_u) > \bar{u}_\rightarrow(a_s)$). Furthermore, let me assign numbers to the parameters and characteristics of the procedures. All parameters are assumed to be one: $\nu_V = 1$, $\nu_I = 1$ and $\nu_S = 1$. The average motivations that the procedures give rise to, are set to $\bar{m}(a_s) = 0$ and $\bar{m}(a_u) = 1$. The pull factors are set to $\bar{u}_\rightarrow(a_s) = 1$ and $\bar{u}_\rightarrow(a_u) = 4$. These values can be inserted into equation (9.11) so that one obtains

$$r(a_s \rightarrow a_u) = 4 \cdot x(a_u, t) \tag{9.27}$$

and

$$r(a_u \rightarrow a_s) = 1 + 2 \cdot x(a_s, t) \ . \tag{9.28}$$

In this case one absorbing state exists; the state in which the whole population applies procedure a_s. In this state the probability to change behaviour (given by equation (9.27)) is zero because $x(a_s, t) = 0$. In the long run the system is found in this state.

However, the system does not gradually converge towards this absorbing state. The behaviour of a population of N individuals can be described by the number $n(t)$ of individuals who apply procedure a_s at each time t. The number of individuals who apply procedure a_u is given by $N - n(t)$. The dynamics of $n(t)$ is analysed below. At each time t three things may happen: $n(t)$ remains constant; one individual switches from applying procedure a_s to applying procedure a_u, which decreases $n(t)$ by one; one individual switches from applying procedure a_u to applying procedure a_s, which increases $n(t)$ by one (simultaneous switches by two individuals are not considered because they are infinitesimally unlikely). A switch of an individual from procedure a_s to a_u occurs with a rate of

$$4 \cdot x(a_u, t) \cdot n(t) \ . \tag{9.29}$$

This rate is the individual rate of changing behaviour multiplied by the number of individuals who may conduct this change, that is, the number $n(t)$ of individuals currently applying procedure a_s (cf. Weidlich 1991). $x(a_u, t)$ is the share of the individuals who applies procedure a_u. It is defined as the number of individuals applying procedure a_u divided by the total number of individuals, i.e. $x(a_u, t) = \frac{N - n(t)}{N}$. Similarly $x(a_s, t) = \frac{n(t)}{N}$ holds. The rate (9.29) represents the probability per time of $n(t)$ of decreasing by one. Therefore, this rate is denoted by $r(n \downarrow, t)$. Inserting $x(a_u, t) = \frac{N - n(t)}{N}$ into equation (9.29) results in

$$r(n \downarrow, t) = \frac{4}{N} \cdot n(t) \cdot (N - n(t)) \ . \tag{9.30}$$

In the same way, the probability $r(n \uparrow, t)$ of $n(t)$ increasing by one, can be calculated. It results in

$$r(n \uparrow, t) = (N - n(t)) + \frac{2}{N} \cdot n(t) \cdot (N - n(t)) \ . \tag{9.31}$$

A comparison of the equations (9.30) and (9.31) shows that downwards changes of $n(t)$ dominate if $n(t)$ is large, and that upwards changes of $n(t)$ dominate if $n(t)$ is small. Upward and downward changes balance each other if $n(t) = \frac{1}{2}$ (inserting $n(t) = \frac{1}{2}$ into equations (9.30) and (9.31) it results $r(n \downarrow, t) = r(n \uparrow, t)$). Thus on average, one should expect half of the population to apply procedure a_u and the other half to apply procedure a_s (this corresponds with the stable state on the level of populations given by Theorem 9.2). However, Theorem 9.3 states that only procedure a_s is applied in the long run, which contradicts the statement that each procedure is used by half the population on average.

To understand the message of both statements (that only procedure a_s is applied and that both procedures are applied by half of the population), the dynamics have to be analysed statistically. To this end, $p(n, t)$ is defined as the probability of finding n individuals applying procedure a_s at time t. The change of this probability over time is given by the master equation (cf. Weidlich 1991)

$$\frac{dp(n, t)}{dt} = \sum_{m=0}^{N} \left[r(m \to n, t) \cdot p(m, t) - r(n \to m, t) \cdot p(n, t) \right] . \quad (9.32)$$

In the present approach, $n(t)$ can only increase or decrease by one each time. Thus one obtains

$$\begin{aligned} \frac{dp(n,t)}{dt} &= r(n \uparrow, t) \cdot p(n - 1, t) + r(n \downarrow, t) \cdot p(n + 1, t) \\ &- r(n \uparrow, t) \cdot p(n, t) - r(n \downarrow, t) \cdot p(n, t) . \end{aligned} \quad (9.33)$$

The process described by equation (9.33) can be illustrated by a Markov chain (see Figure 9.1). Each value of $n(t)$ represents one possible state of the population's behaviour. The system may change from each state to one of the two neighbour-states. $p(n, t)$ assigns a probability to each state; the probability that the state of the system is given by $n(t) = n$ at time t. These probabilities change over time, according to the likelihood of the system switching to a neighbour-state. Thus, the arrows in Figure 9.1 can be also interpreted as probability flows.

It is important to notice that no probability flow exists leading out of the state $n = 0$. Once this state is reached, the system remains there indefinitely (above, this state was identified as the absorbing state of the system). For all other states, it holds that the system changes between these states constantly.

As a consequence, two processes have to be distinguished. First, whenever the system is, which happens with a certain probability, in the state $n = 1$, it changes from $n = 1$ to $n = 0$ with a certain probability. Once in the state $n = 0$, the system locks in because it cannot leave this state. This means that the probability of the system being in the

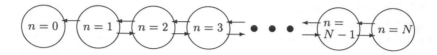

Figure 9.1: *States and possible changes illustrated as a Markov chain*

state $n = 0$ increases constantly with time and finally converges to one, because the increase stops only if the probability $p(1,t)$ of the system being found in state $n = 1$ is zero, implying that the probability of being in another state, except $n = 0$, is zero as well.

Second, as long as the state $n = 0$ has not been reached, the system randomly switches between the other states. To analyse this random process, let me assume that the state $n = 0$ is reached with probability zero (cutting off the transition from state $n = 1$ to state $n = 0$ by setting the rate $r(1 \rightarrow 0, t) = 0$). In this case, the probabilities $p(n, t)$ converge to a stationary probability distribution given by $\frac{dp(n,t)}{dt} = 0$. After inserting this condition in equation (9.33), the resulting set of equations can be solved analytically (the necessary steps are omitted for convenience). For the stationary values $\breve{p}(n)$ results

$$\breve{p}(n) = \breve{p}(1) \cdot \frac{4^{n-1} \cdot \prod_{m=N-m+1}^{N-1} m}{N^{n-1} \cdot n \cdot \prod_{m=N-m}^{N-2} \left(1 + \frac{2m}{N}\right)} \tag{9.34}$$

where $\breve{p}(1)$ is given by the condition

$$\sum_{m=1}^{N} p(m) = 1 . \tag{9.35}$$

The stationary probability distribution given by equation (9.34) is shown in Figure 9.2, for various total numbers N of individuals. Two processes have been identified above: the permanent increase of the probability $p(0,t)$ of the system to be in state $n = 0$ and remain there; and the tendency of the probability distributions of the other states to converge to a distribution given by equation (9.34). The dynamics of the learning depends on the speed of these two processes, especially the speed of the increase of the probability $p(0,t)$. $p(0,t)$ increases more quickly the higher the probability of finding the system in state $n = 1$, and the higher the probability for the last individual applying procedure a_u to abandon this procedure. The probability of the system being in state $n = 1$ is higher the smaller the number N of individuals in the population is (cf. Figure 9.2, where it can be seen that the probability for state $n = 1$ is relatively high in the case of $N = 50$, small in the case of $N = 100$, and almost zero for the cases of $N = 200$ and $N = 500$).

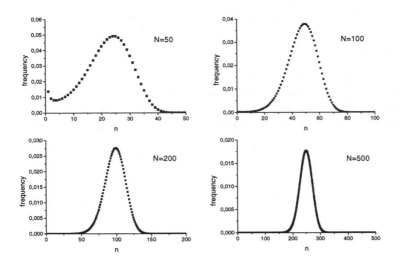

Figure 9.2: *stationary probability distributions for different values of N according to equation (9.34)*

Thus, $p(0,t)$ increases quickly for small numbers of individuals, while it increases slowly for high numbers of individuals (according to Figure 9.2 already for numbers of individuals above 200). In the first case, the system reaches the absorbing state fairly early so that only procedure a_s is applied after a short time with any significant probability. The stable state that characterises the stationary distribution for all other states is unimportant in this case. In the latter, for high numbers N of individuals, $p(0,t)$ increases very slowly. Thus the absorbing state plays a role only in the very long run. In this case, the behaviour of the individuals is sufficiently indicated by the stable state on the level of populations in the short run.

9.3.3 Summary

The above results can be transmitted to the more general situation discussed throughout this chapter, whenever the number of individuals is finite. Some implications include the following:

- In the long run, learning processes always lead to an absorbing state given by Theorem 9.3. Once an absorbing state is reached, the dynamics lock in and do not change again unless the circumstances change. However, the period of time that the system takes to reach an absorbing state may be too long to be relevant in the context of real processes.

- The behaviour in the short run depends crucially on the number of individuals. The higher the number of individuals, the less likely that an absorbing state is reached in the short run (if it is not identical with a stable state, according to Theorem 9.1).

- If a stable state exists according to Theorem 9.1, this is also an absorbing state according to Theorem 9.3. In this case, the state given by Theorem 9.1 is likely to be reached in the short run and, if it is reached, the system remains in this state indefinitely.

- If the stable state on the level of populations is given by Theorem 9.2 (meaning that in the stable state, all procedures are used by some individuals), this state is not an absorbing state (Theorem 9.3 restricts stationary states, meaning absorbing states, to states in which only one procedure is applied). Consequently, this stable state represents the behaviour of the population for approximately as long as no absorbing state is reached. The likelihood of the behaviour on the level of populations to be represented by a stable state according to Theorem 9.2, decreases with time. The higher the number of individuals, the slower this likelihood is to decrease, and the longer the population behaves according to the stable state on average.

This shows that stable and absorbing states are equally important to the understanding of the dynamics of learning in the present approach. Their relevance depends on the time horizon and the number of individuals.

9.4 DIFFUSION OF INNOVATIONS

The calculations and findings above, offer a comprehensive basis for the discussion of the diffusion of innovations, the principal aim of this chapter. The diffusion of an innovation can be modelled within the concept proposed above, as the occurrence of a new procedure at a certain time with the new procedure used by an arbitrary proportion of the population, usually one individual. The studies conducted above allow for immediate discussion of the possible dynamics after the introduction of innovation.

There is much literature on the *diffusion of innovations* (cf. e.g. Rogers 1995 and the references therein) in economics. It is theoretically, as well as empirically, well known that the adoption of innovations follows an S-shaped path with respect to the number of agents who have already adopted the innovation depicted against time. Many different explanations of this feature exist in the economic literature. The most convincing is the one that argues on the basis of an imitative process, where the probability of imitation depends on the number of agents who have already adopted the innovation (cf. Rogers 1995). The model of diffusion proposed here utilises a similar line of arguments, although it contains further aspects. Thus, it will be shown in the following section, that the model above also predicts an S-shaped adoption of new options, besides other possible dynamics.

9.4.1 Mathematics for the Diffusion of an Innovation

An innovation occurs at one point in time. As a consequence, a new alternative procedure is created that was not available before. For convenience it is assumed that the time before the innovation took place, during which no other innovation was made, was long enough for the dynamics to be locked in an absorbing state, if such a state exists. If at least one procedure is always satisfying ($\bar{m}(a) = 0$) for every individual, all individuals use the same procedure when the innovation occurs. Thus, the following analysis is restricted to the case in which all individuals apply procedure a with $\bar{m}(a) = 0$ when the innovation occurs. Allowing for different procedures to be used when the innovation shows up, does not fundamentally change the results of the analysis.

Since the situation is stationary when the innovation shows up, none of the individuals has any motivation to change her/his behaviour. It has to be assumed that one individual adopts the innovation by chance (maybe the individual who invented the new procedure). The

mathematical problem to get the diffusion of an innovation started, however, is also a problem in reality. Many innovations, although they may
be helpful, never get adopted by one single individual. Theoretically, the
problem is solved by simply assuming that one individual uses the new
procedure. Below, the already existing procedure is denoted by a and the
new procedure by $\tilde{a}$. Furthermore, these two procedures are assumed to
be the only procedures available, for convenience (consequently, $A = 2$).
Since the present procedure is always satisfying for every individual, the
dynamics of $x(\tilde{a}, t)$ are given by (cf. equation (9.15))

$$\frac{dx(\tilde{a}, t)}{dt} = -\left[\nu_V + \nu_I \cdot \bar{u}_\rightarrow(a) \cdot x(a, t)\right] \cdot \bar{m}(\tilde{a}) \cdot x(\tilde{a}, t)$$
$$+ \nu_S \cdot \left[\bar{u}_\rightarrow(\tilde{a}) - \bar{u}_\rightarrow(a)\right] \cdot x(a, t) \cdot x(\tilde{a}, t) \tag{9.36}$$

while the dynamics of the share $x(a, t)$ are given by the condition $x(a, t) +$
$x(\tilde{a}, t) = 1$. This condition can also be inserted in equation (9.36) so that
one obtains

$$\frac{dx(\tilde{a}, t)}{dt} = \left[\Delta u - \hat{m}(\tilde{a}) - \hat{u}(\tilde{a} \rightarrow a)\right] \cdot x(\tilde{a}, t)$$
$$- \left[\Delta u - \hat{u}(\tilde{a} \rightarrow a)\right] \cdot x(\tilde{a}, t)^2 \tag{9.37}$$

where the following abbreviations are used:

$$\Delta u = \nu_S \cdot \left[\bar{u}_\rightarrow(\tilde{a}) - \bar{u}_\rightarrow(a)\right] , \tag{9.38}$$

$$\hat{m}(\tilde{a}) = \nu_V \cdot \bar{m}(\tilde{a}) , \tag{9.39}$$

and

$$\hat{u}(\tilde{a} \rightarrow a) = \nu_I \cdot \bar{u}_\rightarrow(a) \cdot \bar{m}(\tilde{a}) . \tag{9.40}$$

The partial differential equation (9.37) can be solved analytically. To
this end, it is transformed into

$$\frac{dx(\tilde{a}, t)}{\left[\Delta u - \hat{m}(\tilde{a}) - \hat{u}(\tilde{a} \rightarrow a)\right] \cdot x(\tilde{a}, t) - \left[\Delta u - \hat{u}(\tilde{a} \rightarrow a)\right] \cdot x(\tilde{a}, t)^2} = dt \tag{9.41}$$

An integration on both sides leads to (the integration is conducted from
time 0 to time t and from share ϵ to share $x(\tilde{a}, t)$, respectively)

$$\frac{1}{\Delta u - \hat{m}(\tilde{a}) - \hat{u}(\tilde{a} \to a)} \cdot \ln\left[\frac{x(\tilde{a}, \tau)}{x(\tilde{a}, \tau) - \frac{\Delta u - \hat{m}(\tilde{a}) - \hat{u}(\tilde{a} \to a)}{\Delta u - \hat{u}(\tilde{a} \to a)}}\right]$$

$$-\frac{1}{\Delta u - \hat{m}(\tilde{a}) - \hat{u}(\tilde{a} \to a)} \cdot \ln\left[\frac{\epsilon}{\epsilon - \frac{\Delta u - \hat{m}(\tilde{a}) - \hat{u}(\tilde{a} \to a)}{\Delta u - \hat{u}(\tilde{a} \to a)}}\right] = t.$$

$$(9.42)$$

The borders of the integration imply that the new procedure is invented at time $t = 0$ and has an initial share of $x(\tilde{a}, 0) = \epsilon$. Equation (9.42) can be transformed to

$$
\begin{aligned}
x(\tilde{a}, t) &= \Big[\tfrac{1}{\epsilon} \cdot \exp\left[-\left(\Delta u - \hat{m}(\tilde{a}) - \hat{u}(\tilde{a} \to a)\right) \cdot t\right] \\
&+ \frac{\Delta u - \hat{u}(\tilde{a} \to a)}{\Delta u - \hat{m}(\tilde{a}) - \hat{u}(\tilde{a} \to a)} \\
&\cdot \left(1 - \exp\left[-\left(\Delta u - \hat{m}(\tilde{a}) - \hat{u}(\tilde{a} \to a)\right) \cdot t\right]\right)\Big]^{-1}.
\end{aligned}
$$

$$(9.43)$$

9.4.2 Features of the Diffusion of Innovations

The above results and equation (9.43) suggest treating several cases separately. To find an adequate classification, the definition of a superior procedure is helpful. A superior procedure a is defined to be a procedure that satisfies equation (9.18). If a superior procedure leads to a motivation $\bar{m}(a) = 0$, it satisfies Theorems 9.1 and 9.3, and supersedes in the population in the short run as well as in the long run (cf. the considerations in the previous section). In the present approach, the procedure a mainly applied at time $t = 0$, is assumed to satisfy $\bar{m}(a) = 0$. It is superior to the innovation $\tilde{a}$ if the following condition holds (cf. equation (9.18) and consider the abbreviations (9.38) to (9.40)):

$$\hat{u}(\tilde{a} \to a) > \Delta u - \hat{m}(\tilde{a}). \qquad (9.44)$$

In this case, I call the innovation inferior. The innovation is superior if it satisfies

$$\hat{u}(\tilde{a} \to a) < \Delta u - \hat{m}(\tilde{a}). \qquad (9.45)$$

$\bar{m}(\tilde{a}) = 0$ implies $\hat{u}(\tilde{a} \to a) = 0$ and $\hat{m}(\tilde{a}) = 0$ so that equation (9.45) results in

$$\Delta u > 0. \qquad (9.46)$$

Thus, the innovation $\tilde{a}$ is superior to the established procedure if it satisfies $\Delta u > 0$.

The dynamics of the diffusion process is given by equation (9.43), assuming an infinite population. In the realistic case of a finite population, equation (9.43) represents an approximation of the average dynamics (cf. the considerations in the previous section). In addition to these dynamics, the exclusive application of one of the procedures represents an absorbing state, if this procedure causes an average motivation of zero. Thus, the established procedure represents an absorbing state.

I distinguish the following four cases:

1) A superior, satisfying innovation:

$$\Delta u > 0 \qquad \wedge \qquad \bar{m}(\tilde{a}) = 0 . \tag{9.47}$$

2) A superior, dissatisfying innovation:

$$\Delta u - \hat{m}(\tilde{a}) - \hat{u}(\tilde{a} \to a) > 0 \qquad \wedge \qquad \bar{m}(\tilde{a}) > 0 . \tag{9.48}$$

3) An inferior, satisfying innovation:

$$\Delta u < 0 \qquad \wedge \qquad \bar{m}(\tilde{a}) = 0 . \tag{9.49}$$

4) An inferior, dissatisfying innovation:

$$\Delta u - \hat{m}(\tilde{a}) - \hat{u}(\tilde{a} \to a) < 0 \qquad \wedge \qquad \bar{m}(\tilde{a}) > 0 . \tag{9.50}$$

Each of these cases will be analysed separately below.

A superior, satisfying innovation

Inserting condition (9.47) (i.e. $\bar{m}(\tilde{a}) = 0$ and therefore $\hat{m}(\tilde{a}) = 0$ and $\hat{u}(\tilde{a} \to a) = 0$) into equation (9.43) results in

$$x(\tilde{a}, t) = \frac{1}{1 + \frac{1-\epsilon}{\epsilon} \cdot \exp\left[-\Delta u \cdot t\right]} \tag{9.51}$$

which is shown in Figure 9.3.

This is the time-path of diffusion known from the theoretical and empirical literature (cf. e.g. Rogers 1995). The old procedure is completely eliminated by the new, it holds that (deduced from equation (9.51))

$$\lim_{t \to \infty} x(\tilde{a}, t) = 1 . \tag{9.52}$$

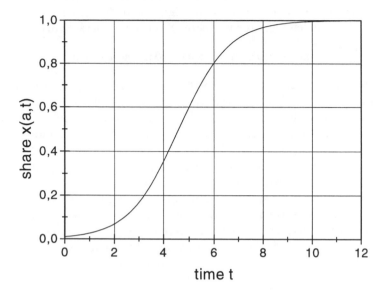

Figure 9.3: *Proportion of individuals applying the new procedure which is superior to the old and introduced at time $t = 0$*

The substitution of the old procedures follows a logistic curve. However, this feature of complete substitution occurs only if $\hat{m}(\tilde{a}) = 0$ (the innovations are always satisfying for everybody) and $\Delta u > 0$ (the pull factor $\bar{u}_{\rightarrow}(\tilde{a})$ that the innovation gives rise to, is higher than the pull factor $\bar{u}_{\rightarrow}(a)$ of the old procedure). Furthermore, as stated above, the procedure established before the innovation took place, represents an absorbing state. Since the diffusion process is a stochastic process, an exclusive application of the old procedure may occur by chance and remains thereafter. Thus, there is a small probability that the innovation does not supersede, although it is superior and satisfying.

A superior, dissatisfying innovation
According to equation (9.43), the application of the procedures converges to

$$\lim_{t \to \infty} x(\tilde{a}, t) = \frac{\Delta u - \hat{m}(\tilde{a}) - \hat{u}(\tilde{a} \to a)}{\Delta u - \hat{u}(\tilde{a} \to a)} \qquad (9.53)$$

if the number of individuals is infinite. According to condition (9.48) the numerator in the fraction on the right-hand side of equation (9.53) is positive. The denominator is greater than the numerator according to

$$\Delta u - \hat{m}(\tilde{a}) - \hat{u}(\tilde{a} \to a) < \Delta u - \hat{u}(\tilde{a} \to a) \qquad (9.54)$$

and, therefore, positive as well, so that $x(\tilde{a}, t)$ converges to a value between zero and one. This means that the diffusion leads to a simultaneous use of both procedures, the old one and the innovation, for an infinite number of individuals. In the case of a finite number of individuals, equation (9.43) approximates the real dynamics sufficiently well only in the short run. In the long run, the dynamics lead to the only absorbing state; the exclusive application of the old procedure.

Thus a superior, dissatisfying innovation may diffuse throughout the population in the short run, in the sense that is used by a certain proportion of the individuals. However, there is always a certain probability that the procedure will be abandoned by all individuals, leading to a neglect of the innovation for ever. Thus in the long run, a superior, dissatisfying innovation disappears (if the procedure used before is always satisfying for every individual), although it may be used for some period of time by some proportion of the population.

An inferior, satisfying innovation
This case is exactly the opposite to a superior, satisfying innovation. Inserting $\bar{m}(\tilde{a}) = 0$ into equation (9.43), equation (9.51) results. However in the present case, $\Delta u < 0$ so that $x(\tilde{a}, t)$ decreases over time and

$$\lim_{t \to \infty} x(\tilde{a}, t) = 0 . \qquad (9.55)$$

Again this only holds for an infinite number of individuals. However, since the exclusive application of the alternative to the innovation by the whole population represents an absorbing state, this state remains constant once it is reached. Nevertheless, there is a small probability that the state in which only the innovation is applied, is reached by chance, a case in which the innovation would remain to be used by all individuals. Thus the innovation may supersede, although this case is very unlikely.

An inferior, dissatisfying innovation
According to condition (9.50),

$$\exp\left[-\left(\Delta u - \hat{m}(\tilde{a}) - \hat{u}(\tilde{a} \to a) \right) \cdot t \right] \to \infty \qquad \text{for } t \to \infty . \qquad (9.56)$$

With the help of equation (9.56), it can be deduced from equation (9.43) that

$$\lim_{t \to \infty} x(\tilde{a}, t) = 0 . \tag{9.57}$$

Thus an inferior, dissatisfying innovation disappears in a population with an infinite number of individuals. Furthermore, an exclusive application of the innovation does not present an absorbing state (because $\bar{m}(\tilde{a}) > 0$ according to condition (9.50)). Consequently the innovation is also abandoned in the long run by a finite number of individuals, with certainty.

9.5 SUMMARY

This chapter presented a second example of an application of routine-based learning. In Chapter 2 it is claimed that general learning routines are applied whenever context-specific knowledge, allowing for a more adequate learning behaviour, is missing. The adoption of innovations is a good example of such a situation. Innovations have the principal characteristic that their usefulness is unknown when they first appear. Therefore, no specific cognitive models exist, allowing evaluation of innovations. Individuals have to rely on information from others who have used the innovation already, and decide whether they adopt this innovation on the basis of their satisfaction with the current procedure they apply. Such a learning routine is described by the VID model.

In the present approach, it is assumed that the individuals are able to switch between different procedures without costs. Given this assumption, the characteristics necessary for an innovation to supersede in a homogenous population of individuals, have been analysed. The most important result is the understanding that we have to be aware that the dynamics in the long and short runs are given by different considerations. In the long run absorbing states play a dominant role. These are all states in which one procedure is exclusively applied that is satisfying for every individual. Absorbing states cause the dynamics to lock in. Once such a state is reached, the system is not able to leave this state again, unless the circumstances change. However, it may be very unlikely for the system to reach one of the absorbing states, so that it may take a very long time until the system locks in, on average. As long as the dynamics have not locked in, the individuals behave stochastically and various different procedures are used in the population simultaneously. In such a case, the average choice of the individuals can be described approximately by the assumption of an infinite number of individuals.

Furthermore, it has been found that an innovation is most likely to substitute the alternative procedures only if it is superior and always satisfying. In such a case, the substitution can be expected to start immediately after the introduction of the innovation, and to follow a logistic curve. However, even if the innovation is superior and always satisfying, such a substitution can not be guaranteed. The present study shows that there is a positive probability that the innovation disappears due to fluctuations. Once the innovation has disappeared, the endogenous dynamics will never bring it back. The same can be said if a satisfying innovation is inferior. Although in such a case, the innovation is unlikely to take hold in the population, there is a positive probability that the innovation would supersede and the superior previously-used procedure disappear. This choice of an inferior procedure is not reversed, once it has been made, not even in the long run.

However, these considerations hold only if the procedures are always satisfying, that is, if the individuals are never motivated to change the procedure they apply. Such a claim is not realistic for several reasons. First, all individuals are different, so that there is seldom a procedure that satisfies everyone. Second, the circumstances, as well as the individual situation, change permanently so that each procedure can be expected to become dissatisfying at some point in time. Third, the aspiration level adapts to the performance of the individuals, so that a procedure that leads to high performance increases the aspirations. Thus it is more realistic to assume not-always-satisfying procedures. In such a case no lock-ins exist. An innovation is able at least to attract some attention in the population. Subsequently a mixture of both, the old and the new procedures, will be applied, with the superior procedure being used by more individuals on the average.

Chapter 10

Associative Learning and the Evolution of Cooperation

In the economic literature, certain learning processes called *associative learning*, are rarely considered. There are a few exceptions (see e.g. Denzau & North 1994, Gößling 1996 or Kubon-Gilke 1997), but, generally cognition, the basic element of associative learning, is regarded to be too complex to be included in a clear-cut mathematical analysis. Economists usually stick to concepts that can be formalised properly and lead to well-defined implications, so that mathematical formulations of associative learning are few and far between.

Nevertheless, associative learning processes play an active role in the context of economic actions. According to their definition in Chapter 2, they are the processes that change cognitive models and these, in turn, determine the way in which individuals decide, or what the applied learning routines look like.

Associative learning plays a role for various economic actions, especially for those seen as important to the individual and requiring a certain understanding of the situation. Examples are: most managerial tasks; the actions of unions; politicians and other representatives of certain groups; the behaviour in the job market; the actions of professionals in the financial market; and various interactions between individuals, especially if they contain strategic elements.

As mentioned above, the modelling of associative learning is still in its infancy and the approaches used are very heterogeneous. Below, a mathematical approach will be used to study the implications of associative learning, in the context of a *prisoner's dilemma*. This approach should rather be seen as containing a proposal of how to deal with cognitive models and associative learning in an economic context than as a well established procedure. This proposal, however, reveals some interesting aspects of dilemma situations not adequately represented in the literature.

In the first section, a short introduction to the prisoner's dilemma, and its presentation in the form of a game, is given. The second section lists some of the explanations in the literature for cooperation to result occasionally in the prisoner's dilemma game. In section three, this game is discussed in relation to the involved learning processes categorised in Chapter 2. Section four proposes a model of the associative learning process relating to the prisoner's dilemma game. Finally, a short summary is given in section five.

10.1   THE PRISONER'S DILEMMA GAME

Research based on *game theory* has been of interest in the social sciences for more than 30 years. One game in particular has attracted much attention and is called the *prisoner's dilemma*. This is a symmetrical 2×2 game (in normal form given by Table 10.1) with the condition $e(\text{exploitation}) > c(\text{cooperation}) > d(\text{defection}) > a(\text{altruism})$.

		column-player	
		cooperation	defection
row-player	cooperation	c c	e a
	defection	a e	d d

Table 10.1: *Payoff matrix in the prisoner's dilemma*

The inherent structure of a prisoner's dilemma game can be explained as follows. Two individuals interact with each other in a situation where each has two possible ways to act; a cooperative one and a competitive one, also often called "defection". If they behave cooperatively, they increase the payoff for the other individual but decrease their own. If they defect, they increase their own payoff while decreasing the payoff for the other. In other words, the individuals pay for the increase of their own payoff by a decrease of that of the other. Let us assume for example, both individuals cooperate and therefore receive a payoff of c. If in this case, one of the individuals intends to improve her/his payoff and defects, (s)he increases her/his own payoff to e but decreases the payoff of the opponent to a.

Furthermore, it is an important prerequisite for the prisoner's dilemma that both individuals are better off if they both behave cooperatively (payoff c) than if they both defect (payoff d). It is best for either individual to defect while the other cooperates (payoff e), and most disadvantageous for either individual to cooperate while the other defects (payoff a).

The prisoner's dilemma game owes the attention that it has attracted, and still attracts, to its inherent conflict between the individual and the collective maximisation of payoff. Since payoff e is higher than c and payoff d is higher than a, it is always better to choose defection independent of the choice of the opponent. Such a behaviour, if both individuals apply the same reasoning, leads to mutual defection, that is, to a payoff of d. If both players cooperate, the payoff would be c for them both, which is higher than the payoff d for defection. It is unlikely that a player faces an opponent who is an altruist and accepts a payoff of a. Consequently, the best payoff a player is able to gain in the long run is the payoff c, if both players cooperate. Hence an incentive exists to establish cooperation. At the same time, as said above, both players are individually better off if they defect. This results in a conflict of motives.

Rational game theory makes a simple prediction for the behaviour occurring in a prisoner's dilemma game: the Nash equilibrium. In the prisoner's dilemma game only one Nash equilibrium exists; the only stable situation is the one where both players defect. This situation is also the ESS in evolutionary game theory. However, empirical as well as experimental evidence (cf. e.g. Rapoport & Chammah 1965, Ostrom 1990 and Ledyard 1995) shows that cooperation may occur. This is usually claimed to be the result of repeated interaction. For a repeated prisoner's dilemma, traditional game theory is only able to restrict the possible behaviour to a certain set that includes mutual cooperation as well as mutual defection.

As a consequence of this inability of game theory to make an unambiguous statement about the occurrence of cooperation, many theories have been proposed that offer different explanations for the evolution of cooperation. Most of the existing explanations for the evolution of co-operation are rather fragmentary. Each author puts forward one single aspect of human behaviour that may be responsible for the occurrence of cooperation, but a comprehensive study of all relevant aspects is missing. The most important proposals are discussed in the next section.

10.2 EXPLANATIONS FOR COOPERATION

10.2.1 Moral Attitudes

Many economists claim that cooperation results from *moral attitudes* or *norms* (cf. e. g. Taylor 1987). Individuals in a prisoner's dilemma game are assumed not to defect because they feel a commitment to treat their opponent fairly. Particularly if their opponents cooperate, the incentive not to defect is high from a moral point of view, because defecting would mean an exploitation of the other. In experiments it has been shown that people have a tendency to behave in the same way as their opponent (cf. e. g. Liebrand 1986). People feel an intrinsic obligation to cooperate, at least if others do the same. If the opponent defects instead, the motivation cooperating decreases and the players stop to cooperate after some time (cf. Lave 1965). These and other results imply that people not only evaluate their own payoffs but also consider the performance of their opponents. Norms and moral attitudes seem to be important, especially in cases of conflicting motives, like the prisoner's dilemma game. However, people differ in their moral attitudes. Selten and Stoecker (1986) found for example, that three of their 35 subjects always cooperated in a finite prisoner's dilemma super-game, while the behaviour of all others converged towards the rationally predicted behaviour of defection. Similar differences in the behaviour of the subjects have been found in other experiments (cf. e. g. Deutsch 1958, Solomon 1960 and Kuhlman, Camac & Cunha 1986).

To do justice to these experimental findings, psychologists developed the notion of motivational attitudes that may be cooperative, individualistic or competitive (cf. Deutsch 1958). C. G. McClintock and E. Van Avermaet (1982) further expanded this notion by the general assumption that players evaluate the outcomes in a game by the sum of their own payoff and the payoff of their opponent, each multiplied by a certain parameter. Dependent on the two parameters, they categorised the motivational attitude of the players into altruism, cooperation, egoism, competition, aggression, sadomasochism, masochism and martyrdom. In experiments, psychologists have shown that such motivational attitudes are quite stable (cf. Kuhlman, Camac & Cunha 1986). The cooperative, competitive and egoistic attitudes have been found particularly frequently. It has been shown that these attitudes have a crucial influence on the establishment of cooperation.

Some scientists even claim that the puzzle of cooperation is solved adequately by the consideration of moral attitudes and norms. However, there are two main obstacles undermining the belief in motivational attitudes as a satisfactory explanation of cooperation. First, motivational attitudes change the payoffs of the game and therefore also its character. In the economic interpretation, payoffs are assumed to include aspects of subjective evaluation of outcomes. Thus, the consideration of motivational attitudes changes the payoffs compared to the monetary payoffs and therefore alters the structure of the game. The game, although it is a prisoner's dilemma game according to monetary payoffs, may no longer be a true prisoner's dilemma game, so that motivational attitudes are not an explanation for cooperation in a prisoner's dilemma game, but do explain why many games (prisoner's dilemma games according to the monetary payoffs), are not true prisoner's dilemma games because individuals have motivational attitudes. Second, the dynamics that are found in experiments cannot be explained by motivational attitudes.

10.2.2 Conditional Strategies

Since the work of R. Axelrod (1987), the notion of strategic behaviour in games has changed the analysis of the prisoner's dilemma game. Axelrod organised a 2×2 tournament in which everybody could submit a strategy. The different strategies were then used to play a prisoner's dilemma repeatedly against each other. Although many people had submitted complex algorithms, a very simple strategy won the tournament, the tit-for-tat strategy (however, this result cannot be expanded to a general setting because the performance of strategies depends on the mixture of strategies taking part in the tournament). The idea of strategic behaviour and the good performance of tit-for-tat was not really new; it had already been stated in earlier works (see e.g. Solomon 1960). But Axelrod's tournament changed game theory in three ways. First, it paved the way for the analysis of repeated games with the help of strategic behaviour. Second, tit-for-tat became a frequently discussed strategy and the level of comparison for everything else. Third, since tit-for-tat is able to evoke cooperation, it inspired a huge amount of work concerning the evolution of cooperation and its underlying reasons.

Before analysing the importance of conditional strategies, like tit-for-tat, for the establishment of cooperation, it is helpful to clarify the terminology. In recent years, the expression "strategy" has become widely used. In evolutionary game theory, every behaviour is denoted by the expression "strategy". Thus, "strategy" is used for fixed behaviours as well as stochastic, with a fixed probability for each alternative and behaviours like tit-for-tat. To avoid any confusion, the expression "conditional strategy" is used here. In my terminology, conditional strategies are behavioural concepts in which the next action depends on both or either the previous behaviour of the individual or the opponent. Tit-for-tat is an example of a conditional strategy in which an individual's behaviour depends only on the previous move of the opponent. Conditional strategies can also be more complex and depend on the whole history of the repeated game. Fixed behaviours or stochastic choices of alternatives are not conditional strategies.

In the literature, two kinds of notations of conditional strategies exist: one is based on a logical structure of if-then relations (cf. e. g. Axelrod 1987), while the other is based on Moore Automata (cf. e. g. Osborne & Rubinstein 1994). Both structures assume that a certain number of previous plays are relevant to the next behaviour. Axelrod (1987), for example, assumes that the players remember three rounds of the repeated game and act on the basis of this history. Consequently, 64 different histories exist that can be denoted by a string of six decisions: $a_r(t-3), a_r(t-2), a_r(t-1), a_c(t-3), a_c(t-2), a_c(t-1) \in \{C, D\}$; ($a_r(t)$ denotes the action of the row-player while $a_c(t)$ denotes the action of the column-player at time t). For each of the possible histories, the conditional strategy defines the response $a_i(t) \in \{C, D\}$. There are 2^{64} conditional strategies in this case. Axelrod found that, in such a case, conditional strategies similar to the tit-for-tat strategy evolve. K. Lindgren (1992) tested, in a similar approach, the robustness of the results, under the assumption that the players make mistakes. In this case the conditional strategies are much more unstable. From time to time, new strategies appear and others disappear. However, most of the time the individuals gain a payoff that is almost as high as the one for mutual cooperation. This means that cooperation is established at least most of the time.

The approaches discussed above are based on the concept of evolutionary algorithms. It is often claimed that evolutionary algorithms describe learning adequately. This has been doubted in Section 3.3 and Brenner (1998) for certain kinds of learning processes. Therefore in the present approach, behavioural rules will be used similar to conditional strategies that are learnt in an associative learning process.

10.2.3 Local Structures

In the last few years, the use of *cellular automata* in game theory has increased tremendously. This is a response to the apprehension that local interactions in large groups have crucial influences on the behaviour of the individuals. In this context, it is usually assumed that individuals imitate the behaviour of other individuals in their own surrounding, which may lead to clusters of individuals behaving equally, and sometimes to the evolution of cooperation in these clusters (cf. Nowak, Latané & Lewenstein 1994, Kirchkamp 1995, Witt 1996 and Eshel, Samuelson & Shaked 1996 who all applied different models of imitation).

Besides the different models of imitation, these approaches can be classified into two categories. Some of the authors considered only the alternative actions that the players are able to choose, cooperation or defection. Other authors considered conditional strategies as possible behaviours.

In the works that considered of conditional strategies, it has been repeatedly shown that local clusters occur, where tit-for-tat or similar conditional strategies applied by some players enforce cooperation, while in other areas defection dominates (cf. Nowak, Latané & Lewenstein 1994). The shares of cooperation and defection depend on the payoffs for each of the outcomes (see Kirchkamp 1995). The results of these approaches, however, offer no truly new insights. Most of the work resulted in rediscovering the same insights into game behaviour that have been found relevant for interactions without local structure. The only exception is the evolution of clusters of behaviour in some cases.

In the approaches without conditional strategies, the players have two options for acting; to cooperate or defect. We would expect that each learning process that increases the average payoff, leads to the Nash equilibrium. Similar to the findings of Ellison (1993), the local structure should only have an influence on the speed of players to find the Nash equilibrium. However, some theoretical works (see Eshel, Samuelson & Shaked 1996 and Witt 1996) show that local interaction may cause results different from Nash equilibria. While, in the work of Witt, the prisoner's dilemma is enriched by a third strategy, in the work of Eshel, Samuelson and Shaked, the players are only able to cooperate or defect; they are not able to apply conditional strategies. Nevertheless, the authors have been able to show that at least 60% of the players cooperate (if the initial state contains at least one group of three neighbours who cooperate) in a one-dimensional local structure (all individuals are located in a line) where each player interacts only with her/his direct neighbours. Similar results can be obtained if a two-dimensional structure is chosen, or if players interact with their neighbours, and the neighbours of their neighbours. Thus the results seem to be robust in terms of changes in the structure.

However, the line of reasoning crucially depends on the fact that the individuals are fixed in their locations and that they are only able to interact with their neighbours. In such a spacial neighbourhood, the neighbours of a neighbour are neighbours as well, or at least neighbours of another neighbour (see Figure 10.1). This allows clusters of cooperating individuals to stabilise themselves. In reality, most relations are rather structured in a network (a network structure is shown in Figure 10.2, for the distinction between these two kinds of structures cf. Nowak, Latané & Lewenstein 1994).

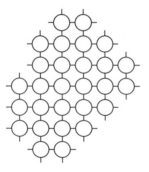

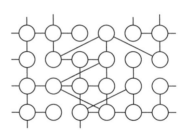

Figure 10.1: *An extract of a spacial structure*

Figure 10.2: *An extract of a network structure*

In a network structure, the enforcement of cooperation or defection depends strongly on the existing links. Cooperation spreads in the population only if a small group of cooperators is able to expand and convince others to cooperate as well. This means that they have to be able to convince defectors at the edge of this group to change their behaviour. To this end, the group of cooperators has to profit from their mutual cooperation. Their payoffs have to be larger than the ones of the defectors outside the group. This holds only if the cooperators interact mainly within the group, that is, with other cooperators, and the defectors interact mainly with defectors outside the group. Consequently, the network structure has to be such that the neighbours of a neighbour have to be neighbours themselves, or at least also neighbours of another neighbour. In other words, groups have to be able to established in such a way that interactions within the group are frequent and interactions with individuals outside the group are rare. This condition is fulfilled in the case of a local structure but not necessarily in the case of a network structure.

10.2.4 Expectations and Mutual Influence

Some authors stress the importance of *expectations* and *reputation* for the evolution of cooperation. The concept is as follows. Players may believe that their actions have an influence on that of their opponents. For example, if they cooperate they may expect the others to do the same, such an assumption is not ungrounded. The mutual influence of players has been repeatedly reported in experiments (see e. g. Lave 1965 and Liebrand 1986). If one of the players cooperates, the other feels some pressure to do the same. However, not everybody feels like that. In the experiment of Solomon (1960), some of the subjects exploited an always-cooperating opponent with the justification that if others are not optimising their payoff, they are therefore responsible for the result themselves. The need for justification points to the existence of norms. People seem to feel uneasy if the others play cooperatively and they themselves defect. Aware of this fact, in turn, players may try to provoke cooperation by starting to cooperate themselves; they may hope that their opponents feel obliged to do the same. The expectations about the influence of their individual behaviour on the behaviour of the others, depends on their experience (cf. Lave 1965) and on the amount of trust in the others (cf. Kuhlman, Camac & Cunha 1986).

On the basis of these experimental findings, one may now claim that cooperation evolves because one of the players hopes to influence the other's behaviour by cooperating, and the other feels obliged to do the same. Glance and Huberman formulated this idea mathematically for social dilemmas (Glance & Huberman 1993). They found that the values of the payoffs, and the expectations about the influence of personal actions on the actions of others, determine whether cooperation occurs. Varoufakis (1996) has proposed a similar reasoning to explain his experimental findings. He claims that the subjects in his game cooperate if they are in the disadvantageous strategic position, because they hope that their opponents feel morally obliged to do the same, in order to be treated the same way when the situation is reversed.

A similar line of reasoning is used by many economists, who argue that cooperation evolves because of the struggle of individuals for reputation (cf. e. g. Klein & Leffler 1981, Shapiro 1983 and Milgrom, North & Weingast 1990).

10.3 LEARNING OF COOPERATION

Each of the above-presented explanations for cooperation considers a different aspect of human behaviour relevant in the prisoner's dilemma game. Although each of these approaches offers some interesting ideas, a more comprehensive understanding of behaviour in prisoner's dilemma games, making it possible to predict behaviour, would be preferable to a collection of several different explanations.

In this case, a more comprehensive approach to behaviour in a prisoner's dilemma game can be realised, using learning behaviour models as a basis for development of strategies, and for the occurrence of cooperation. In such a model, individuals are assumed to learn during the repeated game; this is a fundamental assumption that hardly contradicts any of the above explanations. However, it allows us to proceed with the analysis, starting from the consideration of different motivations of individuals, that is, different learning processes, and to find out which explanations of cooperation are relevant under which circumstances.

The consideration of learning processes implies that a situation occurs repeatedly, or at least that situations faced are sufficiently similar for individuals to regard them as the same. This assumption fits many economic situations. Examples are: the use of common resources; interactions at the work place, the preparedness to help or advise each other; and competition for the market of a good.

Due to the wide variety of real life situations that have the character of a prisoner's dilemma game, behaviour in prisoner's dilemma games is not the same in all these situations. Instead, behaviour depends on the circumstances and the kind of learning processes involved. Thus the prisoner's dilemma game is an ideal example for demonstrating the relevance of the different learning processes distinguished in Chapter 2.

10.3.1 Non-cognitive Learning

Whenever individuals are not cognitively aware of the prisoner's dilemma situation which they face, they learn by reinforcement. The implications of such a learning process in the context of interactions between individuals is studied in Chapter 6 and finally discussed at the end of Section 6.4. There it is claimed that reinforcement learning leads to defection if the payoffs for mutual defection are positive. If, however, the payoffs for mutual defection are negative, the players are repeatedly pushed to avoid mutual defection. Other behaviours are unstable as well, so that there is no behaviour that satisfies all players. In such a case the Bush-Mosteller model predicts permanent changes of behaviour. Permanent changes, however, are likely to attract the cognitive attention of individuals. Therefore if mutual defection causes punishing outcomes, the individuals are most likely reflect about the situation cognitively.

To sum up, individuals learn to defect in a prisoner's dilemma game if there is no incentive to reflect on the game cognitively, and if the payoffs for mutual defection are reinforcing (although the payoffs for mutual cooperation are even more reinforcing).

10.3.2 Routine-based Learning

According to the categorisation of learning processes (cf. Figure 2.1) proposed in this book, individuals who are cognitively aware of a situation may engage in two kinds of learning: routine-based learning and associative learning. Prisoner's dilemma situations are typical examples of those in which both learning processes interact. However, the benchmark situations in which one or the other kind of cognitive learning dominates, are easy to identify by distinguishing a situation in which the players are not aware of the fact that they interact with another individual, and a situation in which they build cognitive models of the behaviour of their opponents. The latter situation is discussed in the next subsection.

If individuals are not aware of the fact that they interact with another individual, they only know about the choice they have between two alternative actions and the payoffs that result from their choice. In this case they have to rely on general learning routines, like the one described by the VID model (such an approach to game behaviour can be found in Brenner 1998b). In the case of the prisoner's dilemma game, the use of a learning routine based on the principle of satificing, occasional variations, and imitation, leads to permanent fluctuations in behaviour (cf. Brenner 1998b) if the payoff for mutual defection is dissatisfying. Thus,

the results of routine-based learning are somehow similar to the results
of non-cognitive learning. However, two fundamental differences exist.
First, whether the payoff for mutual defection is dissatisfying depends
on the experience of the individuals in the past, and on their knowledge
about possible payoffs. If they know about the higher payoffs, obtained
by other individuals or themselves, individuals are not satisfied with
their current results. Thus if mutual cooperation is established between
a subgroup of individuals, the payoff for mutual defection becomes dissatisfying for the individuals who are not able to establish cooperation,
and they will search for other behaviours in the hope of establishing cooperation as well (cf. Dixon 1995). Second, if the aspect of imitation
is accompanied with the learning routine, local structures of neighbours
may allow for the evolution of cooperation (cf. the discussion in Section
10.2.3).

10.3.3   Associative Learning

The situation is principally different if the players are aware of the prisoner's dilemma situation and of the fact that they interact with others.
Cognitive awareness comes into play more strongly and implies that the
individuals build cognitive models of the situation and the relevant circumstances. Since the game is sufficiently understood, the cognitive
models that are built mainly relate to the behaviour of the opponents,
which is unknown. This means that individuals develop beliefs about
the behaviour of others, and the influence that their own behaviour has
on the behaviour of others. These changes of belief or cognitive models,
in time are called "associative learning processes" according to the categorisation of learning processes proposed in this book. The results of
the associative learning processes shape the behaviour of the individuals
and therefore determine whether cooperation is established or not.

   Thus if individuals have an incentive to cognitively reflect on their
behaviour, and if they are aware of the fact that they interact with others,
associative learning processes have to be studied in order to answer the
question of which circumstances lead to cooperation, and which do not.
This will be done in the next section.

10.4 MODELLING ASSOCIATIVE LEARNING

10.4.1 Purview of Cognitive Models

To specify what sort of cognitive models dominate the thinking concerning appropriate action in a prisoner's dilemma game, their purview has to be discussed, according to two features of the situation. First, it has to be distinguished whether individuals learn about the behaviour of one specific opponent or about opponents in general. Second, it has to be distinguished whether individuals learn about the behaviour of opponents in one specific prisoner's dilemma situation or in prisoner's dilemma situations in general. Four situations of learning result from this distinction. Each of them leads to different cognitive structures.

The following analysis is restricted to one specific situation, a situation in which only one kind of prisoner's dilemma is played repeatedly, and the individuals are able to recognise their opponents. Furthermore, it is assumed that each individual plays the prisoner's dilemma game against one opponent several times before the individuals are matched in a new random order. Thus, after a little while, an individual faces a new opponent knowing that (s)he will interact with this opponent for an unknown number of times.

Each time an individual faces a new opponent, it is important for this individual to figure out what sort of behaviour to expect from that opponent, in order to act in an adequate way in the following interactions. To this end, individuals build a cognitive model about their new opponent, models that allow them to classify the opponent and to apply the optimal strategy with respect to this classification. The development and change of these cognitive models is an associative learning process.

The cognitive model of an opponent's behaviour first of all determines the payoff believed possible by an individual. Individuals may believe that it is possible to reach cooperation or, alternatively, to exploit others. They also may believe that cooperation is impossible and that the others intend to exploit them. Thus cognitive models, once they have been developed, allow individuals to judge which payoffs can be reached and which payoffs are impossible. Thus, associative learning in prisoner's dilemma games, in principle, leads to an identification of the payoff attainable through interaction with a certain opponent.

In the prisoner's dilemma game, only four outcomes are possible; these are altruism, defection, cooperation and exploitation. Moral attitudes or other additional preferences that may cause altruism to be desirable (cf. Section 10.2.1), are assumed to be included in the payoffs in the present approach. Consequently if the payoffs, including these aspects, still fulfil the condition ($e > c > d > a$) for a prisoner's dilemma, altruism is not desirable because it leads to the smallest payoff. Furthermore, the payoff for mutual defection (d) can at least be reached, independent of the opponent's behaviour, by always defecting. Thus as mentioned earlier, there are two desirable states for each individual: mutual cooperation or exploitation of the other. It can be assumed that players who are conscious of their interaction with others are also aware of these two desirable states.

As a consequence, once a prisoner's-dilemma-type of interaction is recognised, associative learning aids in identifying which of the states (mutual cooperation and exploitation), can be reached during an interaction with a given opponent. Thus, an individual can classify an opponent into one of the following three types, with respect to the payoffs obtainable.

Suckers: Suckers are opponents who always cooperate from a certain stage of the repeated game onwards (they may be individuals with different moral attitudes so that the game is no prisoner's dilemma for them) so that they can be exploited. Thus, if one player identifies her/his opponent as a sucker, (s)he believes that the highest payoff e can be reached.

Opportunists: Opportunists are opponents who cooperate or defect dependent on the other's behaviour. They intend to establish mutual cooperation but only if their opponent shows the same intention. This means that they cannot be exploited but that mutual cooperation can be established.

Defectors: Defectors are opponents who always defect after a certain stage of the repeated game onwards. This means that neither exploitation nor cooperation can be reached sustainably. All an individual can do is defect as well, in order not to be exploited.

These three types of individuals describe the possible behaviours sufficiently; everyone usually falls into one of these three categories. Reasons for being a sucker or a defector may be different evaluations of the payoffs. In such a case, the game is not a prisoner's dilemma any more. Nevertheless, for one of two interacting individuals it may look like a prisoner's dilemma, while the other always cooperates or always defects, due to her/his subjective evaluation of the outcome. The learning process of one individual is studied below, assuming that this individual regards the game to be a prisoner's dilemma. This individual is called "the player" and behaves, in principle, like an opportunist. Her/his opponents may evaluate the outcomes differently and may be one of the three types. However, the evaluation of the outcomes by the opponent cannot be anticipated by the player, so the player only knows about the different types possible and therefore aims to identify the opponent as one of these types.

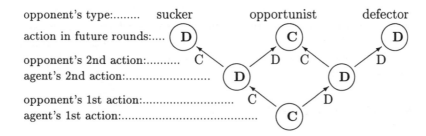

Figure 10.3: *This graph describes an arbitrarily chosen routine. The actions of an individual are given within the circles. The routine starts with the initial behaviour (here D for defection) and proceeds along the arrows according to the actions of the opponent which are written beneath the arrows. Here in the first round the individual cooperates. If her/his opponent cooperates (s)he gets to the circle on the left just above the initial state and defects in the second round (note that the actions of both players in any one round are made simultaneously, the opponent is not able to observe the agent's action before (s)he chooses an action her/himself). If her/his opponent again cooperates in the second round (s)he identifies the opponent as a sucker and defects in the following rounds. If the opponent changes behaviour and defects in the second round (s)he identifies her/his opponent as an opportunist and cooperates from then on. If the opponent cooperates after defecting in the first round (s)he reaches the same state as if the opponent first defects and then cooperates. If the opponent defects in first two rounds, the agent identifies the opponent as a defector and defects subsequently.*

If the opponent is a sucker, a player exploits this opponent by defecting; if the opponent is an opportunist, they offer cooperation to establish mutual cooperation; and if the opponent is a defector, they defect as well, in order not to be exploited themselves. To this end, they have to learn a rule of behaviour in the first rounds, and how to classify their opponent. I call such a rule a "routine"; it is established by associative learning. Such a routine may state: when meeting a new individual, offer cooperation in the first round and defect in the second round and, based on her/his behaviour, identify the person as follows: if the other accepts the offer and cooperates in the second round although (s)he has defected in the first, (s)he is identified as an opportunist; if the other cooperates in both rounds (s)he is a sucker; if the other defects in both rounds, (s)he is a defector (cf. Figure 10.3).

There are also many other plausible learning routines. The cognitive models, built from the associative learning process performed in the past, determine which routine an individual applies. In a theoretical approach, the possible routines have to be defined before the associative learning process is studied.

10.4.2   Cognitive Models and Routines

According to the consideration in Section 3.5, there is a mapping from the set of possible cognitive model into the set of possible behaviours given by routines here. Thus associative learning, although it essentially changes the cognitive models of individuals, can be modelled as if it changes routines. Thus the possible routines have to be defined in the following section, while the appearance of the cognitive models is ignored.

Identification of the opponent

As stated above, the aim of individuals in the short run is to identify the character of their opponent. Three characters are possible; the opponent is a sucker, an opportunist or a defector. The information used for identification are the actions chosen by the opponent in the past. Once the opponent is identified, individuals behave according to this identification; they cooperate if their opponent is an opportunist and defect if their opponent is either a sucker or a defector. This behaviour remains until the opponent changes, or until the current opponent behaves in a way that contradicts this label. In the latter case, the identification rule is changed and identification is started again.

Since cognitive capacity is a scarce resource, it is important to identify the opponent after a small number of actions, because the consideration of a long history of actions is costly in terms of cognitive capacity. A good measure for the cognitive capacity consumed by an identification rule, is the number of rounds needed to identify an opponent's type. Therefore I define:

DEFINITION 10.1 (COMPLEXITY): *A routine is said to be of complexity n if the corresponding identification rule requires the first n actions of the opponent to be observed.*

Considering the example given by Figure 10.3, the identification rule requires that the individual is able to remember the first two actions of her/his opponent. Thus it is a routine of complexity $n = 2$. The complexity measure defined above should not be regarded as a general measure of complexity. It is designed for the present approach only, to simplify argumentation in the following.

Routines and conditional strategies

In Section 10.2.2, the explanation of cooperation, based on the assumption that individuals behave according to conditional strategies, has been presented. In an approach with conditional strategies, individuals are assumed to react to the actions of their opponents (e. g. the conditional strategy tit-for-tat assumes that an individual always acts in the same way as her/his opponent has acted in the previous round). In the case of routines, individuals identify their opponents as a certain type of player according to the opponents' actions, and then act according to this identification. Thus, they also act in response to the actions of their opponents. Furthermore, I described the routines by means of a graph that can be interpreted as a *Moore automaton*, which is also used to describe conditional strategies. From this perspective, each routine defined above is a conditional strategy; however, differences exist between routines and conditional strategies. Although each routine is also a conditional strategy given by a Moore automaton, not every conditional strategy is also a routine. Here the decision and identification routines are restricted to such rules that finally identify the type of opponent after some rounds of playing the same game. Thus routines, as they are defined above, have to converge to a constant identification and a constant behaviour. Moore automata, instead, allow for cyclical behaviour (e. g. two players who apply the tit-for-tat strategy may use one cooperation and one defection each time and alternate always their actions). It is assumed here that individuals cognitively aware of the prisoner's dilemma situation, are able to recognise such a pattern and identify their opponent as a tit-for-tat player, which means the type of player who accepts mutual cooperation, and so they offer permanent cooperation.

This difference between routines and conditional strategies results from different approaches to analysing game behaviour. The concept of conditional strategies is mainly used in connection with evolutionary game theory, in the literature. Evolutionary game theory is based on the process of biological selection. In this context, different behaviours show up by mutations and are therefore arbitrarily chosen, so that every possible strategy may occur. Then biological selection eliminates the less successful ones. The decision and identification routines, on the other hand, are assumed to develop through an associative learning process. This learning process involves a search for meaningful strategies right from the beginning. Thus many routines that are theoretically possible are never used. However, the assumption of associative learning in action makes the analysis more complex, because the reflection about the value of routines has to be approached, in addition to the pure definition of the representation of routines.

10.4.3 Process of Associative Learning

In addition to incorporating the use of different possible routines or conditional strategies employed in a game, the present approach deviates from the evolutionary approaches (cf. e.g. Axelrod and Lindgren 1992) by assuming an associative learning process which is defined in the following manner.

In an associative learning process, not every Moore automaton occurs. Individuals do not just try different cognitive models by chance, and select the appropriate ones according to their correspondence with reality. Individuals start with an initial cognitive model that is transferred to the situation from a similar situation. If a cognitive model has proved to be wrong, individuals change this cognitive model in a meaningful way.

Three aspects are important for the development of cognitive models and the corresponding routine. These include the initial cognitive model, the causes for an abandonment of cognitive models, and the ways in which cognitive models are modified.

The initial state is impossible to understand theoretically, because all the other situations that have been faced by individuals in the past, influence the initial state. Therefore the initial behaviours have to be chosen either according to experimental or empirical knowledge, or arbitrarily. In the latter case, it should be checked whether the arbitrary choice of the initial cognitive models influences the results of the analysis.

Individuals change their cognitive models if they realise the present model is inadequate. The failure of a cognitive model to describe reality, can be easily identified in the present approach. The routine is defined such that it converges to a certain belief about the opponent's behaviour after some time. Once the opponent's behaviour has been identified, the individuals believe in this identification. As long as the opponent behaves correspondingly, the identification rule is confirmed. A behaviour that contradicts the identification falsifies the identification rule.

In addition to the identification rule, routines also determine the behaviour of individuals in the first few rounds, until the opponent is identified. Behaviour can not be falsified, it can only be appropriate or inappropriate. However, it is difficult to judge whether a behaviour displayed in the first rounds is appropriate because this behaviour has two purposes. On the one hand, individuals try not to be exploited in the first rounds or try to exploit others in these rounds. On the other hand it is important to signal the willingness to cooperate early on, if cooperation is to be established. These two motives lead to opposite behaviours. Thus in general, different behaviours in the first few rounds cannot be compared with each other with respect to their appropriateness. It may be assumed that an individual's earlier behaviour is changed if (s)he is exploited too often, if an individual believes there to be a possibility to establish cooperation by changing behaviour, and sometimes by chance.

According to the above three reasons for changing cognitive models and therefore behaviour, the changes themselves may have different features. An individual exploited too much will reduce their cooperation, while an individual believing that chances to establish cooperation have been missed, increases her/his cooperative acts. Random changes occur occasionally too.

If, during the course of the game, the identification rule is falsified, the reaction is generally to alter the identification rule and make a new start on the identification process for the current opponent. The rule change is generally made in such a way that for most of the observations, the identifications stay the same and only the identification for the realised observation, which was falsified, is corrected according to the latest experience. However, this still allows for several changes in most cases. Furthermore, due to the scarcity of cognitive capacity, detailed identification rules are unlikely to be established. Thus the individual tends rather to ignore a falsification of the current identification rule if the opponent's behaviour was correctly identified for a long time. In these cases individuals tend to believe that the opponent's behaviour has changed for some reason. Consequently, they may merely start the identification process, again.

10.4.4   Analysis of Associative Learning in Prisoner's Dilemma Games

To start with the analysis of associative learning in prisoner's dilemma games, it is helpful to analyse the stability of learning by using routines. This means that only one aspect of the three aspects relevant for the changes of cognitive models, is investigated; it is the question of when routines are abandoned.

Falsification of identification rules

As stated above, identification rules are abandoned if they are falsified. A falsification is the most severe obstacle to the stability of an identification rule. Therefore I will analyse which routines are eliminated by falsification. As mentioned above, it is assumed that some individuals in the population perceive the game differently and either always cooperate or always defect. This assumption allows the elimination of some identification rules right from the beginning, because they are falsified by the those opponents who always defect or always cooperate. The identification rules eliminated are all rules identifying an opponent, (who always defected in the past), as a sucker or opportunist. If an opponent is identified as either, the individual expects this opponent to cooperate in the future (suckers always cooperate, while in the case of an opportunist, the individual her/himself cooperates and expects the opponent to do the same). Both cases are falsified by an always-defecting opponent. Similarly, an always-cooperating opponent falsifies all identification rules that identify an opponent, who cooperated in the past, as a defector.

Furthermore, identification rules that are inconsistent are falsified and eliminated quickly. Therefore, all routines identifying an opponent as an altruist, although (s)he defected at least once in the past, are ignored. Similarly, all rules that identify an opponent as a defector, although (s)he cooperated at least once in the past, are eliminated.

As a consequence, possible identification rules are restricted to those defined as meaningful by the following definition:

DEFINITION 10.2: *A routine is meaningful if it satisfies the following three conditions:*

- *An opponent who always cooperated in the past is identified as a sucker or an opportunist.*

- *An opponent who cooperated and defected in the past is identified as an opportunist.*

- *An opponent who always defected in the past is identified as a defector.*

The above conditions reduce the set of possible identification rules enormously and simplify the following analysis of routines.

Routines of complexity $n = 1$

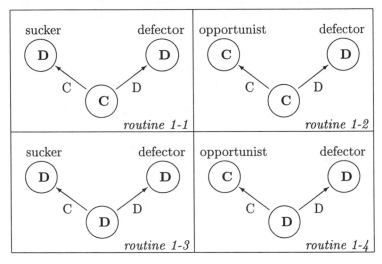

Figure 10.4: *Graphs describing all meaningful routines of complexity $n = 1$ (the structure of representation follows the logic symbolised in Figure 10.3)*

First, this analysis is restricted to routines of complexity $n = 1$. Individuals using such routines classify their opponents immediately after their first action. According to Definition 10.2 of meaningful routines, an opponent who cooperates in the first round can only be identified either as a sucker or as an opportunist. Similarly, opponents who defect in the first round can only be identified as defectors. Note that identification of an opponent as an opportunist who defected in the first round is falsified by all opponents who always defect and is therefore not a meaningful routine.

As a consequence, only two meaningful identification rules exist: one states that opponents cooperating in the first round are altruists; the other states that opponents cooperating in the first round are opportunists. Both identification rules state that opponents defecting in the first round are defectors. Since a routine defines the identification rule as well as the individual's behaviour in the first n rounds, two further situations have to be distinguished; the individuals may either cooperate or defect in the first round. Thus, four routines exist, which are given in Figure 10.4. The aim of the present analysis is to identify which routines may be stable in a population, meaning those which are not falsified. The routines given in Figure 10.4 satisfy the three general conditions given in Definition 10.2, so that they are not falsified by individuals who always cooperate or always defect. However, they may be falsified by opponents who are also applying one of the routines given in Figure 10.4. Let us consider one example to make this point clearer. Assume two individuals are interacting in a prisoner's dilemma game and both apply routine 1-1 as given in Figure 10.4. Both cooperate in the first round, according to this routine. Both identify an opponent who cooperates in the first round as a sucker, which means that both believe their opponent will always cooperate. As a consequence, both defect after round one (as given by routine 1-1). By doing this, however, both falsify the belief of their opponent. Thus, routine 1-1 is falsified by an opponent applying routine 1-1. All pairs of players can be analysed in the same way. The result is

- routine 1-1 is falsified by routine 1-1 and routine 1-4.

- routine 1-2 is falsified by routine 1-1 and routine 1-4.

- routine 1-3 is falsified by routine 1-1 and routine 1-2.

- routine 1-4 is falsified by routine 1-1 and routine 1-2.

This result has an important implication: none of the routines is stable if all four routines are used in the population. Only if routines do not alter by chance but only by falsification, may a state be reached in which one of the three routines 1-2, 1-3 or 1-4 is used by the whole population, so that this state is stable. The pure use of routine 1-1 by the whole population is never stable because it always falsifies itself.

General identification rules

Above, it has been shown that all meaningful identification rules based on one observation are falsified by at least one other rule based on one observation. Thus no routine considering one observation is stable, if we allow all meaningful routines of this complexity to occur in the population. The same holds for all other levels of complexity, as will be proved in the following theorem.

THEOREM 10.1: *Each meaningful routine of a given complexity can be falsified by a meaningful routine of the same complexity.*

Proof: Let us consider an arbitrary chosen routine of complexity n that is used by individual i. The first n moves of individual i influence the behaviour of the opponent j, who also uses a routine of complexity n, for deciding how to proceed after the first n rounds. First, let me assume that the routine of individual i causes individual j to cooperate after the identification phase (i.e. individual j believes individual i to be an opportunist). Then if individual j defects in the first n rounds, individual i has to believe that individual j is a defector, according to Definition 10.2, and this routine is falsified by the cooperation of individual j in round $n + 1$. Thus a routine (the one of individual j defecting in the identification phase) has been found falsifying the routine of individual i, which leads the other to cooperate. Second, let me assume that the routine of individual i causes individual j to defect after the identification phase. Then if individual j cooperates the first n rounds, individual i has to believe that individual j is a sucker or an opportunist (in both cases individual j should continue to cooperate) according to Definition 10.2, so that individual i's routine is falsified by the defection of individual j in round $n + 1$. Thus also for routines that cause the opponent to defect, a routine (the one of individual j cooperating in the identification phase) is found that falsifies such a rule. ∎

As a consequence of Theorem 10.1, routines can only be stable, that is, not falsified by any other routine used within the population, if certain other meaningful routines of the same complexity are never used for some reason. Therefore, stability requires reasons to exist for not using some routines. In some cases such reasons can be found, as for example, in the case of all routines of complexity $n = 1$.

Everybody may agree that routine 1-1 is quite a stupid rule; it identifies every opponent after the first round as a sucker or a defector. Both identifications imply that the appropriate personal action is to defect. Thus an individual using this rule believes that defection is the best action, because there is no possibility they are facing an opportunist. Nevertheless, routine 1-1 requires cooperation in the first round. Consequently, we may claim that routine 1-1 never occurs in a population, so that every routine that is only falsified by routine 1-1, is a stable routine. Unfortunately no such routine (of complexity $n = 1$ that is only falsified by routine 1-1) exists. Hence, on the level of a complexity of $n = 1$, there is no stable routine even if all "stupid" ones are eliminated. Below, routines of complexity $n = 2$ are studied, to see whether the implications of the present model allow for more precise statements on this level.

Routines of complexity $n = 2$

Similar to the calculation of meaningful routines of complexity $n = 1$, according to the conditions given in Definition 10.2, 12 meaningful routines of complexity $n = 2$ exist, which are shown in Figure 10.6.

For the routines given in Figure 10.6 one obtains:

- routine 2-1 is falsified by the routines 2-7 and 2-8.

- routine 2-2 is falsified by the routines 2-3 and 2-4.

- routine 2-3 is falsified by the routines 2-1, 2-2, 2-4, 2-5, 2-6, 2-8, 2-9, 2-10 and 2-12.

- routine 2-4 is falsified by the routines 2-1, 2-2, 2-3, 2-5, 2-6, 2-7, 2-9, 2-10 and 2-11.

- routine 2-5 is falsified by the routines 2-1, 2-2, 2-5, 2-6, 2-7 and 2-8.

- routine 2-6 is falsified by the routines 2-1, 2-2, 2-3, 2-4, 2-5 and 2-6.

- routine 2-7 is falsified by the routines 2-4, 2-8 and 2-12.

- routine 2-8 is falsified by the routines 2-3, 2-7 and 2-11.

- routine 2-9 is falsified by the routines 2-1, 2-2, 2-5, 2-6, 2-7 and 2-8.

- routine 2-10 is falsified by the routines 2-1, 2-2, 2-3, 2-4, 2-5 and 2-6.

- routine 2-11 is falsified by the routines 2-4, 2-8 and 2-12.

- routine 2-12 is falsified by the routines 2-3, 2-7 and 2-11.

Similar to the discussion for routines of complexity $n = 1$, we may try to declare some of the routines inappropriate, and therefore not used for other reasons. For example, routines 2-5 and 2-6 falsify themselves, so they are not sustained, even if the whole population applies them. All other routines described in Figure 10.6 would at least remain un-falsified if everyone were to apply the same routine. Furthermore, routines 2-3 and 2-4 are falsified by nearly all others so that they are unlikely to be used in a μ opulation for long. Excluding these routines results in:

- routine 2-1 is falsified by the routines 2-7 and 2-8.

- routine 2-2 is falsified by no routine.

- routine 2-7 is falsified by the routines 2-8 and 2-12.

- routine 2-8 is falsified by the routines 2-7 and 2-11.

- routine 2-9 is falsified by the routines 2-1, 2-2, 2-7 and 2-8.

- routine 2-10 is falsified by the routines 2-1 and 2-2.

- routine 2-11 is falsified by the routines 2-8 and 2-12.

- routine 2-12 is falsified by the routines 2-7 and 2-11.

This reveals that a reduction of possible routines, by the elimination of some that are unlikely to be used, changes the picture of the associative learning process crucially. For example, in the case above, routine 2-2 is no longer falsified by any of the considered routines (2-3, 2-4, 2-5 and 2-6 are assumed not to occur). Thus it might be claimed that routine 2-2 would supersede in the population. To support this claim, the following mathematical analysis is conducted.

Mathematical approach to meaningful routine of complexity $n = 2$

All meaningful routines of complexity $n = 2$ are described in Figure 10.6. They are denoted by 2-1 to 2-12. Below, each of these routines is assigned to a natural number i from 1 to 12 ($i = 1$ for routine 2-1,... and $i = 12$ for routine 2-12). The share of individuals in a population who apply routine i at time t, is denoted by $x_i(t)$. This share is assumed to change by two processes. First, individuals change their behaviour occasionally by chance. The probability of such a change is denoted by ϵ. Second, routines are abandoned if they are falsified. The probability of a routine being falsified equals the probability that one of the routines falsifying this routine, is used in the population. For example, the probability that routine 2-2 is falsified at time t is given by

$$x_3(t) + x_4(t) . \tag{10.1}$$

Furthermore, the new routine is assumed to be chosen randomly, so that each routine is chosen as the new routine with the same probability. This contradicts the claim, which was made above, that changes in cognitive models, and therefore also changes in routines, are meaningful. Hence it is necessary to point out that the following analysis is a fairly crude approximation of associative learning, and is made only to support the claim that routine 2-2 is, to some extent, superior to the other routines of complexity $n = 2$. Since the assumption of a random choice of routines after falsification weakens superior routines compared with others, the result would be more significant under more realistic assumptions.

Given the above assumption, the probability that a routine i is chosen by an individual who has abandoned her/his former routine, is the same for all and is denoted by $p_0(t)$ (it is the overall probability of an individual abandoning her/his routine at time t divided by 12). Thus, the dynamics of the share $x_2(t)$ of individuals who apply routine 2-2, is given by

$$x_2(t+1) - x_2(t) = p_0(t) - \Big(x_3(t) + x_4(t) + \epsilon\Big)x_2(t) . \qquad (10.2)$$

This means that the application of routine 2-2 increases by $p_0(t)$, and decreases by the probability of routine 2-2 being falsified, plus the probability of an occasional change, both multiplied by the share of individuals who apply routine 2-2 at time t, and therefore become able to abandon it through falsification.

Similarly, the equations for the dynamics of all other shares are obtained:

$$x_1(t+1) - x_1(t) = p_0(t)) - \left(x_7(t) + x_8(t) + \epsilon\right)x_1(t)$$

$$x_2(t+1) - x_2(t) = p_0(t) - \left(x_3(t) + x_4(t) + \epsilon\right)x_2(t)$$

$$x_3(t+1) - x_3(t) = p_0(t) - \left(x_1(t) + x_2(t) + x_4(t) + x_5(t) + x_6(t)\right.$$
$$\left. + x_8(t) + x_9(t) + x_{10}(t) + x_{12}(t) + \epsilon\right)x_3(t)$$

$$x_4(t+1) - x_4(t) = p_0(t) - \left(x_1(t) + x_2(t) + x_3(t) + x_5(t) + x_6(t)\right.$$
$$\left. + x_7(t) + x_9(t) + x_{10}(t) + x_{11}(t) + \epsilon\right)x_4(t)$$

$$x_5(t+1) - x_5(t) = p_0(t) - \left(x_2(t) + x_5(t) + x_6(t) + x_7(t)\right.$$
$$\left. + x_8(t) + \epsilon\right)x_5(t)$$

$$x_6(t+1) - x_6(t) = p_0(t) - \left(x_2(t) + x_3(t) + x_4(t) + x_5(t)\right.$$
$$\left. + x_6(t) + \epsilon\right)x_6(t)$$

$$x_7(t+1) - x_7(t) = p_0(t) - \left(x_4(t) + x_8(t) + x_{12}(t) + \epsilon\right)x_7(t)$$

$$x_8(t+1) - x_8(t) = p_0(t) - \left(x_3(t) + x_7(t) + x_{11}(t) + \epsilon\right)x_2(t)$$

$$x_9(t+1) - x_9(t) = p_0(t) - \left(x_2(t) + x_5(t) + x_6(t) + x_7(t)\right.$$
$$\left. + x_8(t) + \epsilon\right)x_2(t)$$

$$x_{10}(t+1) - x_{10}(t) = p_0(t) - \left(x_2(t) + x_3(t) + x_4(t) + x_5(t)\right.$$
$$\left. + x_6(t) + \epsilon\right)x_2(t)$$

$$x_{11}(t+1) - x_{11}(t) = p_0(t) - \left(x_4(t) + x_8(t) + x_{12}(t) + \epsilon\right)x_2(t)$$

$$x_{12}(t+1) - x_{12}(t) = p_0(t) - \left(x_3(t) + x_7(t) + x_{11}(t) + \epsilon\right)x_2(t) .$$

$$(10.3)$$

The stationary state of these dynamics is given by $x_i(t) - x_i(t) = 0$ for all i. Inserting this condition into equation (10.3), the resulting set of equations can be solved for each value of ϵ. For example, in the case of $\epsilon = 0.001$, the stationary state is given by $\breve{x}_1 = 0.097$, $\breve{x}_2 = 0.394$, $\breve{x}_3 = 0.021$, $\breve{x}_4 = 0.021$, $\breve{x}_5 = 0.027$, $\breve{x}_6 = 0.034$, $\breve{x}_7 = 0.087$, $\breve{x}_8 = 0.087$, $\breve{x}_9 = 0.027$, $\breve{x}_{10} = 0.034$, $\breve{x}_{11} = 0.087$, and $\breve{x}_{12} = 0.087$ which means that the routine 2-2 is used most often.

Thus if individuals do not change their routines frequently by chance, but mostly if their routine is falsified, and only if routines of complexity $n = 2$ are applied, routine 2-2 supersedes in the population. Two individuals applying routine 2-2 establish cooperation.

10.4.5   Implications for the Evolution of Cooperation

The above considerations, as well as the above mathematical analysis, suggest but do not prove, that cooperation is established in a prisoner's dilemma game if the players learn associatively. However, for the mathematical analysis some crucial assumptions have been made to derive this result. First, it has been assumed that individuals apply only meaningful routines of complexity $n = 2$. Second, it has been assumed that none of the individuals attempts to exploit others by trying to convince them to be opportunists with whom cooperation can be established, only to defect later. Third, changes in routines have been assumed to occur if the current routine is falsified or occasionally, due to chance. Other reasons for changes in the applied routines have been ignored.

Given these three assumptions, the above calculations predict cooperation to be the result of associative learning in a repeated prisoner's dilemma game. Whether this result still holds if the above assumptions are altered, is discussed in the following.

Complexity of routines

In the calculations above, only routines of complexity $n = 1$ and $n = 2$ have been considered. The analysis has been restricted to these routines because the number of meaningful routines increases quickly with complexity. However this is not a realistic assumption, because people are able to develop more complex routines than the ones studied here.

A justification for the restriction of routines to those with a complexity $n \leq 2$, may be the scarcity of cognitive capacity. Routines with a higher complexity use more cognitive capacity, so that there should be a tendency for individuals to apply less complex routines. Nevertheless, this tendency does not imply that routines of complexity $n > 2$ are not used. Thus, in general, routines of higher complexity should be analysed. However, there is no reason to believe that an analysis of routines of complexity n ($n > 2$) leads to results different from the ones obtained above. An analysis of conditional strategies in a game theoretic approach, revealed similar results to the ones obtained here (cf. Lindgren 1992). There it is shown, by simulations, that at each level of complexity cooperation is established, while by each change to conditional strategies of higher complexity, cooperation was dismissed for some period of time, then to be later re-established. Similar results seem to be likely in the present approach. As long as all individuals apply routines of the same complexity, the analysis above suggests, but does not prove, cooperation is established. However, some individuals may change to more complex routines and falsify the current routines that lead to cooperation. If the other individuals switch to more complex routines as well, cooperation should be re-established.

This raises the question of why individuals should have an incentive to switch to more complex routines. This question is approached in the next subsection.

Individuals trying to exploit others

Once cooperation is established, only one reason exists for individuals to search for alternative routines, and that is the attempt to exploit others. It was argued above that exploitation does not work in the long run because individuals who learn associatively are able to detect individuals who try to exploit them. However, if the routine of an individual is restricted to a certain complexity, this individual may be exploited. Consider, for example, an individual applying routine 2-2. Routine 2-2 adequately identifies the long run behaviour of the most relevant routines of complexity $n = 2$. However to obtain this result, it was assumed that individuals apply only consistent routines. Let us consider an individual with a routine given by Figure 10.7.

The routine given in Figure 10.7, called routine 2-13 below, is similar to routine 2-2 in Figure 10.6. The only difference is that individuals applying routine 2-13 identify all opponents who have cooperated once and defected once in the first two rounds, as suckers. Playing against any routine given in Figure 10.6, it can be seen that routine 2-13 is only falsified by individuals using routines 2-3 and 2-4, similar to routine 2-2. However, in the cases in which routine 2-2 helps identify the opponent as an opportunist and suggests establishing cooperation, routine 2-13 gives rise to an identification of the other as a sucker, and suggests exploiting her/him. Thus routine 2-13 is able to exploit many routines of complexity $n = 2$ because, at the time the exploitation starts, individuals applying routine 2-13 are already identified as opportunists.

For other levels of complexity, similar "exploiting routines" can be constructed. Playing with an individual who applies a routine of complexity n, the exploiting routine helps to persuade most of the individuals applying a routine of this complexity, after the identification period, that they face an opportunist. Thus the opponent will cooperate after the identification period, while the individual with the exploiting routine will exploit this opponent.

However, through the very act of exploitation, the opponent's routine becomes falsified. Thus the application of an exploiting routine of complexity n, (like the routine 2-13 given in Figure 10.7), while playing a prisoner's dilemma with another individual who applies a routine of the same complexity n, leads to one of two states. First, the opponent may not have been successfully convinced that (s)he plays against an opportunist. In this case, both players defect after the identification phase. Second, the opponent may have been successfully convinced that (s)he plays against an opportunist. In this case, the opponent cooperates and can be exploited. However, this exploitation necessarily falsifies the opponent's routine, so that this player may react in one of three ways, the opponent may ignore the falsification, start to identify the opponent again, or change the applied routine.

In the first case, the exploiting player will manage to get by with her/his exploitation. Falsification is likely to be ignored if it does not happen too often. Thus, exploiting players are most successful if they are the only ones. A large number of exploiting players makes it worth the effort of modifying routines in order to identify exploiting players. Keeping these routines meaningful requires that they have a complexity larger than that of the exploiting routine, because the exploiting routines, as constructed above, are designed to foul all meaningful routines of the same complexity. Thus, detection costs more cognitive capacity than exploitation. As a consequence, detection of those players who exploit has to be more important than exploiting others, if cooperation is to be established. Therefore, the occurrence and sustainability of exploiting routines in a population depends on the differences in payoffs between mutual cooperation (c) and altruism (a) and mutual cooperation (c) and exploitation (e).

However, there is also another obstacle to the exploitation of others. Exploited opponents may react to the falsification of their routine by a new start of their identification process. In this case, if the exploiting player continues to exploit, they will realise that their opponent always defects, and will defect as well. Through this, exploiting players are not detected as individuals who try to exploit others, but as individuals who always defect after at least the second identification phase in all future rounds. In such a case, exploitation works only in the short run, or if the individuals who try to exploit others, do so only occasionally. However, occasional exploitation requires a more complex behavioural routine, which can again be detected by a yet more complex identification rule. Thus exploitation can only be successful in the long run, if the incentive to detect exploiting individuals is low compared with the incentive to exploit others.

If the incentive for the detection of exploitation is high, individuals modify their routine after they have been exploited, that is, after their current identification rule has been falsified, in such a way that the real intention of their opponent is detected and exploitation is prevented, unless the opponent changes her/his routine as well.

Thus, exploitation is only possible for a short time if a strong desire exists between the players, not to be exploited. If, however, exploitation presents only a minor risk to individual payoff, exploitation may be tolerated due to the scarcity of cognitive capacity.

Short run payoffs

Above, it was assumed that individuals change their routines occasionally by chance or if their current routine is falsified. It also might be claimed that individuals change their routines if they are exploited in the first n rounds. Let us take two individuals, one applying routine 2-5 while the other applies routine 2-4. The first individual cooperates in the first two rounds while the latter one defects. From round three on, both individuals will defect. Thus the first individual is exploited in the first two rounds. This may motivate the first individual to search for an alternative routine which is less cooperative in the first n rounds, although the current one was not falsified.

Changes caused by being exploited early on, reduce the share of individuals applying routines that dictate the frequent use of cooperation in the first rounds. Thus, the inclusion of this aspect into the modelling of associative learning, favours routines that lead individuals often to defect in the first rounds. The use of these routines decrease the likelihood of cooperation being established. So the evolution of cooperation is hindered if individuals change their routines frequently, after being exploited in the first rounds.

The personal payoffs in the first rounds are more important for individuals the fewer the number of rounds played with the same opponent. Thus cooperation is more likely to evolve, the greater the number of rounds played with the same opponent. If individuals play many rounds it is important to be identified as an opportunist in order to establish cooperation. This means that establishing a certain reputation is important in this case. If individuals play fewer rounds with each other, the results in the first rounds are more important and mutual defecting occurs more often.

10.5   SUMMARY

The aims of this chapter are twofold; to give some idea of how associative learning processes can be modelled, and to study the evolution of cooperation from a new perspective.

To satisfy the first aim, the modelling of associative learning, cognitive models and plausible routines relevant in a prisoner's dilemma game, are studied. On the basis of these routines a model was set up describing the choice of routines by individuals. Three aspects have been identified as important for the dynamics of these choices (although only two of them have been included in the model itself): the falsification of cognitive models; the obtained personal payoffs; and occasionally random changes. These three aspects seem to be important to every associative learning process. Thus, the concept of associative learning outlined here may also be used in other approaches.

Besides the proposal of a model to describe associative learning processes, a theoretical explanation for a feature claimed to be relevant in the context of prisoner's dilemma games in the literature, the aspect of reputation, has been found to play a role here. Especially in political economy, the aspect of reputation is claimed to be important for the evolution of cooperation in prisoner's dilemma games or social dilemma situations (cf. Section 10.2.4). The present approach arrives at a similar conclusion. In the present terminology, it is important for individuals to identify their opponents correctly and to be identified as opportunists who are willing to cooperate themselves. In addition, the present approach gives some hints about the aspects interfering with these intentions. According to the above calculations, cooperation is negatively affected by a small number of interactions with the same opponent, and by individuals with a strong ambition to exploit others, or circumstances generally leading to a high incentive to exploit.

Although the results of the present approach are well presented in the literature, this approach adds two aspects to the analysis of the evolution of cooperation.

First, the present approach is based on learning processes and a categorisation of these processes into three types: non-cognitive learning, routine-based learning and associative learning. Each of these three learning processes leads to different results in prisoner's dilemma games and each of them occurs under different circumstances. Understanding the circumstances necessary for the different learning processes to occur, allows prediction of which cases cooperation can be established in. According to reinforcement learning (cf. Chapter 6), whenever individuals are not cognitively aware of the prisoner's dilemma situation, cooperation will not occur in the long run. Only through reflection on the situation and behaviour, (which may be motivated by the importance of the situation itself or by the possibility of punishing results), may mutual cooperation be established. Whether it is established or not depends on the incentives given by the payoffs, and the number of times that interaction takes place between the same individuals.

Second, the proposal of an associative learning process and corresponding modelling, offers a new way of treating dilemma situations and also other interactions between individuals. In the context of the prisoner's dilemma games, it has been shown that an analysis of strategic behaviour must not be based on unrealistic assumptions of either an evolutionary process, or the optimality of the behaviour of individuals. A simple, associative, cognitive learning process is able to describe the most important features in prisoner's dilemma games and, in my opinion, seems to be more realistic and more flexible.

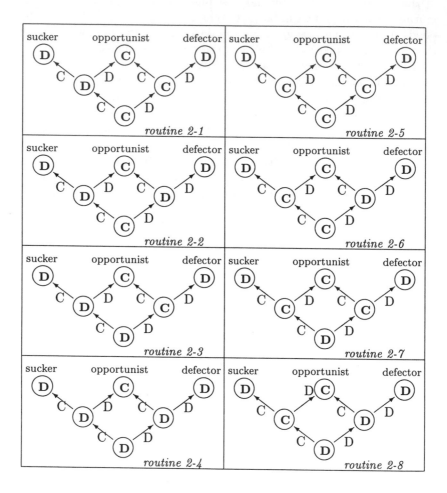

Figure 10.5: *Graphs describing meaningful routines with n = 2 (part one)*

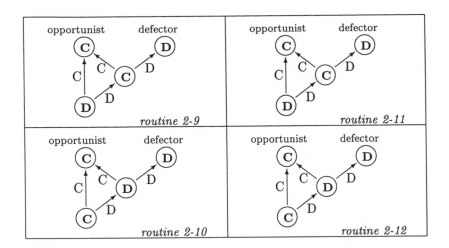

Figure 10.6: *Graphs describing all meaningful routines with n = 2 (part two)*

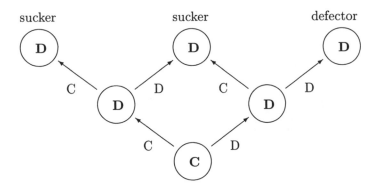

Figure 10.7: *Graph describing a routine similar to routine 2-2 which exploits all opportunists*

Chapter 11

Learning in Economic Research

This book focuses on the categorisation, modelling and application of learning processes in economic contexts. In the introduction it was claimed that the consideration of learning, and the categorisation of types of learning, are necessary for understanding economic behaviour. The importance of a categorisation of learning processes has been shown for the prisoner's dilemma game, where the characteristics of different learning processes determine the dynamics of behaviour, as well as the eventual behaviour of individuals. It has been shown that reinforcement learning leads to results that differ from associative learning. Thus in order to include the proper characteristics of learning in a situation, it is important to categorise learning processes according to the reasons for their occurrence. This work offers strong clues and hopefully some answers to three important issues involving learning in an economic context: the categorisation of learning processes; factors leading to the occurrence of a particular learning process; and ways of modelling these learning processes. The present approach, however, does not offer final clues for modelling learning nor is it the only existing work on the subject. There are other economists who classify learning processes in one way or another (cf. Fudenberg & Levine 1998 and Slembeck 1997). More literature and thoughts about this can be expected to occur in the future. Hence, the present categorisation is only a first proposal which might prove to be adequate or otherwise by further studies. It is a categorisation that seeks to find the relevant circumstances for different learning dynamics to occur. To this end, the present categorisation refers quite a lot to psychological findings. To show that such a categorisation is helpful, learning processes have been studied in five different economic contexts with different learning dynamics being involved. However, learning processes may also be characterised according to the information individuals have about a situation (as claimed by Slembeck 1997) or according to mathematical properties (as proposed by Fudenberg & Levine 1998).

Despite these heterogeneous opinions about the best way to model learning, an increasing number of economists agrees that learning processes do play a significant role in economics and should be studied and considered more comprehensively. Thus, more research on modelling learning in economics can be expected to take place in future. However, such research will remain heterogeneous, at least until one way of modelling learning becomes generally accepted. The main source of knowledge about learning processes nowadays is psychology. But psychological research aims to understand human behaviour and not to provide economists with the required tools and knowledge. Therefore, psychology is able to offer only part of the knowledge necessary for modelling learning in economic contexts. This has led economists to use models based on introspection or common sense, and to conduct experiments with human subjects, to obtain insights on learning themselves. It can be expected that this process will continue; so that the modelling of learning will receive inputs from four areas of research in the near future: psychology; introspection in combination with the necessity to explain certain economic features; experimental economics; and econometric studies. The developments within these four areas of research are outlined above.

Psychological research on learning
In psychology at present, the study of learning process is usually that of cognitive processes. The behaviourist's aim, to explain changes in behaviour for simple repeated situations, is not of much interest to psychologists nowadays. Their aim, instead, is to understand more complex processes, like learning a language. Modelling learning, in this context, means describing the changes of cognitive structures and elements dependent on the experience of a person. This requires the understanding of cognitive processes including the memorising of events and facts, the establishment of associations between cognitive elements and the handling of stored information. Since all these processes take place within the brain, neuro-psychological research has become increasingly important for the understanding of learning.

The psychological research into cognitive learning is a fast developing area of research and can be expected to develop further in the near future. Thus, it is very likely that cognitive psychology will be able to offer more and more insights into learning processes and deepen its understanding of cognitive processes. However psychological research focuses on understanding cognitive learning, and studies most intensively the learning processes of childhood and the acquisition of skills, language and basic knowledge about causes and features of life. In economics, in contrast, the changes of behaviour due to social interaction and experience are of principal interest. If, for example, the dynamics on the stock markets are to be understood, the behaviour of investors must be analysed. This behaviour involves cognitive learning processes that are not based on the establishment of associations but upon the results of interactions with others, individual experience and imagination. These processes, however, do not belong to the core research agenda of psychology. Furthermore, psychologists aim to understand the basic processes of human behaviour. Economists, by contrast, require models of human behaviour that allow for predicting economic actions and therefore, for understanding or predicting economic processes. So there is a huge gap between the research undertaken in psychology and the knowledge required for economic theory. This gap has led economists to conduct experiments themselves and to study human behaviour in the hope of achieving the results they need.

Nevertheless, the developments in psychology will have an influence on the economic notion of learning. With a better understanding of cognitive processes, economists might be willing to consider associative learning processes as well, and not only the simple mechanisms of reinforcement learning and imitation, as they generally do nowadays. In my opinion, cognitive processes, like associative learning, are the keys to a better understanding of much of economic behaviour. However, these processes are very complex and still not completely understood. Psychologists try hard to find out about the mechanisms that shape cognitive models, and it can be expected that they will obtain more and more insights into cognitive processes. These insights should be used to build more realist models of economic agents or to develop an understanding of deviations from rational behaviour, and their causes. Some economists have already begun to consider cognitive processes explicitly, whilst others study the anomalies of economic behaviour. My guess is that the anomalies, the deviations from rational behaviour, are caused by cognitive processes. Thus, both groups of economists should join forces and try to understand these deviations. At the moment, both groups are increasing in size and it can be predicted that cognitive processes and non-rational behaviour will become more frequently considered in the field of economics. However, I do not expect cognitive processes to have a crucial impact on economics before cognitive processes are understood to such an extent that they can be modelled unambiguously in an economic context. Whether psychologists come to this point in the near future cannot be predicted at this stage.

Introspection and economic features

Another source of learning models is introspection and the need for explanations of certain economic features. In the last ten years an enormous number of different learning models has been proposed within economics. Most of them are neither based on empirical evidence nor on psychological findings. These models seem to be inspired by the author's experience or notion of learning, or they seem to be designed to explain economic features. A typical example is the modelling of imitation. Of course there is strong evidence for imitation as such. However, the features of imitation processes are modelled differently by each author. The psychological findings about imitation are generally neglected and the models are designed in such a way that they are either easy to handle mathematically, or cause an interesting or intended result.

It can be expected that more learning models of this kind will appear. However, only a handful of learning models have been considered in general discussion in the past. Thus, most of these models will never become well-known. There is already some tendency to consider only a few basic learning models and a discussion has started about the appropriateness of these models. It is to be hoped that this discussion continues and becomes recognised by all economists working with learning models. However, economists should not search for the most adequate model, since learning models are often designed to describe different processes that occur in different situations. It is necessary to establish a classification of learning processes and a corresponding list of the characteristics that cause certain processes to occur, if learning models are to be used in economics. At the moment, however, most economists dealing with learning search for a simple model of human behaviour that reflects or justifies the simple model of utility maximising behaviour. Such a model will never be able to capture the complex dynamics of human behaviour. Hence, simple models will be a good description of human behaviour only under certain circumstances, and it is important to gather more information about these circumstances. The economic features that are meant to be explained by these various models may be used for testing a system of learning models, but they are not the right building tool to start with if one does not want to end up with a bundle of learning models and no idea of when to use them.

Learning in experimental economics

Experimental economics seems to be the perfect tool to find out more about the usefulness of different learning models; and, indeed, economists have recently started to test learning models in experiments (examples are Roth & Erév 1995 and Erév & Roth 1998), although most experimental economics still deals with static concepts.

The rapidly increasing interests of economists in experiments, is due to a lack in understanding economic behaviour. Many features of economic behaviour have been recognised that cannot be adequately explained assuming utility maximising behaviour, although most behaviour can be modelled as utility maximising. Since psychology does not always offer the missing knowledge, economists have started to investigate economic behaviour themselves, by conducting experiments. Therefore, most experimental economics focuses on behavioural aspects that seem to contradict utility maximising. With time, economists also became interested in the dynamics of behaviour, which means that they started to study learning processes. Some experimental economists proposed specific learning models to describe the dynamics of behaviour in experiments (cf. e. g. Selten & Stoecker 1986 and Roth & Erév 1995) and tested these models in experiments. Thus at the beginning, the models tested were usually those proposed by the authors. At the same time, however, many different learning models have been developed, especially in game theory. So it becomes increasingly common to compare the dynamics of some of these models with experimental data, or compare the predictions of different learning models with respect to their correspondence with experimental data. Other experimental economists study whether some principal features of learning occur in specific economic situations. All these experimental studies, in my opinion, will provide a good basis for a discussion on the use of learning models in economics, although a lot of work has still to be done.

However some very important work has not been started yet. I suspect that, while comparing the predictions of different learning models, each kind of model outperforms others in some experimental settings, whilst it is, itself, outperformed by others in other settings. In other words, as claimed throughout this book, different learning processes exist and they occur under different circumstances. Thus, for experimental economics to contribute to understanding learning processes, it is necessary to consider the possibility of the existence of various different learning processes while designing experiments. The aim of studying learning processes with the help of experiments should be a categorisation of situations and the respective learning processes. This seems to be possible, since both the learning models and the experimental tools are available.

Hence, experimental economics is able to provide two important kinds of insights into learning processes: First, it allows for studying the circumstance that cause certain features of learning to occur. Second, it allows for comparing learning models directly with respect to their predictions. Thus, experimental studies are able to identify adequate ways of modelling different aspects of learning. Whilst the comparison of learning models can already be found in the literature, the aspect of different learning processes has so far been widely neglected. In my opinion, however, studying learning models experimentally is helpful only if learning processes are categorised. Thus there is a great work to be done in this area.

These aspects will probably be tackled in the near future, so that I expect most impulses for the development of modelling learning in economics to come from experimental economics in the next few years.

Empirical study of learning

Another field of economic research that could add to the understanding and modelling of learning processes in economics, is empirical economics. The most natural way to study economic behaviour is to observe real economic action. However such an observation is not easy to conduct, especially if the aim is to collect data on learning. There is not much data about individual economic behaviour and if there is any, there are so many conflicting individual circumstances that it is difficult to focus on one particular feature. Furthermore, the study of learning processes requires that the same situation is faced repeatedly. In reality, only a few situations reoccur with nearly the same characteristics; thus individual data is difficult to obtain. It is more easy to obtain aggregated data. However, since different individuals show different learning processes in the same situation, as it is argued in this book, and also found in some experiments, that aggregated data reflects the sum of a mixture of processes and can hardly be analysed in a fruitful way. These obstacles explain why there have, as far as this author is aware, been no empirical studies of learning in economics, although econometrics is a well developed field of research.

I expect that with an increasing interest in learning processes, some economists will find a way to gather adequate data and analyse it. This would add perfectly to the artificially created data from experiments and expand the knowledge about learning, and its modelling, in economic contexts.

Summary

Economists have become increasingly interested in learning processes in recent years. This process can be expected to continue since there is a strong desire to understand economic behaviour in more detail. At the moment, the study of learning in economics is a very heterogeneous field of research. One of the developments that can be expected in the near future is a concentration of research activities; this concentration should lead to a generally accepted theory. To reach such a theory, two things have to be provided: the categorisation of learning processes; and the experimental and empirical testing of learning models. These two aspects seem to be crucial for achieving a greater understanding of learning processes and the ability to model them in economic contexts. I expect these aspects to be the core of economic research into learning processes.

Bibliography

Adams, R. D. & McCormick, K. (1992), 'Fashion Dynamics and the Economic Theory of Clubs', *Review of Social Economy*, **50**, 24-39.

Alhadeff, D. A. (1982), *Microeconomics and Human Behavior: Toward a New Synthesis of Economics and Psychology*, Berkeley: University of California Press.

Arthur, W. B. (1989), 'Competing Technologies, Increasing Returns, and Lock-in by Historical Events', *Economic Journal*, **99**, 116-131.

Arthur, W. B. (1992), 'Path-dependent Processes and the Emergence of Macro-structure', in U. Witt (ed.), *Evolutionary Economics*, Aldershot: Edward Elgar, pp. 257-266.

Axelrod, R. (1987), 'The Evolution of Strategies in the Iterated Prisoners Dilemma', in D. Davis (ed.), *Genetic Algorithms and Simulated Annealing*, London: Pitman, pp. 32-43.

Bandura, A. (1965), 'Influence of Models' Reinforcement Contingencies on the Acquisition of Imitative Responses', *Journal of Personality and Social Psychology*, **1**, 589-595.

Bandura, A. (1977), *Social Learning Theories*, Englewood Cliffs: Prentice-Hall.

Biel, A. & Dahlstrand, U. (1997), 'Habits and the Establishment of Econogical Purchase Behavior', in G. Guzmán, A. José & S. Sanz, *The XXII International Colloquium of Economic Psychology*, Valencia: Promolibro, pp. 367-381.

Bikhchandani, S., Hirshleifer, D. & Welch, I. (1992), 'A Theory of Fads, Fashion, Custom, and Cultural Change as Informational Cascades', *Journal of Political Economy*, **100**, 992-1026.

Binmore, K. & Samuelson, L. (1994), 'Muddling Through: Noisy Equilibrium Selection', Discussion Paper No. B-275, Sonderforschungsbereich 303, Bonn.

Blume, L. E. & Easley, D. (1982), 'Learning to be Rational', *Journal of Economic Theory*, **26**, 340-351.

Bolles, R. C. (1972), 'Reinforcement, Expectancy, and Learning', *Psychological Review*, **79**, 394-409.

Börgers, T. (1996), 'On the Relevance of Learning and Evolution to Economic Theory', *The Economic Journal*, **106**, 1374-1385.

Börgers, T. & Sarin, R. (1996), 'Naive Reinforcement Learning With Endogenous Aspirations', mimeo, University College, London.

Börgers, T. & Sarin, R. (1997), 'Learning Through Reinforcement and Replicator Dynamics', *Journal of Economic Theory*, **77**, 1-16.

Bray, M. (1982), 'Learning, Estimation, and the Stability of Rational Expectations', *Journal of Economic Theory*, **26**, 318-339.

Brenner, T. (1994), 'An Evolutionary Approach to Decision Making under Uncertainty', Papers on Economics & Evolution #9401, European Study Group for Evolutionary Economics, Freiburg.

Brenner, T. (1995), 'Empirische Modellvalidierung und zeitliche Entwicklung von Entscheidungsprozessen', Dissertation, University of Stuttgart.

Brenner, T. (1996a), 'Learning in a Repeated Decision Process: A Variation-Imitation-Decision Model', Papers on Economics & Evolution #9603, Max-Planck-Institute, Jena.

Brenner, T. (1996b), 'Decision Making and the Exchange of Information', in F. Schweitzer (ed.), *Self-Organization of Complex Structures: From Individual to Collective Dynamics, vol. II*, London: Gordon and Breach, pp. 379-392.

Brenner, T. (1997), 'Reinforcement Learning in a 2×2 Game and the Relevance of Aspiration Levels', Papers on Economics & Evolution #9703, Max-Planck-Institute, Jena.

Brenner, T. (1998a), 'Can Evolutionary Algorithms Describe Learning Processes?', *Journal of Evolutionary Economics*, **8**, 271-283.

Brenner, T. (1998b), 'Learning as an Alternative Concept to Explain Games', mimeo, Jena.

Brenner, T. & Witt, U. (1997), 'Frequency-Dependent Pay-offs, Replicator Dynamics, and Learning Under the Matching Law', Papers on Economics & Evolution #9706, Max-Planck-Institute, Jena.

Brown, G. W. (1951), 'Iterative Solution of Games by Fictitious Play', in T. C. Koopmans (ed.), *Activity Analysis of Production and Allocation*, New York: John Wiley and Sons, pp. 374-376.

Brown, P. M. (1995), 'Learning from Experience, Reference Points, and Decision Costs', *Journal of Economic Behavior and Organisation*, **27**, 381-399.

Bruner, J. S. (1973), *Beyond the Information Given*, New York: Norton.

Bullard, J. & Duffy, J. (1994a), 'Learning in a Large Square Economy', Working Paper 94-013A, Federal Reserve Bank of St Louis.

Bullard, J. & Duffy, J. (1994b), 'A Model of Learning and Emulation with Artificial Adaptive Agents', Working Paper 94-014B, Federal Reserve Bank of St Louis.

Bush, R. R. & Mosteller, F. (1955), *Stochastic Models for Learning*, New York: John Wiley & Sons.

Camerer, C. (1995), 'Individual Decision Making', in J. H. Kagel & A. E. Roth (eds), *The Handbook of Experimental Economics*, Princeton: Princeton University Press, pp. 587-703.

Canning, D. (1995), 'Learning and Social Equilibrium in Large Populations', in A. Kirman & M. Salmon (eds), *Learning and Rationality in Economics*, Oxford: Blackwell, pp. 308-323.

Crawford, V. P. (1995), 'Adaptive Dynamics in Coordination Games', *Econometrica*, **63**, 103-143.

Cross, J. G. (1973), 'A Stochastic Learning Model of Economic Behavior', *Quarterly Journal of Economics*, **87**, 239-266.

Cross, J. G. (1983), *A Theory of Adaptive Economic Behavior*, Cambridge: Cambridge University Press.

Cyert, R. M. & March, J. G. (1963), *A Behavioral Theory of the Firm*, Oxford: Blackwell.

David, P. A. (1985), 'Clio and the Economics of QWERTY', *American Economic Review Proceedings*, **75**, 332-337.

David, P. A. (1997), 'Path Dependence and the Quest for Historical Economics: One More Chorus of the Ballad of QWERTY', Discussion Papers in Economic and Social History, University of Oxford.

Dawid, H. (1996), *Adaptive Learning by Genetic Algorithms*, Berlin: Springer, Lecture Notes in Economics and Mathematical Systems 441.

Day, R. H. (1967), 'Profits, Learning and the Convergence of Satisficing to Marginalism', *Quarterly Journal of Economics*, **81**, 302-311.

Day, R. H. & Tinney, E. H. (1968), 'How To Co-operate in Business without Really Trying: A Learning Model of Decentralized Decision Making', *Journal of Political Economy*, **74**, 583-600.

Dekel, E. & Scotchmer, S. (1992), 'On the Evolution of Optimizing Behavior', *Journal of Economic Theory*, **57**, 392-406.

Denzau, A. & North, D. C. (1994), 'Shared Mental Models. Ideologies and Institutions', *Kyklos*, **47**, 3-31.

Deutsch, M. (1958), 'Trust and Suspicion', *Journal of Conflict Resolution*, **2**, 267-279.

Dixon, H. D. (1995), 'Keeping Up With the Joneses: Aspiration and Experiments Without Random Matching', mimeo.

Easley, D. & Kiefer, N. M. (1988), 'Controlling a Stochastic Process with Unknown Parameters', *Econometrica*, **56**, 1045-1064.

Ebbinghaus, H. (1913), *Memory*, New York: Columbia University.

Eichberger, J., Haller, H. & Milne, F. (1993), 'Naive Bayesian Learning in 2x2 Matrix Games', *Journal of Economic Behavior and Organization*, **22**, 69-90.

Eigen, M. (1971), 'The Selforganisation of Matter and the Evolution of Biological Macromolecules', *Naturwissenschaften*, **58**, 465-523.

El-Gamal, M. A. & Palfrey, T. R. (1995), 'Vertigo: Comparing Structural Models of Imperfect Behavior in Experimental Games', *Games and Economic Behavior*, **8**, 322-348.

Ellison, G. (1993), 'Learning, Local Interaction, and Coordination', *Econometrica*, **61**, 1047-1071.

Erév, I. & Roth, A. E. (1998), 'Predicting How People Play Games: Reinforcement Learning in Experimental Games with Unique, Mixed Strategy Equilibria', *American Economic Review*, **88**, 848-881.

Escalona, S. K. (1939), 'The Effect of Success and Failure Upon the Level of Aspiration and Behavior in Manic-depressive Psychoses', *University of Iowa Studies in Child Welfare*, **16**, 199-307.

Eshel, I., Samuelson, L. & Shaked, A. (1996), 'Altruists, Egoists and Hooligans in a Local Interaction Model', Discussion Paper No. B-341, Sonderforschungsbereich 303, Bonn.

Estes, W. K. (1950), 'Toward a Statistical Theory of Learning', *Psychological Review*, **57**, 94-107.

Festinger, L. (1942), 'Wish, Expectation and Group Standards as Factors Influencing the Level of Aspiration', *Journal of Abnormal Social Psychology*, **37**, 184-200.

Festinger, L. (1957), *A Theory of Cognitive Dissonance*, Stanford, CA: Stanford University Press.

Fishburn, P. C. (1970), *Utility Theory for Decision Making*, New York: John Wiley & Sons.

Foster, D. & Young, P. (1990), 'Stochastic Evolutionary Game Dynamics', *Theoretical Population Biology*, **38**, 219-232.

Foxall, G. (1990), *Consumer Psychology in Behavioural Perspective*, London: Routledge.

Fudenberg, D. & Levine, D. K. (1998), *The Theory of Learning in Games*, Cambridge: MIT Press.

Gale, J., Binmore, K. G. & Samuelson, L. (1995), 'Learning to be Imperfect: The Ultimatum Game', *Games and Economic Behavior*, **8**, 56-90.

Garcia, J., McGowan, B. K., Ervin, F. R. & Koelling, R. A. (1968), 'Cues: Their Relative Effectiveness as a Function of the Reinforcer', *Science*, **196**, 794-796.

Glance, N. S. & Huberman, B. A. (1993), 'The Outbreak of Cooperation', *Journal of Mathematical Sociology*, **17**, 281-302.

Gößling, T. (1996), *Entscheidung in Modellen*, Egelsbach: Hänsel-Hohenhausen Verlag der Deutschen Hochschulschriften.

Güth, W. (1995), 'On Ultimatum Bargaining Experiments – A Personal Review', *Journal of Economic Behavior and Organisation*, **27**, 329-344.

Güth, W. & Yaari, M. E. (1992), 'Explaining Reciprocal Behavior in Simple Strategic Games: An Evolutionary Approach', in U. Witt (ed.), *Explaining Process and Change*, Ann Arbor: University of Michigan Press, pp. 23-34.

Haken, H. (1983), *Synergetics*, Berlin: Springer Verlag.

Hallpike, C. R. (1986), *The Principles of Social Evolution*, Oxford: Clarendon Press.

Harley, C. B. (1981), 'Learning the Evolutionary Stable Strategy', *Journal of Theoretical Biology*, **89**, 611-633.

Hebb, D. O. (1949), *The Organization of Behavior: A Neuropsychological Theory*, New York: Wiley.

Hebb, D. O. (1955), 'Drives and the CNS', *Psychological Review*, **62**, 243-254.

Hegselmann, R. (1996), 'Social Dilemmas in Lineland and Flatland', in W. B. G. Liebrand & D. M. Messick (eds), *Frontiers in Social Dilemmas Research*, Berlin: Springer, pp. 337-361.

Heiner, R. (1988), 'The Necessity of Imperfect Decisions', *Journal of Economic Behavior and Organisation*, **10**, 29-55.

Helbing, D. (1995), *Quantitative Sociodynamics, Stochastic Methods and Models of Social Interaction Processes*, Boston: Kluwer Academic.

Hergenhahn, B. R. & Olson, M. H. (1997), *An Introduction to Theories of Learning*, *5th edn*, Upper Saddle River: Prentice-Hall.

Herrnstein, R. J. (1961), 'Relative and Absolute Strength of Response as a Function of Frequency of Reinforcement', *Journal of the Experimental Analysis of Behavior*, **4**, 267-272.

Herrnstein, R. J. (1970), 'On the Law of Effect', *Journal of the Experimental Analysis of Behavior*, **13**, 243-266.

Herrnstein, R. J. & Prelec, D. (1991), 'Melioration: A Theory of Distributed Choice', *Journal of Economic Perspectives*, **5**, 137-156.

Hey, J. D. (1991), *Experiments in Economics*, Oxford: Blackwell.

Hirshleifer, J. & Riley, J. G. (1992), *The Analytics of Uncertainty and Information*, Cambridge: Cambridge University Press.

Hofbauer, J. & Sigmund, K. (1984), *Evolutionstheorie und dynamische Systeme*, Berlin: Paul Parey.

Hogarth, R. M. (1980), *Judgement and Choice: The Psychology of Decision*, New York: Wiley.

Holland, J. H. (1975), *Adaption in Natural and Artificial Systems*, An Arbor: University of Michigan Press.

Holland, J. H. & Miller, J. H. (1991), 'Artifical Adaptive Agents in Economic Theory', *American Economic Review, Papers and Proceedings*, **81**, 365-370.

Hoppe, F. (1975), 'Das Anspruchsniveau', in H. Thomae (ed.), *Die Motivation menschlichen Handelns*, Köln: Kiepenheuer & Witsch.

Johnson-Laird, P. N. (1983), *Mental Models*, Cambridge: Harvard University Press.

Jordan, J. S. (1991), 'Bayesian Learning in Normal Form Games', *Games and Economic Behavior*, **3**, 60-81.

Jordan, J. S. (1995), 'Bayesian Learning in Repeated Games', *Games and Economic Behavior*, **9**, 8-20.

Kalai, E. & Lehrer, E. (1993), 'Rational Learning Leads to Nash Equilibrium', *Econometrica*, **61**, 1019-1045.

Kandel, E. R. & Schwartz, J. H. (1982), 'Molecular Biology of Learning: Modulation of Transmitter Release', *Science*, **218**, 433-443.

Kelley, H. H. & Thibaut, J. W. (1978), *Interpersonal Relation. A Theory of Interdependence*, New York: John Wiley & Sons.

Kimble, G. A. (1961), *Hilgard and Marquis' Conditioning and Learning (2nd edn)*, Englewood Cliffs: Prentice Hall.

Kirchkamp, O. (1995), 'Spatial Evolution of Automata in the Prisoner's Dilemma', Discussion Paper No. B-330, Rheinische Friedrich-Wilhelms-Universität Bonn.

Klein, B. & Leffler, K. B. (1981), 'The Role of Market Forces in Assuring Contractual Performance', *Journal of Political Economy*, **89**, 615-641.

Koffka, K. (1963), *Principles of Gestalt Psychology*, New York: Harcourt, Brace, and World.

Köhler, W. (1925), *The Mentality of Apes*, London: Routledge & Kegan Paul.

Kreps, D. M. (1990), *Game Theory and Economic Modelling*, Oxford: Clarendon Press.

Kubon-Gilke, G. (1997), *Verhaltensbindung und die Evolution ökonomischer Institutionen*, Marburg: Metropolis-Verlag.

Kuhlman, D. M., Camac, C. R. & Cunha, D. A. (1986), 'Individual Differences in Social Orientation', in H. A. M. Wilke, D. M. Messick & C. G. Rutte (eds), *Experimental Social Dilemmas*, Frankfurt am Main: Peter Lang, pp. 151-176.

Lancaster, K. (1966), 'Allocation and Distribution Theory: Technological Innovation and Process', *American Economic Review*, **56**, 14-23.

Latané, B. (1981), 'The Psychology of Social Impact', *American Psychologist*, **36**, 343-356.

Lave, L. B. (1965), 'Factors Affecting Co-operation in the Prisoner's Dilemma', *Behavioral Science*, **10**, 26-38.

Ledyard, J. O. (1995), 'Public Goods: A Survey of Experimental Research', in J. H. Kagel & A. E. Roth (eds), *The Handbook of Experimental Economics*, Princeton: Princeton University Press, pp. 111-194.

Lewin, K. (1963), *Feldtheorie in den Sozialwissenschaften*, Bern: Huber.

Lewin, K., Dembo, T., Festinger, L. & Sears, P. S. (1944), 'Level of Aspiration', in J. M. Hunt (ed.), *Personality and the Behavioral Disorders*, New York: Ronald.

Leibenstein, H. (1976), *Beyond Economic Man: A New Foundation for Microeconomics*, Cambridge: Harvard University Press.

Liebrand, W. B. G. (1986), 'The Ubiquity of Social Values in Social Dilemmas', in H. A. M. Wilke, D. M. Messick & C. G. Rutte (eds), *Experimental Social Dilemmas*, Frankfurt am Main: Peter Lang, pp. 113-133.

Lindgren, K. (1992), 'Evolutionary Phenomena in Simple Dynamics', in D. Farmer et. al. (eds), *Artifical Life II*, Santa Fe Inst.: Proceedings of the second workshop on the synthesis and simulation of living systems, pp. 295-312.

Lindsley, D. B. (1951), 'Emotion', in S. S. Stevens (ed.), *Handbook of Experimental Psychology*, New York: Wiley, pp. 473-516.

Lintner, J. (1965), 'The Valuation of Risk Assets and the Selection of Risky Investments in Stock Portfolios and Capital Budgets', *The Review of Economics and Statistics*, **47**, 13-37.

Ljung, L. & Söderström, T. (1983), *The Theory and Practice of Recursive Identification*, Cambridge: MIT Press.

MacIntegre, S. H. & Miller, C. M. (1992), 'Social Utility and Fashion Behavior', *Marketing Letters*, **3**, 371-382.

Marcet, A. & Sargent, T. J. (1989), 'Convergence of Least Squares Learning Mechanisms in Self-Referential Linear Stochastic Models', *Journal of Economic Theory*, **48**, 337-368.

March, J. G. (1988), 'Variable Risk Preferences and Adaptive Aspirations', *Journal of Economic Behavior and Organization*, **9**, 5-24.

Marimon, R. (1993), 'Adaptive Learning, Evolutionary Dynamics and Equilibrium Selection in Games', *European Economic Review*, **37**, 603-611.

Markowitz, H. M. (1959), *Portfolio Selection: Efficient Diversification of Investments*, New York: Wiley.

Markowitz, H. M. (1991), 'Foundations of Portfolio Theory', *Journal of Finance*, **46**, 469-477.

Maslow, A. H. (1970), *Motivation and Personality*, New York: Harper & Row.

Maynard Smith, J. (1982), *Evolution and the Theory of Games*, Cambridge: Cambridge University Press.

McClintock, C. G. & Van Avermaet, E. (1982), 'Social Values and Rules of Fairness: A Theoretical Perspective', in V. J. Derlega & J. Grzelak (eds), *Cooperation and Helping Behavior*, New York: Academic Press.

Menger, C. (1968), *Gesammelte Werke, 2nd edn*, Tübingen: J. C. B. Mohr.

Milgrom, P. R., North, D. C. & Weingast, B. R. (1990), 'The Role of Institutions in the Revival of Trade: The Law Merchant, Private Judges, and the Champagne Fairs', *Economics and Politics*, **2**, 1-23.

Milgrom, P. R. & Roberts, J. (1991), 'Adaptive and Sophisticated Learning in Normal Form Games', *Games and Economic Behavior*, **3**, 82-100.

Miller, N. E. & Dollard, J. (1941), *Social Learning and Imitation*, New Haven: Yale University Press.

Nash, J. F. (1950), 'Equilibrium Points in n-Person Games', *Proceedings of the National Academy of Sciences (US)*, **36**, 48-49.

Nowak, M. A. & May, R. M. (1993), 'The Spatial Dilemmas of Evolution', *International Journal of Bifurcation and Chaos*, **3**, 35-78.

Nowak, A., Latané, B. & Lewenstein, M. (1994), 'Social Dilemmas Exist in Space', in U. Schulz, W. Albers & U. Mueller (eds), *Social Dilemmas and Cooperation*, Berlin: Springer-Verlag, pp. 269-289.

Oechssler, J. (1995), 'An Evolutionary Interpretation of Mixed-Strategy Equilibria', Humboldt University Discussion Paper No. 26, Berlin.

Osborne, M. J. & Rubinstein, A. (1994), *A Course in Game Theory*, Cambridge: MIT Press.

Ostrom, E. (1990), *Governing the Commons*, Cambridge: Cambridge University Press.

Pasche, M. (1997), 'Explaining Violations of Bayesian Inference', Diskussionspapier Reihe B, Nr. 97/01, Friedrich-Schiller-Universität Jena.

Pavlov, I. P. (1953), *Sämtliche Werke, Bd. IV*, Berlin: Akademie-Verlag.

Piaget, J. (1976), *Die Äquilibration der kognitiven Strukturen*, Stuttgart: Klett.

Ramstad, Y. (1994), 'On the Nature of Economic Evolution', in L. Magnusson (ed.), *Evolutionary and Neo-Schumpeterian Approaches to Economics*, Boston: Kluwer Academic Publishers, pp. 65-121.

Rapoport, A. & Chammah, A. M. (1965), *Prisoner's Dilemma*, Ann Arbor: University of Michigan Press.

Rapoport, A. & Guyer, M. (1966), 'A Taxonomy of 2x2 Games', *General Systems*, **11**, 203-214.

Rechenberg, I. (1973), *Evolutionsstrategie: Optimierung technischer Systeme nach Prinzipien der biologischen Evolution*, Stuttgart: Frommann-Holzboog Verlag.

Rescorla, R. A. & Wagner, A. R. (1972), 'A Theory of Pavlovian Conditioning: Variations in the Effectiveness of Reinforcement and Nonreinforcement', in A. H. Black & W. F. Prokasy (eds), *Classical Conditioning II*, Englewood Cliffs: Prentice Hall.

Révész, P. (1973), 'Robbins-Monro Procedure in a Hilbert Space and Its Application in the Theory of Learning Processes I', *Studia Scientiarum Mathematicarum Hungarica*, **8**, 391-398.

Robinson, J. (1951), 'An Iterative Method of Solving a Game', *Annals of Mathematics*, **54**, 296-301.

Rogers, E. M. (1995), *Diffusion of Innovations, 4th edn*, New York: The Free Press.

Roth, A. & Erév, I. (1995), 'Learning in Extensive Form Games: Experimental Data and Simple Dynamic Models in the Intermediate Run', *Games and Economic Behavior*, **6**, 164-212.

Samuelson, L. (1994), 'Stochastic Stability in Games with Alternative Best Replies', *Journal of Economic Theory*, **64**, 35-65.

Sargent, T. J. (1993), *Bounded Rationality in Macroeconomics*, Oxford: Clarendon Press.

Schlag, K. H. (1998), 'Why Imitate, and If So, How? A Boundedly Rational Approach to Multi-armed Bandits', *Journal of Economic Theory*, **78**, 130-156.

Scitovsky, T. (1992), *The Joyless Economy, revised edn*, New York: Oxford University Press.

Sears, R. R. (1942), *Success and Failure: A Study of Motility*, New York: McGraw-Hill.

Seidl, C. & Traub, S. (1995), 'The Relevance of Irrelevant Alternatives and Other Tales', Discussion Paper No. 50, Institut für Finanzwissenschaft und Sozialpolitik, Kiel.

Selten, R. & Stoecker, R. (1986), 'End Behavior in Sequences of Finite Prisoner's Dilemma Supergames', *Journal of Economic Behavior and Organization*, **7**, 47-70.

Shapiro, C. (1983), 'Premiums for High Quality Products as Returns to Reputations', *Quarterly Journal of Economics*, **98**, 659-679.

Shapley, L. S. (1964), 'Some Topics in Two-Person Games', in M. Dresher, L. Shapley & A. Tucker (eds), *Advances in Game Theory*, Princeton: Annals of Mathematic Studies No. 52, pp. 1-28.

Simon, H. A. (1957), *Administrative Behavior*, New York: The Macmillan Company.

Simon, H. A. (1978), 'Richard T. Ely Lecture. Rationality as Process and as Product of Thought', *American Economic Association*, **68**, 1-16.

Simon, H. A. (1987), 'Satisficing', *The New Palgrave Dictionary of Economics*, **Vol. 4**, London: Macmillan Press, 243-245.

Skinner, B. F. (1938), *The Behavior of Organisms*, New York: Appleton.

Slembeck, T. (1997), 'A Behavioral Approach to Learning in Economics – Towards a Theory of Contingent Learning', Working Paper No. 316, Department of Economics, University of Pittsburgh.

Solomon, L. (1960), 'The Influence of Some Types of Power Relationships and Game Strategies upon the Development of Interpersonal Trust', *Journal of Abnormal and Social Psychology*, **61**, 223-230.

Symons, D. (1992), 'On the Use and Misuse of Darwinism in the Study of Human Behavior', in J. H. Barkow, L. Cosmides & J. Tooby (eds), *The Adapted Mind*, New York: Oxford University Press, pp. 137-162.

Taylor, M. (1987), *The Possibility of Cooperation*, Cambridge: Cambridge University Press.

Thibaut, J. W. & Kelley, H. H. (1959), *The Social Psychology of Groups*, New York: Wiley.

Thorndike, E. L. (1932), *The Fundamentals of Learning*, New York: AMS Press.

Tolman, E. C. (1949), *Purpose Behavior in Animals and Men*, New York: Century-Crofts.

Tooby, J. & Cosmides, L. (1992), 'The Psychological Foundations of Culture', in J. H. Barkow, L. Cosmides & J. Tooby (eds), *The Adapted Mind*, New York: Oxford University Press, pp. 19-136.

Underwood, B. J. (1948), 'Retroactive and Proactive Inhibition after Five and Forty-eight Hours', *Journal of Experimental Psychology*, **38**, 28-38.

van Laarhoven, P. & Aarts, E. (1987), *Simulated Annealing: Theory and Applications*, Dordrecht: Reidel Publishing Company.

Varoufakis, Y. (1996), 'Moral Rhetoric in the Face of Strategic Weakness: Modern Clues for an Ancient Puzzle', mimeo.

Vaughan, W. & Herrnstein, R. J. (1987), 'Stability, Melioration, and Natural Selection', in L. Green, J. H. Kagel (eds), *Advances in Behavioral Economics, vol. 1*, Norwood: Ablex, pp. 185-215.

Venkatesan, M. (1966), 'Experimental Study of Consumer Behavior Conformity and Independence', *Journal of Marketing Research*, **3**, 384-387.

Walker, C. M., Roberts, E., Burgoyne, C. & Webley, P. (1997), 'A Natural History of Personal Financial Information Management: First Results of a Diary Study', in G. Guzmán, A. José & S. Sanz, *The XXII International Colloquium of Economic Psychology*, Valencia: Promolibro, pp. 118-125.

Watson, R. I. & Rayner, R. (1920), 'Conditioned Emotional Reactions', *Journal of Experimental Psychology*, **3**, 1-14.

Weibull, J. W. (1995), *Evolutionary Game Theory*, Cambridge: The MIT Press.

Weidlich, W. (1991), 'Physics and Social Science – the Approach of Synergetics', *Physics Reports*, **204**, 1-163.

Weidlich, W. & Haag, G. (1983), *Concepts and Models of a Quantitative Sociology*, Berlin: Springer Verlag.

Weidlich, W. & Brenner, T. (1995), 'Dynamics of Demand Including Fashion Effects for Interacting Consumer Groups', in A. Wagner, H.-W. Lorenz (eds), *Studien zur Evolutorischen Ökonomik III*, Berlin: Duncker & Humblot, pp. 79-115.

Weise, P. (1993), 'Eine dynamische Analyse von Konsumtionseffekten', *Jahrbücher für Nationalökonomie und Statistik*, **211**, 159-172.

Wilkie, W. L. (1994), *Consumer Behavior, 3rd edn*, New York: John Wiley & Sons.

Witt, U. (1986a), 'How Can Complex Economic Behavior Be Investigated? The Example of the Ignorant Monopolist Revisited', *Behavioral Science*, **31**, 173-188.

Witt, U. (1986b), 'Firms' Market Behavior under Imperfect Information and Economic Natural Selection', *Journal of Economic Behavior and Organization*, **7**, 265-290.

Witt, U. (1987a), 'How Transaction Rights Are Shaped to Channel Innovativeness', *Journal of Institutional and Theoretical Economics*, **143**, 180-195.

Witt, U. (1987b), *Individualistische Grundlagen der Evolutorischen Ökonomik*, Tübingen: J. C. B. Mohr.

Witt, U. (1989), 'Wissen, Präferenzen und Kommunikation – eine ökonomische Theorie', *Analyse und Kritik – Zeitschrift für Sozialwissenschaften*, **11**, 94-109.

Witt, U. (1991a), 'Evolutionary Economics – an Interpretative Survey', Papers on Economics & Evolution # 9104, European Study Group for Evolutionary Economics, Freiburg.

Witt, U. (1991b), 'Economics, Sociobiology, and Behavioral Psychology on Preferences', *Journal of Economic Psychology*, **12**, 557-573.

Witt, U. (1996), 'Bounded Rationality, Social Learning, and Viable Moral Conduct in a Prisoners' Dilemma', in M. Perlman & E. Helmstädter (eds), *Behavioral Norms, Technological Progress and Economic Dynamics: Studies in Schumpeterian Economics*, Ann Arbor: Michigan University Press, pp. 33-49.

Witt, U. (1997), '"Lock-in" vs. "Critical Masses" – Industrial Change Under Network Externalities', *International Journal of Industrial Organization*, **15**, 753-773.

Wuketits, F. M. (1990), *Gene, Kultur und Moral*, Darmstadt: Wissenschaftliche Buchgesellschaft.

Yin, G. & Zhu, Y. M. (1990), 'On H-Valued Robbins-Monro Processes', *Journal of Multivariate Analysis*, **34**, 116-140.

Young, P. (1993), 'The Evolution of Conventions', *Econometrica*, **61**, 57-84.

Index